ESSAYS IN LABOUR HISTORY

Elliott & Fry Ltd

GEORGE DOUGLAS HOWARD COLE

ESSAYS IN LABOUR HISTORY

In memory of G. D. H. Cole
25 September 1889–14 January 1959

EDITED BY

ASA BRIGGS
*Professor of Modern History,
University of Leeds*

AND

JOHN SAVILLE
*Senior Lecturer in Economic History,
University of Hull*

With recollections of G. D. H. COLE by
Ivor Brown, Hugh Gaitskell,
Stephen K. Bailey and G. D. N. Worswick

LONDON
MACMILLAN & CO LTD
NEW YORK · ST MARTIN'S PRESS
1960

Copyright © Macmillan & Co Ltd 1960

MACMILLAN AND COMPANY LIMITED
London Bombay Calcutta Madras Melbourne

THE MACMILLAN COMPANY OF CANADA LIMITED
Toronto

ST MARTIN'S PRESS INC
New York

PRINTED IN GREAT BRITAIN

CONTENTS

G. D. H. COLE *Frontispiece*

Foreword vii

RECOLLECTIONS OF G. D. H. COLE

i. G. D. H. COLE AS AN UNDERGRADUATE 3
 By Ivor Brown

ii. AT OXFORD IN THE TWENTIES 6
 By Hugh Gaitskell

iii. WHAT COLE REALLY MEANT 20
 By Stephen K. Bailey

iv. COLE AND OXFORD, 1938–1958 25
 By G. D. N. Worswick

ESSAYS IN LABOUR HISTORY

1. THE LANGUAGE OF 'CLASS' IN EARLY NINETEENTH-CENTURY ENGLAND 43

 By Asa Briggs, Professor of Modern History, University of Leeds

2. NINETEENTH-CENTURY CO-OPERATION: FROM COMMUNITY BUILDING TO SHOPKEEPING 74

 By Sidney Pollard, Lecturer in Economics, University of Sheffield

3. CUSTOM, WAGES, AND WORK-LOAD IN NINETEENTH-CENTURY INDUSTRY 113

 By E. J. Hobsbawm, Lecturer in History, Birkbeck College, University of London

4. THE SOCIALISTS OF THE POLISH 'GREAT EMIGRATION' 140

 By Peter Brock, Lecturer in History, University of Alberta

Essays in Labour History

		PAGE
5.	THE *BEE-HIVE* NEWSPAPER: ITS ORIGIN AND EARLY STRUGGLES	174

  By Stephen Coltham, Staff Tutor, University of Oxford Extra-Mural Delegacy

6. PROFESSOR BEESLY AND THE WORKING-CLASS MOVEMENT   205

  By Royden Harrison, Staff Tutor, Department of Extra-Mural Studies, University of Sheffield

7. THE ENGLISH BRANCHES OF THE FIRST INTERNATIONAL   242

  By Henry Collins, Staff Tutor, University of Oxford Extra-Mural Delegacy

8. HOMAGE TO TOM MAGUIRE   276

  E. P. Thompson, Staff Tutor, Department of Extra-Mural Studies, University of Leeds

9. TRADE UNIONS AND FREE LABOUR: THE BACKGROUND TO THE TAFF VALE DECISION   317

  By John Saville, Senior Lecturer in Economic History, University of Hull

INDEX   351

FOREWORD

THESE recollections and essays were written to be presented to G. D. H. Cole on the occasion of his seventieth birthday, 25 September 1959. He died, however, on 14 January 1959. He had approved and given his support to the idea of this book, and it now becomes a memorial volume.

Among those who have helped with the production of this book, we wish to thank Mrs. Margaret Cole, whose advice and encouragement have been much appreciated; Mrs. Susan Horsley, who assisted with the proof reading; and Mr. John Farrell, Assistant Librarian of the University of Hull, who compiled the Index.

A. B.
J. S.

Recollections of G. D. H. Cole

(i)

IVOR BROWN

G. D. H. COLE AS AN UNDERGRADUATE

When I entered Balliol in 1909, with two abominable little rooms over the Front Porch, there was more handsomely and spaciously housed in the Garden Quad an undergraduate with a reputation for socialism, conversation, and hospitality. This was the old Pauline, George Douglas Howard Cole. Nobody called him George; nor, at that time, was he known as Douglas. Many people called him O. This strange abbreviation was due to the methods of address used in his forms of speech by one of the College staff, Mr. Pusey. We were expected then to collect our weekly bills in Hall, answering Mr. Pusey's roll-call. Three names, all later on to be illustrious, came together on his list, H. J. Paton, P. Guedalla, and G. D. H. Cole. Mr. Pusey was not wasting his breath on consonants. What he seemed to read out was 'A. Arlar. O.' O has since been Douglas, never George, to many, but in a world that has given up initials for Christian names, he has remained G. D. H.

I found that O, a year my senior, had already established a reputation for sundry activities or lack of them. He did not, I think, greatly please his tutors, but he never failed to satisfy the examiners. It was understood that he did not, perhaps could not, ride a bicycle, that he never travelled abroad, and that he never went to bed before dawn. On the positive side it was alleged, and I did not doubt the allegation, that he had read more books in various tongues than any other of his age — or even of almost any age. He was essentially adult; one did not feel that he had recently been at school or that he had ever been at school. St. Paul's was far away and long ago. Yet this maturity had nothing to do with solemnity. He mixed both his learning and his propaganda with hilarity.

He played no college games. But I subsequently played lawn-tennis with him at Ealing and badminton at Hampstead. He wrote and published poetry. Since printing was then so cheap, to produce in paper covers a book of verse was a fairly common practice. It needed self-confidence to do so, for fellow-undergraduates were likely to spend a shilling on the product and then go readily into business as critics. I remember one line of Cole's which was much quoted, not without a smile.

Love is the anaesthetic of the soul.

It can be said in its defence that poets then wrote both metrically and intelligibly.

With F. K. Griffith, from Marlborough, Cole edited a red-covered magazine called *The Oxford Socialist*. I was invited to write for it and then had my piece, very properly, rejected. It did not disturb me : I did not deem myself to be in his class as essayist or agitator. Griffith subsequently became an M.P. (Liberal) for one of the Middlesbrough divisions. Cole never went to Westminster ; he was too busy in Tothill Street, headquarters of the Fabians and their Research Department, his particular centre of activities, to be concerned with the legislative proceedings in adjacent premises. Griffith became, while a socialist, President of the Union. Cole did not bother with this form of oratory and intrigue, though he could have won that chair with ease, had he cared to do so. There would have been the Balliol Vote behind him as well as the support of socialists in other colleges. The Balliol Vote was large, loyal, regardless of party, and well organised. Freshmen were coaxed to join the Union : were they not potential voters ? We ran in a series of presidents of all parties, Griffith as socialist, Guedalla as liberal, and Barrington-Ward (later editor of *The Times*) and Walter Monckton (later almost everything) as tories. But Cole continued to address meetings outside that arena and to practise his journalism.

Amid the general dalliance of undergraduate life he was immensely active in a multifarious way, taking the curriculum in his stride as he proceeded by way of firsts in Classical Mods.

and Greats to a Prize Fellowship at Magdalen. He was not one of the Pure Classics who snapped up the Hertford, Craven, and Ireland university scholarships for which Balliol classical scholars and exhibitioners were entered, almost as routine, by their tutors. His interests were too many and too urgent outside the academic field ; inside it he preferred philosophy.

His was a dark, dynamic presence. The women undergraduates, whose knowledge of the males was then limited to admiring or contemptuous glances in lecture-rooms, could hardly have failed to be struck with a fascinated awe, if he attended lectures, which may not have been often. They could purchase and read his poetry and possibly refuse to agree that love is the anaesthetic of the soul.

I owe much to O. He did not introduce me to undergraduate politics, since I was a socialist at school. But he caused me to read much that I would not otherwise have read and he explained to me what philosophy was about in a way that my tutors never managed to do. He had 'digs' with a Balliol coterie in Holywell and later, by himself, in Bath Place before he moved on to Magdalen, with august premises looking out upon the Deer Park ; there he mingled party-giving with politics which outranged those of the existing Labour Party ; they included serious attention to Guild Socialism ; but I am moving outside the years *in statu pupillari*.

I remember that any company which he entered seemed quickened by his coming and that any group to which he spoke felt a rise in the intellectual temperature. But he could be most icy if he chose and he chose to be so in Chapel. Attendance on Sundays was then compulsory, and Cole, like many others of us, appearing under protest and taking no part in the proceedings, was magnificent in his aloofness and formidable in his non-participation. But it is not as a silent non-worshipper that I chiefly remember him, but rather as a talker on summer evenings in the Quad — we did have full summer in May then — or in any fireside company on winter nights. He was the spirit of animation and conviction. He spoke with an authority to which his chief claim was that you had to listen ; yet he never monopolised talk, drawing others out as he led them on.

(ii)
HUGH GAITSKELL

AT OXFORD IN THE TWENTIES

OXFORD in the middle twenties was gay, frivolous, stimulating, and tremendously alive. The political and economic anxieties of the immediate post-war years were over. The gloom of the Great Depression and the horrors of the Nazis were yet to come. Nobody had heard of Hitler. The Spanish Civil War was ten years off. Mussolini had strutted on to the stage but was regarded as only a minor blot. There were still hopes that the League of Nations might work.

True, unemployment was over 10 per cent — an appalling figure by today's standards — but this was much less than it had been; there was not so much worry about getting jobs after finishing at the university.

It was a brief, blessed interval when the lives of the young were neither overshadowed by the consequences of the last war nor dominated by the fear of a future one. Most of us sighed with relief and settled down to the business of enjoying ourselves.

These were the days of 'Oxford Bags', of high-necked jumpers, of exotic shantung ties and wild parties. But we could also take some pride in our literary and intellectual standards. Graham Greene was writing short stories in an undergraduate magazine. Emlyn Williams was a star at the O.U.D.S. At the Playhouse, Oxford's repertory theatre, a young actor called John Gielgud was making his name. Peter Quennell, John Betjeman, Cecil Day-Lewis, W. H. Auden were to be seen around.

Politics, to tell the truth, were rather at a discount. We were in revolt all right — against Victorianism, Puritanism, stuffiness of any kind, but most of us weren't sufficiently bitter — or perhaps sufficiently serious — to be angry young men.

There is another reason why our revolt was not, somehow, 'angry'. In our earlier years at school we had been subjected to much war-time propaganda and experienced in an unusually intense fashion the pressures of the community on the individual. Such pressures were both cruder and, at the same time, less generally accepted during the 1914–18 War than in the second World War. Our reaction against all this, as soon as we reached the heavenly freedom of Oxford, took the form of an outburst of scepticism, a mistrust of dogma, a dislike of sentimentality and of over-emotional prejudices or violent crusades.

We were, therefore, suspicious of general ideas, especially when these involved some mystical, collective, common good. We preferred the happiness of the individual as the only acceptable social aim. As for personal values, truth was our supreme object and intellectual integrity was the greatest of virtues.

Of course, this was not the whole of Oxford. There were also the 'hearties' who concentrated on games, the quiet scholarly types who worked the whole time, and the average conventional undergraduates who did a little of each. But it was the gay 'intellectuals' who set the tone of Oxford in those years and earned for them the name of 'the roaring twenties'.

To this Oxford Douglas Cole, accompanied by his wife Margaret and their two small daughters, Jane and Ann, returned in 1925 after an absence of ten years.

In some respects the atmosphere cannot have been congenial to them. Margaret was a Cambridge girl and, as she has confessed, never cared much for Oxford. Douglas was, of course, from Oxford, but he was very much a product of the first decade of the twentieth century. He was an enthusiast and a romantic. True he had been and was (and for that matter remained) a rebel. He had stormed not only at the whole social and economic structure of capitalism and the conventional Establishment of post-Edwardian times but also at the dominant intellectual leadership of the labour movement. He had denounced the Webbs and the orthodox Fabians in the most violent and bitter terms. He had done all this — and become famous in the process — before he was 30. But he had been very much a rebel with a cause — the 'cause' of Guild Socialism.

And this cause, although violently opposed to a traditionally orthodox cause such as, say, Tory Patriotism, at least resembled it in being avowedly and consciously emotional. Indeed part of Douglas Cole's case against the older Labour leaders was that their approach to socialism was cold, dull, mechanical, and over-rational. If he also objected that 'Fabianism' meant over-centralisation and too much power for the state, his own theory exalted not the individual but the group — a concept just as suspect to the Oxford of the twenties, to which he now returned.

Moreover, Douglas had not just played the part of an intellectual in the past ten years. As secretary of the Labour Research Department he had been one of the leading figures on the left of the labour movement. Indeed, for a few stormy months at the end of the war he had wielded so much influence with the trade unions that he was talked about as a possible leader of a British revolution.

To be sure the tide had since receded; the atmosphere had changed; and after being more or less squeezed out of the Labour Research Department by the communists, he had retreated into adult education and away from active politics. Nevertheless, the contrast between his own ideas, the experiences he had been through in the previous decade and the outlook of the young men he found at Oxford on his return must have seemed to him remarkable. He might have thought us a pallid, bloodless, over-intellectual, self-centred crowd, ridiculously out of touch with the great movements of the day. Yet, I do not recall that this was really his reaction. While he and Margaret, unlike some dons, played little part in the social life of the undergraduate world, they never became impatient with our frivolities or resented our somewhat more detached attitude to social issues.

We were not, in any case, detached all the time. For not

At Oxford in the Twenties

long after the arrival of the Coles there burst upon us the General Strike.

It was on account of the Strike that I first came to know Douglas and Margaret. I had been reading some socialist theory as well as economics — Tawney, the Webbs, Marx (about half of volume i of *Das Kapital*), J. A. Hobson, Hugh Dalton, but I did not at that time follow day-to-day politics at all closely. Thus for me, as I think for many others, the impact of the Strike was sharp and sudden, a little like a war, in that everybody's lives were suddenly affected by a new unprecedented situation, which forced us to abandon plans for pleasure, to change our values and adjust our priorities.

Above all we had to make a choice. And how we chose was a clear test of our political outlook.

The vast majority of undergraduates went off to unload ships and drive trams or lorries. For me this was out of the question. All my sympathies were instinctively on the side of the miners, the unions, the Labour Party, and the Left generally. It was their cause I wanted to help.

But how to help? Someone, possibly Evan Durbin, already a practised speaker and active politician, or John Dugdale must have told me about the Coles. Anyway I went to their house in Holywell where they had set up a University Strike Committee which was working with the official Oxford City Trade Union Committee and also providing a kind of unofficial employment exchange for those undergraduates who wanted to do something to help the strikers.

What could I do? Precious little. Speak at meetings? God forbid! Organise? Absolutely no experience. Had I got a car? No. Could I by any chance drive a car? Yes, I had learnt the year before. Then perhaps I could drive John Dugdale's. I knew him personally; he was a pupil of Douglas's; but as he was taking his 'schools' in a few weeks he could not spare much time. John agreed to let me drive his snub-nosed Morris when he himself was not available. So with this plan and the sponsorship of the Coles I went off to the Oxford Strike Committee Headquarters, got myself enrolled as a driver and received my instructions. When available I was to take speakers to meetings in the Oxford area. But my main job was to act as driver to Margaret Cole who was the liaison officer between the Oxford Committee and the T.U.C. in London, and to bring back our copies of the *British Worker*, the strike broadsheet, printed on the *Daily Herald* presses. I was even given a union card (Printers and Papermakers), fully paid up, to get me through the pickets and crowds in Fleet Street.

Margaret and I must have driven to London and back three or four times during those ten days. A few incidents stand out clearly in my memory. The car stopping on Huntercombe Hill with the radiator boiling; waiting in Eccleston Square while Margaret was in the T.U.C. offices and hearing an old gentleman mutter as he passed 'what a crowd' and add, as he realised where he was, 'what a crew!'; giving Will Thorne a lift to the House of Commons and the difficulty of getting his vast bulk in and out of the little Morris; going with Margaret to see the Tawneys in Mecklenburgh Square and being surprised to find the famous socialist wearing his old sergeant's jacket from the first World War; trying vainly to climb into college one night when we arrived back after 12 (later I was to find an easier way), and being in consequence fined £1 despite a fierce verbal protest to the Warden of the College — H. A. L. Fisher — that he was shockingly biased against the strikers and those who were helping them.

But, alas, though Margaret must have taught me during those drives a great deal about the personalities of the movement, its recent history and the whole set-up, I do not hold much of our conversation clearly in my memory. Perhaps because this was the beginning of four or five years of especially close association with the Coles, I cannot separate what was said in those days of May 1926 from many other later discussions.

After the collapse of the Strike, there followed the long-drawn-out agony of the miners' lock-out. We collected money for them and argued hotly with the more conventional about the merits of striking and the whole system. In Holywell, at the Coles's house, there were gatherings of the faithful —

At Oxford in the Twenties

brought closer together by the Strike — Evan Durbin, Colin Clark, Gilbert Walker, John Parker, Rachael Stewart, Robert Henriques, and Anthony Bowlby must have been among those present.

The Strike and what followed led in my case to an important decision — to take as my special subject in the 'Modern Greats' degree, 'Labour Movements' — with Douglas as my tutor.[1]

I can recall very vividly the wonderfully stimulating quality of those tutorials. Douglas treated one as completely adult — a research worker rather than someone to be pushed through an examination. I wrote perhaps a dozen essays for him and for each of these there was a prodigious reading list. I remember once finishing an essay at 4 A.M., reading it to Douglas at a tutorial at 9 A.M. and being so impressed and fascinated by our discussion that on receiving at the end of the hour my next subject with the usual colossal list of books, I went, despite the need for sleep, straight off to the Bodleian and started work on it.

This enthusiasm which Douglas stirred in me about the subject was due partly to his immense personal charm, partly to his remarkable erudition and partly, I think, to his deep interest in the characters and personalities about whom we were talking — William Cobbett, Francis Place, Robert Owen, William Lovett, and many others. Douglas was interested in such persons not just because of the influence they had upon their times but as people. He would talk about them as if he knew them well, disliking some and liking others. His favourite was certainly Cobbett. He loved this brilliant, forthright pamphleteer with his hatred of sham and evasions, his colossal energy, his robust language and his passion for the English countryside. These were qualities which Douglas himself held in highest esteem. The special edition of *Rural Rides* upon which he was working at this time was a labour of love.

---

[1] In effect 'Labour Movements' really meant the history of the British Labour Movement. For my part I regard Douglas Cole's work in this field as being especially outstanding. Although he was not a pure specialist, the breadth of his knowledge and his sense of perspective made him a very fine teacher of social and economic history.

Soon after I had gone down from Oxford, Douglas and I went on two walking tours — not very extensive — three days each — nor very fast — 20-25 miles a day. Again, I do not recall the detail of what we talked about. But I do remember learning some things about him which might not be so obvious to those who only heard his brilliantly lucid lectures, sat under his efficient chairmanship, or met him round the table on some committee.

We walked in Southern England — and this was no accident. Like George V, Douglas never cared much for 'abroad'. I emphasise *Southern* England. I do not recollect his showing much enthusiasm even for Yorkshire dales, Welsh mountains, Cheviot Hills, or Scottish lochs. But he loved Southern England, especially the Home Counties — the Downs and the meadows; the old villages and the woodlands. And not by anything he said but by his own obvious feeling for it he taught me to appreciate far more than before the quiet, unspectacular loveliness of the typical English countryside.

He also taught me to like walking, which I had hitherto looked upon as a tiresome chore. Indeed if I had not been so flattered at being asked to accompany such a famous companion, I doubt if I would have gone on a walking tour at all. As it was, I remember asking him how it was possible not to bump into cars and people on hard roads all the time in the Home Counties and being surprised to find with Douglas's help and an ordnance survey map that one could easily avoid such horrors for hours on end.

However much on the intellectual plane Douglas was an internationalist, emotionally — and he never attempted to hide it — he was profoundly attached to England. He was not even a little Englander — really a little Southern Englander!

I made one other discovery about Douglas during these walks. At the time it rather shocked me, though looking back I see now that I should have expected it. I discovered how much more he hated the liberals than the tories. This came out vividly when we were walking past the grounds of the Highclere Estate near Newbury (which belongs to the Earl of Carnarvon). At this point Douglas, to my astonishment, launched into a panegyric of the English aristocracy. It might not have been wholly serious, but it did, I think, reflect a certain nostalgia for pre-industrial Britain. One can trace this same backward look in his writings on Guild Socialism as well as in his love of William Morris (very much a favourite too) and his respect for Hilaire Belloc.

Alongside this strong strain of resistance to rationalism and utilitarianism, this anti-intellectualism and even the odd respect for tory traditionalism, he also had, like all socialists, a deep and passionate hatred of social injustice. But sometimes in our talks this led not so much to a calm appraisal of policy as to a virtually nihilistic attitude to society. 'There ought to be', he once said to me, 'a revolution of some kind every few years whatever it's about'. And though I expressed strong dissent about this, he still maintained half-seriously at least that revolution, even if it led to bloodshed, was something desirable in itself. Yet, personally, he was the most non-violent of men.

While as his pupil and friend I was aware of these unusual contrasts in his attitude as well as of his far better-known socialist convictions, I never thought of him in the least as a prophet with a message, at whose feet we sat and whose disciples we became. I doubt if he ever wanted to play that kind of role. In later years when he became better known and more established in Oxford, he must, through his lectures and tutorials, have influenced the minds of many younger men and women towards his own political outlook. But I do not think his relationship with his students was ever like that of Harold Laski, for example, with his. In my time at any rate there was nothing of the sort. I should say that Douglas himself was much too sensitive, self-critical, and even sardonic to play the part of 'The Master' at all willingly.

We disagreed quite frequently — not on economic history or when I was his pupil, but in the years which followed, on socialist doctrine and policy. I suppose that these differences were really differences of temperament, since he was, as I have said, much more emotional and I was much more of a rationalist. One of my most treasured memories is of a tremendous argument we had when he was writing in — I think — 1929,

The Next Ten Years in British Social and Economic Policy. I was attacking Guild Socialism because it was both unrealistic and really directed to what were false aims. One must, I said, always come back to the happiness of the individual. Eventually we went to bed. The next morning Douglas said he had been thinking about it all night and decided I was right. I was deeply touched and absurdly pleased when later the preface to the book contained a moving reference to our tussle. But I mention this episode to show the complete equality which Douglas accorded to unknown young men half his age.

Apart from being a brilliant tutor and a warm-hearted friend of the young, Douglas impressed me enormously — as he did everybody — with his prodigious intellectual energy, the wide range of his interests and the speed with which he worked. In view of his sheer literary output it may seem superfluous to stress this. Margaret picks on his ability to write without stopping as his most extraordinary quality. I agree, but it was not the number of books he had written and was writing which struck me most. It was other, smaller things. I have never known anyone who could write so many letters in his own hand on his knee so fast and without stopping, or even correcting what he had written. On and on he would go — doing what most of us find extremely tedious, pausing only to pick up an envelope, address it, stick it down and drop it on the growing pile on the floor beside him.

I have also known few men who could speak so fluently and clearly on so many different subjects. I remember once being taken by him to a meeting of the Political Economy Club in London where he was to talk on 'Local Government Reform'. He spoke without notes with great brilliance and incomparable lucidity for about forty-five minutes. Even this well-informed audience did not seem to think there was much more to say after he had finished. Yet Local Government was not by any means a subject on which he was a specialist. Indeed until that evening I did not realise he knew very much about it at all.

In the years during which I saw most of Douglas and Margaret, there were two activities in which (apart from academic work, historical writing, detective stories, weekly journalism, and bringing up children!) they were especially interested — adult education and socialist research. It so happened that in a small way I was involved with them in both. They had turned to adult education after the end of the post-war militant phase in the labour movement when before returning to Oxford, Douglas had held for a short time the post of Director of Tutorial Classes at London University. And when he came to Oxford with the post of Reader in Economics he continued to take two tutorial classes a week.

In part their interest in adult education was non-political. Teaching in and organising adult classes, helping to bring non-vocational education to those who had had no secondary education, was simply the way in which they thought they could best serve their fellow-citizens at that time. But they were also moved by the need to educate and train the men and women from whom would come the future leadership of the movement. I remember Douglas once saying to me that W.E.A. tutors were in many respects the true missionaries of today — doing the kind of job which at one time the churches used to do.

He himself, typically, was not content to take and organise classes or to write books especially for these classes. Recognising that one of the keys to success was decent pay and conditions and a proper status for the tutors he also built up and led their trade union, the Tutors' Association, not at all the kind of thing which a man of his eminence would have been expected to bother with.

It was through Douglas that I myself became a W.E.A. tutor — as my first job after leaving Oxford. This was a turning-point in my life at which Douglas exercised for better or worse a decisive influence upon me. So I think I should tell the story.

I had got a 'first' — though only after a long *viva* — and had to make up my mind what to do. I did not want to do the 'conventional' things — Civil Service, Bar, etc.; indeed I had worked hard for a 'first' in my last year, virtually since the General Strike, in the hope that it would give me the freedom to choose something different. But what? Douglas invited me to dine with him at Les Gourmets restaurant in Gerrard Street and we discussed the situation. He suggested two possibilities — either research with him — probably on some part of the history of the labour movement — or adult education. If I chose the latter there was a job going in Nottingham which he thought I could get. I was tremendously pleased with this second idea. I was anxious to earn my own living and be on my own. Having heard Douglas talk about the W.E.A. I had sometimes wondered if I could do this sort of job but thought it probably beyond me. Yet there I was being offered a start at once. So I plumped for it, and on the strength of Douglas's recommendation, got the Nottingham post. It was my experiences there — especially in the coalfields — which were to turn me later towards active politics.

This change in my life meant that for a time I was less closely in touch with Douglas and Margaret. However, a year later, I moved down to London, having got a job at University College, and took a flat in Great Ormond Street. The Coles, who had to be in London quite often, wanted a *pied-à-terre* and rented my back room. This helped me out financially and gave me a chance of seeing some more of them.

That brings me to the second major activity of theirs of which I have spoken — socialist research. Some background must be sketched in here. The election of 1929 seemed to us at the time a wonderful, almost miraculous victory. We had done so much better than I (perhaps because most of my speaking had been in Marylebone !) had thought possible. We paid little, no doubt far too little, attention to the absence of a clear majority. It was enough for us that Labour was in power again, and for the first time held the largest number of seats. Now hopes for peace could be high, we would clear the slums — and, above all, tackle the unemployment. . . .

Then came the slump. The break in the autumn was followed by a steady, remorseless decline. Month by month the unemployment mounted — and with it came fearful disappointment and disillusionment. The government seemed incapable of stopping the rot or indeed of grappling with the situation at all. It was natural, if a little unfair, to conclude that they and Labour Members of Parliament generally were incapable of doing their job because they were unprepared. And it did not seem that Transport House was any better.

The Coles decided something must be done about it. Beginning in 1930 and stretching over about two years, they organised several conferences at Easton Lodge in Essex, the home of Lady Warwick, a well-known socialist who had been a great Edwardian beauty and friend of Edward VII and subsequently a close friend of H. G. Wells. To these were invited people drawn from different sections of the labour movement: M.P.s, dons, writers, trade unionists. Among those who came were Bertrand Russell, H. N. Brailsford, Leonard Woolf, Stafford Cripps, Harold Laski, Hugh Dalton, Arthur Pugh, Ernest Bevin, and many others. It was the Coles, however, who organised and ran the conferences. Their most important outcome was the formation of two new organisations, the Society for Socialist Information and Propaganda (SSIP, pronounced 'Zip') and the New Fabian Research Bureau (NFRB). SSIP was an avowedly propaganda body — for in this field too it was felt that the party had also failed badly. It soon took on a decidedly left-wing tinge and after some internal struggles was transformed into the Socialist League, which under Stafford Cripps's influence later joined the United Front with the communists and was consequently disaffiliated from the party.

Although the Coles had launched SSIP and were keen on it at first, they devoted far more of their energies to the NFRB. It was realised from the start that if it was to have any influence in the party, it must steer clear of internal controversy and refrain from forming policies of its own. It was to be a research service of a genuine objective kind. And such it turned out to be.

The decision to set it up was a natural one in view of the obvious failure of the Labour Government and the desperate desire for new thinking after the 1931 election disaster. The need for it sprang from the almost moribund character of the older Fabian Society which for some years had failed to produce any new ideas worthy of the name.

This is not the place to write the history of the NFRB. But

about it three things can be said. First it served to harness the intellectual energies of many younger socialists to the practical issues of policy confronting the party; in so doing it brought them together and put them in touch with the older leaders. Secondly, it led on to the reinvigoration of the Fabian Society after the merger of the two bodies in 1938. Thirdly, it would never have existed if it had not been for Douglas and Margaret who founded it and cherished it throughout the thirties and made it into a force whose influence was to be felt in post-war years, when quite a few of those who had been connected with it were members of the Labour Government. In the remarkable story of the Cole partnership NFRB will not be the least of their achievements.

There is one last question which, looking back to the 1920s, I should perhaps try to answer about Douglas Cole. Why did he not go into active politics? It can be said that in his earliest and most famous contribution to socialist thought he was tilting against the emphasis on purely political institutions. It can be added that judging by the things he has said about them he never much liked politicians! Nevertheless, Douglas would not have denied that in Great Britain political power must be the major instrument by which to achieve the ideals of democratic socialism.

Certainly his friends would have rejoiced had he gone into politics. I remember at the time how excited and pleased we were when in 1930 he became prospective Labour candidate for the King's Norton division of Birmingham. It was before the 1931 débâcle and the seat was a marginal one. We felt he was badly needed in Parliament, where the Labour Party could well do with the reinforcement which Douglas's brains and ability would bring them. But he gave up the candidature after only a few months. No doubt it was partly for reasons of health. Yet I am sure that this was not the decisive thing. I remember his telling me at the time that 'he could not bear all the awful competition and the limelight'. I think that this and all that it implies was much more important.

The truth is that Douglas would have found utterly distasteful much that is unavoidable in a politician's life. I do not mean the simplification of complex issues : few people have been so successful in doing this or have done so much of it ; his work for adult education speaks for itself. He would have disliked, rather, having to try to please so many people, having to pretend to tolerate those he really found intolerable, having to overcome his natural shyness and develop into a good mixer. He would have rebelled against the compromises which from time to time working in a team must involve. But above all I think he would have objected to any idea of playing on people's emotions, even trying to convey to others in a way which would move them the deep emotions with which he himself was affected. For it was another contrast in Douglas that being in so many respects less intellectual and more emotional in his approach to politics than most of my generation, he would nevertheless shrink from displaying emotion before any audience of even the smallest size. I cannot think of any speech of his which I have heard in which he did not keep to the dry, hard track of intellectual reasoning.

It seems to me that it was these personal qualities of sensitiveness and inner restraint which more than anything else held him back from being either a politician — or for that matter a prophet. I do not think we should regret it. It was a quality which his friends and admirers especially valued in him. Moreover, the labour movement will always need thinkers as well as doers, planners as well as politicians. Douglas Cole's contribution in the past half-century to the history, thought, and education of the movement has been on such a massive scale that it could hardly have been matched by the most impressive parliamentary triumphs or the most successful Ministerial record.

(iii)

STEPHEN K. BAILEY

WHAT COLE REALLY MEANT

LIFE in midpassage is too filled with demands and routines to permit much personal reflection. One is conscious that the years are ticking by; that the children are mushrooming; that parents and other older friends are now gone, or have themselves become dependent; that sooner than expected the sharp, cutting edge of one's own psyche has been slightly dulled by time and fate; and that the great questions of purpose and meaning of life remain as intractable as ever.

But 42 is not an age for reminiscing or for metaphysical speculation. It is an age for load-carrying. It is an age when formative influences have hardened; when intelligence has become the great rationaliser as well as modifier of moral habit and prejudice; when disappointments in others are increasingly equalised by disappointments in one's own performance and possibilities; when, with Cecil Rhodes, one interrupts activity only to lament the amount to be done and the short time in which to do it.

But I find that in those few minutes when I *can* pause to scan the sky, the bright stars are not precepts but people — people who have lived life ahead of me and who have communicated by the example of their works, and by the ineffable grace of gentleness and poise, that the years ahead are not only endurable, but, with effort and dedication, rich and meaningful.

It strengthens me, age 42, to think of Douglas Cole, age 50. (When I am 62 I shall think of G. D. H. Cole, as I saw him last, then in his sixty-ninth year, working quietly in his room in All Souls, the burnished steel of intellect and moral purpose shining through an honestly-earned but vast weariness. But in this paper, Cole is 50.)

G. D. H. Cole is a towering and somewhat frightening figure to a newly matriculated American at Oxford. His erudition is legendary; his productivity, superhuman; his smoking, incessant; his lecturing, brilliant; his anti-Americanism, notorious. Ogden Nash once accused the English of loving their colonies and hating their colonials. Cole operates in reverse. He loves Americans but hates America. It takes no time at all to discover that his image of the United States is often outrageous and partial; that what he hates is the social injustices, personal indignities, and ruthlessness of untamed capitalism, and that the word 'America' is for him simply a handy verbal symbol for those evils. It takes almost as little time to discover that his friendlier image of the U.S.S.R. is utterly incongruous with his personal hatred of violence and his devotion to individual liberty. It takes a little longer to discover that although he knows a vast amount about democratic theory and institutions, he can never reconcile himself completely to the necessary compromises and accommodations of democracy. One senses, for example, that he dislikes Burke not only because Burke 'pitied the plumage and forgot the dying bird', but because Burke viewed reason as a lowly handmaiden rather than as sovereign. (Sitting passively under a gargantuan gramophone horn, Cole smokes at my concluding sentences on Burke and Paine, and then says rather cheerily, 'Of course, I hate Burke'.)

It is ironic that Cole's stubborn propensity to divide the world into good guys and bad guys, good systems and bad systems, is a peculiarly American failing. But in Cole the failure is the necessary shadow of a light so strong and an affirmation so incandescent that the weird shapes on the wall only draw attention to the beauty of the object elongated in reflection. For the overpowering effect of Cole as a teacher is his capacity to convey the message that reason and compassion are man's twin glories; that the evils of the world are amenable to rational correction by the construction and pursuit of ideal forms and norms; that ideas are the only civilised weapons of power; that prescription exists only to be fearlessly challenged; that education can free the lowly, and tame the arrogant; that history can teach.

These are not unfamiliar themes; some of them, in the short run at least, may seem naïve. But Cole gives them a strange authority by his self-mastery. The very crispness of his personality takes the edge off his prejudices and dislikes. He is utterly devoid of self-pity. ('Excuse me, Bailey, it is time for my needle. Diabetes, you know.') And both the crispness and the absence of self-pity are manifestations of a mind constantly in control. Cole never voices an opinion which seems extraneous to a formal system of thought peculiarly his own. Every idea is pregnant with well-ordered premises, even if some premises turn out upon examination to be unacceptable to the listener.

Cole teaches without technique, without even what would be called in the advertising jungle of the 1950s, the 'soft sell'. His erudition is never paraded in pomp. Surely few minds in the twentieth century have been tidier or fuller.

The tutorial starts promptly and pleasantly. Questions, comments, criticisms appear with such briskness and kindness that one is encouraged to excellence.

'Hyndman', I read from my essay, 'was an orthodox Marxist.'

'Excuse me, Bailey; but what do you mean by the word "orthodox"?'

Bailey is not sure what he means by 'orthodox', but a lesson is learned that words have value beyond style, that precision is an intellectual virtue.

'Rousseau was fundamentally a Platonist', I read from another essay.

'I'm sorry, Bailey, but this seems to me to say everything and nothing. Let us pause and consider for a moment.'

Bailey is not chastised. He is urged to think. It is not Cole who is superior, but Bailey's sober second thought.

'Bailey, I think you have a typographical error here. The year was not 1812 but 1821. The date is important because the Napoleonic wars did not end until 1815, and the situation you

What Cole Really Meant

describe was part of the post-war slump.'

The date is important only as it suggests events and sequences which are important.

'Bailey, I don't remember the exact wording of the Act, but let me check.' Cole leaps from his chair, strides with the accuracy of a homing bee to a tiny volume in an undifferentiated section of a vast collection of books, thumbs with incredible speed to the legislation in question, and reads the appropriate passage.

Again the lesson is precision, but added are the lessons of unselfconscious humility, and the utility of a personal library.

Cole tutors in Political Theory, Economic Theory, Economic Institutions, Labour Movements since 1815, and Social and Economic History. He is at his best in Political Theory and Social and Economic History. He is frank about his dislike of Economic Theory, and one senses a slight *ennui* in his handling of Economic Institutions. Even in Social and Economic History, although enormously effective in tutorials, he is more effective as a lecturer. Standing on the platform in a crowded lecture hall in Schools, eyes closed, machine on, Cole projects the sweep of the industrial revolution and its meaning in human terms. Whatever the influence of Marx upon Cole's thinking, his lectures belie a simple determinism. Rich in biography — Defoe and Wilkes, Cobbett and Place, Owen and O'Connor, Morris and Hardie — his lectures are testaments to man as creator as well as creature. And what stirs him particularly is compassionate man — not the compassion of paternalism, but the compassion of a moral conviction that ugliness and human suffering and ignorance and ruthless exploitation are unspeakable evils.

In no field does Cole make a greater impression than in Political Theory. Neither he nor I know in 1938 that some day I will become mayor of an American city, and will find his Political Theory the most practical knowledge at my command. Cole's non-Hegelian interpretation of Rousseau's General Will becomes an ethical proposition of ruling dimensions in my subsequent life, and makes me forever impatient with definitions of the public interest which view man solely as appetite.

But Cole is more than lecturer and tutor. Writer of detective stories, of 'intelligent guides', of profound essays, popular biographies, social histories, Fabian tracts, *New Statesman* leaders; Labour candidate for Oxford University, who would have been horrified at the thought of personal political victory; one of the towering intellectual leaders and institution-builders of the national Labour Party; one of Britain's pioneers in workers' education; Cole nevertheless always seems to have time to spend informally with students. And it is in these informal contacts — tea, sherry, the Master's Discussion Group — that a special quality appears. Hidden in shyness, sheltered in matter-of-factness, protected by hedgerows of cool and clipped rationality, is a spirit so wistful, so delicate, so ineffably kind, so fundamentally lacking in contentiousness, so sensitive to the aspirations and needs of others, as to make one weep in gratitude and wonder. This is the Cole which many of his professional colleagues have never seen, or been allowed to see. This is the Cole which withered by contrast the embattled pundit by the same name. This is the Cole which was never consciously revealed.

But this is the image which is freshest after twenty years. With all gratitude for his brilliance and for his intellectual inspiration and guidance, I am most grateful for having known a poised and beautiful spirit.

This is what Cole really meant.

(iv)
G. D. N. WORSWICK

COLE AND OXFORD, 1938–1958

THE Faculty of Social Studies in Oxford, according to the official university *Gazette*, has some two hundred members. Symbols *ph*, *p*, and *e* against each name denote the sub-faculty, of philosophy, politics, or economics, to which each member is attached. The exact rules which determine the affixing of these symbols no doubt lie somewhere deep in the university statutes, but roughly they denote the central interest, in research or teaching of college tutors, university professors, readers and lecturers, and so on. Most members have only one symbol. Pairs are not unknown, *ph*, *p* ; or *p*, *e* : though none — is this significant ? — *ph*, *e*. Among all two hundred names only one carried a triple pennant *ph*, *p*, *e*, G. D. H. Cole, M.A., All Souls. This surely is significant. In his teaching, his writing, and his many public and political activities, Cole always represented in his person the idea of the seamless web of social studies.

From 1925 to 1944 Cole was Fellow of University College and University Reader in Economics : from 1944 until his retirement in 1957 he was Chichele Professor of Social and Political Theory. As author he could be labelled economist, historian, political philosopher, sociologist — and there may be some to whom he is most familiar as half of a well-known writer of detective stories. This unitary view of social studies was consciously affirmed, was clearly apparent in his writings, and manifested itself in innumerable ways in Cole's approach to the study of society. Though the cast of Cole's mind seemed perhaps more purely intellectual and scholarly than many 'non-political' dons, he always placed great emphasis on political and social action.

I have been asked to write about Cole in Oxford after the beginning of the second World War, and though I shall confine myself almost entirely to university matters, I shall be hard put to it to keep within my allotted space. But for many G. D. H. Cole meant the political writer and pamphleteer, the chairman of the Fabian Society, the active organiser of conferences and socialist societies, or the adult educationist. Indeed it may come as a surprise that despite his prodigious industry on the national and international stage it is still in keeping to regard him as an Oxford man who made an important contribution to his university, not only by his writing and teaching, but by an amount of administrative activity in the Social Studies Faculty, in the Delegacy for Extra-mural Studies, and the Delegacy for Social Training, to mention only a few, which would daunt even the most ardent university committeeman, who finds no time to write or even to go to a polling-booth.

When my story begins Cole's position in the university was less influential in the faculty and in administration than it was to become, but already enormously influential among undergraduates. He lectured on a wide range of subjects and drew large audiences. My own first sight of Cole was at a lecture on trade unions. I was astonished then, and never ceased later to admire his wonderful ability to lecture *extempore* (perhaps he had notes, but he never seemed to be looking at them) and yet to keep everything in proper balance. At the end one saw how well planned it all was, but while he was speaking one was conscious only of a fascinating and often exciting narrative. He gave much time and help to the Labour Club, whose 'Popular Front' line he wholly approved and did much to engender. The Cole group, which met on Wednesday evenings in Cole's room in University College, and consisted of undergraduates from all colleges, mostly reading P.P.E. and History but with a fair sprinkling of others, who read and discussed papers with Cole as an informal chairman, was at its peak. In one form or another the Cole group lasted throughout Cole's career in Oxford. He himself was obliged from time to time to take a less active part in the last twenty years, and when he retired from his chair in 1957, he wound it up. But in the late thirties it was thought of by many of its members as far the most exciting and educative experience of their Oxford life. Some undergraduates would take a lot more trouble over a paper for the Cole group than over a whole term of weekly tutorial essays.

In the earlier thirties he had been instrumental in forming the Thursday Lunch Club, in which some of the younger economists and other dons discussed the problems of world depression and unemployment. But he played no part in the formation of the Oxford Economists' Research Group, whose studies of the rate of interest, and of cost and price behaviour can claim an important part in the development of economics. No doubt this was mainly because in the later thirties Cole was looking outwards, to the Spanish War and the rise of fascism in Europe, but it was partly, I suspect, because he was out of sympathy with the main stream of academic economics. To his way of thinking the enthusiasm for Keynes's *General Theory of Employment, Interest and Money* was quite excessive : all Keynes was doing was to re-state what Hobson had said some thirty years before. In any case the whole business was only tinkering : the structure of capitalism had developed cracks far deeper and wider than could be papered over with mere changes in monetary and budgetary practice. As for business behaviour, he thought the orthodox methods of analysis, with their diagrams and semi-mathematical techniques, altogether too narrow and fiddling to be of use in understanding the harsh realities of monopoly capitalism.

What brought him into the centre of social studies research in Oxford, however, was less any intellectual reappraisal than the second World War. In October 1937 Lord Nuffield made an offer to the university to establish a new College 'to bridge the separation between the economist, the political theorist, the student of government and administration on the one hand, and on the other hand the business man, the politician, the civil servant and the local government official, not to mention the ordinary man and woman', and he went on to make certain suggestions about the kinds of things such a College might do and the way in which it might be run.[1] Besides undertaking research the College might provide opportunities for experts in the various practical fields to co-operate with those engaged in theoretical study, through the appointment of part-time Fellows from government and industry, and through 'expert' conferences. The founder hoped that a strong connection with the Dominions could be established, and that there should be provision for Dominion graduates to reside in the College. To begin with the College and its endowment should be under the direct control of the Hebdomadal Council. To start it off Lord Nuffield gave the site and £1 million (less a small amount being simultaneously given for another purpose). The later story of the College, whose building is now nearly complete, and which has recently entered into full collegiate independence, does not concern us here. A powerful university committee, under the chairmanship of the Vice-Chancellor, A. D. Lindsay, was appointed in 1937, and in the following June Mr. H. B. Butler (later Sir Harold Butler) was appointed Warden. In May 1939 six Visiting Fellows and six Faculty Fellows were appointed. The Faculty Fellows were non-stipendiary appointments of persons already holding college Fellowships or other university posts. The first six were G. D. H. Cole, R. L. Hall, H. R. F. Harrod, R. C. K. Ensor, J. S. Fulton, and Miss Margery Perham. In August 1939, on her appointment to a Readership in Colonial Administration, Miss Perham became at the same time the first Official Fellow of Nuffield College.

But within a month these beginnings were sharply interrupted and policy was reduced to the single question whether the whole project should be put into cold storage for the duration of the war. There could, of course, be no question of a new building, and the Warden himself was one of the first to be called to war-time service, as Regional Commissioner for the South of England. In May 1940, however, the Warden put forward a proposal that the College should undertake research into problems of reconstruction. The tense military

---

[1] Perhaps it should be mentioned that the suggestions outlined in the official offer were not for a college of technology which Lord Nuffield originally had in mind. But that is a different story.

situation postponed consideration of this idea, but by November 1940 it was decided to go ahead, and a plan of work was drawn up for a Nuffield College Social Reconstruction Survey. The subjects of study were to be :

(a) The redistribution of industry and population brought about by the war.
(b) The effects of war conditions on the working of the public social services.
(c) The human effects of evacuation, industrial migration, and other war-time changes in the conditions of living.
(d) The bearing of all these factors on the general problems of social and economic reorganisation and on the practical efficiency of democratic institutions including both government and voluntary agencies.

A committee was appointed, with Cole as Chairman and Director of the Survey. The Survey started in some chilly rooms in the Indian Institute, and soon after further premises were acquired at 17/19 Banbury Road. Contact was to be established with the Institute of Statistics Committee and together these two were to constitute a war-time research committee.

The method of inquiry was novel. In the spring of 1940 Sir William Beveridge had been asked by the government to undertake a Manpower Survey, a task completed in a remarkably short time and a fine example of those great British qualities, unpreparedness and the capacity to improvise. With Cole as his assistant, Beveridge had called upon universities (principally social science departments) and other voluntary agencies to provide local investigators. With little more than a letter of introduction these investigators interviewed employers, employment exchange managers, and others, dug out statistics, and surveyed like anything. I can vouch, as a very junior volunteer in the Survey, for thoroughness. Driving between interviews along an Oxfordshire country lane, my chief suddenly stopped the car, crying 'There goes a tramp, what's *he* doing ?' Cole's idea was to carry out the Nuffield Survey with some of the local investigators already drawn together by the Manpower Survey. A small central staff was appointed both to disseminate statistical and other information to local investigators, who, incidentally, were all honorary, and to receive and collate the reports from them.

Without access to data the Survey would have been stillborn, but full government support was provided through the Minister without portfolio responsible for Reconstruction (Mr. Greenwood) and the Minister of Works and Buildings (Lord Reith); and in the first instance a Treasury grant was made of £5000, though the greater part of the expense of the Survey was met from College funds. (Total expenditures on the Survey were in the end about £46,000. Treasury grants provided £15,000 and the remainder was almost entirely found from College funds.)

The Reconstruction Survey was not the whole of the wartime research in which Nuffield College was engaged. The Second Programme consisted of Miss Perham's colonial research, which was kept quite distinct. In 1942 the College expanded into the field of international economic reconstruction. This work was, however, also kept distinct from the Survey, and was carried out in the Institute of Statistics, being supervised by a committee with representatives from the Nuffield College Committee, the Institute of Statistics, and also Chatham House (part of which was housed in Balliol until late in the war).

In June 1942 Mr. H. B. Butler was appointed British Minister in Washington but he still remained Warden (he resigned the Wardenship in October 1943). Cole was simultaneously appointed to a new post of Sub-Warden, and besides remaining Director of the Survey, took over the chairmanship of the International Committee. Within less than a year of his appointment as Sub-Warden the Treasury stopped its grant (April 1943): in September 1943 Cole resigned his post as Sub-Warden of Nuffield College and in January 1944 his post as Director of the Survey: he also resigned his Faculty Fellowship of the College. The Survey continued at the centre throughout 1944, but solely to tidy up and to bring to publication certain parts of the work which had been undertaken. Its effective work was done under Cole's direction in three short years from early 1941 to the end of 1943. What did it achieve and why was it so quickly strangled ?

Of the work which finally was published there were two kinds. A big study of the *Prospects of the Industrial Areas of Great Britain*, two volumes of *Studies in Industrial Organisation* and a book on *Voluntary Social Services* were supplemented by a few smaller studies, of holiday trades, for example. This work was published over the names of individual authors, who were employed on the central staff in Oxford, or else local investigators, though in varying degrees other members of the survey staff contributed. These might be fairly classed as primarily 'academic' studies. Then there was the series of Reports, on subjects such as Employment Policy and Organisation of Industry after the War, the Problems of Scientific and Industrial Research, and various aspects of Education. It would be a mistake however to regard these simply as 'other publications'. The organisation of expert conferences [1] which preceded these reports constituted a substantial part of the work of the central survey staff. The conferences, usually held in Balliol College, were attended by distinguished university men and women, civil servants, both permanent and temporary, industrialists, and others. Much background documentation had to be prepared by the staff : the whole proceedings were recorded and then smaller committees of experts would prepare a draft Statement, which ultimately was published, with the names of those who had taken part in the conference. Though it was made clear that no signatory was bound to every argument and opinion expressed in the Statement, nevertheless the very fact that they did sign gave them great authority. Cole's own contribution to this side of the work cannot be over-estimated. The conference climate varied from dull respectability to high drama, as when Balogh pricked the balloon of the Bretton Woods scarce currency clause in the presence of some of those who had negotiated the agreement. Dull or exciting, Cole would sum up. His extraordinary memory, his intellectual tidiness and his power of lucid exposition were fully displayed,

[1] There were, besides, regular conferences at which the local investigators and the central staff met to discuss problems of the Survey.

perhaps the most remarkably when the conference had appeared to be least interesting and purposive. Ideas and arguments which had seemed at the time trivial and disconnected were, like the scrappy themes of a symphony by Sibelius, drawn together into a final statement of overwhelming clarity and force. It was said by some that in these summaries and in his drafting Cole slipped in too much of himself. This view was both uncharitable and wrong.

In political and social matters the great British public is, it has been said, torpid and sluggish — but from time to time, like some slumbering beast, it rumbles and snorts and heaves its bulk into some new and more comfortable position. That it did so in 1945 is now history. Cole, more sensitive to the stirrings and stretchings of the beast than some of his critics, sensed this, and sensed too that in the higher ranks of government and industry there was an exceptional receptiveness to ideas of change. What he did was to bring these ideas into the open and then to mould them into those understatements so necessary for Englishmen when they are being most bold. For with all the drafting, changing, and compromising the Statements are not exactly clarion calls; but they retain a breadth of vision, firmness, and humanity which contrast strongly, and rather sadly, with the bleak and bankrupt pessimism of our latter-day experts such as the Cohen Council.

Why did the Survey not go from strength to strength? There were difficulties from the start. It was one thing to have central government approval: it was another to extract statistical and other information from individual Ministries. Some co-operated wholeheartedly. But there were others who had their own ideas about security and who thought that the number of days in the week should be kept a closely guarded military secret. Then, it was said, there was a danger that the 'restricted' information might get to refugee economists, of whom there was indeed a distinguished group in Oxford. (Hence the complicated administrative arrangements for the work of the International Committee.) There were criticisms of the quality of the work being carried on, and it was these which appear to have been the official justification for the withdrawal of Treasury support in 1943.

It is not easy to say how valid these criticisms were, since only part of the work of the Survey was ultimately published. When the Treasury grant was withdrawn the Nuffield College Committee asked Professor A. L. Bowley, Professor G. N. Clark, and Professor D. H. Macgregor to form a special committee of inquiry into the whole work of the Survey. This committee gave a favourable report on the work produced and justified the College committee's confidence in the conduct of the Survey. No doubt not all the work was always of the highest possible standard. It could hardly have been otherwise. Many of the ablest economists in Oxford were already in the forces or in Ministries when the Survey was formed. By the accident of the war, a small number of outstanding European economists had come to work in Oxford, but the government's own rules forbade their use. Again, one can argue that the scope of the Survey was too wide, and too many projects were studied. But this would not have been a serious objection if more resources had been made available.

My own guess is that the reasons for withdrawing the grant were altogether more fundamental. In the earlier years the Survey was started precisely because the Ministries were entirely preoccupied with the war and constructing an effective war economy. No one who mattered had a moment to spare for reconstruction. By 1943 the war economy was under way, and there was time to breathe and to think of the future. The departments began to have ideas of their own. Not that the government's own efforts in the matter of forming and guiding opinion proved ultimately superior. (The Employment Policy White Paper of 1944, for example, compares poorly with the Nuffield Statement.) But anyway they did not want some outside body barging about. Nor can one escape the thought that Cole's avowed socialism might have occurred to some as a good reason for winding up the Survey. Cole's battles were not confined to the Treasury and government front: despite the clean bill of health subsequently given him by the committee of inquiry, there were rumblings in higher university circles. Throughout this time, the framework of Nuffield

College had been kept in being, and even developed. From time to time new Visiting Fellows were appointed, Mr. Harold Clay and Mr. Samuel Courtauld, for example. In October 1942 Field-Marshal Smuts and Mr. J. C. Winant were made Honorary Fellows. The time was approaching when the College would be able to set about building its premises, and establishing its position in a peace-time university. But what was that position to be? Was the College to emerge as a kind of continuation and expansion of the Survey, with the Fellows conducting research in the framework of some general plan? Or was it to be a body of Fellows, chosen for their individual ability, pursuing studies of their own choice and in their own manner, with no attempt to link up either the subjects or the methods of inquiry? There are respectable arguments for both these approaches. Since the latter was already well provided for in Oxford by the existing colleges, one might have thought that the balance might profitably be tilted in favour of experiment. But authority in Oxford tends to be conservative, distrustful of novelty. Moreover the choice of approach could hardly be separated from the choice of a new Warden.

To add to his difficulties Cole was by no means a fit man. He would never rest or spare himself, but even his iron will could not prevent his being laid low on critical occasions by the illness which dogged him all these years. He would brush aside any suggestion that he should drive himself less hard and it was only in recent years that he allowed himself to acknowledge the curb which ill-health imposed upon his tremendous activity. He fought valiantly to save the Survey, but the opposition was too strong. At the beginning of 1944 he had severed all connection with the Survey and with the College. The central staff of the Survey was kept in being for a further period to bring to publication parts of the work which had been undertaken. Under the new Warden, Sir Henry Clay, appointed in May 1944, the College continued to hold a number of conferences of the type which Cole had pioneered, but this side of the College's activities quickly died out, although one or two have been held in more recent years. Cole, it is true, was very soon back in the counsels of the College, as a Professorial Fellow, and in 1957 on his retirement as professor he became a research Fellow ; but the leadership in the creation of Nuffield College, as it is today, was in other hands.

Before the war there had been two professorships for the Politics sub-faculty, the Gladstone Professorship in Political Theory and Institutions, and the Montague Burton Professorship of International Relations. On the resignation of Sir Arthur Salter from the former, in 1944, an earlier decision to 'split the Gladstone chair' was brought into effect. K. C. Wheare was elected Gladstone Professor of Government and Public Administration and Cole was elected the first Chichele Professor of Social and Political Theory. Both professorships are attached to All Souls College. This duumvirate was to reign until 1957 (when by a coincidence the retirement of Cole occurred at the same time as the election of Wheare as Rector of Exeter), and it was a very happy one.

Cole had made his home in London, and he made it clear from the outset that he was not going to give up his London activities. He never spent vacations in Oxford, and during term he always spent the first part of the week in London. This was not to mean, however, that he confined himself to his statutory duties of giving a certain number of lectures in each year. As I try to record what Cole actually did do in the next twelve years I find it almost incredible that he packed all this activity into one half of the week. Officially the supervision of graduate studies is a matter for Faculty Boards : in practice this work falls to a considerable extent on professors. Cole took his full share of interviewing and advising candidates, and of actual supervision, in an astonishingly wide range of topics. Occasionally one comes across students who complain that they never had enough attention from their supervisor : such complaints were never made about Cole.

The Faculty Board has numerous sub-committees and Cole was an active member of most of them, and chairman of several. It fell to him to present the reports of the committee which supervised the Diplomas in Economic and Political Science and in Public Administration. The former is largely taken by men and women from Ruskin College and the Catholic

Workers' College, and the latter by students of the Delegacy for Social Training. In all this he invariably showed an astonishing mastery of the smallest detail. He was a vigorous member of the Standing Committee for the Institute of Statistics.

He was a member of the governing body of two colleges,[1] All Souls and once more of Nuffield to which he was elected professorial Fellow. As if this was not enough he was one of the two or three most active members of the Delegacy for Extra-mural Studies and was academic adviser to Ruskin College. No doubt with age and experience a formidable load such as this can be carried lightly enough, provided one does not try to *do* too much. But Cole constantly appeared as an innovator, bubbling over with new ideas and suggestions.

When the Clapham Committee's recommendations were followed by a large U.G.C. grant 'earmarked' for the expansion of Social Studies, Cole was at the centre of the discussions of the form which this expansion should take. He was especially concerned in promoting the Lecturership in Industrial Relations, and not only did he promote a post in sociology, but did a great deal of work of all kinds to help the Pilot Survey of Oxford undertaken by Mr. Mogey, the Lecturer in Sociology.

Perhaps the best measure of the sheer volume of practical work which Cole did in his years as professor came when he retired and when his place had to be filled in committees too numerous to describe. Time and again it proved necessary to call on two or three to take up a load hitherto carried on a single back.

In the twenties and thirties Cole had made for himself a unique position in the labour movement. He never sought political office — indeed he rarely attended a Labour Party Conference, even as a visitor. But he was continuously consulted by the leaders of the Labour Party and of the trade unions. After 1945 he never exerted such unique influence on current policy. It was not that he was replaced by anyone

[1] The general Oxford rule is that one may not be a member of more than one college governing body at a time. An exception in the case of Nuffield College was possible until 1958, when the College received its Charter.

else, rather that circumstances changed. The 1945 Parliamentary Labour Party contained not only a number of professional economists, many of whom had indeed learned much from Cole, but also men who had during the war acquired firsthand experience of government in the war-time civil service. A Labour Government commanded vastly greater resources for inquiry and consultation than the Labour Opposition of pre-war days. Then, too, though Cole himself was the most ardent advocate of the view that the practical measures needed to cope with the reconstruction of the British economy in a war-torn world were the same as those which would hasten the transformation of the economy into a fully socialist one, this consideration was by no means so obvious to others. Cole found himself increasingly out of sympathy with labour leaders preoccupied with the balance of payments, production, and efficiency, to the neglect of socialist ideals.

In 1945 he decided to break the rule he had set for himself, to keep out of the political arena, and stood for Parliament, as a candidate for one of the two Oxford University seats. He was supported by the university constituency Labour Party, but he did not seek endorsement as an 'official' Labour candidate. On the other hand he would not stand purely as an 'independent' which so often had meant simply being rather more conservative than the official Conservatives. His poll, of 3414 original votes against 6771 for Sir Arthur Salter and 5136 for A. P. Herbert, was a good one for so uncompromising a socialist candidate. Cole himself had thought there was little hope of a win, and since he had no personal wish for limelight he was much less disappointed than his friends who had hoped that his particular brand of independence might prove especially valuable in the first post-war parliamentary years.

Almost as if he regarded this innocent flirtation with practical politics as a warning of more serious things, in 1946 he cut away from many public activities. He resigned from the chairmanship of the Fabian Society, whose research and other activities he had directed with great vigour since 1939: although he was to return to active work in the Society in the last years of the Labour Government. He was, as I have already suggested, out of sympathy with the 'technocratic' tendencies among labour leaders and intellectuals and felt the need to withdraw completely from involvement in current questions. Nonetheless he continued to write with force on current problems, in his books and in the *New Statesman*, and in recent years he set out to organise socialist intellectuals in an international society, although eschewing any idea of formulating a programme. To think, to teach, and to write, and to leave political action to others; this remained his guiding principle after the second world war.

The history of the British labour movement cannot be fully understood without an appreciation of the strand of socialist *faith* which runs unbroken. As a historian Cole had always known this, and in turn he came to personify it. With such profound conviction, matched as it was with outspokenness and a high degree of moral courage, it is not surprising that he aroused misgivings and opposition in the predominantly conservative university of the inter-war years. Such opposition merely fired him to greater efforts. Given enough time for reason to do its work, it must inevitably dissolve. After 1945 he became, willy-nilly, a highly influential member of the university establishment, and he had plenty of colleagues who voted Labour and did not regard him as a dangerous firebrand. Not that he was satisfied with the prevailing intellectual climate of logical analysis and empirical inquiry. For the latter indeed he had an appetite as strong as his socialist faith. But as he made clear in his *Socialist Economics* he was convinced that social research must be guided by certain value judgments, which he set out as twelve postulates of socialist economics. Cole's conviction that it was possible to school one's thinking and to guide one's action according to principles was very profound. There were many times when his friends and colleagues, less gifted and less sure of their motives, felt that inflexible principle had overridden good judgment. Cole disdained the ordinary arts of committee manoeuvring: and, heaven knows, the *pure* committee man can be a tiresome nuisance. One sometimes wonders, however, whether the cold rays of pure reason are sufficient, even among dons.

Cole and Oxford, 1938–1958

In the last twenty years Cole moved over to the centre of the government of social studies in Oxford, but intellectually he still remained somewhat isolated. The cautious and meticulous linguistic analysis of Oxford philosophers had no appeal for him, and though he approved the increasing emphasis upon applied economics, one sensed that he regarded the deliberate circumscription of their field by economists as a wilful disregard of the complexities of social behaviour. His dislike, even disdain, for the 'professional specialisms' which flourish today sprang partly from the heart — he felt that the human purpose of all this detailed research was being lost sight of — but partly it arose, paradoxically, from his own extreme versatility. The specialists put themselves in blinkers because they wish to pursue a particular road and want to avoid distractions on either side. That the subtler refinements which this makes possible may sometimes produce results which have far-reaching importance did not seem to impress Cole. He regarded the blinkers merely as obscurantist devices of scholasticism, getting in the way of a synoptic view of the landscape. It is not unfair to say that when he set out in his inaugural lecture to delimit the scope of 'social and political theory', he came out with the answer — everything, or very nearly everything. I think, incidentally, that it was this all-embracing attitude which partly explains why, although he gave lectures and seminars in social and political theory, Cole never attempted to write any principal work in this field. He continued to write books on practical economics and politics, primarily addressed to the layman — to the W.E.A. student shall we say — and steadily continued his historical researches into socialism and socialist thought, extending his range to the international plane. He had already prepared for himself, before he became professor, a vast programme of research which would have kept him busy even without the persistent interruptions of ill-health. I suspect too that to concentrate on 'social and political theory' might to him have appeared as a concession to the 'professional specialist' view of research which he so much deplored.

Be that as it may, only a man of truly outstanding gifts

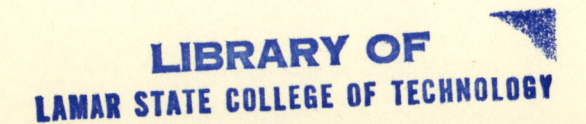

could have attempted work of the scope which Cole always did, or could have dared to adopt his intellectual position. It is not surprising that he occasionally showed traces of intellectual arrogance and intolerance. What is so extraordinary is that despite his own virtuosity and quickness of mind he could be so encouraging, so patient and so helpful to students and colleagues of much humbler powers. We all know how much he wrote. Not everyone knows, except his grateful pupils and friends, how much he read, of theses, drafts of articles, and books. If you sent him something he would not merely tell you what he thought of it, but would accompany his reply with meticulous and invariably pointed comments. Nothing was too large or too small.

Cole was a man of many roles, in all of which he made an outstanding contribution. I have tried to describe some of the things he did, and the position he occupied in Oxford in the last twenty years. He was a great man, of high ideals, who never sought for himself honours or personal aggrandisement. As a thinker and writer he never spared his opponents. But he was quite without malice. Ironically, perhaps, for one who had such a profound belief in principle and the power of reason, his greatest influence may prove to have been through his own goodness.

Essays in Labour History

1

ASA BRIGGS

THE LANGUAGE OF 'CLASS' IN EARLY NINETEENTH-CENTURY ENGLAND

THE concept of social 'class' with all its attendant terminology was a product of the large-scale economic and social changes of the late eighteenth and early nineteenth centuries. Before the rise of modern industry [1] writers on society spoke of 'ranks', 'orders', and 'degrees' or, when they wished to direct attention to particular economic groupings, of 'interests'. The word 'class' was reserved for a number of people banded together for educational purposes [2] or more generally with reference to subdivisions in schemes of 'classification'.[3] Thus the 1824 edition of the *Encyclopædia Britannica* spoke of 'classes of quadrupeds, birds, fishes and so forth, which are again subdivided into series or orders and these last into genera'. It directed its readers to articles on 'Animal Kingdom' and 'Botany'. By 1824, however, the word 'class' had already established itself as a social label, and ten years later John Stuart Mill was to remark:

They revolve in their eternal circle of landlords, capitalists and labourers, until they seem to think of the distinction of society into

[1] In its modern sense the word 'industry', used with reference not to a particular human attribute, but to a complex of manufacturing and productive institutions, was itself a new word in the late eighteenth century. See R. Williams, *Culture and Society* (1958), p. xv. Adam Smith was one of the first writers to use the word in this way: he did not use the word 'class' in the sense discussed in this essay.

[2] It was later used by the Methodists to refer to 'class' meetings, a usage which was later borrowed by early nineteenth-century 'Political Protestants' and Chartists.

[3] Daniel Defoe, who usually wrote in terms of 'orders', 'ranks', and 'degrees', on a few occasions used 'class' in contexts where he was referring to social classification. See, for instance, *Review*, 14 April 1705, 21 June 1709. Smith also referred (incidentally) to 'classes of people' in his account

those three classes as if it were one of God's ordinances not man's, and as little under human control as the division of day or night. Scarcely any one of them seems to have proposed to himself as a subject of inquiry, what changes the relations of those classes to one another are likely to undergo in the progress of society.[1]

The word 'class' has figured so prominently in the subsequent development of the socialist — and of other social — vocabularies that a study of the origins and early use of the term in Britain is not simply an academic exercise in semantics. There was no dearth of social conflicts in pre-industrial society, but they were not conceived of at the time in straight class terms. The change in nomenclature in the late eighteenth and early nineteenth centuries reflected a basic change not only in men's ways of viewing society but in society itself. It is with the relationship between words and movements — in an English context — that this essay is concerned.

I

Eighteenth-century English society was hierarchical, and was often conceived of in terms of a pyramid with the 'common people', those without rank or 'dignity' at the base. The 'meer labouring people who depend upon their hands', as Defoe called them, were never without defenders,[2] but social orthodoxy had little use for 'the gross and inconsistent notion' of equality.[3] Skilled artisans had their own grades of 'superiority' and 'inferiority',[4] while between the 'nobility' and the 'commonalty' were the growing numbers of 'middling people' or 'middling sorts' whose praises were frequently sung in an

of 'the three great orders of society' in his *The Wealth of Nations*, Book I, chapter 11.

[1] *Monthly Repository* (1834), p. 320.

[2] For one of the most important strands in the defence, see C. Hill, 'The Norman Yoke' in J. Saville (ed.), *Democracy and the Labour Movement* (1954).

[3] For an early eighteenth-century criticism of it and an alternative analysis of society, see D. Defoe, *Of Royall Educacion* (written 1728-9).

[4] Francis Place complained in the early nineteenth century of the indiscriminate jumbling together of 'the most skilled and the most prudent workmen with the most ignorant and imprudent labourers and paupers' when the term 'lower orders' was used. 'The difference is great indeed,' he went on, 'and in many cases will scarce admit of comparison.' *Place Papers*, British Museum, Add. MSS. 27,834, f. 45.

age of increasing wealth and mercantile expansion. The most successful of them were easily absorbed into the 'gentry', that most English of social groupings, and chapter xxiv of Defoe's *Complete English Tradesman* (1726) was entitled 'Extracts from the genealogies of several illustrious families of our English nobility, some of which owe their rise to trade, and others their descent and fortunes to prudent alliances with the families of citizens'.[1]

The element of mobility in the social system — based on what Adam Smith and Malthus after him called 'the natural effort of every individual to better his own condition'[2] — was often stressed by social commentators, particularly those who drew a sharp distinction between England and the continent. There were two other very different elements, however, which were given equal attention and were especially emphasised by the first generation of writers to condemn the social 'disintegration' consequent upon the rise of factory industry. The first of them was what Cobbett called 'the chain of connection' between the rich and the poor[3] and the second was what Southey described as 'the bond of attachment'.[4] The use of the nouns 'chain' and 'bond' is as eloquent (in retrospect) as the choice of 'connection' and 'attachment', but Cobbett and Southey in their different ways were praising the past in order to condemn the present. 'Connection' was associated not only with a network of social obligation but with gentle slopes of social gradation. It implied that every man had his place within an order, but that the order allowed for declensions of status as well as bold contrasts. To those who were willing to disturb that order Cobbett exclaimed, 'You are for reducing

[1] Cp. P. J. Grosley, *A Tour of London, II* (1772): 'The mixture and confusion . . . between the nobility and the mercantile part of the nation, is an inexhaustible source of wealth to the state, the nobility having acquired an accession of wealth by marriage, the tradesmen make up for their loss by their eager endeavours to make a fortune, and the gentry conspire to the same end by their efforts to raise such an estate as shall procure a peerage for themselves or their children'. For nineteenth-century statements of a similar point of view, see below, p. 72.
[2] *The Wealth of Nations* (1776), Book IV, chapter 9.
[3] *Political Register*, 14 April 1821.
[4] R. Southey, *Sir Thomas More: or, Colloquies on the Progress and Prospects of Society* (1829), p. 47.

the community to two classes: Masters and Slaves'.[1] 'Attachment' was directly associated both with 'duty' — the 'duty' appropriate to 'rank' — and with dependence, and thereby with 'charity', 'deference', and 'subordination'. 'The bond of attachment is broken', wrote Southey in 1829, 'there is no longer the generous bounty which calls forth a grateful and honest and confiding dependence.'[2]

Before the industrial revolution of the 1780s there were many signs of tension and contradiction both in society and in contemporary writings about it. The growth of population, the problem of 'indigence', the enclosure movement in the villages, the increase in home and foreign trade, and the emergence of 'radical' ideas in politics preceded the development of the steam-engine. It was the steam-engine, however, which was the 'principal factor in accelerating urban concentration' and 'generalising' the labour force.[3] It was the steam-engine also which inspired both the optimistic panegyrics of man's 'conquest of Nature' and the critical analyses of the contradictions and conflicts of the new society. The extent of the contradictions and the conflicts was clearly appreciated before the term 'industrial revolution' was coined. John Wade, the author of the *History of the Middle and Working Classes* (1833), one of the first attempts to put the facts of the recent past into historical perspective, wrote as follows:

> The physical order of communities, in which the production of the necessaries of subsistence is the first want and chief occupation, has in our case been rapidly inverted, and in lieu of agricultural supremacy, a vast and overtopping superstructure of manufacturing wealth and population has been substituted. It is to this extraordinary revolution, I doubt not, may be traced much of the bane and many of the blessings incidental to our condition — the growth of an opulent commercial and a numerous, restless and intelligent operative class; sudden alternations of prosperity and depression — of internal quiet and violent political excitement; extremes of

---

[1] *Political Register, loc. cit.*   [2] *Sir Thomas More, loc. cit.*
[3] For the social impact of the change from water power to steam power, see G. D. H. Cole, *Studies in Class Structure* (1955), pp. 28-30.   Marx, *Capital*, i, Part IV, chapter 13, quoted A. Redgrave, a factory inspector, who argued that 'the steam-engine is the parent of manufacturing towns'. (Everyman edition, i, 1930, p. 398.)

Language of 'Class' in Early Nineteenth-century England

opulence and destitution ; the increase of crime ; conflicting claims of capital and industry ; the spread of an imperfect knowledge, that agitates and unsettles the old without having definitely settled the new foundations ; clashing and independent opinions on most public questions, with other anomalies peculiar to our existing but changeful social existence.[1]

The use of the word 'class' and the sense of class that made the use increasingly meaningful must be related to what Wade called both 'the bane' and 'the blessings' of the new society. The development of factory industry often broke 'the bond of attachment', substituting for it what Carlyle was to call a 'cash nexus'.[2] The continued existence of factory paternalism checked but did not reverse this process. At the same time with the breaking of the bond there was increasing pressure to secure 'union' among the workers themselves. The demand not only for union at the factory or the local level but for 'general union', the story of which has been told by Professor Cole,[3] was directly related to the story of the emergence of a self-conscious 'working class'. Cobbett, who was one of the most forthright advocates of the old social system operating in an ideal form, saw clearly that once that system had been destroyed, 'classes' would be ranged against each other :

> They [working men] combine to effect a rise in wages. The masters combine against them. One side complains of the other ; but neither knows the *cause* of the turmoil, and the turmoil goes on. The different trades combine, and call their combination a GENERAL UNION. So that here is one class of society united to oppose another class.[4]

The same consequence followed on the growth of industrial cities, where the 'masses' were segregated and left to their own devices. A few years before Disraeli used the phrase 'two

---

[1] J. Wade, *History of the Middle and Working Classes* (1842 edn.), Preface, p. 1.

[2] This phrase, which was used by Disraeli, the authors of the *Communist Manifesto*, and many of the novelists and reviewers of the 1840s, was first used by Carlyle. As early as 1829 he wrote in his essay *Signs of the Times* that 'Cash Payment' was becoming the 'sole nexus' between man and man. Later, the shorter term became something of a slogan.

[3] *Attempts at General Union* (1953), originally published in 1939 in the *International Review for Social History*.

[4] *Political Register*, 27 August 1825.

nations', a distinguished preacher spoke in very similar terms at a chapel in Boston across the Atlantic:

> It is the unhappiness of most large cities that, instead of inspiring union and sympathy among different 'conditions of men', they consist of different ranks, so widely separated indeed as to form different communities. In most large cities there may be said to be two nations, understanding as little of one another, having as little intercourse, as if they lived in different lands. . . . This estrangement of men from men, of class from class, is one of the saddest features of a great city.[1]

It was a theme which was to be taken up frequently in nineteenth-century argument, and which dominated Engels's picture of Manchester in the 1840s. 'We know well enough', Engels wrote, 'that [the] isolation of the individual . . . is everywhere the fundamental principle of modern society. But nowhere is this selfish egotism so blatantly evident as in the frantic bustle of the great city.'[2] But the 'disintegration of society into individuals' was accompanied by the carving out of classes. 'The cities first saw the rise of the workers and the middle classes into opposing social groups.'[3]

Forty years before Engels, Charles Hall had stressed the snapping of 'the chain of continuity' in society and stated clearly for the first time the central proposition of a class theory of society:

> The people in a civilised state may be divided into different orders; but for the purpose of investigating the manner in which they enjoy or are deprived of the requisites to support the health of their bodies and minds, they need only be divided into two classes, viz. the rich and the poor.[4]

The sharp contrasts of industrialism encouraged the restatement of theories of society in these terms. In one sense 'class' was a more indefinite word than 'rank' and this may have been among the reasons for its introduction.[5] In another

---

[1] W. E. Channing, *A Discourse on the Life and Character of Rev. Joseph Tuckerman* (Boston, 1841), pp. 7-8.
[2] *The Condition of the Working Class in England* (tr. W. O. Henderson and W. H. Chaloner, 1958), p. 31.   [3] *Ibid.* p. 203.
[4] C. Hall, *The Effects of Civilisation on the People in European States* (1805), p. 3.
[5] Williams, *op. cit.* p. xv.

sense, however, employment of the word 'class' allowed for a sharper and more generalised picture of society, which could be provided with a historical and economic underpinning. Conservatives continued to prefer to talk of 'ranks' and 'orders' — as they still did in the middle of the nineteenth century [1] — and the old language co-existed with the new, as it did in the words of the preacher quoted above, but analysts of the distribution of the national income [2] and social critics alike talked increasingly in class terms. So too did politicians, particularly as new social forces were given political expression. The stormiest political decade of early nineteenth-century English history, that which began with the financial crisis of 1836 and the economic crisis of 1837, was the decade when class terms were most generally used and 'middle classes' and 'working classes' alike did not hesitate to relate politics directly to class antagonisms.

There was, however, an influential social cross current which directed attention not to the contrasting fortunes and purposes of 'middle classes' and 'working classes' but to a different division in industrial society, that between 'the industrious classes' and the rest. Those writers who were more impressed by the productive possibilities of large-scale industry than afraid of social 'disintegration' dwelt on this second division. St. Simon's demand for unity of 'the productive classes' against parasitic 'non-producers' [3] had many parallels as well as echoes inside England. Patrick Colquhoun, whose statistical tables were used by Robert Owen and John

[1] The *Quarterly Review*, which continued to refer to 'attachment' and 'continuity' in many of its articles on the social system even in the second half of the nineteenth century, referred in 1869 (vol. cxxvi, p. 450) to 'lower-middle class', adding hastily, 'We must apologize for using this painful nomenclature, but really there is no choice'.

[2] Writers on the national income were among the first to have to consider how best to describe the various sections of the population. 'Political arithmetic' and social classification went together.

[3] See G. D. H. Cole, *Socialist Thought, The Forerunners, 1789–1850*, pp. 42-3, for the distinction *les industriels* and *les oisifs*. The word 'industry' itself had a special significance for St. Simon (see his *L'Industrie* (1817), and there were socialist undertones beneath many of the words derived from it. See the fascinating, pioneer article by A. E. Bestor, 'The Evolution of the Socialist Vocabulary' in the *Journal of the History of Ideas*, ix (June 1948).

Gray,[1] attempted to divide industrial society into a productive class whose labour increased the national income and a 'diminishing class' which produced no 'new property'. When he argued that 'it is by the labour of the people, employed in various branches of industry, that all ranks of the community in every condition of life annually subsist',[2] he was not stating, as Gray later did, that manual labour created all wealth. Owen, who occasionally wrote in what were coming to be regarded as conventional terms of the 'upper', the 'middle', and the 'working classes', more usually conceived of society in the same terms as Colquhoun:

There will be, therefore, at no distant period, a union of the government, aristocracy, and non-producers on the one part and the Industrious Classes, the body of the people generally, on the other part; and the two most formidable powers for good or evil are thus forming.[3]

The same conception influenced radical politics. The *Extraordinary Black Book*, also borrowing from Colquhoun and mixing up the language of 'class' and 'orders', maintained that

The industrious orders may be compared to the soil, out of which every thing is evolved and produced; the other classes to the trees, tares, weeds and vegetables, drawing their nutriment, supported and maintained on its surface.... When mankind attain a state of greater perfectibility ... [the useful classes] ought

---

[1] Owen constructed visual aids to illustrate Colquhoun's tables, a set of eight cubes exhibiting a 'General View of Society', the working classes being represented at the base by a large cube whilst the apex was formed by a small cube, representing the Royal family and the aristocracy. See F. Podmore, *Robert Owen* (1906), pp. 255-6. John Gray's *A Lecture on Human Happiness* (1825) set out the case that labour received only one-fifth of its produce, the rest being appropriated by the 'unproductive' classes.

[2] *A Treatise on the Wealth, Power and Resources of the British Empire* (1814). Colquhoun's attempt — in his own words — 'to show how ... New Property ... is distributed among the different Classes of the Community' — had socialist implications which he did not draw out. He believed that poverty was necessary in society, that Malthus's population doctrine was sound, and that improved 'social police' would hold society together. Yet just as Ricardian economics were used to develop a socialist theory of value, so Colquhoun's statistics were used to propound a socialist analysis of distribution. Behind both Ricardo and Colquhoun was Adam Smith. For Smith's account of 'productive' and 'unproductive' labour, see *The Wealth of Nations*, Book II, chapter 3.

[3] 'Address to the Sovereign', printed in *The Crisis*, 4 August 1832.

Language of 'Class' in Early Nineteenth-century England

to exist in a perfect state. The other classes have mostly originated in our vices and ignorance . . . having no employment, their name and office will cease in the social state.[1]

Thomas Attwood, who in favourable social and economic circumstances in Birmingham, tried to unite 'middle' and 'working classes' in a single Political Union,[2] also believed that what he called 'the industrious classes' should secure political power. 'The ox is muzzled that treadeth the corn.'[3] It was only after the Reform Bill of 1832 had failed to satisfy his hopes — and only then for a short period of time — that he claimed that 'in a great cause, he was content to stand or fall with the workmen alone' even if the middle classes, to which he belonged, were against him.[4]

II

Before turning to 'working-class' critics of both Owen and Attwood and to the statement of class theory in specifically working-class perspectives, the terms 'upper class' and 'middle class' require more careful and detailed examination. The phrase 'higher classes' was used for the first time by Burke in his *Thoughts on French Affairs* in 1791, significantly only when the position of the 'higher classes' seemed to be threatened not only in France but in England. It was an exhortatory phrase in much of the Evangelical literature of the last decade

---

[1] *The Extraordinary Black Book* (1831 edn.), pp. 217-18. Colquhoun was described as 'a bold, but, as experience had proved, a very shrewd calculator'. (*Ibid.* p. 216.)

[2] For the significance of his thought and work against a European background, see my article, 'Social Structure and Politics in Birmingham and Lyons' (1825-48) in the *British Journal of Sociology*, i, March 1950.

[3] Report of the Proceedings of the *Birmingham Political Union*, 25 January 1830. The Declaration of the Union drawn up on this occasion claimed that the House of Commons 'in its present state' was 'too far removed in habits, wealth and station, from the wants and interests of the lower and middle classes of the people to have any just views respecting them, or any close identity of feeling with them'. It went on to complain of the over-representation of the 'great aristocratical interests', only nominally counter-balanced by the presence of a few 'rich and retired capitalists'. The National Political Union, founded in London in 1831, also proclaimed as one of its purposes, 'to watch over and promote the interests, and to better the condition of the INDUSTRIOUS AND WORKING CLASSES'. (*Place Papers*, Add. MSS. 27,791, f. 184.)

[4] *Birmingham Journal*, 17 January 1836.

of the century. When the French Revolution challenged the power of aristocracies and in England traditional duties seemed to be in disrepair, there was a need to re-define them. It was in this mood that Thomas Gisborne, clergyman friend of Wilberforce, published his *Enquiry into the Duties of Men in the Higher Rank and Middle Classes of Society in Great Britain* in 1795. There was much literature of this kind in the 1790s. Hannah More, Cobbett's 'old bishop in petticoats',[1] was an indefatigable supporter of 'the old order', and her tracts, some of which were specially addressed to 'Persons of the Middle Ranks', 'were bought by the gentry and middling classes full as much as by the common people'.[2]

The phrase 'middle classes', which antedates the phrase 'working classes',[3] was a product, however, not of exhortation but of conscious pride. As early as the 1780s attempts had been made to create new organisations which would uphold the claims of the new manufacturers. Pitt's commercial policy goaded manufacturers to set up the General Chamber of Manufacturers in 1785:

> Common danger having at length brought together a number of Manufacturers in various branches, and from various places, and their having felt the advantages resulting to each from unreserved conferences and mutual assistance, they are now persuaded, that the prosperity of the Manufacturers of this kingdom, and of course that of the kingdom itself, will be promoted by the formation of a general bond of union, whereby the influence and experience of the whole being collected at one common centre, they will be the better enabled to effect any useful purposes for their general benefit.

---

[1] *Political Register*, 20 April 1822.

[2] Letter to Zachary Macaulay, 6 January 1796, quoted by M. G. Jones, *Hannah More* (1952), p. 144. These tracts were regarded as 'antidotes to Tom Paine', 'Burke for Beginners.'

[3] Gisborne's *Enquiry* was certainly one of the first publications to use the term 'middle classes'. In 1797 the *Monthly Magazine*, founded by Richard Phillips and John Aikin to 'propagate liberal principles', spoke of 'the middle and industrious classes of society' (p. 397). The phrase 'working classes' seems to have been used for the first time by Robert Owen in 1813 in his *Essays on the Formation of Character*, later reprinted under the more familiar title *A New View of Society*, but it was a descriptive rather than an analytical term ('the poor and working classes of Great Britain and Ireland have been found to exceed 12 millions of persons'). He used the term frequently in letters to the newspapers in 1817 and in 1818 he published *Two Memorials on Behalf of the Working Classes*.

Language of 'Class' in Early Nineteenth-century England

In eighteenth-century terms this was the mobilisation of a new economic 'interest', an interest which failed to maintain its unity in the immediate future. It was something more than that, however. 'The manufacturers of Great Britain', their statement began, 'constitute a very large, if not a principal part of the community ; and their industry, ingenuity and wealth, have contributed no small share towards raising this kingdom to the distinguished and envied rank which she bears among the European nations.'[1] The word 'class' was not used, as it was used freely and unashamedly by the Anti-Corn Law League half a century later, but what was whispered in private in the 1780s was shouted on the platform in the 1840s.

There were several factors encouraging the development of a sense of middle-class unity where hitherto there had been a recognition of (imperfect) mutual interest. First in time was the imposition of Pitt's income tax, which entailed the common treatment of a group of diverse 'interests' by the government. Second was the impact of the Napoleonic Wars as a whole, which laid emphasis on the incidence of 'burdens', burdens which seemed to be of unequal weight for the owners of land and the owners of capital. Adam Smith had already distinguished clearly between these two 'interests' or 'orders' as he called them (and, indeed, a third 'interest', that 'of those who live by wages' as well), but he did not concede the claims of the merchants and 'master manufacturers' : in his opinion, they were more concerned with their own affairs than with the affairs of society as a whole. 'Their superiority over the country gentlemen is, not so much in their knowledge of the public interest, as in their having a better knowledge of their own interest than he has of his.'[2] Between 1776 and 1815, however, the numbers and wealth of the 'owners of capital' increased, and both their public grievances and their public claims were advocated with energy and persistence.

It is not surprising that a sense of grievance stimulated talk

[1] *Sketch of a Plan of the General Chamber of Manufacturers of Great Britain* (1785).
[2] Smith's general account of the division of the 'annual produce' of land and labour is given at the end of the last chapter (11) of Book I of *The Wealth of Nations*. For Smith's view of the 'labourer', see below, p. 62.

of 'class', and there are many expressions of it in the periodicals of the day. 'Why rejoice in the midst of rivers of blood', asked a writer in the *Monthly Repository* in 1809, 'while the burden of taxation presses so heavily on the middle classes of society, so as to leave the best part of the community little to hope and everything to fear?'[1] Four years later the same magazine demanded immediate peace 'for the relief of those privations and burdens, which now oppress every class in the community, including the poor and middle classes'.[2] The *Oxford Dictionary* gives 1812 as the first occasion on which the phrase 'middle class' was used — in the *Examiner* of the August of that year — and in the twentieth century the example has a very familiar ring — 'such of the Middle Class of Society who have fallen upon evil days'.

By 1815, however, statements about the 'middle classes' or the still popular term 'middle ranks' often drew attention not to grievances but first to the special role of the middle classes in society as a strategic and 'progressive' group and second to their common economic interests.

As early as 1798 the *Monthly Magazine* sang the praises of 'the middle ranks, in whom the great mass of information, and of public and private virtues reside'.[3] In 1807 the *Athenaeum* eulogised 'those persons whom the wisest politicians have always counted the most valuable, because the least corrupted, members of society, the middle ranks of people'.[4] Such magazine comments had an element of editorial flattery about them, but beneath the flattery was a keen awareness of social trends. The growing reading public included large numbers of people who belonged to the 'middle classes',[5] and their views were considered to be the main expression of the new 'public opinion'. It was not difficult, indeed, to argue, as James Mill did in his *Essay on Government*, that 'the class which is universally described as both the most wise and the

---

[1] The *Monthly Repository* (1809), p. 501.
[2] *Ibid.* (1813), p. 65.
[3] The *Monthly Magazine* (1798), p. 1. It referred to the 'ignorant apathy' of the 'lowest classes'.
[4] *The Athenaeum* (1807), p. 124.
[5] See R. D. Altick, *The English Common Reader* (Chicago, 1957), p. 41.

most virtuous part of the community, the middle rank' was the main opinion-making group in a dynamic society and would control politics 'if the basis of representation were extended'.[1] In the diffusion of Utilitarian ideas in the 1820s this case was frequently argued. The middle classes, 'the class who will really approve endeavours in favour of good government, and of the happiness and intelligence of men', had to unite to bring pressure upon the aristocracy. Their philosophy, like their wealth, depended on 'individualism', but their social action had to be concerted. 'Public opinion operates in various ways upon the aristocratical classes, partly by contagion, partly by conviction, and partly by intimidation: and the principal strength of that current is derived from the greatness of the mass by which it is swelled.'[2]

Politicians could not remain indifferent to this language, particularly when it was backed by wealth and increasing economic authority. One of the first to appreciate the need to win the support of the 'middle classes' was Henry Brougham. While the Luddites were engaged in what Engels later called 'the first organised resistance of the workers, as a class, to the bourgeoisie',[3] the 'middle classes' were being mobilised in a campaign to abolish the Orders-in-Council. Brougham, 'the life and soul' of the agitation, was later in his life to produce his celebrated equation of the 'middle classes' and 'the People'. 'By the people, I mean the middle classes, the wealth and intelligence of the country, the glory of the British name.'[4] During the Reform Bill agitation of 1830–2

---

[1] *An Essay on Government* (ed. E. Barker, 1937), pp. 71-2. The essay was completed in 1820. There is a remarkable and significant contrast between the method and style of Mill's argument and the form of his dogmatic and defiant concluding sentence. 'It is altogether futile with regard to the foundation of good government to say that this or the other portion of the people, may at this, or the other time, depart from the wisdom of the middle rank. It is enough that the great majority of the people never cease to be guided by that rank; and we may with some confidence, challenge the adversaries of the people to produce a single instance to the contrary in the history of the world.' (*Ibid.* p. 73.)

[2] James Mill in the *Westminster Review*, i, October 1824.

[3] Engels, *op. cit.* p. 243.

[4] This quotation is given in the *Oxford Dictionary*. In introducing the Reform Bill Lord John Russell talked of changing the House of Commons from 'an assembly of representatives of small classes and particular interests' into 'a body of men who represent the people'.

many similar statements were made by Whig leaders who were anxious, in Durham's phrase, 'to attach numbers to property and good order'.[1] Even the aristocratic Grey, who feared the Political Unions with their propaganda for unity between the middle classes and the working classes, chose to appeal 'to the middle classes who form the real and efficient mass of public opinion and without whom the power of the gentry is nothing'.[2] The Whigs wished to hitch the middle classes to the constitution to prevent a revolution: a section of the extreme radicals wanted to associate them with the working classes to secure a revolution. In the tense atmosphere of the years 1830 to 1832 it was not surprising that advocates of cautious change insisted that 'any plan [of Reform] must be objectionable which, by keeping the Franchise very high and exclusive, fails to give satisfaction to the middle and respectable ranks of society, and drives them to a union, founded on dissatisfaction, with the lower orders. It is of the utmost importance to associate the middle with the higher orders of society in the love and support of the institutions and government of the country.'[3] The language as much as the content of this statement reflects a traditionalist view not only of politics but of society.

The relationship between 'public opinion' and the growing strength of the 'middle classes' was recognised even when there was an absence of political crisis. Sir James Graham, at that time an independent but later a member both of the Whig committee which drafted the Reform Bill and of the Conservative cabinet which proposed the repeal of the corn laws, remarked in 1826:

I know no bound but public opinion. The seat of public opinion is in the middle ranks of life — in that numerous class, removed from the wants of labour and the cravings of ambition, enjoying the advantages of leisure, and possessing intelligence sufficient for the

---

[1] Quoted by N. Gash, *Politics in the Age of Peel* (1953), p. 16.
[2] Grey made this remark outside Parliament. See Henry, Earl Grey (ed.), *The Correspondence of the Late Earl Grey with His Majesty King William IV* (1867), i, p. 376.
[3] H. Cockburn, *Letters on Affairs of Scotland*, quoted by Gash, *op. cit.* p. 15.

formation of a sound judgement, neither warped by interest nor obscured by passion.[1]

The remark echoes Aristotle rather than Mill,[2] but it was one version of an extended argument. Another, more cogent, was set out in a historically important but neglected treatise *On the Rise, Progress, and Present State of Public Opinion in Great Britain and Other Parts of the World* (1828). Its author, W. A. Mackinnon, generalised from recent experience.[3] His book began with a 'definition' of the 'classes of society' and went on to describe how the rise of the 'middle classes' led to the growth of wealth and freedom :

> The extent or power of public opinion ... resolves itself into the question whether ... a community is possessed of an extensive middle class of society, when compared to a lower class; for the advantages called requisites for public opinion, cannot exist without forming a proportionate middle class. ... In every community or state where public opinion becomes powerful or has influence, it appears that the form of government becomes liberal in the exact proportion as the power of public opinion increases.[4]

Mackinnon related the recent rise of the 'middle classes' to what was later called 'the industrial revolution' :

> Machinery creates wealth, which augments the middle class, which gives strength to public opinion; consequently, to allude to the extension of machinery is to account for the increase of the middle class of society.[5]

In a footnote to this passage he drew attention to the magnitude of the changes in his own life-time :

> That the results arising from the improvement of machinery and

[1] Sir James Graham, *Corn and Currency* (1826), p. 9. Graham appealed to the landed proprietors to unite as 'the manufacturing and commercial body' had done, and to frame their actions in accordance with 'public opinion' and 'the interest of the community'.

[2] It also recalls a passage in Defoe's *Robinson Crusoe* — 'Mine was the middle state or what might be called the upper station of low life ... not exposed to the Labour and sufferings of the Mechanick part of Mankind, and not embarrassed with the Pride, Luxury, Ambition and Envy of the Upper Part of Mankind.'

[3] William Mackinnon was a member of parliament almost continuously from 1830 to 1865. His book on public opinion was rewritten in 1846 as a *History of Civilisation*. Mackinnon was one of the first writers to relate the rise of the 'middle classes' to the 'progress of civilisation'.

[4] *On the Rise, Progress, and Present State of Public Opinion* (1828), pp. 6-7.

[5] *Ibid.* p. 10.

its increase, are almost beyond the grasp of the human mind to define, may seem probable from the change that has and is daily taking place in the world.

Finally, he pegged class divisions to the distribution of property:

> The only means by which the classes of society can be defined, in a community where the laws are equal, is from the amount of property, either real or personal, possessed by individuals. As long as freedom and civilisation exist, property is so entirely the only power that no other means, or choice is left of distinguishing the several classes, than by the amount of property belonging to the individuals of which they are formed.[1]

Not only the amount of property was relevant in shaping class consciousness after 1815, but the kind. The prolonged but intermittent battle for the repeal of the corn laws encouraged social analysis in class terms: at the same time, particularly in its last stages, it sharpened middle-class consciousness and gave it highly organised means of expression.

The kind of social analysis set out in T. Perronet Thompson's *Catechism on the Corn Laws* (1826) was immediately popular for its content as much as for its style of exposition. The theory of rent was used to drive a wedge between the 'landlords' and the rest of the community, often with as much force as the labour theory of value was used in working-class arguments. Rent was defined as 'the superfluity of price, or that part of it which is not necessary to pay for the production with a living profit'. Adam Smith's argument that 'the landed interest', unlike the manufacturing interest, had a direct concern in 'the affairs of society as a whole' was turned on its head. The landlords were described by the repealers as selfish monopolists, who used the corn laws to protect their own selfish interest against the interests of the community. No vituperation was spared. There were two other particularly interesting questions and answers in the *Catechism*. '*Q*. That we must reconcile conflicting interests. *A*. There can be no conflict on a wrong. When the question is of a purse unjustly given, it is a fallacy to say we must reconcile conflicting interests, and give the taker half. *Q*. That the relation between the land-

---

[1] *On the Rise, Progress, and Present State of Public Opinion* (1828), p. 2.

lords and others, arising out of the Corn Laws is a source of kindly feelings and mutual virtues. *A.* Exactly the same was said of slavery.'[1]

Between the publication of the *Catechism* and the formation of the Anti-Corn Law League in 1839 there was a lull in the agitation. The League, however, was a uniquely powerful instrument in the forging of middle-class consciousness. 'We were a middle-class set of agitators', Cobden admitted, and the League was administered 'by those means by which the middle class usually carries on its movements'.[2] When the battle for repeal had been won Cobden asked Peel directly — 'do you shrink from the post of governing through the *bona fide* representatives of the middle class ? Look at the facts, and can the country be otherwise ruled at all ? There must be an end of the juggle of parties, the mere representatives of tradition, and some man must of necessity rule the state through its governing class. The Reform Bill decreed it : the passing of the Corn Bill has realised it.'[3] Such a bold statement demonstrates that by 1846, not only had the phrase 'middle class' established itself as a political concept, but those people who considered themselves as representatives of the middle classes were prepared to assert in the strongest possible language their claim to political leadership.

Behind the League was middle-class wealth and what Disraeli in *Coningsby* (1844) called 'the pride of an order'.[4] There was also what had recently been called 'a strong belief in the nobility and dignity of industry and commerce', a kind

---

[1] For the background of the *Catechism* and its importance in the struggle for repeal, see L. G. Johnson, *General T. Perronet Thompson* (1957), chapter 8, and D. G. Barnes, *A History of the English Corn Laws* (1930), pp. 210-12.

[2] J. Morley, *The Life of Richard Cobden* (1903 edn.), i, p. 249.

[3] *Ibid.* pp. 390-7. In his reply Peel was careful to avoid all reference to 'class'.

[4] Disraeli also referred to 'classes'. When Coningsby went to Manchester, 'the great Metropolis of Labour', he 'perceived that [industrial] wealth was rapidly developing classes whose power was imperfectly recognized in the constitutional scheme, and whose duties in the social system seemed altogether omitted'. (Book IV, chapter 2.) In conversing with Milbank he had already 'heard for the first time of influential classes in the country, who were not noble, and yet were determined to acquire power'. (Book II, chapter 6.) He referred to 'the various classes of this country [being] arrayed against each other'. (Book IV, chapter 12.)

of businessmen's romantic movement :

> ... trade has now a chivalry of its own ; a chivalry whose stars are radiant with the more benignant lustre of justice, happiness and religion, and whose titles will outlive the barbarous nomenclature of Charlemagne.[1]

This kind of rhetoric was usually accompanied by attacks on 'aristocratic tyranny', 'hereditary opulence', and 'social injustice', and by the declaration that 'trade shall no longer pay a tribute to the soil'. At the same time, it was necessary to supplement it — for political purposes — by an appeal to the 'working classes' ('joint victims' of the 'monopolists') and by an attempt to win over tenant farmers and to draw 'a broad distinction ... between the landed and the agricultural interest'.[2] The case for repeal had to be stated in different terms from those employed in Manchester in 1815, when the narrow economic interests of the manufacturers were the main staple of the published argument.[3] In Morley's famous words, 'class-interest widened into the consciousness of a commanding national interest'.[4] The argument was radically different in its tone and its implications from that advanced by the General Chamber of Manufacturers in the 1780s. Again Morley has caught the mood as the Leaguers themselves liked to interpret it :

> Moral ideas of the relations of class to class in this country, and of the relations of country to country in the civilized world, lay behind the contention of the hour, and in the course of that contention came into new light. The promptings of a commercial shrewdness were gradually enlarged into enthusiasm for a far-reaching principle, and the hard-headed man of business gradually felt himself touched with the generous glow of the patriot and the deliverer.[5]

---

[1] H. Dunckley, *The Charter of the Nations* (1854), p. 25. Quoted by N. McCord, *The Anti-Corn Law League* (1958), p. 24.

[2] A phrase of Cobden, quoted *ibid.* p. 145.

[3] The early advocates of free trade in 1815 'took the untenable and unpopular ground that it was necessary to have cheap bread in order to reduce the English vote of wages to the continental level, and so long as they persisted in this blunder, the cause of free trade made little progress'. W. Cooke Taylor, *The Life and Times of Sir Robert Peel* (1842), p. 111.

[4] Morley, *op. cit.* i, p. 180.

[5] *Ibid.* p. 182.

III

The glow was not always infectious, and although the League had some success in attracting the support of 'the working classes of the more respectable sort',[1] it was confronted in the provinces with the first large-scale self-consciously 'working-class' movement, Chartism. Relations between Chartists and Leaguers often demonstrated straight class antagonism. Mark Hovell quotes the story of the relations between the two groups in Sunderland. The Leaguers asked the local Chartist leaders, moderate men who agreed that the corn laws were an intolerable evil, to join them in their agitation. They replied that they could not co-operate merely on the merits of the question :

> What is our present relation to you as a section of the middle class ? — they went on — It is one of violent opposition. You are the holders of power, participation in which you refuse us ; for demanding which you persecute us with a malignity paralleled only by the ruffian Tories. We are therefore surprised that you should ask us to co-operate with you.[2]

This attitude was not shared by all Chartists in all parts of the country — actual class relations, as distinct from theories of class, varied from place to place — but it was strong enough and sufficiently persistent to ensure that Chartists and Leaguers were as violently opposed to each other as both were to the government. Indeed, middle-class claims both of the rhetorical and of the economic kind helped to sharpen working-class consciousness, while fear of independent working-class action, tinged as it was with fear of violence, gave middle-class opinion a new edge. To men like Ebenezer Elliott, the Corn Law Rhymer, who believed as part of the same programme in repeal, suffrage extension, and class conciliation, the 'middle classes' were being assailed on two sides. On the one side was 'the tyranny of the aristocracy' : on the other was 'the foolish

---

[1] A phrase used in a letter from a repealer in Carlisle, quoted by N. McCord, *op. cit.* p. 97. There was strong working-class support in Carlisle for Julian Harney, who preached a very different gospel to that of the League. See A. R. Schoyen, *The Chartist Challenge* (1958), p. 72.

[2] Quoted by M. Hovell, *The Chartist Movement* (1925 edn.), pp. 215-16.

insolence of the Chartists, which has exasperated into madness the un-natural hatred which the have-somethings bear to the have-nothings'.[1]

Chartist theories of class and expressions of class consciousness have recently been scrutinised.[2] In this essay more attention will be paid to the concept of a 'working class' before it was proclaimed in eloquent language by William Lovett and the London Working Men's Association in 1836.

Adam Smith often showed considerable sympathy in his writings for the 'workman', but the sympathy was frequently accompanied by statements about the workman's powerlessness. 'Many workmen could not subsist a week, few could subsist a month, and scarce any a year without employment.' Nor did their 'tumultuous combinations' do them much good. 'The interposition of the civil magistrate', 'the superior steadiness of the masters', and 'the necessity which the greater part of the workmen are under of submitting for the sake of the present subsistence' were handicaps to concerted action.[3] In addition Smith was impressed by the limitations on the effectiveness of political action on the part of the 'labourers':

> Though the interest of the labourer is strictly connected with that of the society, he is incapable either of comprehending that interest, or of understanding its connection with his own. His condition leaves him no time to receive the necessary information, and his education and habits are commonly such as to render him unfit to judge even though he was fully informed. In the public deliberations, therefore, his voice is little heard and less regarded, except upon some particular occasions, when his clamour is animated, set on, and supported by his employers, not for his, but their own particular purposes.[4]

Between 1776 and 1836 such a diagnosis, warmed as it was by human sympathy, began to be increasingly unrealistic. The combined effect of the French and industrial revolutions was to direct attention not to the powerlessness of the labourer but to the potential power of the 'working classes', whether hitched to the 'middle classes' or, more ominously, relying on their

---

[1] Quoted by Johnson, *op. cit.* p. 233.
[2] See Schoyen, *op. cit.*; A. Briggs (ed.) *Chartist Studies* (1959), chapter 9.
[3] *Wealth of Nations*, Book I, chapter 8.
[4] *Ibid.* Book I, chapter 9.

own leaders. In the early 1830s, when political radicalism was often blended with labour economics in a lively brew, critics of 'working class' claims, like Peter Gaskell, talked of the dangers of the growth of a dual society hopelessly torn apart:

> Since the Steam Engine has concentrated men into particular localities — has drawn together the population into dense masses — and since an imperfect education has enlarged, and to some degree distorted their views, union is become easy and from being so closely packed, simultaneous action is readily excited. The organisation of these [working-class] societies is now so complete that they form an 'imperium in imperio' of the most obnoxious description. . . . Labour and Capital are coming into collision — the operative and the master are at issue, and the peace, and well-being of the Kingdom are at stake.[1]

The same case was argued in Henry Tufnell's extremely interesting study, *The Character, Objects and Effects of Trades Unions* (1834), which expressed horrified alarm at the ramifications of a secret and hidden system of trade-union authority, based on its own laws with 'no reference to the laws of the land'. Like Gaskell, Tufnell argued that —

> Where combinations have been most frequent and powerful, a complete separation of feeling seems to have taken place between masters and men. Each party looks upon the other as an enemy, and suspicion and distrust have driven out the mutual sentiments of kindness and goodwill, by which their intercourse was previously marked.[2]

Leaving on one side the merits of Tufnell's assessment of earlier industrial relations,[3] there has been a marked shift of

---

[1] Gaskell to Lord Melbourne, 16 April 1834 (Home Office Papers 40/32). Gaskell, whose book *The Manufacturing Population of England* (1833) was freely used by Engels, had a diametrically opposed view of the correct answer to the 'social problem'.

[2] H. Tufnell, *The Character, Objects and Effects of Trades Unions* (1834), p. 2, p. 97.

[3] Gaskell shared his tendency to idealise social relations before the industrial revolution. 'The distinctions of rank, which are the safest guarantees for the performance of the relative duties of classes, were at this time in full force' (*op. cit.* p. 20). Engels, who did not make use of this sentence, borrowed direct from Gaskell in the 'Historical Introduction' which forms the first chapter of his book, and thereby over-rated 'patriarchal relationships' and 'idyllic simplicity'. He broke sharply with Gaskell, however, in his conclusion. Workers before the rise of steam power 'know nothing of the great events that were taking place in the outside world. . . . The

emphasis since *The Wealth of Nations*. The shift was marked even in the far shorter period between the end of the Napoleonic Wars and the Reform Bill crisis. James Mill, who in his *Essay on Government* stated categorically that 'the opinions of that class of the people, who are below the middle rank, are formed, and their minds are directed by that intelligent and virtuous rank, who come the most immediately in contact with them . . . to whom they fly for advice and assistance in all their numerous difficulties, upon whom they feel an immediate and daily dependence',[1] was bemoaning in 1831 the spread of 'dangerous doctrines' among 'the common people' which would lead to a 'subversion of civilised society, worse than the overwhelming deluge of Huns and Tartars'. In a letter to Brougham he exclaimed :

> Nothing can be conceived more mischievous than the doctrines which have been preached to the common people. The illicit cheap publications, in which the doctrine of the right of the labouring people, who say they are the only producers, to all that is produced, is very generally preached, are superseding the Sunday newspapers and every other channel through which the people might get better information.[2]

A pamphlet published by an 'approved source', the Society for the Diffusion of Useful Knowledge, warned that such doctrines, apparently 'harmless as abstract propositions', would end in 'maddening passion, drunken frenzy, unappeasable tumult, plunder, fire, and blood'.[3]

While James Mill was finishing off his *Essay on Government*, there had already been published what seems to be one of the first English working-class manifestos to talk straight language of 'class'. *The Gorgon*, published in London in November 1818, set out a series of four objections to an argument which was being frequently employed at that time that 'workmen must be expected to share the difficulties of their employers

---

Industrial Revolution . . . forced the workers to think for themselves and to demand a fuller life in human society' (*op. cit.* p. 12).

[1] *Essay on Government*, p. 72. He added the words 'to whom their children look up as models for their imitation, whose opinions they hear daily repeated, and account it their honour to adopt'.

[2] Quoted by A. Bain, *James Mill* (1882), p. 365.

[3] 'The Rights of Industry' (1831), *passim*.

and the general distress of the times'. The language of eighteenth and nineteenth centuries overlaps in the statement of their second objection, as it does in much of the socialist literature of the 1820s:

> To abridge the necessary means of subsistence of the working classes, is to degrade, consequently to demoralise them; and when the largest and most valuable portion of any community is thus degraded and demoralised, ages may pass away before society recovers its former character of virtue and happiness.[1]

Their other objections — the last of them related to the lack of political representation — were frequently reiterated by later working-class organisations. What Mill most complained of in 1831 — the spread of the doctrine of the right of the labouring people to the whole produce of labour — still needs a more systematic examination than historians have given it. The story of the development of formal labour economics in the 1820s is relatively well charted,[2] but the story of popular social radicalism is as yet only partly explored. The two stories are related, but they are not the same. Cobbett's postwar demand for the restoration of the dignity of labour in a changing society [3] merged with Owen's demand for an end to 'the depreciation of human labour',[4] and theories of radical reform of parliament and economic co-operation were often seen not as alternative ways to working-class emancipation but as pointers to complementary areas of working-class action.

[1] The statement in *The Gorgon* (28 November 1818) is printed in full in G. D. H. Cole and A. W. Filson, *British Working-Class Movements, Select Documents, 1789–1875* (1951), p. 159.

[2] The road leads back before Adam Smith, but Ricardo's *Principles of Economics* (1817) was the greatest single milestone. Smith used the phrase 'the whole produce of labour' (Book I, chapter 8), but claimed that the labourer had only been able to secure it in a primitive society and economy, 'the original state of things'. Ricardo (with important qualifications) based his general theory of value on 'the quantity of labour realised in commodities'. William Thompson (*An Inquiry into the Principles of the Distribution of Wealth, most Conducive to Human Happiness* [1824]) and Thomas Hodgskin (*Labour Defended* [1825]) anticipated Marx in using the theory as part of a socialist analysis.

[3] *Political Register*, 2 November 1816. 'The real strength and all the resources of a country, ever have sprung and ever must spring, from the *labour* of its people.'

[4] See 'Labour, the Source of All Value' in *A Report to the County of Lanark* (1820). Owenism has been studied far less than Owen.

As early as 1826 a speaker in Manchester claimed that 'the purpose of parliamentary reform was to secure to the labourer the fruits of his own labour . . . and to every British subject a full participation in all the privileges and advantages of British citizens'.[1] John Doherty and his supporters in industrial Lancashire continued to argue that 'universal suffrage means nothing more than a power given to every man to protect his own labour from being devoured by others', and urged that parliamentary reform would be of little value to the masses of the population unless it was accompanied by social action to guarantee to the workmen 'the whole produce of their labour'.[2] The same views were being canvassed in the London Rotunda in 1831 and 1832 and were often expressed in the pages of the *Poor Man's Guardian*.[3] During the agitation for the Reform Bill the National Union of the Working Classes, founded in 1831, identified political oppression and social injustice:

> Why were the laws not made to protect industry, but property or capital? Because the law-makers were compounded of fund and landholders, possessors of property, and the laws were made to suit their own purposes, being utterly regardless of the sources from which the property arose. . . . Had the producers of wealth been the makers of laws, would they have left those who made the country rich to perish by starvation?[4]

As far as the leaders and members of the National Union of the Working Classes were concerned — numerically they were extremely small, and on many points they were divided[5] — it did not need disillusionment with the results of the Reform Bill of 1832 to make them distinguish clearly between the interests of the 'middle classes' and the 'working classes'. The distinction was made on economic grounds before 1832.

---

[1] *Wheeler's Manchester Chronicle*, 28 October 1826.
[2] Home Office 52/18. A letter from a Preston correspondent to the Home Secretary encloses a pamphlet, *A Letter from one of the 3730 Electors of Preston to his Fellow Countrymen*. See also Doherty's pamphlet, *A Letter to the Members of the National Association for the Protection of Labour* (1831).
[3] *E.g.* 16 February 1833. 'Universal suffrage would give the power to those who produce the wealth to enjoy it.'
[4] *Ibid*. 24 December 1831.
[5] For the division between 'Huntites' and 'Owenites', see *ibid*. 4 February 1832.

Language of 'Class' in Early Nineteenth-century England

The 'working classes', the argument ran, were victims of the industrial system, yet they constituted a majority in society. They did not receive that to which they were legitimately entitled: the rights of property were the wrongs of the poor.[1] They could only secure their proper place in society, however, by concerted action, what was called in the language of the day — with both economic and political reference — 'union'. History could be employed to support their claims,[2] but the claims could be understood without difficulty in their immediate context, an industrial system founded on 'competition' instead of 'co-operation'. There was an urgent need for 'the elite of the working classes'[3] to communicate their ideas and solutions to the rest. As one popular lecturer on co-operation in Lancashire put it:

About one third of our working population ... consists of weavers and labourers, whose average earnings do not amount to a sum sufficient to bring up and maintain their families without parochial assistance. ... It is to this class of my poor fellow creatures, in particular, that I desire to recommend the system of co-operation, as the only means which at present, seem calculated to diminish the evils under which they live.[4]

Owen might be suspicious of the mixing of his doctrines with those of popular radical reformers[5] and continue to talk of the need to create an ideal class of 'producers' which included both workmen and employers, but the social and political situation was beyond his control. It was not only the National Union of Working Classes which talked in class terms. At

[1] *Ibid.* 26 January 1833.
[2] The old Saxon/Norman theme (see above, p. 44, n. 2) was still raised. In a London debate in 1833 on the notion that 'until the laws of property are properly discussed, explored and understood by the producers of all property the wretched condition of the working classes can never be improved', more than one spectator referred to 'the misappropriation' of the Norman Conquest and its aftermath. (*Ibid.* 18 May 1833.)
[3] This phrase, which has often been used with reference to the London Working Men's Association, was employed in the *Poor Man's Guardian*. Describing the fourth Co-operative Congress, the newspaper reporter said that it was comprised of 'plain but intelligent workmen ... the very elite of the working classes'. (*Ibid.* 19 October 1833.)
[4] F. Baker, *First Lecture on Co-operation* (Bolton, 1830), p. 2.
[5] He sharply condemned 'a party of Owenites of the Rotunda or desperadoes' and said that he had never been to the London Rotunda (*Union*, 17 December 1831).

the third Co-operative Congress held at the Institution of the Industrious Classes in London in 1832 several speakers described operatives and employers as separate and hostile forces,[1] while in the pages of the *Pioneer*, which first appeared in September 1833, there were many signs of differences of opinion between the editor, James Morrison, and Owen on questions of class. The first number of the *Pioneer* had a 'correct' Owenite editorial,[2] but Morrison soon proclaimed the independence of the 'working class' from the 'middle men'.[3] In one striking passage he declared:

> Trust none who is a grade above our class, and does not back us in the hour of trial. . . . Orphans we are, and bastards of society.[4]

In writing the detailed history of working-class movements of the 1830s, culminating in Chartism, it is necessary to separate out different strands.[5] For the purposes of this essay, however, emphasis must be placed on the element of class consciousness which in various forms was common to them all. Bronterre O'Brien, who was identified with three of the main movements — the struggle for Reform in 1831 and 1832, trade unionism, and Chartism — described this element as follows:

> A spirit of combination had grown up among the working classes, of which there has been no example in former times. . . . The object of it is the sublimest that can be conceived, namely — to establish for the productive classes a complete dominion over the fruits of their own industry. . . . Reports show that an entire change in society — a change amounting to a complete subversion of the existing 'order of the world' — is contemplated by the work-

---

[1] See *The Crisis*, 28 April 1832.

[2] 'The Union [the Grand National Consolidated Trade Union] is a well-organised body of working men, bound together by wise and discreet laws, and by one common interest. Its object is to affect the general amelioration of the producers of wealth, and the welfare of the whole community. Its members do not desire to be at war with any class, neither will they suffer any class to usurp their rights.' (*Pioneer*, 7 September 1833.)

[3] *Ibid.* 21 June 1834. 'The capitalist,' he wrote (21 December 1833), 'merely as a property man, has no power at all, and labour . . . regulated by intelligence, will in a very few years, be the only existent power in this and in all highly civilised countries.'

[4] *Ibid.* 22 March 1834.

[5] See for the various strands, *Chartist Studies*, especially chapter i, 'The Local Background of Chartism'. It is important to note that at the local level many working-class activists joined several movements, caring less about doctrinal differences than leaders or writers.

ing classes. They aspire to be at the top instead of at the bottom of society — or rather that there should be no bottom or top at all.[1]

In the bitter rivalry between Chartists and Leaguers there was class consciousness on both sides, although a section of the Chartists came to the conclusion that they would be able to accomplish nothing without middle-class support and the Leaguers were always compelled to look for working-class allies. Tory traditionalists disliked the language of 'class' from whichever quarter of society it came. Peel, prime minister in the critical years of the century, would have nothing to do with it. During the middle years of the century, the language of class was softened as much as social antagonisms themselves, but it burst out again in many different places in the years which led up to the second Reform Bill of 1867.

IV

There were some affinities, on the surface at least, between eighteenth-century views of society and those most frequently canvassed in the 1850s and 1860s. Attention was paid not to the broad contours of class division, but to an almost endless series of social gradations. The role of deference even in an industrial society was stressed, and the idea of a 'gentleman', one of the most powerful of mid-Victorian ideas but an extremely complicated one both to define and to disentangle, was scrutinised by novelists as much as by pamphleteers. The case for inequality was as much a part of social orthodoxy as it had been a hundred years before. 'Almost everybody in England has a hard word' for social equality, wrote Matthew Arnold in 1878.[2] The language of 'interests' enjoyed a new vogue both in the world of politics and outside. It was perhaps a sign of the times that the Amalgamated Society of Engineers, founded in 1851, did not claim that it was its duty to secure the objects of a 'class' but rather 'to exercise the same control over that in which we have a vested interest, as the physician who holds his diploma, or the author who is protected by his

---

[1] *Poor Man's Guardian*, 19 October 1833.
[2] Essay on 'Equality' in *Mixed Essays* (1878), p. 49.

copyright'.[1] The term 'labour interest' figured prominently in political discussion at all levels. A distinction was drawn even by radical politicians between the articulate 'labour interest' and the 'residuum', the great mass of the working-class population. The concept of the 'residuum', indeed, was useful to writers who wished to write off the 'condition of England question' of the 1840s as something dead and done with.

Against this background 'class' came to be thought of as a rather naughty word with unpleasant associations. *The Times* in 1861 remarked that 'the word "class", when employed as an adjective, is too often intended to convey some reproach. We speak of "class prejudices" and "class legislation", and inveigh against the selfishness of class interest.'[2] One of the most influential of the people who inveighed was Herbert Spencer. In a chapter with the significant title 'The Class Bias' he wrote:

> The egoism of individuals leads to an egoism of the class they form; and besides the separate efforts, generates a joint effort to get an undue share of the aggregate proceeds of social activity. The aggressive tendency of each class thus produced has to be balanced by like aggressive tendencies of other classes.[3]

The word 'balance' was one of the key words of the period both in relation to politics and to society.

It is not surprising that during these years three main points were made about 'class' in England. First, England was a country where there was a marked degree of individual mobility and this made class divisions tolerable. Second, the dividing lines between classes were extremely difficult to draw. Third, there were significant divisions *inside* what were conventionally regarded as classes, and these divisions were often more significant than divisions *between* the classes. Taken together these three points constituted a description rather than an analysis. The description was compared, however, with descriptions of the state of affairs in other countries, the

---

[1] Quoted in J. B. Jefferys (ed.), *Labour's Formative Years* (1948), p. 30.
[2] *The Times*, 10 August 1861.
[3] H. Spencer, *Principles of Sociology* (1873), p. 242.

Language of 'Class' in Early Nineteenth-century England

United States or France, for example, or even India.[1] Whereas during the 1840s both middle-class and working-class politicians (and most writers on society) had argued about 'class' in general terms, relating what was happening in England to what was happening in other countries,[2] during the middle years of the century most of the arguments were designed to show that England was a favoured special case.

The 'facts' of individual mobility were stated eloquently and forcefully by Palmerston in his famous speech during the Don Pacifico debate in the House of Commons in 1850:

> We have shown the example of a nation, in which every class in society accepts with cheerfulness the lot which Providence has assigned to it; while at the same time every individual of each class is constantly striving to raise himself in the social scale — not by injustice and wrong, not by violence and illegality, but by preserving good conduct, and by the steady and energetic execution of the moral and intellectual faculties with which his Creator endowed him.[3]

Only two years after the revolutions of 1848 and the waning of Chartism the language of politics was changing. The values were the same as those described by Beatrice Webb at the beginning of *My Apprenticeship*:

> It was the bounden duty of every citizen to better his social status; to ignore those beneath him, and to aim steadily at the top rung of the ladder. Only by this persistent pursuit by each individual of his own and his family's interest would the highest general level of civilisation be attained.[4]

The rungs of the ladder did not move: it was individuals who were expected to do so. 'Individuals may rise and fall by

---

[1] See, for instance, Walter Bagehot's essays on Sterne and Thackeray reprinted in *Literary Studies* (1873) where he distinguished between social systems founded upon caste and those founded upon equality. The English system of 'removable inequalities' was preferable to both.

[2] The leaders of the London Working Men's Association, for example, had clearly stated in addresses to working men in America, Belgium, and Poland that there were common interests among 'the productive millions' in all parts of the world and that it was 'our ignorance of society and of government — our prejudices, our disunion and distrust' which was one of the biggest obstacles to the dissolution of the 'unholy compact of despotism'. See W. Lovett, *Life and Struggles* (1876), p. 152.

[3] Quoted in J. Joll (ed.), *Britain and Europe, Pitt to Churchill* (1950), pp. 124-5.

[4] B. Webb, *My Apprenticeship* (1950 edn.), p. 13.

special excellence or defects', wrote Edward Thring, the famous public school headmaster, 'but the classes cannot change places'.[1]

The metaphor of 'ladders' and 'rungs' proved inadequate for the many writers who wished to emphasise the blurring of class dividing lines in mid-Victorian England. 'Take any class of Englishmen, from the highest to the lowest', wrote the young Dicey in a stimulating essay, 'and it will be found to mix, by imperceptible degrees, with the class below it. Who can say where the upper class ends, or where the middle class begins?'[2] Arnold, who was quick to catch the 'stock notions' of his age, some of which he believed in himself, referred in *Friendship's Garland* to 'the rich diversity of our English life . . . the happy blending of classes and character'.[3] Other writers described 'intermediate classes' bridging the chasms of class antagonism.

Finally, divisions within classes — the presence of what were sometimes called 'sub-classes' — were stressed. The 'middle classes', which Cobden had struggled to pull together during the 1840s, separated out into diverging elements after 1846, and the plans of the more daring spirits of the Manchester School to carry through a 'middle-class revolution' were never realised.[4] To cross the 'moral and intellectual' gulf between

[1] Rev. E. Thring, *Education and School* (1864), p. 5.
[2] *Essays on Reform* (1867), p. 74. Dicey added that 'in criticising a theory of class representation, the words "classes", "orders", or "interests", must be constantly employed'. Such employment, in his view, gave an undue advantage to the view criticised, for 'the very basis on which this view rests is not firm enough to support the conclusions grounded upon it'. For a parallel question of a later date about the social position of 'working men' see C. Booth, *Life and Labour of the People, East London* (1889), p. 99.
[3] *Friendship's Garland* (1897 edn.), pp. 49-50. One aspect of the blending, which deserves an essay to itself, was the association of the industrial and agricultural 'interests'. 'Protection,' wrote a shrewd observer, Bernard Cracroft, 'was the only wall of separation between land and trade. That wall removed, the material interests of the two classes have become and tend to become every day more indissolubly connected and inseparably blended.' (*Essays on Reform*, p. 110.)
[4] Cobden himself came to believe in the 1860s that 'feudalism is every day more and more in the ascendant in political and social life. . . . Manufacturers and merchants as a rule seem only to desire riches that they may be enabled to prostitute themselves at the feet of feudalism.' (Quoted by Morley, *op. cit.* ii, chapter 25.) He was very critical of the alliance of the industrial and the landed 'interest', and on one occasion in 1861 wrote to a friend, 'I wonder the working people are so quiet under the taunts and

the skilled workers and unskilled, wrote Henry Mayhew, was to reach 'a new level . . . among another race'.[1] In some respects, at least, dividing lines seemed to be sharper at the base of the social pyramid than towards the apex.

The political debate which followed the death of Palmerston in 1865 and ended with the passing of the Second Reform Bill two years later led to a revival of interest in the problems and terminology of 'class'.[2] It was the change in economic circumstances in the 1870s and 1880s, however, and the disturbance of the mid-Victorian social balance which shifted the debate on to a wider front. An understanding of the new phase which was opening during the late Victorian years depends on a thorough examination of the phrase 'working classes' in a context of socialism. Whatever else may be said of the new phase, one development is incontrovertible. The language of 'ranks', 'orders', and 'degrees', which had survived the industrial revolution,[3] was finally cast into limbo. The language of class, like the facts of class, remained.

insults offered to them. Have they no Spartacus among them to head a revolt of the slave class against their political tormentors?' (quoted *ibid.* ii, chapter 30).

[1] H. Mayhew, *London Labour and the London Poor*, i (1862), pp. 6-7. Cp. T. Wright, *Our New Masters* (1873): 'Between the artisan and the unskilled a gulf is fixed. While the former resents the spirit in which he believes the followers of "genteel occupations" look down upon him, he in his turn looks down upon the labourers.' (P. 5.)

[2] See below, p. 220, for a remarkable letter written by Professor Beesly on the day Palmerston died.

[3] Traditionalists employed the old language in some of the mid-century debates about education, *e.g.* P. Peace, *An Address on the Improvement of the Condition of the Labouring Poor* (Shaftesbury, 1852), p. 15. 'Children must be instructed according to their different ranks and the station they will probably fill in the graduated scale of society.' A similar thought was expressed quite differently by Sir Charles Adderley in 1874. 'The educating by the artificial stimulus of large public expenditure, a particular class, out of instead of in the condition of life in which they naturally fill an important part of the community, must upset the social equilibrium.' (*A Few Thoughts on National Education and Punishment*, p. 11.)

2
SIDNEY POLLARD

NINETEENTH-CENTURY CO-OPERATION: FROM COMMUNITY BUILDING TO SHOPKEEPING*

THE history of the British co-operative movement in the nineteenth century may be divided into two periods: the first, beginning with the publications of Robert Owen in the second decade of the century, rising to a peak of influence in the years 1828–34, and ending, with the failure of Queenwood, in 1846; and the second, heralded by the foundation of the Rochdale Equitable Pioneers' Society in 1844, registering an expansion around the year 1850 and becoming fully established about ten years later. The foundation of the English wholesale society in 1863 and of its Scottish counterpart in 1868 set the seal of consolidation on this chapter of co-operative history, and since those years the movement has enjoyed an unbroken record of growth and development.

Superficially, the activities of co-operators were not too dissimilar in these two periods. In both, they were found opening stores, establishing co-operative productive workshops, wholesale agencies, and other ancillary organisations, and in both they claimed to be working for higher aims of social amelioration and moral and intellectual improvement of the working classes. Yet, delving below the surface, it soon becomes apparent that these similarities hide fundamental differences, above all of aim and inspiration, which place the two phases of the movement far apart. It is the purpose of this

* Thanks are due to the Education Executive of the Co-operative Union and to Mr. R. L. Marshall, O.B.E., M.A., the Principal, for permission to use the library of the Co-operative College in the preparation of this paper.

Co-operation: from Community Building to Shopkeeping

essay to describe these differences and to attempt to account for them in the context of nineteenth-century social history.

I

The first phase of the movement stood wholly under the influence of Robert Owen, direct and indirect, acknowledged and unacknowledged. The development of Owen's ideas is well authenticated in his own voluminous writings, and it is clear that he arrived, at an early stage, at a remarkably complete and self-consistent social philosophy[1] which was adopted, in greater or lesser part, by all who called themselves 'Co-operators' or 'Socialists'.

Although Owen was bound to have been influenced by the mental climate of his day, he owed little to the direct teaching of others. Apart from the underlying assumption that the social system ought to produce the greatest happiness of all, his ideas were mainly formed as a response to two practical problems he was forced to solve: first, the creation of an efficient labour force in his factories, and secondly, the bane of unemployment and pauperism, especially after 1815.

He came upon his first problem early in his career, when, at the age of 18, he had to supervise forty workmen in a trade unknown to him,[2] and he met with it again at Drinkwater's factory and, above all, at New Lanark. He found that by kindness and tact, by forethought and a high degree of intuitive psychology, he could transform an idle, intemperate, vicious, and immoral proletariat into a contented, moral, and well-conducted group of workers, and his successes as an educator of children were greater still. This led him to the conviction of the infinite pliability of human character, expressed in his motto, 'man's character is made *for*, not *by* him' and to the further conclusion that only happy and moral surroundings would produce a happy and moral people. The competitive capitalism around him, red in tooth and claw, was clearly not a suitable background.

[1] It was firmly established by 1817. See *A New View of Society* (1817) and *Report to the County of Lanark* (Glasgow, 1821).
[2] Robert Owen, *Life of Owen* (1920), p. 31.

The problem of unemployment attracted his notice as early as 1813, but it became more pressing in 1816.[1] Owen was among the first to recognise the effects of machinery, at times even exaggerating its influence by imputing to other industries the productivity increases of cotton spinning.[2] During the war, he declared, mechanical and chemical invention had gone on unheeded, as the struggle swallowed up all the increase in output; with the peace, the artificial markets fell away, and labour, displaced by machinery, became unemployed. This was inevitable under competition — in John Gray's later, oft-quoted theorem, competition added to the two 'natural' limitations on wealth, namely productive capacity and human needs, yet a third, namely competition, which kept it much below either [3] — and caused the paradox of increasing misery in the midst of growing productive power. Given the industrial advance of England, poverty was not only wicked, it was also unnecessary.[4] Already, every man could produce more than enough to keep himself and his family in comfort, and this could easily be proved by setting all paupers to work on sufficient land and capital, exchanging their products with each other in villages or communities of 300-2000 persons to enjoy some of the benefits of the division of labour, and trading their surplus with the outside world. Instead of wastefully subtracting from the national product by living on the Poor Rates, they would be adding to it, yet live in greater comfort than now.

These two theories could easily be combined, and their perfect complementarity gave Owen his strong conviction which for the rest of his life he never found reason to change. For these villages or communities, necessarily based on co-operation rather than competition, would form the ideal surroundings to create happy and moral men, whose life would be so superior to anything that had gone before, that they would attract new

[1] G. D. H. Cole, *Robert Owen* (1925), pp. 131-2; Owen, *Life of Owen*, p. 222.
[2] E.g. *Co-operative Magazine*, i (1826), p. 247; *Magazine of Useful Knowledge and Co-operative Miscellany* (referred to subsequently as *Co-operative Miscellany*), i (1830-1), p. 49.
[3] John Gray, *A Lecture on Human Happiness* (1825), pp. 56, 61-4; William Pare, in *Co-operative Miscellany*, i (1830-1), pp. 17-18.
[4] H. L. Beales, *The Early English Socialists* (1933), p. 9.

Co-operation: from Community Building to Shopkeeping

converts and form new communities, until the whole world was transformed.[1] In this system, the 'new moral world', there would be no cause for envy or profiting by the failure of others. Labour, by direct exchange, would get the full value of its product (for Owen, like almost every other contemporary, held to the labour theory of value), Malthus's objections could easily be brushed aside, and, the correct 'scientific' foundations being laid,[2] the morality, happiness and wealth of the world's population would necessarily follow.[3]

The various organisations and individuals who came under Owen's influence naturally stressed different parts of this new gospel. Many of the Owenists, and this was particularly true for the period before 1828 and after 1834, emphasised the moral side of the teaching, or the development of character and education, or the 'rational' or 'scientific' approach to questions which religion had hitherto declared to be taboo. Politicians baffled by the effects of an industrialism still beyond their ken, and noble philanthropists led by the Duke of Kent, were mainly interested in the promise of ending pauperism. Many of those, however, who entered heart and soul into the movement, and thousands of working men among them, fastened on the one practical proposal to be found in it: the creation of mixed agricultural and industrial communities of 'united labour and community of property'. The early co-operators, 'worldmakers', as Holyoake called them,[4] were essentially community builders. 'Let it be clearly understood', resolved the London Co-operative Congress of 1832, 'that the grand ultimate object of all co-operative societies, whether engaged in trading, manu-

---

[1] Britain, it was estimated, might be wholly converted in 20-25 years, *Co-operative Magazine*, i (1826), p. 385.

[2] *E.g.* Robert Owen, 'The Science of Society', *Transactions of the Co-operative League*, Part III (1852), p. 76.

[3] Owen's writings on this subject seldom had the merit of conciseness. Good summaries will be found in H. M'Cormac, *The Best Means of Improving the Moral and Physical Condition of the Working Classes* (1830), pp. 23-4; (William Pare), *Address at the Opening of the Birmingham Co-operative Society* (Birmingham, ?1828); G. D. H. Cole, *Socialist Thought, The Forerunners 1789-1850* (1953), p. 90 ff., and *Robert Owen*, pp. 168-171; C. R. Fay, *Life and Labour in the Nineteenth Century* (1920), p. 73; F. Podmore, *Robert Owen*, i (1906), pp. 116-18, 265 ff.

[4] G. J. Holyoake, *The History of Co-operation*, i (1906 repr.), pp. 15, 41.

facturing, or agricultural pursuits, is community on land.'[1]

But the gospel, with all its perfection, had one major deficiency: there was no clear and obvious way of setting the new world in train. Since moral reformation and economic justice mutually depended on each other, neither could in strict logic be brought about without the pre-existence of the other. Owen himself, though he asserted that simple self-interest would provide the initial capital for an investment as safe and desirable as a new community, largely hoped for philanthropy, and it is true that virtually all the communities that were established or came very close to establishment in the years to 1832, at Orbiston, Exeter, Ralahine, Assington, Cork, Dublin,[2] and Owen's settlement at New Harmony depended on the subscriptions by rich individuals, as essentially New Lanark had also done.

Owen's calculations of the capital needs of a community of viable size were very generous, and he assumed at different times that £100,000 to £200,000 would be required for each. In order to find sums of this order of magnitude, it was either necessary to persuade the government or the Poor Law Authorities to take an interest in his scheme, or to look for wealthy subscribers who would either form joint-stock companies or act as trustees, holding the communal property as security. Owen tried both approaches. Even in his earliest essays on the 'Formation of Human Character' he proposed that the public authorities should advance the capital, for employing

[1] F. Hall and W. P. Watkins, *Co-operation* (Manchester, 1934), p. 71; C. R. Fay, *Co-operation at Home and Abroad*, i (5th edn., 1948), pp. 274-5; Lloyd Jones, *The Life, Times and Labours of Robert Owen* (4th edn., 1905), p. 304.
[2] For Orbiston, see Podmore, *Robert Owen*, ii, p. 359; G. D. H. Cole, *A Century of Co-operation* (1944), p. 21; M. Beer, *A History of British Socialism*, i (2nd edn., 1929), pp. 206-11; *Reports of the Practical Society* (Edinburgh, 1821-2); A. Combe, *The Sphere for Joint-Stock Companies* (Edinburgh, 1825); *The Register of the First Society of Divine Revelation at Orbiston* (Orbiston, 1825-7). For Dublin, *Co-operative Magazine*, i (1826), p. 136, and ii (1827), pp. 250-1. For Cork, *Co-operative Magazine*, i (1826), pp. 297-8, 314-20; Podmore, *Robert Owen*, ii, pp. 381-2. For Assington, *Co-operator*, viii (1868), p. 801; ix (1869), pp. 39, 753. For Exeter, *Co-operative Magazine*, i (1826), pp. 136, 155, 226, 265, 297; ii (1827), pp. 22-4; Benjamin Jones, *Co-operative Production*, i (Oxford, 1894), p. 62. For Ralahine, E. T. Craig, *The Irish Land and Labour Question* (1882); William Pare, *Co-operative Agriculture* (1870).

Co-operation: from Community Building to Shopkeeping

the unemployed, as a form of pauper relief, and this demand was repeated again and again after his plan for communities had matured,[1] but despite the great interest taken in his proposals,[2] and the reasonable hope of such assistance on several occasions, no help was actually forthcoming. He next turned to private subscriptions, and in 1819 and again in 1822 sums of some £50,000 were promised, but Owen considered these insufficient even for one community.[3] The appeals to the wealthy and the influential had failed.

But if those who were comfortably off had remained indifferent to Owen and his schemes, there were many among the working classes who had not. 'There was so much that was true in his analysis of current evils, so much that was practicable at the heart of his vision, so much that was common to his aspirations and theirs, that even the difficulties of communication in a country still largely illiterate and not yet equipped with either railways or a popular Press, could not keep him and them apart.'[4] Owen became, despite himself, the leader of the new working-class socialism 'because his ideas were the one coherent expression of a widespread sentiment'.[5] As early as 1821 George Mudie, a Scottish printer, had collected a group of working-class Owenists around him and even established a small settlement in London.[6] His journal, the *Economist*, and Combe's writings in Edinburgh were spreading co-operative ideas, and the establishment of the London Co-operative Society in 1824 united many of the most thoughtful and influential of the artisans of London in a propagandist body which successfully maintained its position against the political economists in 1825 and began to issue a widely read monthly

[1] Even during the excitements of 1832, Owen hoped for £5 million from the State for his proposed co-operative ventures. Beer, *History of British Socialism*, p. 323.

[2] Owen, *Life of Owen*, p. 290 ff.

[3] Attempts were again made in 1835 and 1837 to interest groups of capitalists in these schemes, but without success. Lloyd Jones, *Robert Owen*, pp. 282, 309.

[4] Beales, *Early English Socialists*, p. 62.

[5] Cole, *Robert Owen*, p. 193.

[6] For Mudie's settlement see Podmore, *Robert Owen*, pp. 350-5; Catherine Webb, *Industrial Co-operation* (Manchester, 4th edn., 1910), pp. 54-7; G. D. H. Cole and A. W. Filson, *British Working-Class Movements, Select Documents 1789–1875* (1951), pp. 207-9.

journal, the *Co-operative Magazine*, in 1826. To Owen's own writings were added those of William Thompson, Abram Combe, John Gray, and others, and 'the difficulties of communication' were being rapidly broken down, in London and several other towns, at least.

As the hopes of help from the wealthy receded, the working-class co-operators began perforce to look to their own resources. Sums of the order of magnitude of Owen's requirement were much beyond their powers, but more recent estimates had put the needs much lower; Vesey, of Exeter, had even promised to settle 2000 people for a mere £5000.[1] The difference largely lay in the fact that while Owen intended to complete all the building and provide all the equipment before the population moved in, the new plan envisaged the merest minimum housing for a pioneer group, which would then build up the settlement for the others while living as a community.

On this basis the London Co-operative Society proposed in 1825 to establish a settlement within fifty miles of London on £5000. Even that sum was beyond working-class resources, and the Society planned, therefore, to create three classes of shareholders: those subscribing £100, who would join only when the settlement was complete (or who would remain mere investors, drawing 5 per cent interest); those subscribing £40, who would join only after the first year's harvest was brought in; and those subscribing £10, who would go in as pioneers to prepare the ground for the others.[2]

By the middle of 1826, it had become clear that even these modest sums would not be forthcoming. Working men could not even supply £10, and the affluent could not be expected to show much enthusiasm. Support would have to come from those 'who give their labour for what they receive, those who are weary of the present system, who have been groaning under the miseries inseparable from that system, those who have long struggled against the strong tide of opposing events, and who

[1] B. Jones, *Co-operative Production*, p. 62; also *Co-operative Magazine*, iii (1828), pp. 42-6.
[2] *First Community of Mutual Co-operation, Commenced April 1825*, J. Corss, Secretary (1825); also in Appendix to Gray, *A Lecture on Human Happiness*.

are anxious to seize any probable plan that promises a speedy and effectual remedy from the evils they contend with'. It was necessary, the workers were told, to 'do for yourselves'.[1] As a last resort, the 'Co-operative Community Fund Association' was formed, to collect £1250 from fifty subscribers, who would each subscribe 4s. per week for 2½ years, to produce shares of £25 each. After one year, when £500 had been collected, a start would be made on the land and the buildings, and these would be ready for occupation eighteen months later.[2] Any sum higher than 4s. per week would have excluded working men ; any lower sum would have put the realisation too far into the future.

This scheme, however, also threatened to fail. 'Intelligent mechanics', wrote 'Henricus' in the *Co-operative Magazine*,[3] who had 4s. a week to spare, were too well off to think of communities, and some of those who had begun their subscriptions might be obliged by bad trade to suspend them at any time. Could nothing be done to speed the first community, save another appeal to the middle classes that was likely to remain fruitless ? In despair, the *Co-operative Magazine* suggested in January 1827 lowering subscriptions still further, down to 6d. per week, while an 'intelligent mechanic' of Brighton (William Bryan) suggested savings groups of forty-eight men, who would subscribe 1d. per week each, to meet the requirements of one man, and when his share of £25 were paid up, they would continue, providing the share for a second man, and so on.[4] A brief calculation will show that this method would take 120 years to settle all the members of the group, and even contributions of 3d. or 6d. per week would take far too long to expect poor men with irregular earnings to keep up their payments. The co-operators seemed to have come to an impasse ; lack of finance was destroying the hopes of communal settlement.

---

[1] From the address which led to the establishment of the C.C.F.A., *Co-operative Magazine*, i (1826), p. 309 ; and *ibid.* ii (1827), pp. 27-30.
[2] Podmore, *Robert Owen*, p. 380 ; *Co-operative Magazine*, i (1826), pp. 224 ff., 308-14.
[3] *Ibid.* ii (1827), p. 149.
[4] *Ibid.* pp. 29, 156, 225.

At this juncture, about March-April 1827, a solution seems to have occurred simultaneously to two men, one in Brighton and the other in London. 'I merely throw this out as a hint', William Bryan wrote from Brighton on 18 March 1827, but could not funds be rapidly accumulated 'in any moderate-sized town' by co-operation in the spending of money? If fifty households, spending £50 per year, could do their own retailing, making 10 per cent profit, they would have painlessly saved £260 per annum for the community fund. In the same issue of the *Co-operative Magazine*, 'C. F. C.', the founder, reported on 16 April 1827 the formation of an 'Auxiliary Fund' to help out the C.C.F.A. by using the profits of a small producer's co-operative, but above all by a 'repository' for retail trading. 'The plan of raising them [funds for a planned community] by profits on trade is one of the easiest which can be designed, because they can be so raised without putting the parties concerned to any expense, more than they are compelled to be at present. . . . The person laying out the pound [per week at the depot at 36 Red Lion Square] might not be able to contribute sixpence a week to a regular fund, yet by purchasing at his own *depot* he may contribute two or three shillings, without making any sacrifice over what he must do if he laid out his cash anywhere else.' Funds could be accumulated faster still if the store were open to the general public as well.[1]

The idea of accumulating funds quickly and painlessly at the expense of what were believed to be the extortionate profits of shopkeepers caught on rapidly. A store was quickly established in Brighton by the 'Co-operative Benevolent Fund Association', of which Bryan was the secretary,[2] and it was from Brighton that Dr. William King propagated the new

[1] *Co-operative Magazine*, ii (1827), pp. 223-6.
[2] From Brighton, the 'Sussex General Co-operative Trading Organisation', another society, reported in February 1828 an even more ambitious scheme, whereby the community funds were to benefit not only by the profits of a store, but also by those of a printing shop, the sales of the members' own productions through the store and from direct sales of members (who were independent handicraftsmen and shopkeepers) to each other, from which they undertook to contribute 5 per cent to the funds. *Co-operative Magazine*, iii (1828), pp. 67-8.

system of raising funds in his influential paper, *The Co-operator*, which began publication in May 1828. The classical outline of this 'Brighton system' of co-operation will be found in its sixth issue, for October 1828: the methods of attaining 'independence by means of a common capital' consist, 'first in a weekly subscription, of not less than sixpence, to the common capital: and secondly, in employing those subscriptions in a different way from what is usually done — namely, not in investment, but in trade: thirdly, when they have accumulated sufficiently, in manufacturing for the society: and lastly, when the capital has still farther accumulated, in the purchase of land and living on it as a community'.[1] It will be noted that there is an intermediate stage between storekeeping and communal settlement, in which the funds are boosted by self-employment, or co-operative production, in order to benefit the working men not only by the profits of trade, but also by those of production, to give them 'the whole of the produce'. Dr. King also proposed to associate with the society, even before its settlement, weekly meetings, friendly benefits, and education.

Thus did storekeeping enter the co-operative movement.[2] Shopkeeping was by no means an end in itself: 'to these early co-operators the word co-operation was synonymous with brotherly love; the petty trading profits were an earnest of liberty for themselves and their children; and the grocery store appeared as an antechamber to the millennium'.[3] To describe, at that time, storekeeping as a co-operative end would have been as justifiable as making a raffle for church funds the occasion of describing the running of a lottery as one of the aims of the church: both were thought of as convenient ways of providing funds for higher purposes. 'In Dr. King's co-operative theory the wagon of joint shopkeeping is hitched to the star of a noble social ideal.'[4]

[1] A good summary will also be found in Heaton's statement to the Birmingham Co-operative Congress, October 1831, quoted in G. D. H. Cole, *Attempts at General Union* (1953), pp. 92-3, and in Cole and Filson, *Select Documents*, pp. 209-11.
[2] Earlier co-operative stores, corn mills, and bakeries were isolated efforts which in no sense constituted part of a movement.
[3] Podmore, *Robert Owen*, p. 391.
[4] Hall and Watkins, *Co-operation*, p. 59.

Nor was this ideal forgotten when the movement spread outwards from London and Brighton to engulf the most advanced and responsible sections of the working classes in all the main centres of population in 1829 and 1830. Even the sober William Lovett 'was induced to believe that the gradual accumulation of capital by these means would enable the working classes to form themselves into joint-stock associations of labour, by which . . . they might ultimately have the trade, manufactures, and commerce of the country in their own hands'.[1] *The Birmingham Co-operative Herald*, in its first number in April 1829, urged the formation of retail trading societies on the Brighton model to accumulate funds, 'adding the difference or profit to a common stock (for it is a fundamental rule of these Societies never to divide any portion of the fund, but to suffer it to accumulate till it becomes sufficient to employ all the members thereon)'. The First Armagh Co-operative Society, founded in February 1830, laid it down in its rules that 'the capital shall in no case be touched, but allowed to accumulate for the ulterior object which the Society has in view'. The first Co-operative Congress, held at Manchester in 1831, determined to collect resources from 200 societies to establish a community, and John Finch, of Liverpool, addressing the third Co-operative Congress in 1832, could still state that the existing societies had two main objects, education and the collection of capital.[2]

Perhaps the best contemporary account was given by the Scottish Owenist, Alexander Campbell, in a letter dated 26 January 1831:

These societies are generally composed of the working classes; and their capital, held in small shares, payable in instalments, is to be applied to the following objects :—The purchasing at wholesale prices of such articles of daily consumption as the members require, and retailing out to them and others at the usual retail prices, adding all profits to stock for the further object of giving employment for

[1] William Lovett, *Life and Struggles of William Lovett*, i (1920 edn.), p. 42. Cf. also Graham Wallas, *Life of Francis Place, 1771–1854* (1898), pp. 269-71.

[2] Fay, *Life and Labour*, p. 61 ; *Rules of the First Armagh Co-operative Society* (Armagh, 1830), Law iii/1 ; Lloyd Jones, *Robert Owen*, p. 249. See also Cole, *Robert Owen*, pp. 195, 197 ; Holyoake, *History of Co-operation*, ii, p. 615.

Co-operation: from Community Building to Shopkeeping

members who may be either out of work or otherwise inefficiently employed, and thereby still increasing their capital to obtain their ultimate object — the possession of the land, the erection of comfortable dwellings and asylums for the aged and infirm, and seminaries of learning for all, but more especially for the formation of superior character for their youths, upon the principles of the new society as propounded by Robert Owen.[1]

Indeed, so firmly planted had this idea become, that in March 1830 the British Association for Promoting Co-operative Knowledge, a London propagandist body formed in 1829 and largely responsible, with Dr. King, for spreading the ideas of co-operation in those years, found it necessary to take Dr. King himself to task in these words for appearing to betray his own ideal in the issue No. 22 of the *Co-operator*, for 1 February 1830:

The grand aim of co-operative societies is *not* to combine to raise the wages of its members by buying at wholesale prices and selling the same for ready money, as stated . . . but, on the contrary, to raise a capital sufficient to purchase and cultivate land and establish manufactories of such goods as the members can produce for themselves, and to exchange for the production of others; likewise to form a community, thereby giving equal rights and privileges to all.[2]

It was, perhaps, not surprising that Owen, returning from abroad, at first 'looked somewhat coolly on those "Trading Associations", and very candidly declared that their mere buying and selling formed no part of his grand "Co-operative Scheme"',[3] but when he realised their significance as the practical means towards the realisation of his New Moral World, he put himself enthusiastically at the head of what was

[1] Quoted in William Maxwell, *The History of Co-operation in Scotland* (Glasgow, 1910), pp. 58-9.
[2] The protest was signed by G. R. Skene, Secretary of the B.A.P.C.K. Quoted in T. W. Mercer, *Co-operation's Prophet* (Manchester, 2nd edn., 1947), pp. 28-9.
[3] Lovett, *Life of Lovett*, p. 44, also Holyoake, *History of Co-operation*, i, p. 73. It is noteworthy that Owen reverted to his hostility to 'making profit by joint-stock retail trading' in the later 1830s, when the surviving co-operative societies had become mere stores. 'It is high time to put an end to the notion,' he wrote on the occasion of a visit to Carlisle in November 1836, 'very prevalent in the public mind, that this is the Social System which we contemplate, or that it will form any part of the arrangements in the New Moral World.' Podmore, *Robert Owen*, p. 453.

rapidly becoming a large and powerful movement. Reliable statistics are scarce, and many societies were short-lived, but there is little doubt that after the rapid growth of 1830 and 1831 there were up to 500 societies in existence, with at least 20,000 members, with several journals and frequent, though often ill-attended, Co-operative Congresses and innumerable local meetings to propagate and discuss their ideas, to hearten each other by reports of their progress, and to exert united pressure on other bodies.[1]

It is doubtful whether any of these hundreds of small local co-operative societies, had they been allowed to develop, would have had the self-restraint to permit sufficient capital to accumulate in order to establish themselves in communities, without earlier distribution of the funds on one or another pretext ; or whether, had they indeed accumulated something like £25 per member, their members would still have been sufficiently hostile to the existing capitalist system in which such progress could be made, to leave it for the unknown blessings of communal settlement. But the experiment was never tried, for between 1832 and 1834 the co-operative societies, by their innocuous entry into production, were swept up in a storm which began with the Labour Exchanges and the conversion of some small trade unions to the principle of co-operative production, and ended with the Operative Builders' syndicalist organisation and the establishment of the Grand National Consolidated Trades Union.[2] This, Owen's most famous creation, attempted for a time to unite the militant trade unions and the idealistic co-operative societies in one grand tide, only to dash itself against the rocks of disunity, lack of funds, lack of leadership and government persecution, and to leave behind more remnants of trade unions and co-operative societies which took years of patient labour and a

[1] Some estimates and discussions will be found in Lloyd Jones, *Robert Owen*, p. 248 ; Hall and Watkins, *Co-operation*, p. 67 ; Podmore, *Robert Owen*, p. 396 ; Holyoake, *History of Co-operation*, i, pp. 100-1, and ii, pp. 476-7 ; B. Jones, *Co-operative Production*, i, pp. 77-80 ; Cole, *Century of Co-operation*, pp. 23-6 ; Joseph McCabe, *Life and Letters of George Jacob Holyoake*, i (1908), p. 179 ; *Co-operative Miscellany*, i (1830-1), p. 33.

[2] The best accounts of these developments will be found in Cole, *General Union*, and R. W. Postgate, *The Builders' History* (1923).

new approach to build themselves up again.

Owen had at first only reluctantly been drawn into this movement.[1] He was initially attracted to it by the practice of several small London societies of carpenters, tailors, shoemakers, and similar trades of setting their unemployed members to work on materials bought out of union funds and out of special weekly subscription, and of bartering their products in a primitive 'bazaar' at Hatton Garden and later at Portland Road and at Gothic Hall, New Road — an idea first suggested by the working of the 'Auxiliary Fund'.[2] Owen took up the idea of a bazaar or 'Labour Exchange', which he himself had propagated in earlier years,[3] in some lectures at the Grays' Inn Road Institution, a building offered to him free of charge by an enthusiast, and combined it with his theories for fair exchanges and of labour notes to express them, and with the vision of universal application by co-operative producers. The idea was enthusiastically taken up by his working-class audiences, and they insisted on starting a 'Labour (Produce) Exchange' before the capital or preparations Owen thought necessary had been completed.[4]

Though ultimately a failure, the 'Labour Exchange' enjoyed great initial success in the then serious state of unemployment in London. For a time, Owen began to see in associations of producers, trading by means of these Exchanges, the medium of transforming the system of society, to the neglect, perhaps, of village settlements. A second Exchange was opened in Birmingham, and Owen and his disciples, travelling about the country, inspired the planning of others in Sheffield, Glasgow, Barnsley, and elsewhere, while Liverpool already had a wholesale depot for co-operative commodities. In these travels, addressing working-class audiences, Owen became caught up in the discussions about the strikes then raging in many indus-

---

[1] This is the distinct impression given by his account, 'Memoranda relative to Mr. Owen', in *New Moral World*, i (1834–5), pp. 395-6, 401-3.
[2] Cf. *Co-operative Magazine*, ii (1827), pp. 230-1.
[3] Lloyd Jones, *Robert Owen*, p. 270.
[4] E. Nash, 'The Gray's Inn Road Equitable Labour Exchange', *Transactions of the Co-operative League*, Part II (1852), pp. 33-7 ; C. R. Fay, *Life and Labour*, pp. 62-3 ; Lovett, *William Lovett*, i, p. 48 ; B. Jones, *Co-operative Production*, i, p. 88.

tries, and in particular, the Lancashire builders' dispute. Under his influence, the powerful Operative Builders transformed themselves into a guild for co-operative self-employment at the 'Builders' Parliament' of September 1833, and in Birmingham, where Owenism was strongest, they set about erecting a Guildhall; in October, a meeting of trade unions and co-operative societies decided to form the 'Grand National Moral Union of the Useful and Productive Classes', and in February 1834 the Consolidated Union was founded which claimed up to 800,000 members. None of these survived the end of the year.

Long before the year was out, however, Owen had turned his back on these organisations. The brief aberration [1] into trade-union action was over, but during its collapse the co-operative movement was seriously weakened. Even those co-operative societies which survived became largely isolated from each other, and mostly divided their profits or capital, several becoming simple joint-stock companies. The Owenite socialists who retained their cohesion increasingly turned their attention to the reformation of religion, morals, and education, and to building 'Halls of Science', by means of grandly named associations scattered in fragile local groups. Their last practical effort again ran true to type: out of the pounds of middle-class sympathisers, and the pence, collected weekly, of the working-class membership, a fund was raised and used in 1839 to establish the Queenwood communal settlement in Hampshire. Its ignominious failure in 1846 spelt the end of the first phase of British Co-operation.

It would be misleading to maintain that all the co-operators in this period were motivated solely by the hope of communal living on Owenite principles. It is one of the strengths of the co-operative idea that its appeal to human beings, then as now, is at many different levels. At the lowest, it offers immediate advantages in employment, saving and pure goods for sale, without any special demands on the members; next, it offers

[1] '[Owen's] connection with the great Trades Union uprising of these years had been, in a sense, an accident. He was by nature neither a Trade Union organiser nor a revolutionary leader, but a prophet', Cole, *General Union*, p. 151.

Co-operation: from Community Building to Shopkeeping

the social and educational values of collaborating with others on a local basis ; further, it was expected to put all the paupers to useful work, and increase national output ; at a higher level still, it proposed to offer the attractions of communal, harmonious relationships in life and work ; it offered justice in the distribution of wealth ; it promised a rational, happy, and moral social commonwealth ; and at its highest, it presented a new religion which could combine the aspirations of the soul with a rational explanation of society, and promised to lift the life of man on to a higher plane of existence. 'The co-operative store and the co-operative workshop', wrote Lloyd Jones,[1] 'have in them the power of practically satisfying the narrowest, as well as the highest, ambitious spirit. To the man who only looks for profit, it gives profit, — to the man who seeks to realise the imagining of the philanthropist, it gives the power to do so by its gains, and in this light it claims encouragement from all classes of social reformers.'

Many co-operators, even in that heroic age, looked no further than their immediate profits. Others, particularly those in the trade unions, fastened on some aspects of it that would assist them in their day-to-day struggle. Some co-operative societies perhaps never seriously intended to found communities in a New Moral World.[2] And even those socialists who wholeheartedly endorsed the higher objectives, who were often 'the most skilled, well-connected, and intelligent of the working class',[3] did not always keep their eyes glued to the distant horizon. Yet the power of Owenism should not be underrated. Its basic concepts and its main conclusions, the right of every man to happiness, the right to the whole produce of labour, the right to work, to knowledge, to social equality, the longing for a social system that would encourage man to help man instead of competing against him — these and others touched a chord in almost every artisan and labourer who lived

[1] Lloyd Jones, 'Co-operative Stores and Co-operative Workshops', *Transactions of the Co-operative League*, Part III (1852), p. 93.
[2] Beer, *History of British Socialism*, i, p. 184 ; T. W. Mercer, *Towards a Co-operative Commonwealth* (Manchester, 1936), p. 25.
[3] According to police reports. G. J. Holyoake, *History of the Rochdale Pioneers* (10th edn., 1907), p. 8.

through the dark days of the industrial revolution. There may have been relatively few who became full members of cooperative societies, but the sympathies of all went with them unless they were diverted by religious intolerance; even in its impotence after 1834, Owen's Association of All Classes of All Nations was said to have 70,000-100,000 members, or more probably, sympathisers, and its proselytising activities were prodigious. In two and a half years, in 1839-41, 2½ million tracts were distributed, ten missionaries were maintained,[1] and 1450 lectures delivered in a year, the Sunday lectures being attended by up to 50,000 people weekly, — and this at a time when Chartist and Anti-Corn Law agitations were at their height.

Co-operation had its idealists and its materialists even then, or rather, its members were swayed by ideals and material gains in different proportion: no one, perhaps, is wholly without the divine spark; but the ideal which inspired them then was that of social communities.

All the fervour and earnestness of the early Co-operative Societies was not . . . about Co-operation, as it is now known, but about communistic life. The 'Socialists' so frequently heard of then were Communists. They hoped to found voluntary, self-supporting, self-controlled industrial cities, in which the wealth created was to be equitably shared by all whose labour produced it.[2]

II

The magnitude of the gulf that separates the community builders of the first half of the century from the storekeepers of the second is to some extent obscured by the bridge of a transition period around 1850. In it, three developments were of particular importance: the Redemption Societies, the activities of the Christian Socialists, and the foundation and

[1] Hall and Watkins, *Co-operation*, p. 64; Podmore, *Robert Owen*, ii, pp. 468-9, 506; Ramsden Balmforth, *Some Social and Political Pioneers of the Nineteenth Century* (2nd edn., 1902), p. 84; Holyoake, *History of Co-operation*, i, p. 244; Lloyd Jones, *Robert Owen*, pp. 294-5. All these figures may be exaggerated, but the arguments put forward against them by Canon C. E. Raven, *Christian Socialism, 1848-54* (1920), p. 52, are too weak to merit serious attention. See also Beatrice Potter (Webb), *The Co-operative Movement in Great Britain* (4th edn., 1897), p. 51.

[2] Holyoake, *History of Co-operation*, ii, p. 615.

Co-operation: from Community Building to Shopkeeping

consolidation of the Rochdale Pioneers' Society.

The Redemption Society of Leeds, the first in the field and the leading one throughout, was established in 1846 to carry out a purely Owenist social programme, but with the important proviso that it sought to avoid religious controversy, the bane of the latter-day Owenists.[1] The emphasis was on the need to employ all resources and to retain for the worker the whole produce of labour in order to end poverty and raise the working class morally and intellectually, and the means to this end were to be found by providing the worker with his own capital, and ultimately to establish communal settlements. The final aim was 'the transformation of the whole of capitalist society into a socialist commonwealth'.[2]

When vast bodies of the people are deprived of the means of labouring for their bread, [ran the address of the Society adopted at its annual meeting on 3 January 1848], they not only cease to produce wealth for the Community at large, but they are necessarily fed at the same time from the diminishing stores of the country. . . . Hence it is evident that this distressing state of things is oppressive to all, and all must therefore feel an interest in a remedy. Community of property has been proved by practice to supply this remedy, and fortunately it can be accomplished in this country without improperly interfering with the property or opinions of any. . . . With its funds it [the Redemption Society] will purchase property in suitable localities, for it intends to effect a beneficial union between agriculture in its most improved forms and manufactures and the arts in their highest development; thus combining under one great and common proprietory — production, distribution and consumption, not neglecting education. . . . Not only will community of property be an immediate benefit to those located, but it will gradually, as its possessions increase, begin to diminish the pressure on the labour market, and the poor rates. It will do this simply by giving a greater amount of labour than before upon a given surface of land,[3] and by creating a greater amount of wealth in proportion to the labour employed, and as a certain consequence cheaper production and increased consumption.[4]

---

[1] *Herald of Redemption*, i (1847–8), pp. 2-3.
[2] J. F. C. Harrison, *Social Reform in Victorian Leeds, the Work of James Hole, 1820–1895* (Leeds, 1954), p. 14; *Herald of Redemption, passim*; C. Webb, *Industrial Co-operation*, p. 19.
[3] This was Owen's stock answer to Malthusian criticism.
[4] *Herald of Redemption*, i (1847–8), p. 108.

The similarity with the former socialist programmes was, indeed, striking, despite the influence of Chartism with its primacy of politics over economics in the town in which the *Northern Star* was issued ; and apart from a more sophisticated statement of the labour value theory — a reflection, perhaps, of the teaching of J. F. Bray [1] — the Leeds Redemptionists were fully in the old co-operative tradition. Their means of finance was a 1d. a week subscription, collected from hundreds of members by district collectors. The society was fortunate, for not only was it well established before it was hit by the depression of 1847 — a circumstance favouring the Rochdale Pioneers also — but in August 1847 it was offered a farm at Garnlwyd, in South Wales, on which it could attempt a settlement. Its hopes of raising £6 a head from its 500 supporters for its development proved optimistic, but with smaller resources agriculture, building, and some handicrafts were undertaken by a handful of settlers, subsidised by the society, until its decline and ultimate demise in 1855 put an end to the scheme.

At the height of its power, the Leeds Redemption Society had considerable influence, and by its monthly paper, the *Herald of Redemption* (later named the *Herald of Co-operation*), which bore the motto : 'Labouring Capitalists, not Labourers and Capitalists' and which ran for 19 numbers from January 1847, it kept in touch with other co-operative and communistic societies, as well as with its sister societies in Bury, Norwich, and Stockport and branches in Bingley, Birstall, Barnsley, North Cave, Hull, London, and Pudsey.[2]

Despite its strong association with the earlier co-operative movement, which mark it clearly as of the same tradition, there are yet unmistakable characteristics in this movement which point to the co-operative framework of the second half of the century. It was not only that there was an absence of Owenist millenial raving, a stronger trait of practical common sense, and better organisation ; but the redemptionists also appeared

[1] J. F. Bray, *Labour's Wrongs and Labour's Remedies* (1839, L.S.E. Reprint, 1931).
[2] Harrison, *James Hole*, p. 2. Subscriptions came in also from about twenty other places, *Herald of Redemption, passim*. For the societies in Bury and Stockport, see B. Jones, *Co-operative Production*, i, pp. 96-100.

to have more elbow room and a bigger stake in the existing system. Though their own subscriptions were only 1d. per week, this was collected and accounted for regularly ; and many of its members joined the Leeds Corn Mill from its inception in 1847, for which much larger resources were required. There were signs, even in the Leeds of that day, that the bad old times were coming to an end, and of the Redemption Society, as of one of its leaders, James Hole, it might be said that it stood midway between the social ideals of 1846–8 and the conditions of the later 1850s and the 1860s.[1]

The work of the Christian Socialists in this period is in a sense outside the development traced here, for the divines and the lawyers who undertook to change society by means of co-operative workshops were not only remarkably innocent of any knowledge of the social sciences or of the life of the industrial proletariat (as distinct from the London sweated trades), but even of earlier and contemporary co-operative efforts.[2] Their co-operative workshops, like most of those which they later persuaded working men to finance, had uniformly disastrous results, and their most valuable services were of a kind which members of the professional classes are by nature best fitted to render : the sponsorship of legislation, especially the Industrial and Provident Societies' Act of 1852, and education, above all the foundation of the London Working Men's College.[3]

These services, as well as the contact gradually established with the existing co-operative societies to which they were helped by such working-class leaders as Walter Cooper and Lloyd Jones, did place the Christian Socialists to some extent within the tradition even in the middle of the century, while from the 1860s onward some of them, led by J. M. Ludlow, E. V. Neale, and Thomas Hughes, played a leading part in the national co-operative movement. In their most active period 1848–52 they also clearly reflected the transitional nature of

[1] Harrison, *James Hole*, p. 26.
[2] Raven, *Christian Socialism*, especially pp. 112, 138, 140, 158, 215 ; E. R. A. Seligman, 'Owen and the Christian Socialists', in *Essays in Economics* (New York, 1925), p. 40 ; Cole, *Century of Co-operation*, pp. 97, 102, and *Socialist Thought*, pp. 293, 296.
[3] Raven, *Christian Socialism*, p. 340 ff. ; J. F. C. Harrison, *History of the Working Men's College 1854–1954* (1954).

those years, for while their protest was against the conditions which largely came to an end with the 1840s, their remedies assumed standards of responsibility and respectability of working men,[1] and an acquiescence in a basically capitalist system, which truly belonged only to the second half of the century.

In the early history of the Rochdale Pioneers, the transition finds its true epitome, for while they inspired and led the co-operative movement in the second phase, their beginnings are firmly rooted in the first period, that of Owenite community building. As their fame spread, several of the old Owenists claimed to have given them their initial impetus and ideas,[2] but it is not necessary to make any assumption of outside Owenist influence: many of the original pioneers had been Owenists, and the others were active in the other social movements of the day. One of them had been to Queenwood, they sent to Queenwood for advice, and their first secretary, James Daly, soon after emigrated to seek a community in the New World, only to be killed by cholera on the way.[3]

Thus their Owenite background is not in doubt, and it emerges clearly from their famous 'objects', enunciated at the outset, which were based largely on the writings of William Thompson.[4] These included the raising of capital in one-pound shares, the establishment of a store, the building or purchase of houses, the employment of unemployed members or of those 'who may be suffering in consequence of repeated reduction in wages', and as a next step,

the society shall purchase or rent an estate or estates of land, which shall be cultivated by the members who may be out of employment, or whose labour may be badly remunerated. And further, that as

---

[1] *E.g.* the evidence given by Ludlow, Neale, Hughes, and Lloyd Jones to *S.C. on Investments for the Savings of the Middle and Working Classes*, 1850, xix, especially Qs. 101, 105, 204-7, 216, 447, 965-77.

[2] Holyoake, *History of the Rochdale Pioneers*, pp. 68, 71, 268; McCabe, *George Jacob Holyoake*, i, p. 180.

[3] See especially Cole, *Century of Co-operation*, pp. 37-65, 84; Lloyd Jones, *Robert Owen*, pp. 244-5, 427; McCabe, *Holyoake*, i, p. 182; Holyoake, *History of the Rochdale Pioneers*, p. 82 ff.; *Co-operator*, vii (1866-7), p. 553, viii (1868), p. 452.

[4] Mercer, *Towards the Co-operative Commonwealth*, p. 31.

Co-operation: from Community Building to Shopkeeping

soon as practicable, this society shall proceed to arrange the powers of production, distribution, education and government, or in other words to establish a self-supporting home of united interests, or assist other societies in establishing such colonies.

And lastly, they hoped to open a temperance hotel.

The ideas are clearly Owenist, and the sequence of operations is that of the Brighton model. 'In essentials, the "objects" of the Rochdale Pioneers did not differ fundamentally from those "castles in the air" which so fascinated the enthusiasts of an earlier day.' Their programme was a 'systematic and orderly scheme of social rebuilding', envisaging 'voluntary associations enlarging into a Co-operative Commonwealth'.[1] They 'set out originally to create, not a mere shop for mutual trading, but a Co-operative Utopia'. 'Their intention was to raise funds for community purposes. . . . Their object was the emancipation of labour from capitalist exploitation. They had no idea of founding a race of grocers, but a race of men.'[2]

But this was in 1844, not in 1830, and the germs of a new outlook were already there. They are most evident in the Pioneers' most famous action: the decision to pay dividends on purchases, after paying interest on capital. It represented the first major breach with Owenism, and one that proved fatal to its ultimate ideal. It implied a new outlook not only by assuming that members needed a special inducement to trade with their own store, while in earlier societies members were expected to patronise the store for the sake of the community funds;[3] it also implicitly recognised that the surpluses gained by trade, when market prices were charged, were the members' as individuals and not the society's. Though it might be argued that the funds thus accumulated from dividends not paid out could still be used for the society's purposes (and they were, in fact, so used in expanding their shopkeeping activities), only a proportion of the dividends was in fact kept in, and con-

---

[1] *Ibid.* p. 36.
[2] Cole, *Century of Co-operation*, p. 2; Holyoake, *History of Co-operation*, ii, p. 616.
[3] This was the ideal. Some societies, in fact, ruled that all the trading, or a certain proportion of it, must be done with the store as a condition of membership.

temporaries, at least, sensed or knew that it spelt the end of community projects. 'The early co-operators', even in Rochdale in the 1820s and 1830s, 'having a world-amending scheme in view, foresaw that money would be required for that purpose, and this led them to adopt a plan of saving all they gained . . . though it was . . . not likely to be so popular with members generally . . . who prefer to know what they save, and to have it at once.'[1] The conviction of the early co-operators was firm on this point, as is shown by the resolution of the London Co-operative Congress of 1832 :

The capital accumulated by such associations should be rendered indivisible, and any trading societies formed for the accumulation of profits with a view to the merely making a dividend thereof at some future period cannot be recognised by this conference as identified with the Co-operative world nor admitted into the great social family which is now rapidly advancing to a state of independent and equalised community.[2]

There were a few societies which ignored this at the time,[3] but most followed the Birmingham Co-operative Society who incorporated this principle of William Pare in their rules : 'Nothing in the way of profits of trade, or any part of the capital shall ever be divided among the members, as Community of Property in Lands and Goods is the great object of this Society'.[4] The surviving rules of other societies of that time usually show similar provisions, and it remained a cardinal principle with the Leeds Redemptionists and other societies [5] even some years after the foundation of the Rochdale store.

The first step along the new road, represented by dividend on purchases, was not a conscious repudiation of the old gods.

---

[1] Holyoake, *History of the Rochdale Pioneers*, pp. 148-9. 'The present division of profits is no doubt a great inducement with many,' wrote Dr. King sadly from Brighton in 1864, 'although it weakens the accumulation of capital.' *Co-operator*, iv (1863-4), p. 146. See also Cole, *Century of Co-operation*, p. 69.

[2] Quoted in Hall and Watkins, *Co-operation*, p. 71. See also Fay, *Co-operation at Home and Abroad*, pp. 274-5, and Mercer, *Towards the Co-operative Commonwealth*, p. 40.

[3] Cole and Filson, *Select Documents*, p. 432.

[4] *Rules of the Birmingham Co-operative Society* (Birmingham, 1828), Rule 39.

[5] *Herald of Redemption*, i (1847-8), pp. 36-7 ; Harrison, *James Hole*, p. 15 ; *Co-operative Commercial Circular*, ii (1854-5), p. 101.

Co-operation: from Community Building to Shopkeeping

More likely, it was a practical device, designed to create confidence and attachment among new members, without the realisation that the ends were being subtly changed by changing the means. The first step having been taken, others followed. The leaders and inspirers became more and more involved in the practical operations of their successful store and its branches. At no time was there a deliberate break with the past, but the ideals of justice, of fair dealing, of banishing poverty and want, were gradually transferred to the day-to-day operation of distribution and, before long, production in Rochdale, while the ultimate ideal of community life receded ever farther into the dim future, even among the leaders.[1] Meanwhile, the successful co-operative society was being swamped by members who were attracted by the immediate benefits, without necessarily believing in any social ideal whatever.

This second process was most evident in the development of the Rochdale Co-operative Manufacturing Society, an offshoot of the store, which the majority of recent members transformed into a simple profit-making joint-stock company in 1862 by abolishing the bounty on labour over the bitter protests of the old Pioneers' leaders.[2] But these leaders themselves transferred their idealism increasingly to more mundane and immediate issues, a process best followed in their statements in the annual Almanack, read avidly by co-operators all over the country.

In 1855, for example, it was still stated that 'the emancipation of the working classes from poverty and degradation, by enabling them to reap the fruit of their own industry, is the ultimate object of co-operative societies', and this was to be achieved by self-employment and 'agricultural operations' with finally 'community of property'. But already there is much stress on immediate benefits. By 1860, however, the object had changed: 'the present co-operative movement does not

---

[1] Cole, *Century of Co-operation*, p. 89.
[2] *Ibid.* p. 90. *Co-operator*, iii (1862–3), p. 70; Percy Redfern, *John T. W. Mitchell* (Manchester, 1923), pp. 28–9. 'I verily believe that if all who hold the bounty theory in Rochdale could be enrolled in one company, they would scarcely be able to carry on a ginger beer establishment,' wrote a critic at the time, B. Jones, *Co-operative Production*, i, p. 263.

seek to level the social inequalities which exist in society as regards wealth', but merely to get some capital, accumulated in retail trading, in order to allow the workman to carry on his own trade without exploitation. In the same year, William Cooper, the respected spokesman of the Rochdale Pioneers, stressed that co-operative workshops were mainly beneficial because they raised wages and, by acquainting workers with the problems of capital-owning, made disputes less likely. It was in 1860, also, that Abraham Howarth, the president of the Pioneers' Society, made his famous statement that 'The Co-operative Movement ... [joins] together the means, the energies, and the talent of all for the benefit of each' by 'a common bond, that of self-interest'.[1]

They had already travelled a long way since their Owenist days, and it must be remembered that these statements were made by the idealist founders, not by members of the dividend-hunting majority. 'It must be admitted,' judged Gide, 'that the Rochdale Co-operators, although disciples of Owen, showed themselves thorough individualists and made an appeal to personal interest the great motive force of the Movement.'[2]

III

As Rochdale thought today, so the whole co-operative world thought tomorrow, for in the 1850s and 1860s the Pioneers' Society completely dominated the northern societies that were being established by the hundred, and it did so not only by virtue of its experience, but also by virtue of mere size. Its corn mill supplied a large number of other societies, for some years it acted as wholesalers for surrounding stores, and it took the lead in conferences which established the wholesale society, which debated insurance, and which influenced the passing of the Act of 1862.

The farther the co-operative inspiration radiated from Rochdale, the more diffuse did the initial Owenist impetus

---

[1] *Co-operative Commercial Circular*, ii (1854–5), p. 126; *Co-operator*, i (1860–1), pp. 6, 22; Cole, *Century of Co-operation*, pp. 95–6: Holyoake, *History of the Rochdale Pioneers*, pp. 94, 161.

[2] Quoted in J. Reeves, *A Century of Rochdale Co-operation* (1944), pp. 1–2.

become. The Model Rules for societies, adopted by the Lancashire and Yorkshire Conference in 1862, laid down the objects of using domestic consumption to allow saving and employing these savings to set labour to work, in order to strengthen the bargaining power of labour in other firms and set a standard for them ;[1] there was no longer any mention of superseding capitalist employment altogether.

The undoubted material success of the Rochdale Pioneers led not only to widespread imitation : it also brought forth, out of their obscurity, surprisingly large numbers of other societies, retailing, productive, baking, and corn milling, which had been formed earlier in the century, and some even before 1800, by occasions as diverse as strikes, high prices of food or the Owenist inspiration of 1828–34, and which claimed no ulterior motives beyond those of immediate savings and, in a few cases, friendly benefits.[2] They had felt no close affinity with the Owenist groups ; but they felt at home in the new, practical, dividend-paying movement, which had 'success' emblazoned on its banner and which filled its journals, the *Co-operative Commercial Circular*, the *Co-operator*, and the *Co-operative News*, with much practical advice and little social philosophy.

Not that the old world-shaking idealism was quite dead. Some of the old Owenite stalwarts, like Dr. Henry Travis, E. T. Craig, and William Pare, were still active, writing and lecturing, and recounting the glories of the old ideology, and there were occasional responses from the provinces, where humbler old Owenists watched with mixed feelings the success of a co-operative movement which they could hardly recognise in its new guise.[3] But they were beating the air. It could not be

[1] B. Jones, *Co-operative Production*, i, p. 145.
[2] Some details of these societies will be found in Cole, *Century of Co-operation*, pp. 14-15, 149-50 ; Holyoake, *History of Co-operation*, ii, pp. 483-8, 630 ; B. Jones, *Co-operative Production*, i, pp. 9, 34-7, 81-6, 127, 152-78 ; William Maxwell, *History of Co-operation in Scotland, passim* ; *Herald of Co-operation*, i (1847-8), p. 87 ; *Co-operative Commercial Circular*, i (1853-4), p. 7 ; *Co-operator*, iii (1862-3), p. 63 ; iv (1863-4), p. 72 ; v (1864-5), p. 33.
[3] *Ibid.*, ii (1861-2), pp. 35-7, 124-5, 191 ; iii (1862-3), p. 86 ; vi (1865-6), pp. 140, 156 ; viii (1868), pp. 389, 481, 791 ; B. Jones, *Co-operative Production*, i, p. 146 ; ii, pp. 736-7 ; Redfern, *J. T. W. Mitchell*, p. 36.

said that they were often directly opposed: William Pare had his Owenist resolution accepted at the first of the new series of congresses in 1869,[1] but after having been passed, it was quickly forgotten.

The difference from the old movement was not that there were those in it who only looked for immediate personal advantage. Even in 1830 there were some to whom co-operation appealed only at its lowest level, though with the more rapid growth and success after 1850 there was a larger proportion of them:

'We have seen enough of Communism,' exclaimed one of them, 'enough of the Utopian ridiculous mummery of Socialism. . . . We don't want it; we have seen the new moral world, and don't like it. . . . Let Co-operation be what it is. . . . Let it inculcate no other spirit but gratitude to God, loyalty to our Sovereign, love to our country, and good-will to all mankind . . . in the cause of constitutional competitive co-operation.'[2]

The main difference was that those who had ideals, had *different* social ideals from those which moved the Owenists. They wanted higher standards of living, greater economic independence for working men, fair dealing in pure goods, the end of indebtedness, perhaps even social security. 'Modern Co-operation . . . means a union of working men for the improvement of the social circumstances of the class to which they belong. As defined by secretaries of certain societies, it is the working man's lever, by which he may rise in the world.'[3] These were not ignoble ideals; but unlike those of the earlier socialist-co-operators (the two terms had then been interchangeable) they assumed the continuance of a mainly capitalist economic system.

It should not be assumed that the 'individualists', led by

---

[1] *Co-operator*, ix (1869), pp. 185, 241-3, 423-4, 433-6, 739.

[2] William Smith of Bridgnorth in *Co-operator*, ii (1861-2), p. 68; cf. also Alfred Bowen, *ibid.* and in other issues: iii (1862-3), pp. 39, 87; iv (1863-4), pp. 83-4; ix (1869), pp. 257-9; Lloyd Jones, 'Co-operative Stores', *Trans. Co-operative League* (1852), p. 90; Jules Lechevalier, *Prospects of Co-operative Associations in England* (1854), pp. 46-7.

[3] Prize Essay in *Co-operator*, vii (1866-7), p. 357; cf. also definitions, *ibid.* vii (1866-7), p. 55; *Co-operative Commercial Circular*, i (1853-4), p. 5; J. M. Ludlow and Lloyd Jones, *The Progress of the Working Class, 1832-1867* (1867), p. 132.

Co-operation: from Community Building to Shopkeeping

some of the Christian Socialists and some of the most influential co-operative figures, like Neale, Ludlow, Hughes, Holyoake, and Lloyd Jones, who urged co-partnership and bonuses on labour and accused the retail societies of betraying Co-operation for not following their advice, had higher ideals than the leaders of the stores movement. On the contrary: the plans of the consumers' societies appeared 'practical' by comparison only because theirs were impracticable. In search for immediate gain they were willing to be far more catholic, not to say indiscriminate, than the consumers' stores. When it is realised that one of their main arguments for 'co-partnership' was that it would lead to greater exertions by labour and thus to higher profits to shareholders,[1] it will not be surprising to learn that for years they were led to quote as a praiseworthy example Messrs. Briggs scheme, which was merely a cynical attempt to raise profits by working the men harder and breaking the power of the trade union.[2] Yet that scheme was described as much more favourable to the workers in its distribution of bonus than Greening's own works,[3] in which most of the Christian Socialist leaders were interested. Their opposition to allowing the 'profits . . . to be dribbled away in bonuses' [4] was not caused by their desire to see them applied to the establishment of a co-operative commonwealth, but merely to the development of co-operative workshops.

The best of the co-operators of all shades were men of goodwill and men with a social conscience, who had found a power-

[1] 'When the public begin to understand what really takes place [in profit sharing],' Holyoake explained to the Social Science Congress in Sheffield, 'they will cease to regard this new plan of the partnership of labour as a philanthropic one; they will estimate it as a new form of enlightened commercial shrewdness which pays.' *Co-operator*, vi (1865–6), p. 154; also *ibid*. vii (1866–7), pp. 412–13. E. O. Greening, in his prospectus, claimed that bonus sharing 'has been found to induce zealous co-operation by them [the workers] in the promotion of the interests of the company, to lessen the chances of disputes and strikes, and to result in larger production and greater and more regular profits'. B. Jones, *Co-operative Production*, ii, p. 499; also i, pp. 222-4, 267.

[2] At the very outset, Briggs suggested that after a period of low dividends because of disputes with their workers, the purpose of co-partnership was to 'induce them to work more steadily, and strive to promote their masters' good'. B. Jones, *Co-operative Production*, ii, p. 494.

[3] *Co-operator*, vii (1866–7), p. 232.

[4] *Co-operative Commercial Circular*, ii (1854–5), p. 111.

ful means of social amelioration, but were essentially reconciled to the existence of capitalism as such. What was true of them was even more true of the bulk of the membership. These men still had their distant ideals, as men have had in all ages. But these, as far as they were co-operative in inspiration, had dissolved into misty vagueness. Nothing is more striking than the contrast between the firm outlines of the New Moral World and the shapeless yearnings of the latter-day co-operators,[1] whether inspired by religion or not, as soon as they leave the firm ground of profitable storekeeping.

IV

The principal difference between the co-operative movements of the first and the second half of the century may now be re-stated. The former regarded the stores and their associated workshops as temporary means towards the grander object of the ending of the capitalist social system and its replacement by a New Moral World, a type of socialism in which hardly any of the existing institutions and social relationships would survive in a recognisable form. The latter saw in the stores and workshops themselves the promises and the fulfilment of a better world, in which to all intents and purposes the continuance of capitalism, with its capital owners and wage earners, was implicity taken for granted.

Can we go further and ask why the Owenists held the ending of capitalism to be desirable and inevitable, while the men of Rochdale, a generation later, not only accepted its continuance, but also expected to improve their position materially under it? To put the question in this form is virtually to answer it.

To workmen of the first half of the century, and to those

[1] Benjamin Jones, collecting innumerable definitions of co-operation in this period, could find only one common inspiration, namely the desire for justice, itself a vague concept; *Co-operative Production*, chapter xxiv. See also *Co-operator*, ii (1861–2), pp. 17, 163; iii (1862–3), p. 84; Edward Carpenter, *Co-operative Production* (1886). The principles of the Christian Socialists, adopted in full by the Northern Co-operative Conference in the 1860s, ran as follows: '1. That human society is a body consisting of many members, the real interests of which are identical. 2. That true workmen shall be fellow-workers. 3. That a principle of justice, not of selfishness, must govern our exchanges.'

who sympathised with them, it was axiomatic that the capitalist system that they knew would bring nothing but insecurity, poverty, and misery. It was the unspoken assumption of every economic discussion of the age. The subsistence theory of wages was common not only to the apologists of the system, the political economists, but also to their Socialist critics; it accorded perfectly with the experience of the working classes; and it was part of that experience that this 'subsistence level', in the Britain of the industrial revolution, was a desperately low level indeed.

'Incredible and indescribable are the miseries of the poor', wrote Dr. M'Cormac, the Armagh Owenist, in 1831. 'Their wailings are for ever in my ears; day by day the spectacle of their sufferings and their dreadful misery rends my feelings. Were I for a time inclined to forget them, some new scene of wretchedness would be sure to rivet my attention to the subject.' 'The misery and degradation of [their] condition are too well known to require either description or comment', remarks John Gray in his famous lecture. 'How many of you are in suffering and wretchedness'; the *Co-operative Magazine* addressed its readers in 1827, 'joyless, without comfort, labouring to exhaustion, starving! That all of you either are so, or in danger of being so, no one need remind you; — you yourselves too fully feel it.' 'Society appears to be labouring under a disease', the Leeds *Herald of Redemption* opened its first number even in 1847, 'complicated by poverty, ignorance and crime. . . . This country presents the strange, the awful fact, that a quantity of men placed upon an earth teeming with fruitfulness — men endowed with mind, and industry, and ten cunning fingers — might turn out to have a less [sic] chance of maintaining their existence, than the cattle and the untamed denizens of the air.'[1]

Not only was the mass of the population, of a country increasing visibly in wealth, condemned to heart-breaking poverty, but its condition was further deteriorating, a process

---

[1] *An Appeal on Behalf of the Poor* (Belfast, 1831), p. 3; John Gray, *A Lecture on Human Happiness*, p. 46; *Co-operative Magazine*, ii (1827), pp. 28-9; *Herald of Redemption*, i (1847-8), pp. 1-2. Cf. also Lloyd Jones, *Robert Owen*, p. 254.

ascribed by Owen to the spread of machinery which displaced labour. This, too, was well within the experience of most.

England, as to the great majority of her population, was in times when she was not near so splendid or so rich a land, much happier than she is at present.

That we are in a gradually progressing state of deterioration and decline, no person can doubt, who is at all conversant with past and existing facts. . . . In our own times we have reached the point whence our downward progress has been greatly accelerated. . . . We hear, and we know, quite enough to satisfy every reasonable man, that whatever may have been the relief brought by the creations of [this] summer, and the various sources of employment and sustenance to which they gave birth, there is — there can be — no real and permanent improvement in the situation of the great mass of the productive classes of society.

The amount of human misery has become fearfully enlarged: week by week a new class of sufferers is added — new aspects of crushing poverty are continually being exhibited — and such is now the accumulation of misery endured by thousands of skilled and industrious labourers, that no conceivable alteration for the worse can take place.

On the continent, in America, indeed the world over, the effect of machinery is deepening the impression. The industrious artizans have a destroying enemy before and a devouring element behind them. In their front is iron, merciless capital grinding them down — behind is yawning destitution waiting to swallow them up.[1]

This was the background of the co-operative movement, as well as of Chartism, of militant trade unionism, of the Short-Hour Movement, and of others, and it is no accident that they ebbed and flowed in those years with the ebb and flow of prosperity and depression. But those who had drunk of the Owenist fountain, were not to be put off by the palliatives of other prophets, nor with free trade, emigration, or moral regeneration in due course. 'The political economy of Rationalism asks why in the meantime must our labourers die, why be trampled down in competition's race ? Will that be solid happiness bought with misery and death ? Shall we pave the highways of commerce with toil-worn bones ? Why not achieve

---

[1] *Co-operative Magazine*, i (1826), p. 222 ; *Co-operative Miscellany*, i (1830–1), p. 4 ; *Herald of Redemption*, i (1847–8), p. 105 ; G. J. Holyoake, *Rationalism, a Treatise for the Times* (1845), pp. 45-6.

Co-operation: from Community Building to Shopkeeping

the independence within our reach by the location of our artizans on our untilled land — and learn to live at home ?'[1]

In the time of their oppression the workers could, and did, clutch at any hope, at any promise held out, but the Owenist promise was the most complete and was satisfying, both in its immediate measures and in its ultimate hopes of transformation. It was one of its strengths that it did not turn its back on machinery and modern industrial organisation, as so many other 'Utopian' movements did, but put them at the very base of its social philosophy. Owen's ascendancy over the minds of so many princes and politicians in the years of his triumphs, in 1817 to 1819, was precisely that he had succeeded in fitting the new machinery into the picture of his world, whereas they had not. Mechanical power was something new in the history of the world, he taught, and social institutions must change accordingly to take account of it.

The immediate causes which make . . . change certain and necessary are the overwhelming effects of new scientific power, and the rapid increase in knowledge among all classes of men. The former will soon render [unaided] human labour of little avail in the creation of wealth; while the latter will make evident to the people the absolute necessity which has thus arisen for them to give a different direction to their powers, and will inform them also, how the change is to be effected.[2]

Far from realising that the new capitalism was precisely the social framework which industrialism had tailored to its measure, Owen assumed confidently that its days were numbered. Next to despair born of grinding poverty, it was the belief in the speedy collapse of capitalism — still only young, still viewed as a chapter in history with a beginning and an end, not, as later, as a permanent framework — which gave Owenist co-operation its main impetus.

Thus the co-operative experiments were carried out 'in the midst of a gloomy atmosphere and full forebodings of the impending bankruptcy of capitalism. Socialism, at its birth,

[1] Holyoake, *Rationalism*, p. 45.
[2] *First Memorial to the Governments of Europe and America, September 20, 1818*, in Robert Owen, *The Life of Robert Owen*, iA (1858), p. 210; also *Report on the Poor, March 1817*, ibid. pp. 54-7.

inbibed the dogma that industrialism meant short spells of prosperity, followed by chronic crises, pauperisation of the masses, and the sudden advent of the social revolution'. In Holyoake's terse phrase, 'the social seers expected that the "old immoral world" was played out'.[1]

In their own eyes, the new vision of the Owenists was anything but Utopian. Capitalism, it seemed to them, could not last, for it failed to grasp the opportunities of the new science. Instead of enriching the population of this country, it impoverished it, instead of greater happiness, it created greater misery, poverty, and vice. All indications pointed to the transformation into a co-operative world of 'equal exchanges' without exploitation, without crises or unemployment, and without needless suffering, and the men who were to bring it into existence were those who had least to hope for from the present system, the 'productive classes', the oppressed classes, the poor.

Contrast this world picture with the position after 1850. The bulk of the heavy investment of the industrial revolution had been completed, and it at last began to show returns; wages began to rise remarkably quickly and consistently. Factory conditions were eased, the reform of town conditions began. If the real improvement was unmistakable, the expectations of further improvement were greater still, and they were not disappointed in the 1860s, despite the Cotton Famine and the panic of 1866. In the minds of the workers, British capitalism was unconsciously transformed from a system which drove the masses into ever deeper ruin into one which offered hopes of progress, slow perhaps and inadequate, but progress still, and the most skilled and intelligent of them, the natural leaders of opinion, had begun to acquire a stake in the country.

The crises of the years 1846–7 in many ways represented the turning-point. At the time, they were seen as only the latest, and the worst, of those harbingers of depression with which the working class had become so familiar. Those were the years of the Redemption Societies, of Christian Socialism,

---

[1] Beer, *History of British Socialism*, i, p. 182; Holyoake, *History of Co-operation*, i, p. 230.

of revolution on the Continent and the last great Chartist demonstration in Britain. But the recovery which began slowly in 1849 was of a different kind from those that went before. It ushered in the period of mid-Victorian prosperity. This explains the 'transitory' nature of the co-operative organisations of the day. Conceived in the despair of the forties, the Leeds Redemption Society and the associations planted by the Christian Socialists (including the engineering workshops which for a time had caught the imagination of the leaders of the new A.S.E.) petered out in the better times of the early fifties, while the Rochdale Pioneers and several of the other Redemption Societies turned themselves into prosperous dividend-paying store associations.

The worst period of economic misery was over. The edge of the industrial system was slightly blunted by the Factory Acts of 1847 and 1850, and the Public Health Act of 1848. In the triumphant outburst of commercial prosperity which began about 1850, both the idealism and the struggles of the working classes were for a time almost forgotten. The energy of the working classes was diverted from political agitation into building up co-operation and trade unionism on a firm financial basis.[1]

As far as his co-operative societies were concerned, the rise above the animal level of subsistence of the previous era gave the workman much greater freedom of movement. Dividend on purchases did help the Rochdale type of society to survive and grow and accumulate capital, in contrast with the Owenist societies of earlier days, but a more important cause was the wider margin of expenditure of the artisan : in the five years to the end of 1848, the Pioneers' membership had grown to 140, and their capital to £397, not very different from the typical figures of 1830–2 ; in the next five years, to the end of 1853, however, they had grown to 720 and £5848, respectively, a capital of £8 per member — a different scale altogether from the Owenist days. While the community builders laboriously collected their funds in pennies and sixpences, the *Co-operator*, when appealing for shares for the Printing and Publishing

---

[1] R. H. Tawney, in Introduction to Lovett, *Life of Lovett*, pp. xxviii-ix. Cf. also Cole, *Century of Co-operation*, p. 11 ; Holyoake, *History of Co-operation*, ii, p. 230.

Society, could write in 1861 : 'the poorest son of toil is not shut out, the shares being £1 each'.[1] The thousands of pounds subscribed by working men in those years for stores, corn mills, and cotton mills show that the statement was not over-optimistic.

Co-operators, perhaps more than others, were conscious of this growing prosperity. Among the first, and the best, of the many works which began to appear before long, extolling the rising standards of the working classes and contrasting them with the grim poverty of the first half of the century, was a work by two of the leading co-operative propagandists, J. M. Ludlow and Lloyd Jones.[2] 'The history of the English working man may be summed up in one word — progress', J. C. Farn, another well-known co-operative speaker, told a Lancashire audience in the midst of the Cotton Famine in 1863, and the editor of the *Co-operator* commented : 'We admit that the condition of the labourer is better than it was of yore, in many respects ; but in regard to his power of providing for the future, Co-operation alone lifts him above the power of the slave and the savage', and he added, significantly : 'we believe it is possible by means of co-operation for working men to obtain more wages with less work'.[3]

For with the advent of better times the second assumption of the Owenists had also changed : the speedy collapse of capitalism was no longer expected. Not only was the system stronger and able to deliver the goods, but the first generation of factory workers which had seen its rise had passed away, and the new industrial system was taken for granted as permanently established ; the task of working-class organisation was merely to establish the best possible positions within it. Co-operation became a 'lever'[4] for rising within it, not for abolishing it ; it was the time when co-operators became 'next-step takers'.[5] 'The new Co-operation was no longer a gospel of revolt, much less of revolution. It took colour from its environment, and

[1] *Co-operator*, i (1860–1), p. 161.
[2] Ludlow and Jones, *The Progress of the Working Class, 1832–1867* (1867).
[3] *Co-operator*, iv (1863–4), p. 146 ; v (1864–5), p. 97.
[4] See p. 100 above.
[5] Holyoake, *History of Co-operation*, ii, p. 582.

Co-operation: from Community Building to Shopkeeping

developed as . . . a field for the investment of working-class savings as well as an expression of the Victorian ideals of self-help.[1]

The charge was not consciously made, but it was there nevertheless. Co-operation was claimed to improve the worker's position in wage bargaining, to allow him to become a saver and an investor. Profits were in principle fervently defended, and co-operation was lauded as making working men respectable, law-abiding, and property-owning citizens.[2] When co-operative societies began to invest in railway and canal shares on a large scale, when leading co-operators became active in the Liberal Party and co-operation was earnestly discussed and supported at meetings of the Social Science Associations and of the British Association for the Advancement of Science,[3] it was clear that the movement had become one of the accepted and respectable institutions of Victorian England.

The parallel course taken by the trade union movement, with the A.S.E. playing the part of the Rochdale Pioneers, is, indeed, most striking, though the co-operatives enjoyed their legal blessings much earlier.[4] There was not only the obvious similarity in the growth of the annual membership figures, the concentration of strength in the same trades and the same areas of the country, and the fact that the first national congresses of both movements, destined to be the beginnings of unbroken series after many earlier attempts, occurred within a year of each other:[5] the two movements were also organically connected. From the early co-operative links, especially in 1833-4, to the innumerable attempts of trade unions to establish co-operative workshops in the late 1840s and the joint organisation of Drury's National Associations of United Trades for the Protection, and for the Employment, of Labour

---

[1] Cole, *Robert Owen*, p. 229.
[2] E.g. *Co-operative Commercial Circular*, i (1853-4), pp. 41-4 ; Hall and Watkins, *Co-operation*, pp. 340-1 ; C. Webb, *Industrial Co-operation*, p. 86.
[3] B. Jones, *Co-operative Production*, i, p. 8 ; Cole, *Century of Co-operation*, pp. 183, 188 ; *Co-operator*, ii (1861-2), p. 83 ; iv (1863-4), pp. 83-4.
[4] Cole, *Century of Co-operation*, pp. 125-6, and *Robert Owen*, p. 229 ; Fay, *Life and Labour*, pp. 52-3.
[5] Potter, *Co-operative Movement*, p. 188 ff.

in 1846, to the co-operative interest of the A.S.E. in 1851–2, and the trade union links with the Co-operative Congresses in 1869 and 1876,[1] their constantly renewed association showed that both were but different aspects of the same working-class movement. Both had learnt to live with the capitalist system, and both centred their aspirations on raising the working man's share within it.

V

It might be considered that the two co-operative movements that were divided by the watershed of 1850 were so divergent in object and inspiration as to constitute, in fact, two separate lines of development. It was true, of course, that the name remained the same, that several of the leading figures, notably G. J. Holyoake, Lloyd Jones, William Pare, and E. T. Craig, spanned both periods with their working lives, and that several societies survived from the earlier phase to enter, suitably changed, into the heritage of the later. To establish true continuity, however, deeper affinities must be found. If we can discover a continuous thread running through the two phases which showed such fundamental differences in many of their most important aspects, we shall have discovered much of the specific contribution of co-operation to the social history of the British people.

In the first place, co-operation was conceived and organised as a purely working-class movement, though inevitably in the conditions of the time it had many middle-class leaders. The ill-starred attempts, inspired by the 'individualists', to bring in middle-class mills and profit-sharing schemes remained without lasting significance and rapidly came to an end with the formation of the Co-operative Productive Federation of genuine producers' co-operatives in 1882. The objects of co-operation were always to improve the conditions of the working classes.

[1] *E.g.* G. D. H. Cole and R. W. Postgate, *The Common People 1746–1938* (1938), pp. 310-11 ; B. Jones, *Co-operative Production*, i, pp. 98-9, 133-7, 343-4 ; Cole, *General Union*, p. 157, and *Century of Co-operation*, pp. 99-101, 108-9 ; Harrison, *James Hole*, p. 13 ; Hall and Watkins, *Co-operation*, pp. 342-4 ; Raven, *Christian Socialism*, especially pp. 222-57, 309-11.

Co-operation: from Community Building to Shopkeeping

Secondly, despite its mundane concerns with flour, soap, and candles, co-operation has always been concerned with more than mere material improvements, even though these were always recognised as essential first steps. It has, since the days of Owen, stressed the morally educative influences of collaboration as against the selfish motives of competition, it has sought to implement educational and ethical aims, and it has aimed to make not only a wealthier but a better people. The educational effects of self-rule have been recognised since the leadership passed out of the hands of Owen into that of the Owenists, and the movemen thas always been unquestionably democratic.

Thirdly, as its name implies, it has always stressed the powers of co-operation. Alone, the working man was always helpless against the powers which assailed him; united with others, he could acquire education, accumulate capital, organise large businesses, and ultimately, perhaps, employ himself. By co-operation the working class would learn the value of self-help.

All these were common to other working-class movements also, and they firmly establish co-operation within that general tradition. But there was yet a fourth characteristic, which not only marked off co-operation from the other movements within that tradition, but also provides the essential continuity between the first and second phase of its history. Whereas the long tradition of state socialism and of political action was for changing society as a whole by rule from the centre, the co-operator attempted to take himself out of society, to seek his own solution without troubling with those who would stay behind in the old world. This explains the essential voluntaryism of the movement.

A community settlement, wrote Dr. M'Cormac in 1830, 'can be quite self-sufficient, *independently of all the world besides*'. 'Co-operators', stated Dr. King in 1828, 'ask nothing from anyone but to be let alone, and nothing from the law but protection', while the *Co-operative Magazine* repeatedly referred to settlements as 'places of refuge', 'a house of comfort for the wretched of the land'. The co-operative scheme, declared Hawkes Smith in 1839, 'infringes no rights, attacks no existing accumulation of property, [and] endangers the safety of no public or private morals'. And in the second phase of the movement, Holyoake contrasted state socialism with co-operation, which was 'the discovery of the means by which an industrious man can provide his own dinner without depriving anyone else of his'. 'The modern co-operator,' concluded Ernest Aves, 'is . . . more than any other, trying to carve out from the whole a sphere that shall be determined by his own scheme of things.'[1]

The differences in the economic and social environment before and after 1850 very largely account for the differences in the methods and aims of the co-operative movement,[2] as they have determined their changes since and are likely to do in the future. Throughout, however, it has remained a movement for working-class emancipation, promising spiritual and material gains by working together, and relying on persuasion and precept only.

[1] H. M'Cormac, Introduction to *Rules of the First Armagh Co-operative Society*, 1830, p. 14; Holyoake, *History of Co-operation*, ii, pp. 594, 606; *Co-operative Magazine*, ii (1827), p. 124; *New Moral World*, vi (1839), p. 670; Ernest Aves, *Co-operative Industry* (1907), p. 12. Cf. also Seligman, 'Owen and the Christian Socialists', *Essays in Economics*, p. 56, and Cole, *Century of Co-operation*, p. 12.

[2] Cf. Reeves, *Rochdale Co-operation*, p. 2.

3
E. J. HOBSBAWM

CUSTOM, WAGES, AND WORK-LOAD IN NINETEENTH-CENTURY INDUSTRY

THE basic principle of the nineteenth-century private enterprise economy was to buy in the cheapest market and to sell in the dearest. For the employer to buy labour in the cheapest market implied buying it at the lowest rate per unit of output, *i.e.* to buy the cheapest labour at the highest productivity. Conversely, for the worker to sell his labour in the dearest market meant logically to sell it at the highest price for the minimum unit of output. Obviously it was to the advantage of the bricklayer to get 7d. for an hour which meant the laying of 50 bricks rather than 100. The ideal situation envisaged by classical economics was one in which the wage-rate was fixed exclusively through the market without the intervention of non-economic compulsion on either side. For the employers this implied having a permanent reserve army of labour at all required grades of skill, for the workers permanent full, or rather over-full, employment. It also implied that both sides would be actuated by market motives: the employers by the search for the highest possible profit (which implied the lowest possible labour cost), the workers by the search for the highest possible wage (which implied complete responsiveness to wage-incentives). Gross though these over-simplifications are, they nevertheless represent the relevant parts of that simple theoretical model of a self-regulating market economy to which many economists and businessmen aspired and which they believed to be largely in operation.

The point was, that neither employers nor workers completely recognised the rules of this game or what they implied. This was partly due to the fact that they were unrealistic. Thus even the workers most open to wage-incentives are so only up to a point : social security, comfort at work, leisure, etc., compete with money. But it was also due to a tendency to base economic behaviour not on long-term rational analysis, but on custom, empiricism, or short-term calculation. In this article I propose to discuss some of the effects of this on nineteenth-century labour productivity.[1] The conclusions of this discussion may be summarised as follows :

1. There are two main watersheds in the nineteenth-century history of the employment of industrial labour : one, probably, in the decades around the middle of the century, the other towards the end of the Great Depression. Both mark changes, or the beginning of changes, in the attitude of both workers and employers. Both, incidentally, coincide with turning-points in the evolution of other aspects of the economy.

2. The first marks the *partial* learning of the 'rules of the game'. Workers learned to regard labour as a commodity to be sold in the historically peculiar conditions of a free capitalist economy ; but, where they had any choice in the matter, still fixed the basic asking price and the quantity and quality of work by non-economic criteria. Employers learned the value of intensive rather than extensive labour utilisation and to a lesser extent of incentives, but still measured the degree of labour utilisation by custom, or empirically — if at all.

3. The second marks the *complete* learning of the rules of the game. (It does not matter, for our purpose, that by this time the ideal model of a self-regulating market economy was, except perhaps in the international money market, ceasing to be even approximately realistic.) Workers began to demand what the traffic would bear and, where they had any choice, to measure effort by payment. Employers discovered genuinely efficient ways of utilising their workers' labour time ('scientific management').

[1] *Labour productivity* is usually a synonym for *output per man-hour* or some similar unit. Such a use normally fails to distinguish between those changes in output due to machinery and those due to other causes, *e.g.* changes in organisation, in staffing, in the efficient utilisation of the time, effort, and skill of the workers. In this paper the term applies *exclusively* to the second type of change. In practice, of course, the two kinds of change generally go together and are hard to separate.

Custom, Wages, and Work-load in Industry

I

How did workers in the early industrial economy decide what wages and conditions to accept and what effort to put into their work, assuming that they had any choice? They have rarely told us, so that we are forced into conjecture, based partly on observation, partly on the analysis of the scattered historical data.[1]

No initial problem of wage determination arose for the unskilled or those in abundant supply. They had to take (if men) a subsistence wage, or one fixed so as just to attract them away from (say) farm labour.[2] (Women and children of course got less than subsistence, but since their rate was normally fixed in relation to the male wage, we may neglect them.) The fact that the wages of unskilled labour were fixed at or around subsistence costs is overwhelmingly attested by theorists, industrialists, and historians. We may therefore take the subsistence wage of the unskilled or plentiful labourer or farmhand as the point of reference, in relation to which all other grades fixed their own positions. We must neglect problems arising out of the payment of wages in kind. 'Subsistence' was, of course, not a physiological absolute, but a conventional category varying at different times and in different places.

The characteristic skilled worker in pre-industrial crafts would expect to get ideally about twice as much as the common labourer, a differential of great antiquity and persistence, for we can find it in Diocletian's price- and wage-fixing as in that of the English J.P.s under Henry VI and Charles II, in eighteenth-century Italy, in France, in the Barcelona building trades

---

[1] J. W. F. Rowe, *Wages in Practice and Theory* (1928), and Barbara Wootton, *The Social Foundations of Wage Policy* (1955), suggest ways of tackling this problem.

[2] *E.g.* P. W. Kingsford, *Railway Labour 1830–1870* (Ph.D. Dissertation, London Univ. Library), p. 145. A useful discussion of the basis of this 'district rate' for labour from the management's point of view is in *Journal of Gas Lighting*, lii (1888), p. 286. It forms part of a series on 'The Management of Workmen'. For some factors tending to raise this 'district rate' above the strictly economic minimum, cf. R. Newman, 'Work and Wages in East London Now and Twenty Years Ago' (*Charity Organisation Review* (July 1887), p. 273); Charles Booth, *Life and Labour* ... 2nd ser. v, p. 365 ff.

of the nineteenth century, and doubtless elsewhere. (These are, of course, *rates* not *earnings*.) In fact, the skilled man normally tended to get rather less than this differential, especially when unable to restrict entry from the unskilled grades, and more when entry was effectively restricted, as when the skilled man was white, the unskilled coloured. In practice the relation between the rates of the pre-industrial labourer and craftsman — say the mason and his labourer — was more likely to be two to three or three to five, than one to two.[1]

How would a skilled man fix his wage standard in relation to other skilled men ? The calculations here, though tacit and often unconscious, were rather complex. On the one hand each worker would regard himself as belonging to a particular stratum — say of craftsmen as distinct from labourers — and would therefore expect a wage conforming to its social status : masons, tilers, and carpenters would expect to earn wages of the same rough order of magnitude, as would smiths, engineers, skilled tailors, and shoemakers. On the other hand within each stratum or industry there was a well-defined hierarchy, though it is not always clear whether this represented earning capacity or whether earnings reflected it. Thus the coachmakers in 1837

are not an equal body, but one composed of classes taking rank one after the other . . . the body-makers are first on the list ; then follow the carriage-makers ; then the trimmers ; then the smiths ; then the spring-makers ; then the wheelwrights, painters, platers, bracemakers and so on. The body-makers are the wealthiest of all and compose among themselves a species of aristocracy to which the other workmen look up with feelings half of respect, half of jealousy. They feel their importance and treat the others with various consideration : carriage-makers are entitled to a species of condescending familiarity ; trimmers are considered too good to be despised ; a foreman of painters they may treat with respect, but working painters can at most be favoured with a nod.[2]

[1] E. Young, *Labor in Europe and America* (Washington, 1876) ; L. Dal Pane, *Storia del lavoro in Italia — secolo XVIII* (Milan, 1944), App. III ; H. Sée, *Histoire écon. de la France*, ii, p. 179 ; Angel Marvaud, *La Question sociale en Espagne* (Paris, 1910), p. 426. For differentials in Britain, E. J. Hobsbawm, 'The Aristocracy of Labour in 19th-century Britain', in J. Saville (ed.), *Democracy and the Labour Movement* (1954).

[2] W. B. Adams, *English Pleasure Carriages* (London, 1837), pp. 188-9.

Custom, Wages, and Work-load in Industry

Similar hierarchies are attested for the new industries, in Alsace, Lancashire, the engineering workshops, and elsewhere.[1] No doubt status reflected wage differences, or wage differences hardened into custom ; but workers did not clearly distinguish between these and the status they believed to be attached to the job : a compositor who did not get a higher wage than, say, a local tailor would regard himself as ill-served, whatever the relative demand for each on the market.

Traditional differentials were, of course, less important in new industries and in those dominated by piece-work (except in so far as the original bidding price for various grades of labour had been set with reference to the previously existing wage-scale). It is dangerous to exaggerate the role of custom in the wage-structure of a fully industrial economy as some recent students have done, though custom undoubtedly somewhat distorted it. (After all, the standards by which workers judged a wage to be acceptable or not were not the only factor in fixing them.) The point is, that the wage-structure of a developed capitalist economy was not formed in a void. It began as a modification or distortion of the pre-industrial wage-hierarchy and only gradually came to approximate to the new pattern ; more quickly in areas of acute labour shortage or glut, in economies dominated by sharp business fluctuations, than in others ; and certainly more quickly in those economies which succeeded in destroying or disorganising the self-defence organisations of small producers or pre-industrial workers. However, the important thing to bear in mind is that the *worker's* wage calculation remained for long, and still to some extent remains, largely a customary and not a market calculation.

One important result of this was that employers almost certainly got their skilled labour in the nineteenth century at less than market cost. This applies not only to countries with a generally low wage-level such as Germany and Belgium, but

[1] *E.g.* Volz, 'Die Fabriksbevoelkerung des Oberelsass im Jahre 1850' (*Ztschr. f. d. ges. Staatswissenschaft*, vii, p. 136) : 'Der Drucker hasst den Stecher, dieser faehrt stolz an jenem vorueber ; der Zeichner und der Maler spricht mit Verachtung von Spinnern . . .' and the various remarks about the refusal of 'mechanics' to abandon their status even under great economic pressure in Charity Organisation Society, *Special Committee on Unskilled Labour* (1908), *e.g.* pp. 102, 112.

also to Britain. It seems clear that, even allowing for the sharp cyclical fluctuations to which they were subject, ironfounders and engineers in Britain before, say, 1840, lived in a wonderful seller's market and could have demanded much more than the rate of 30s. or so which engineers in Lancashire got in the 1850s.[1] Obviously competition between small firms and the absence of effective unions played its part, as did the fact that the men demanded some of their extra price in terms of non-economic satisfactions, such as independence of supervision, dignified treatment, and mobility. Nevertheless the essential modesty of their demands — the greater, the more traditional and hierarchical their society — was and remains important, as any Australian coming to this country is willing to attest.

Since we can only speculate on 'what the traffic would bear' in those days, we cannot of course measure the size of the bonus which employers drew from their workmen's unwillingness to charge it. One would guess that it was at least as great as the bonus they had drawn in the eighteenth century from Professor Hamilton's 'profit-inflation'. It also seems likely that their views on individual productivity were affected by it. The worker's labour effort, or standard of output per unit of time, was also determined by custom rather than market calculation, at any rate until he began to learn the rules of the game. The ideal of 'a fair day's work for a fair day's pay' had, and has, little in common with the ideal of buying in the cheapest and selling in the dearest market. The criteria for a fair day's work are probably too complex for a cursory analysis. They depended partly on physiological considerations (*e.g.* the working speed and effort which a man might maintain indefinitely, allowing for rests during and between working days or shifts); on technical ones (*e.g.* the nature of the jobs he could be expected to do in the course of a day or shift); on social ones (*e.g.* the need for a team to work at the pace which allowed slower members to keep up and in turn earn a fair day's wage); on moral ones (*e.g.* the natural pride a man has in doing a job

---

[1] J. B. Jefferys, *The Story of the Engineers* (1945), p. 23; D. Chadwick, 'On the Rate of Wages in Manchester and Salford ... 1839–1859' (*Journ. Stat. Soc.*, xxiii, 1859).

as well as he can); on economic ones (*e.g.* how much work can earn a 'fair wage'); on historic ones and doubtless on others. They were enforced by powerful collective pressure.[1] In fact, as we know, such standards were so well accepted that — where workers had the choice — there was often no major difference between time and piece-rates: each could be translated into the other with little difficulty. The employer of time-workers knew roughly how much piece-output he would get, the employer of piece-workers (as Adam Smith observed)[2] knew that he was not likely to get more than the standard output for the accepted working week from them, though they might get it done in fewer days. What statistics we have tend to show that in non-mechanised industries output tended to fluctuate about a level trend. Productivity in the Ruhr mines (except for the period 1796–1802 and the early 1830s) remained pretty steady from 1790 to 1850 at between 87 and 97 per cent of the 1850 level. In the Halle coppermines it averaged 12-13 tons per man-shift for each trade cycle period between 1800 and 1850.[3] In French coal-mining it was equally stable between 1834 and 1852.[4] This level was not necessarily the highest obtainable, but it is likely that workers laboured as hard as they could, or were traditionally expected to do, subject to the proviso that they felt themselves to be getting a 'fair' wage and that work did not interfere with their comfort at work and at leisure. Of course raw workers, forced labour, or others set to do uncongenial or untraditional work for which they had no customary standard, and were not trained or practised, workers feeling themselves to be underpaid, or unable to take any pride in their labour naturally worked only as hard as they had to. But pleasure in work is commoner than one thinks. De Man's inquiries in the 1920s

---

[1] *E.g.* Mr. Dent's evidence — a building foreman — on such collective levelling in *Special Ctee. on Unskilled Labour, loc. cit.* p. 104.

[2] *Wealth of Nations*, cap. viii (Cannan (ed.) i, pp. 83-4). Cf. also F. Smith, *Workshop Management* (n.d., ? 1884), p. 1: 'For convenience sake time is computed as the equivalent of work done'.

[3] J. Kuczynski, *Geschichte der Lage der Arbeiter in Deutschland* (6th edn., Berlin, 1954), i, pp. 112-16.

[4] Ministère des Travaux Publics, *Statistiques de l'industrie minérale* (Paris, 1935).

showed that in Germany 67 per cent of skilled workers and even 44 per cent of unskilled ones said they felt more pleasure than distaste for their work.[1] The moral stigma against slacking was and remained very great among such groups. The employer who took over such pre-industrial types of workers, or those who modelled themselves on them, could be fairly sure to get as much work per time-unit out of them initially as was socially expected, unless or until he introduced the criteria of the market economy. Naturally such rigidity of output could be troublesome where he required productivity to increase rapidly, or workers to adjust themselves to rapidly changing work-processes.[2]

It is therefore clear that skilled workers, indeed perhaps all workers who felt some self-respect and were not goaded into revolt, did not apply market criteria to the measurement of their efforts. Unskilled ones were of course habitually overdriven and underpaid, but employers did not expect more than the absolute minimum of voluntary work from them anyway, and relied — perhaps wrongly, before the age of modern mass production — on discipline or 'driving' to get as much effort as could be expected of them.[3]

II

Somewhere about the middle of the century we observe a conscious adjustment of skilled workers to the 'rules of the

[1] H. De Man, *Joy in Work* (1928). However, it must be noted that the pioneer German investigations of A. Levenstein into this question give diametrically opposite results (*Die Arbeiterfrage*, Munich, 1912). 60·5 per cent of his sample of miners, 75·1 per cent of his textile workers, and 56·9 per cent of his metal-workers (all working on payment by results) expressed distaste for work, 15·2, 7·1; and 17 per cent respectively, active pleasure.

[2] Cf. some of the complaints of American employers against British skilled workers, e.g. R. T. Berthoff, *British Immigrants in Industrial America 1790-1950* (Harvard, 1953), p. 66. But possibly also the converse complaints of British employers and foremen about Americans, that they did no work without specific incentives, e.g. *Special Ctee. on Unskilled Labour*, pp. 108-9.

[3] Geo. White, *A Treatise on Weaving* (Glasgow, 1846), complains that there is too much purely coercive labour management, and ascribes this partly to the poor quality of labour, partly to the fact that 'such a state of society where, as with us, labour generally exceeds the demand for it, has a tendency to beget indifference to its improvement and it becomes treated as a state of things in necessary association together' (pp. 330-1). The syntax is obscure, but the general drift is clear.

game', at least in Britain. Thus unions began in the 1840s to recognise the peculiar nature of the trade cycle in their provisions for unemployment and a little later to develop the characteristic policies of the 'new model' unionism: restriction of entry, maximum labour mobility between areas of slack and full employment, emigration benefit, the systematic use of friendly benefits, and so on.[1] As we know, the economic theory behind these policies aimed at the creation of a permanent scarcity of skilled labour, so as to raise its market price. Again, as we shall see, skilled workers as well as employers in the 1850s and 1860s tended to favour the shortest possible forms of hiring contract so as to enable either side to bargain for better terms with the least possible delay. But, even if allowing for the exceptions to *laissez-faire* which unions naturally clung to (especially legal protection and trade unionism), this was only a partial adaptation to free market bargaining. The criteria of a 'fair wage' remained customary in many industries, those of a 'fair day's work' equally inflexible. Indeed some unions combined *laissez-faire* bargaining with strict penalisation of bad work, as did the boilermakers.[2]

The period which followed the Great Depression may have seen a more fundamental change of attitude, as it saw a more fundamental revolution in the economy and in the structure of the labour force. In the first place, as Rowe has shown, certain groups of workers — *e.g.* the railwaymen — for the first time began to demand what the traffic would bear. In the second place there was, in a number of industries in various countries, a very marked slackening in individual productivity, all the more striking in contrast with the very rapid rise of the third quarter of the century. Thus in French coal-mining output per man-day (underground workers, 1900 = 100) rose from 62 in the 1840s to 100 in 1887–95, after which it fell slowly to 95 in 1909–14. In Germany productivity per worker in hard coal-mining rose from 45 in 1844–52 to 101 in 1887–94

[1] S. and B. Webb, *Industrial Democracy*, *passim*; J. B. Jefferys, *op. cit.*; A. Youngson Brown, 'Trade Union Policy in the Scots Coalfields 1855–1885' (*Ec. Hist. Rev.*, 2nd ser., vi, 1, 1953); E. J. Hobsbawm, 'The Tramping Artisan' (*Ec. Hist. Rev.*, 2nd ser., iii, 3, 1951).

[2] R.C. on Labour, Group A, 1893–4, xxxii, Qs. 20, 769.

(1900 = 100) after which it remained roughly stable until 1913.[1] Output per head in British and Belgian mining, in the London building trades, and Lancashire cotton-spinning from the 1890s on showed similar tendencies.[2] Even if we allow where necessary for the effect of diminishing returns, or the increase of non-productive workers sometimes comprised in these totals, or the shortening of hours, the tendency remains suggestive enough. In one or two cases it has been specifically put down to a certain slackening in the men's individual labour effort.[3] It is at least possible that certain groups of workers now began systematically to allow their output to sink unless held up by incentives, or else that the weakening of older forms of labour discipline or tradition produced the same result.

Although industrial militants like Tom Mann developed the theory of free market bargaining by varying the worker's labour effort in the 1890s,[4] conscious and systematic slacking of this kind was no doubt rare. When proposed it met with a great deal of moral indignation not only — naturally, if illogically — from employers, but from skilled workers themselves and their sympathisers.[5] The tendency to slack undermined the workers' self-respect even if it improved his market position; and self-respect is a much more fundamental thing

---

[1] J. Kuczynski, *Short History of Labour Conditions in France* (1946), p. 179; *Short History of Labour Conditions in Germany* (1945), p. 151. It may be observed that these calculations command confidence because their results do not fit well into their author's general thesis.

[2] M. Saitzew, *Steinkohlenpreise u. Dampfkraftkosten* (Leipzig, 1914), p. 141; G. T. Jones, *Increasing Return* (Cambridge, 1933), p. 90; Jewkes and Gray, *Wages and Labour in Cotton Spinning* (Manchester, 1935), p. 42 ff.

[3] *E.g.* in the building industry. Early complaints that employers have difficulty in getting 'a day's work for a day's wages' and that workers are lazier than they used to be, are referred to in J. M. Ludlow and Lloyd Jones, *Progress of the Working Class 1832–1867* (1867), p. 267 ff., but the discussion is too vague to allow us to judge what, if any, weight there was in these complaints.

[4] Cf. 'If labour and skill are "marketable commodities" then the possessors of such commodities are justified in selling their labour and skill in like manner as a hatter sells a hat or the butcher sells beef. . . . If (the housewife) . . . will only pay two shillings, she will have to be content with an inferior quality of beef or a lesser quantity.' (*What Is Ca' Canny?*, leaflet issued by the International Federation of Ship, Dock, and River Workers, 2 October 1896.) Cf. also E. Pouget, *Le Sabotage* (Paris, n.d.), chapter 2: 'La "Marchandise" travail'. The question is discussed, *à propos* of the alleged fall in productivity in this period, by Saitzew, *op. cit.* p. 155.

[5] *E.g.* S. and B. Webb, *The Decay of Capitalist Civilisation* (1923), p. 162.

than the historically evanescent categories of the free market economy.

Between 1880 and 1914, therefore, employers began to lose the advantages which they had hitherto enjoyed owing to the workers' ignorance of the 'rules of the game' or their unwillingness to play it, and from which they had drawn considerable benefits. Sometimes, as in British cotton-spinning, quasi-monopoly cushioned them against the effects of this loss;[1] sometimes not. We must therefore turn to the employers' side of the picture.

III

If the failure to learn or apply the rules of the game caused workers often to work harder and for less money than they need theoretically have done, the employers' failure to learn or apply them caused them to utilise the labour they hired with remarkable inefficiency.

In considering the behaviour of nineteenth-century entrepreneurs we must naturally distinguish between what might be inefficient today, but could be rationally justified under then prevailing conditions, and what could not. (We need not agree with the rational justifications of early employers, but need merely recognise that they were rational.) The early industrial entrepreneur believed, not without some justification, that his labour force was largely impervious to monetary incentives, reluctant to work in the way which suited him, or indeed to enter his employ at all. As Townsend observed in 1780:

> The poor know little of the motives which stimulate the higher ranks to action — pride, honour and ambition. In general it is only hunger which can spur and goad them on to labour.[2]

And, we might add, discipline which could keep them at it. It was therefore logical for employers to use compulsion, non-economic as well as economic, to recruit the labour force and to keep it at work. Hence the first half of the nineteenth century is anything but *laissez-faire* in its labour relations. In

[1] Jewkes and Gray, *op. cit.* p. 45.
[2] (J. Townsend) *Dissertation on the Poor Laws by a Well-Wisher of Mankind*, J. R. McCulloch (ed.), *Scarce and Valuable Economical Tracts* (1859), p. 404.

Britain it saw the codification of the Master and Servant Law, which penalised breaches of contract more harshly for men than for masters,[1] the systematic if not always effective outlawing of trade unions and strikes — the repeal of the Combination Acts made relatively little difference to this — a marked taste for long-term and inelastic labour contracts like the miner's annual or monthly bond,[2] and that ruthless piece of legal-economic coercion, the New Poor Law. Elsewhere similar devices were common.

These things were in part rationally justifiable in terms of contemporary theory, though not wholly so ; for employers were only too willing to abandon *laissez-faire* when it did not suit them. Thus annual bonds, though understandable as a response to local labour shortages, as in the eighteenth-century mines, were not easily defensible by a disciple of Adam Smith. However, what is not justifiable is the extraordinary neglect of the problem of productivity and efficient labour utilisation. Broadly speaking, employers assumed that the lowest wage-bill for the longest hours meant the lowest labour cost per unit of time ; that the workers' effort could not be much increased above a given norm, though they were often too lazy to reach this ; that the problem of productivity was essentially one of mechanisation combined with discipline ; and that incentives were mainly useful as an auxiliary to this, if at all. Handbooks for industrialists and managers, though devoting much attention to the economic utilisation of raw materials, neglected the problem of labour management almost completely.[3]

[1] D. Simon, 'Master and Servant', in J. Saville (ed.), *Democracy and the Labour Movement* (1954), p. 160 ff.
[2] Its history is told in *The History of the Miners' Bond in Northumberland and Durham*, by Hylton Scott (typescript in the Newcastle Public Library).
[3] Of the handbooks on cotton-spinning I have consulted, the following confine themselves to workshop calculations, in some instances omitting even wage calculations : W. Etchells, *The Cotton Spinner's Companion* (Manchester, 1827) ; G. Galbraith, *The Cotton Spinner's Companion* (Glasgow, 1834) ; A. Kennedy, *The Practical Cotton Spinner* (Edinburgh, 1845) ; Daniel Snell, *The Manager's Assistant, being a condensed treatise on the cotton manufacture* (Hartford, Conn., 1850). (R. Scott) *Scott's Practical Cotton Spinner and Manufacturer* (3rd edn., London and Manchester, 1851) considers the problem of payment for spinners and advises keeping pay-books in a form suitable for the calculation of productive efficiency — 2 pages out of 395. The only book worthy of its name, J. M. (J. Montgomery), *The Carding and Spinning Master's Assistant or the Theory and Practice of*

Custom, Wages, and Work-load in Industry

This is, of course, to oversimplify the part played by incentives in the early entrepreneur's scheme. They were in fact widely used, partly in the form of piece-wages, partly in that of subcontract. Yet neither was inconsistent with the view summarised above. The subcontractor was a form of entrepreneur, and entrepreneurs were of course responsive to incentives. Moreover, he set the pace for those under him who did *not* enjoy incentives, and indeed the prevalence of subcontracting appeared to make incentives to the workers themselves largely unnecessary, except in the case of genuine collective task-wages fixed by gangs. The piece-master, charter-master, or whatever he was called, the skilled craftsman — spinner, plater, or smelter — who paid his unskilled assistants himself as often as not on straight time-rates, the foreman or ganger who, almost invariably, worked on a commission basis or as subcontractor : [1] these set the pace and the rest had no option but to follow it.

Nor was payment by results itself (as distinct from subcontract) conceived primarily as a means of raising productivity, but as a means of stopping it from falling below the norm. As Dr. John's Welsh ironmaster claimed, it was the only way to ensure that workers 'did their duty' when they could not be effectively supervised.[2] Or, to quote M. Ponson of Liège :

> Day work is the most disadvantageous method in mines, because the workers, having no interest to work actively, mostly slacken the sum of their efforts as soon as supervision ceases.[3]

Indeed we have examples of deep pits being sunk on time-wages for the first few hundred feet, while supervision was possible,

---

Cotton Spinning (Glasgow, 1832), treats the problem of labour management — in 3 or 4 pages — essentially as one of 'uniform good order and proper authority' (p. 221). Of the weaving handbooks, C. C. Gilroy, *The Art of Weaving* (1845), is purely technical and historical, and Geo. White, *op. cit.* (Glasgow, 1846), considers the management of the hands one of the four non-weaving matters which must be mastered, but devotes only 5 pages to it (pp. 329-34) as against 16 to the selection of yarn, 31 to various calculations connected with the work, and 9 to warping on hand-looms.

[1] Cf. D. Schloss, *Methods of Industrial Remuneration* (1892), chapter xii.
[2] A. H. John, *The Industrial Development of South Wales* (Cardiff, 1950), p. 80.
[3] A. T. Ponson, *Traité de l'exploitation des mines de houille* (Liège, 1854), iv, p. 120.

but on piece-rates thereafter.[1] In general, if an *increase* in effort was required it was got by 'driving', though this might imply giving incentives to a limited number of 'wheel-horses'. Naturally grades of workers who resisted disciplined supervision — *e.g.* skilled craftsmen — could not be so treated.[2]

This argument does not apply in the same way to industries which had always been paid by results, for instance the domestic industries in which piece-work was a degenerate form of the price which formerly independent artisans had been paid for the sale of his product, or in occupations directly modelled on such industries.

Though this attitude cannot be justified, it can be understood. The combination of ultra-cheap wage-costs with standard customary labour efforts gave employers a considerable surplus, once workers were trained and experienced ; larger perhaps than they might have got by high wages and more intensive efforts. Thus Belgian coal-miners were worse paid than those in the Ruhr ; their output per manshift between 1886 and 1910 was consistently 30 to 40 per cent below the Germans. But over the same period (1892–1910) the labour cost of Belgian coal, measured as a percentage of its pithead price, was less : 53·9 against 55·9 per cent.[3] Again, small works may be able, perhaps by close supervision and other factors, to have lower labour costs than all but very large and efficient works : at any rate Rostas's figures for British industry in 1937 seem to suggest this.[4] Most early works were small, and where this was so and capital was short entrepreneurs might think it good policy to utilise the abundant factor, labour, rather than the scarce one, even at the cost of some labour inefficiency per worker. Lastly it seems probable that even

---

[1] A. T. Ponson, *Traité de l'exploitation des mines de houille* (Liège, 1854) iv. But Ponson also advises incessant supervision, where possible, even when excavations are paid by the cubic metre (i (1852), pp. 320-1).

[2] However, the wise employer or foreman would also take account of local custom among workers for, even when this was not based on practical considerations arising out of local experience, 'l'abandon des habitudes invétérées des ouvriers est chose difficile à obtenir', and not to be imposed except when absolutely necessary, in the view of Ponson (*op. cit.* ii, p. 598).

[3] Saitzew, *loc. cit.* pp. 141, 175-6.

[4] L. Rostas, *Productivity, Prices and Distribution* (Cambridge, 1937), p. 37.

Custom, Wages, and Work-load in Industry

with little incentives, unskilled or simple work can be utilised much more efficiently than skilled or complex work, simply because its pace can be more effectively supervised and controlled, whether by man or machine. A standard American textbook of 'scientific management' estimates that unskilled labour and routine clerical jobs directly supervised in small groups work at 50 per cent efficiency, semi-skilled machine-operators at 38-40 per cent, skilled all-round mechanics at 30 per cent, and highly skilled all-round men such as tool-makers at 25-28 per cent.[1] But this does not alter the fact that for each wage-unit paid employers got much less than they might have done, and were largely unaware that this was so.

Again, the combination of an unskilled and untrained labour force and mechanisation tended to blind them. Raw labour could not be expected to be efficient anyway : one must budget with low *per capita* output. The increase in output due to technical innovation was so vast that it was easy to forget how much greater it might have been with efficient exploitation. 'By the aid of mechanical fingers', exclaimed Dr. Ure,[2] 'one Englishman at his mule can turn off daily more yarn than 200 of the most diligent spinsters of Hindostan.' It seemed not to matter that they might have turned out more, because few entrepreneurs realised the potential economies of really efficient labour exploitation. The *Carding and Spinning Master's Assistant* of 1832 warned employers against rearranging their machinery once installed, even if they found the arrangement to be less than ideal, since the costs of reorganisation would probably exceed the savings.[3] Yet this was a patent mistake. It is perhaps impossible, at any rate without long and laborious work, to make an estimate of such inefficiency, but we have at least a guide to it in the Report of the U.N. Commission on Latin American Textile Industries (1950), some of which are extremely archaic. This pioneer study attempts to separate the inefficiency due to obsolete or defective machinery from that due to other factors, chiefly bad organisation — *e.g.* over-

---

[1] L. P. Alford, *Cost and Production Handbook* (New York, 1942), p. 1333.
[2] *Dictionary of Arts, Manufactures and Mines* (1863 edn.), i, p. 529.
[3] *Op. cit.* p. 218.

staffing, in other words inefficient labour utilisation. It concludes that both are equally important causes of inefficiency. In Brazil and Ecuador, the most technically old-fashioned of the industries studied, reorganisation would improve efficiency more than new investment. 'Contrary to what has always been supposed,' says the report, 'bad organisation and administration affect productivity as much as the traditional shortage of capital.'[1] No historian of early industrial Europe will be in the least surprised at this discovery.

The temptations of a cheap labour economy made employers equally reluctant to recognise their inefficiency when it was pointed out to them. Admittedly few were prepared to instruct industrialists in scientific management except the rare scientist like Charles Babbage.[2] On the other hand, the fact that low wages and long hours were not necessarily identical with the lowest labour costs was proved time and again in business, and could indeed be observed. Brassey gave wide publicity to his proof.[3] As Lujo Brentano pointed out, even the experience of the great wage rise of 1872 proved it, though he was regarded as enunciating a paradox and many observers flatly refused to believe their eyes.[4] Owen's New Lanark had made the point decades before. The judicious Ponson, who gave statistics for output per man-day for coal-hewers of 113 pits in four countries whose shifts ranged from six to fifteen hours, concluded in 1853, without any detectable philanthropic bias, that eight hours would seem a reasonable average shift at the coal-face.[5] But as late as 1901, 80 per cent of all Belgian workers still laboured in excess of eleven hours.[6] When in 1889 unions forced the British gas industry to adopt three eight-hour shifts

[1] The report is summarised in *International Labour Review*, August 1952.
[2] *On the Economy of Machinery and Manufactures* (1832). Babbage, incidentally, also strongly urged incentive payments in the form of profit-sharing.
[3] T. Brassey, *On Work and Wages* (1873), *passim*. The subject seems first to have attracted wide attention during discussions on the shortening of the working day or week. Cf. 'By exacting seven days' work you get less than six days' labour. This is a truth widely verified.'—The superintendent of machinery of the Eastern and Continental Steam Packet Co., quoted in John T. Baylee, *Statistics and Facts in Reference to the Lord's Day* (1852), p. 68.
[4] L. Brentano, *Ueber d. Verhaeltnis v. Arbeitslohn u. Arbeitszeit zur Arbeitsleistung* (2nd edn., Leipzig, 1893).   [5] Ponson, *op. cit.* iv, 275-82.
[6] *Handwoerterbuch der Staatswissenschaften*, article 'Arbeitszeit'.

instead of two twelve-hour ones, the industry believed itself to be facing (*a*) a net loss in efficiency and (*b*) a completely unprecedented method of working; but several gasworks in the country had operated on eight-hour shifts for up to fifty years, their results were available to inspection, and the industry happened to be one in which technical discussion was particularly lively and informed.[1]

This resistance to knowledge is also understandable. In practice greater labour efficiency implied higher wages and shorter hours. But in the first place no businessman likes to raise his costs unless he is certain to recover them, and entrepreneurs had no cast-iron guarantee. In the second, it was undesirable to encourage workers to demand higher wages and shorter hours, for where would such demands stop? It was safer, if less efficient, to stick to the old ways, unless pressure on profit-margins, increased competition, the demands of labour or other inescapable facts forced a change. But the periods of major economic adjustment after the Napoleonic Wars and the slump of 1873 subjected employers to just this kind of pressure, and hence led to major modifications in the method of labour utilisation. In the post-Napoleonic period the effect was delayed, since employers first attempted to exhaust the possibilities of cutting labour costs by extending hours and cutting money wage-rates. During the Great Depression (1873–96) new methods tended to be adopted more quickly. Roughly speaking, the mid-century brought the beginning of the substitution of 'intensive' for 'extensive' labour utilisation, the latter part of the Great Depression the beginning of the substitution of rational for empirical 'intensive' utilisation, or of 'scientific management'.

[1] *The Journal of Gas Lighting*, liii (1889), 894, professed itself to be unaware of any town where the three-times-eight-hour shift system was in vogue, though in fact (*loc. cit.* pp. 953, 1000, 1043) it had been functioning for fifteen years in Burnley, for eighteen in Hull, for twelve in Bristol, and for at least nine in Birkenhead, not to mention Dundee and Liverpool, where the system went back 'forty or fifty years' (*loc. cit.* l (1887), pp. 109-10). Similar ignorance of well-established practices by leading business-houses is combated by (J. Lilwall), *Practical Testimonies to the Benefits Attending the Early Payment of Wages* . . . (Early Closing Association, 1858), which prints an impressive list of London firms paying on Fridays and/or giving a Saturday half-holiday.

IV

Though it is very probable that the efficiency of labour utilisation rose after the 1840s, this is not easy to establish statistically. However, it is clear that the system of labour relations in Britain underwent fundamental changes, and analogous ones are observable elsewhere (for instance, in Napoleon III's legalisation of strikes). Non-economic compulsion virtually disappeared with the decline of the miners' bond and other long contracts, the abolition of the Master and Servant Laws and the full legalisation of trade unionism. We can trace the extension of short-hiring contracts in the 1850s, particularly in Scotland,[1] but also in a variety of local building-trade agreements. Piece-mastering and subcontract, those almost invariable concomitants of rapid capitalist industrialisation in its early stages, may well have passed their peak, at any rate in the older industries.[2] Modifications in the Poor Law (*e.g.* in 1867) also tended to turn it from an instrument of labour coercion into one of relief.[3] As often as not these legal changes ratified a *de facto* situation. Obviously the substitution of a willing for an unwilling bargain was likely to improve the morale of skilled operatives, and hence their productivity. (This was more important in doctrinaire *laissez-faire* countries than where paternalism was widespread, as in German heavy

---

[1] *E.g.* W. H. Marwick, *Economic Developments in Victorian Scotland* (1936), pp. 147-8 ; *Proc. Industrial Remuneration Conference* (1885), p. 106 ; *Sel. Ctee. on Master and Servant* (1866), xiii, 1281-1320, 2320 ff., 701-15, 469 ff., 562 ff. ; National Association for the Promotion of Social Science, *Report on Trade Societies* (1860), pp. 290, 332-3 ; N.A. Prom. Soc. Sci., *Papers and Discussions on Social Economy* (1863), pp. 24, 37 (hours system among masons and in Scotland) ; Webb Collection, *Coll EA 31* (British Library of Political Science), MS. pp. 258-64 (hours system introduced among Birmingham Bricklayers, 1865), p. 311 (unsuccessful Glasgow strike against it, 1849) ; R. W. Postgate, *The Builders' History* (n.d.), p. 209. F. Smith, *Workshop Management* (n.d., ? 1884), originally addressed to builders and cabinet-makers, observes that payment by the hour 'gradually but certainly' supersedes payment by the day against the opposition of the workers (p. 32).

[2] Except, of course, on the Continent where this *was* the period of early industrialisation and hence of the expansion of piece-mastering and sub-contract. Cf. L. Bernhard, *Die Akkordarbeit in Deutschland* (Leipzig, 1903), *passim*.

[3] P. Aschrott, *The English Poor Law System* (1888), Pt. I, sect. xii-xiii.

industry, but this is not the place to discuss these interesting differences.) More important, the movement to shorten hours gained ground, partly through legislation, partly through private arrangements and bargains, as in the Saturday half-holiday, which came into fairly wide use from the 1840s among the builders and in some parts of the provinces, and in London from the mid-fifties.[1] Shorter hours virtually obliged employers to raise productivity, and the fact that this could be done was now more widely appreciated.

We know so little about systems of management and wage-payment that it is dangerous to generalise about them, especially in view of the incredible complexity of the industrial scene. Only three facts are at all certain. First, that from the 1830s on the economists, who had previously discussed systems of wage-payment only incidentally — as in Adam Smith, Malthus, Say, and Sismondi — began to pay systematic attention to them. From the end of the 1830s economic treatises normally contained a special section on the form of wage-payments.[2] Where writers had been neutral about, or slightly hostile to, piece-rates, they now became very enthusiastic about them, *e.g.* McCulloch and Michel Chevalier.[3] Second, employers in several countries showed a marked tendency to extend payment by results — *i.e.* incentive payments — initially mostly in combination with subcontracting and piece-mastering. All this led Marx to the familiar view that payment by results was the type of wage system best suited to capitalism.[4] Since we have no reliable statistics, we cannot estimate the success of these efforts. Sometimes they failed, as among British engineers and

[1] On the general literature of sabbatarianism, which multiplied from the middle forties, cf. R. Cox, *The Literature of the Sabbath Question*, ii (Edinburgh, 1865). On the activities and successes of the Early Closing movement, J. R. Taylor, *Government, Legal and General Saturday Half Holiday* (4th edn., 1857); John Lilwall, *The Half Holiday Question* (1856); (J. Lilwall), *loc. cit.* (1858), which deal mostly with London, but contain incidental information about the (earlier) progress of the movement in the provinces. Of the London firms practising early closing and giving dates of its introduction, most claim to have started it within the last three years, practically all in the 1850s.

[2] I owe this point to L. Bernhard, *op. cit.* pp. 3-8.

[3] Cf. McCulloch, *Statistical Account*, ii, 43, who goes so far as to ascribe the superiority of English industry to the prevalence of piece-work.

[4] *Capital*, i (1938 English edn.), p. 561 ff.

builders.[1] Sometimes they succeeded, as when Krupps introduced piece-work after 1850 together with mass production,[2] or when new coal-fields such as those of South Wales paid most of their workers by results, while in older fields (as in the North-east) only certain grades such as coal-getters had been so paid.[3] But the tendency — observed in the British factory inspectors' reports — is not in doubt.[4] It was vastly accelerated by the massive construction of the railways, which was paid almost entirely by results, and helped to spread the principle of piece-work widely, *e.g.* into German agriculture,[5] and into the building industry. Lastly, it is clear that the reluctance to increase money-wages diminished. Money wage-rates took a marked turn upwards in most West European countries after the mid-century, and the first timid defences of a 'high wage economy' could be heard.[6] However, we are pretty much in the dark about the actual increase in labour efficiency, and it is clear that vast areas of industry remained resolutely 'old fashioned'.

After 1880 we sail much less uncharted waters. Since this was precisely the period when labour efficiency came to be considered a subject of special study, at least as important as that of the efficient use of equipment and raw material, it attracted the researcher, the engineer, the government department, and other suppliers of historical material.

The main incentive to change came from the well-known

---

[1] Jefferys, *op. cit.* p. 63 ; Postgate, *op. cit.* p. 149.
[2] R. Ehrenberg, Kruppstudien III (*Thuenen-Archiv*, iii, pp. 53, 89 ff.).
[3] G. D. H. Cole, *The Payment of Wages* (1928 edn.), p. 10.
[4] Cf. Leonard Horner's observation in 1851 on 'the proportion [of piece-work] to fixed weekly wages being daily on the increase'.
[5] L. Bernhard, *op. cit.* p. 39 ff.
[6] Partly as a means of avoiding the political radicalisation of the workers, as by Mundella (W. H. Armytage, *Mundella*, 1951, p. 23) and later by Joseph Chamberlain, but also on grounds of productivity, *e.g.* Brassey and John Ward, *Workmen and Wages at Home and Abroad* (1868), a great believer in the truths of political economy : 'An opinion is entertained, by a considerable number of persons, that high wages tend to generate habits of idleness and dissipation amongst workmen. This opinion rests upon very uncertain and inconclusive data. Wages are the reward and encouragement of industry, which, like every other human quality, increases in proportion to the encouragement it receives. Where wages are high, we generally find the workmen more active, diligent, and persevering than where they are low' (p. 216).

tendency of profit-margins to decline in the Great Depression. This is also the period when imperfect competition made itself felt on a large scale, when the 'second industrial revolution' got under way, and when a powerful labour movement emerged in several countries, composed, moreover, of workers who increasingly knew the 'rules of the game'. Whether pressure from competition or from labour was more important in turning employers' thoughts towards labour efficiency is uncertain. A case has been made for both.[1] From our point of view labour pressure is the more interesting, though it must be borne in mind that the increasing scale and complexity of industrial production made firms more vulnerable to it than they had previously been, as well as making old methods of labour management less applicable. As one of F. W. Taylor's disciples put it : 'We used to drive workers, but — especially if they are skilled — . . . they do not have to stand it'.[2] One reason why they did not need to, as a historian of scientific management observes, was that there now had to be 'a substitute for the effective supervision characteristic of the small shop'.[3]

'Scientific management' was the result.[4] In its initial phases, with which we are here concerned, it consisted of three main elements :

(*a*) a careful analysis of the production process, its break-up into simple segments and the establishment of labour norms for each ;

(*b*) a system of costing which enabled the firm to discover the labour cost of each operation and to keep it under constant observation ;

(*c*) the elaboration of systems of incentives or supervision capable of making workers labour at maximum intensity. For practical purposes this then meant payment by results.

[1] C. B. Thomson, *Scientific Management* (Harvard, 1914), p. 684 ff. ; N. Brisco, *The Economics of Efficiency* (N.Y., 1914), p. 5. Cf. also F. Smith, *op. cit.* (1884), p. 2, 'In these days of excessive competition, it is more than ever necessary that the employer should obtain the full equivalent of what he spends in wages'. [2] Thompson, *loc. cit.* p. 685.

[3] H. S. Person, *Scientific Management in American Industry* (N.Y., 1929), p. 7.

[4] H. B. Drury, *Scientific Management* (Columbia, 1915), for a brief outline and history of the American movement in its earliest stages.

In practice these were generally combined with mechanisation, though this is not theoretically essential. It is possible to have mechanisation without conscious scientific management as in the early nineteenth century, and scientific management without capital investment in new machines. To begin with, scientific management shared the old view that there was an optimum labour effort, the manager's job being to stop workers from falling below it. But in abandoning custom and tradition scientific management discovered that the optimum effort was so much higher than had been believed possible, and thus in practice became a set of methods for raising rather than for maintaining effort.

All this involved considerable changes in the behaviour of employers. We can follow the evolution of their thought — or rather of that of production engineers — in the debates of the American Society of Mechanical Engineers from about 1886. They began as a search for incentives to replace the effective supervision or 'driving' of earlier days. Hence their first concern was with the elaboration of new forms of payment by results, and the main methods at present in vogue — the premium bonus systems of the Halsey and Rowan types, the Taylor, Gantt, etc. — were invented in the following decade. The engineers were then led into a consideration of costing systems; and indeed in some countries the cost-accountants were the real pioneers of the movement, as in Britain, where Fells and Garcke (two young members of the Fabian Society, interestingly enough) published their *Factory Accounts* in 1887.[1] Thence the discussions naturally turned to organisation and management itself, and it was at this point that Frederick Winslow Taylor intervened, henceforth to dominate the whole movement.

Before 1914 and outside the U.S.A. we are still hardly concerned with scientific management in the modern sense — rationalisation based on time-and-motion study and suchlike. However, in a more empirical way even this was implicit in mass production by specialised machines or processes which

[1] L. Urwick and E. F. L. Brech, *The Making of Scientific Management*, ii (1946), pp. 22, 90, 148. The value of payment by results as against time-wages for costing is stressed in, *e.g.*, C. Heiss, 'Die Entlohnungsmethoden in der deutschen Metallindustrie' (*Schmollers Jahrb.*, xxxvii, 1913), p. 1479.

now expanded greatly; particularly where labour was the expensive factor. Innocent of Taylorism the Bristol boot-and-shoe employers, who devised the 'team system' around 1890, applied his principles. They subdivided the process and made sure that the team was 'waited upon hand and foot and never kept waiting for anything, whereas when they have to "shop" their own work a waste of time is involved'.[1] Any new process automatically involved such labour-costing. Where it was carried out by cheap and docile labour, as in many new consumer-goods factories, this was not important, because wage costs were in any case low. However, the core of the new industrial revolution was an industry which had been hitherto overwhelmingly operated on a semi-handicraft basis by self-reliant and highly paid workers: metals and engineering. Here the transition to the new system had to be thought and fought out much more consciously than elsewhere. Nor is it surprising that in consequence the metal-workers, hitherto rather conservative, became in most countries of the world the characteristic leaders of militant labour movements. The history of such movements since the British lock-out of 1897 can be largely written in terms of the metal-workers, so much so that — for instance — the anti-war movements of 1916–18 followed a pace set almost exclusively by them. (We need merely think of Merrheim's union in France, the Berlin shop stewards, the British shop stewards, the Putilov works in Petrograd, the Manfred Weiss works in Budapest, the Turin and Milan metal-workers.)

However, if rationalisation was in its infancy, payment by results and incentive schemes made their way rapidly. In Britain they were imposed on the Amalgamated Society of Engineers by 1903, after bitter conflicts in the 1890s, and increased steadily up to the 1914 war.[2] Armstrong-Whitworth

---

[1] *Report of Factory Inspectors for 1894*, p. 213; S. and B. Webb, *Industrial Democracy*, p. 399. Cf. also the advice by F. Smith, *op. cit.*, to the same effect, for 'every minute [the craftsmen] spend away from their proper occupation [is] so much loss to the employer', and the advisability of having specialised semi-skilled labour trained for each machine (pp. 5-6, 13-14).
[2] Jefferys, *op. cit.* pp. 129-30, 154-5; M. L. Yates, *Wages and Labour Conditions in British Engineering* (1937), pp. 86, 88, 98.

went over to scientific management before 1900; Siemens-Schuckert in Vienna adopted premium bonus in that year.[1] The rapid spread of payment by results is not in doubt. In Britain 5 per cent of all engineering and boilermaking workers were on it in 1886, 27·5 per cent in 1906. (Among turners: 6-7 per cent in 1886, 46 per cent in 1914; among machine-men: 11 per cent in 1886, 47 per cent in 1913.[2]) We can frequently observe the change from time- to piece-wages, as in the Lorraine ironworks — especially the larger ones [3] — British railway workshops,[4] the German railways, and elsewhere.[5] Even where piece-wages had long been the rule, as in cotton, the Great Depression brought significant modifications. At the very least — as in the Bolton spinning list of 1887 — it produced a general systematisation of piece-rates; but it could also lead to the frank recognition of 'speed-up' as an element in piece-wages, as in Oldham, where joint-stock companies predominated.[6]

The object of such innovations was, of course, to lower labour cost per unit of output. If this was not achieved, the employer gained nothing by intensification of labour except perhaps some general savings in capital and labour in other sections of production. Backward or docile workers presented no problem. Ideally it might be possible to 'drive' them simply by the speed of the machine or the effectiveness of supervision, paying them flat time-rates and appropriating the entire gain. This, the so-called 'continental system'[7] was sometimes applied, *e.g.* when the Coventry ribbon trade went over to factory production in the 1850s and in many early

[1] *S.C. on Govt. Contracts* (2469); J. Deutsch, *Auslese u. Anpassung in den Siemens-Schuckert Werken, Wien* (Schriften des Vereins f. Sozialpolitik, vol. cxxxiv).

[2] Yates, *op. cit.* p. 98; Wage Census of 1906, Cd. 5814 (1911) p. 15.

[3] A. Carbonnel de Canisy, *L'Ouvrier dans les mines de fer . . . de Briey* (Paris, 1914), pp. 81-2; L. Bosselmann, *Entloehnungsmethoden in d. suedwestdeutsch-luxemburgischen Eisenindustrie* (Berlin, 1906), p. 144.

[4] A. Williams, *Life in a Railway Factory* (1916).

[5] A. Zimmermann, 'D. Arbeitstarifvertrag im Deutschen Reich' (*Schmollers Jahrb.*, xxxi, 1907, p. 339), Dora Landé, *Arbeits- u. Lohnverhaeltnisse i. d. Berliner Maschinenindustrie* (Schriften des Vereins f. Sozialpolitik, vol. cxxxiv, 1910) and much other German literature.

[6] Jewkes and Gray, *op. cit.* p. 60 ff., 82 ff.

[7] *R.C. on Labour*, Group C, 1893-4, xxiv, Qs. 33296-9.

Custom, Wages, and Work-load in Industry

boot-and-shoe factories.[1] The widespread practice of bribing 'bell-horses' or 'chasers' as pace-makers for the rest also evaded the problem of incentive payments. Slightly less helpless or stupid workers might be paid a simple bounty or premium for all production in excess of the norm, irrespective how much. Until the weavers' unions stopped it, this system was much used in Lancashire.[2] Yet strong or 'educated' workers had to be given more realistic incentives, otherwise they would merely go 'canny'.

The overwhelming importance of payment by results at this stage therefore reflects largely the fact that employers now had to operate with a working class which knew the 'rules of the game' and would make effort proportionate to reward; whether or not it was organised in unions. This also discouraged ordinary piece-work; for under such a system labour costs were only lowered by periodic rate-cutting, always an unpopular process. Hence all the new systems of payment by results tended to make payment automatically regressive, *i.e.* paid for each increment of production at a lower rate than for the preceding increment; a fact generally, and often intentionally, obscured by their immense complexity. But though the lowering of labour costs thus became automatic and tacit in theory, in practice this rarely happened. Firms rarely had enough skilled efficiency experts or rate-fixers to price jobs for good and all. Mass production was rarely so standardised that goods remained the same for long periods. Technical methods and products changed. The new payment schemes therefore often failed to secure tranquil adjustments. They might even, as in engineering, create those constant conflicts over the pricing of new jobs or machines which have made the fortune of shop stewards. Hence the modern tendency to revert to flat time-wages (based, however, on a much more scientifically calculated and controlled output norm per time-unit), as in the American motor industry.[3] However, before 1914 scientific management and the extension of payment by results still went

---
[1] S. and B. Webb, *Industrial Democracy*, p. 397 ff., 401 n.
[2] Schloss, *op. cit.* p. 53.
[3] Twentieth Century Fund, *How Collective Bargaining Works* (N.Y., 1942), pp. 611-12, 930-2; R. Mossé, *Les Salaires* (Paris, 1952), p. 58.

together, as the writings of Alfred Marshall bear witness.[1]

There is hardly any need to demonstrate the results of the new methods. Jewkes and Gray have calculated the extent of speed-up in cotton-spinning between 1876 and 1906, their estimates tallying with those given at the time by the Royal Commission on the Depression of Trade.[2] However, the actual saving in labour cost — 23 per cent between 1876 and 1886 — was halted thereafter by the resistance of the operatives. The increase of output per head which followed a change from time to result wages — and that of accidents which also frequently ensued — is so obvious as hardly to need documenting. Our American textbook estimates the efficiency of piece or premium work at 78 per cent as against the percentages for time-work quoted earlier.[3] A single example from our period should suffice. In the Belgian glass industry output per man remained stable at 750-800 foot-units during the 1890s; rose by about 25 per cent until 1903 when payment by results was introduced, together with a lengthening of the working day; and thereafter shot up, with fluctuations, to about 300 per cent of the 1890 and 200 per cent of the 1903 level by 1909.[4] Employers were at last aware of the fantastic savings in labour cost which scientific labour utilisation could bring. It is at least arguable that the tapping of this reserve by efficient exploitation was as important for the continued progress of the economy as the reduction of other costs.[5]

In this summary discussion I have necessarily and deliberately oversimplified. Thus I have concentrated on one aspect of incentive schemes — regressive piece-work wages — to the exclusion of various other methods of achieving substantially

---

[1] *Industry and Trade*, Book 2, cap. xii.
[2] Jewkes and Gray, *op. cit.* pp. 41-2; *Royal Commission on the Depression of Trade*, quoted in Schulze-Gaevernitz, *D. Grossbetrieb* (1895), p. 117.
[3] Alford, *op. cit.* p. 1333.
[4] E. Mahaim, *Untersuchungen ueber Preisbildung: Belgien* (Schriften des Vereins f. Sozialpolitik, vol. cxliv B), p. 269. (The book is in French.)
[5] And that the superiority of American industry over British was largely due to it. Cf. the pregnant observation, made in 1872, that in Britain 'labour-saving' meant something which *displaced* labour, while in the U.S.A. it meant something which *cut down* time or labour on a given job. (J. Richards, *A Treatise on . . . Woodworking Machines*, London and New York, 1872, pp. 55-6.)

the same results; sometimes, as in the case of Taylor's own system, at the expense of other firms by skimming the cream off the local labour market. Moreover, I have concentrated on one aspect of scientific management, the actual direct saving of labour-time per worker, rather than on other aspects which, though capital- rather than labour-saving, have a very direct bearing on the efficient use of labour-time also; for instance, various shiftwork and continuous work systems which were also greatly reformed and expanded in the period after 1880, partly in response to labour pressure for shorter hours.[1] I have also illustrated the argument mainly from a few Atlantic seaboard countries, in order to avoid complicating the discussion further by considering major differences in the chronology of industrial development. The object of this simplification is to direct attention to the main conclusions, as set out earlier. These are obviously very tentative. Until much further work has been done on nineteenth-century work-loads and output per man, they cannot be satisfactorily verified. Such studies ought to distinguish, so far as possible — as research has often failed to do — between the various cost-reducing effects of mechanisation and other forms of reorganisation in the division of labour, in the ways attempted by the U.N. Commission for the Latin American Textile Industry. This will involve considerable work, and the co-operation of students with good engineering and accounting as well as historical qualifications, for it will involve the analysis of working processes and the cost accounts of many individual works. Perhaps because the available material rarely throws much light on individual work-efforts and because historians are rarely qualified to undertake such analyses, the importance of the changes to which this paper has tried to direct attention, has been somewhat underrated.

[1] P. Boulin, *L'Organisation du travail dans les usines à feu continu* (Paris, 1912), and J. Rae, *Eight Hours Work* (1894), for developments in our period.

4
PETER BROCK

THE SOCIALISTS OF THE POLISH 'GREAT EMIGRATION'

THE history of socialism during the seventy-five years which elapsed between the outbreak of the French Revolution and the founding of the First International has received much attention during recent years. Books and articles in plenty have been written on the theories of the French Utopians and their disciples who, from the eighteen-thirties onwards, were active in the United States, Germany, Belgium, Italy, and Spain. The early British socialists and the German pre-Marxians have also been studied in detail; while the representatives of socialist ideas in Russia during this period are becoming increasingly well known in the West. Among the Poles, too, contemporary schools of socialist thought had many adherents who in books, pamphlets, and journals, sought to spread the new gospel, adapting it in the process to Polish conditions. Studies of their lives and works have been published by later writers, especially since the last war. But the fact that almost all this material is in the Polish language has unfortunately meant that it is virtually unknown in the West.

There is little trace of socialist doctrines in Poland before the insurrection against the Russians which broke out in the Congress Kingdom in November 1830. Its failure in the following year meant the destruction of the far-reaching autonomy which this part of Poland had enjoyed as a result of the decisions of the Congress of Vienna. The military defeat, combined with the humiliation which had been inflicted on the country by the partitions of the previous century, caused many thinking Poles to meditate on the causes of the national calamities and to subject traditional political and social concepts to searching criticism. After the uprising a large number not only of the country's political and intellectual leaders, but of the educated classes, went into exile. At its height the 'Great Emigration' (1831–63) may have numbered nearly ten thousand persons. The majority of the exiles took up residence in France; but there were also smaller groups in England, Belgium, and elsewhere. After only a few months two rival political camps arose to compete for the allegiance of the *émigrés*. The conservatives, under the leadership of Prince Adam Czartoryski, remained united. But the democrats soon split up into a number of warring factions. The most important of these was undoubtedly the Polish Democratic Society, formed in March 1832,[1] which played a leading role in the eighteen-thirties and forties in the conspiratorial work being carried on in the homeland.

The restoration of Poland's independence by armed insurrection was the avowed object of the whole emigration. The means to achieve this, and the social and political conditions which were to prevail after liberation, were the subject of fierce debate. Controversy raged in particular around the problem of peasant emancipation, since the failure to enlist the support of the peasantry in an overwhelmingly agricultural country like Poland was considered to have been one of the main reasons for the insurrection's failure. Both the conservatives and most of the democrats advocated variations of the same policy, that is to say, of *uwłaszczenie*, of granting the peasants property rights over the land they had previously cultivated as serfs. Under such schemes the estates of the landowning class would be left untouched. The Prussian government had already inaugurated emancipation; but the more enlightened Poles of all camps hoped that in the Austrian and Russian provinces, at least, emancipation would come not by governmental decree but from the Poles themselves.

A small minority of the *émigrés* put forward an alternative

[1] No history of the Society has so far been published. For its political and social ideas, see B. Baczko, *Poglądy społeczno-polityczne i filozoficzne Towarzystwa Demokratycznego Polskiego* (Warsaw, 1955). A selection from its publications is given in *Towarzystwo Demokratyczne Polskie: Dokumenty i pisma*, ed. Baczko (Warsaw, 1954).

policy — collective ownership of the land and all the resources of the country — and they had their disciples in the home country, where conditions usually made open advocacy of socialist doctrines out of the question. It was to the teachings of the French Utopians, with whom they had come into contact after leaving their native land — and above all to Lamennais and the Saint-Simonians — that they owed many of their basic concepts.[1] But, citizens of a country where industry was only in its infancy and where the urban proletariat and bourgeoisie played only a very subordinate role, they had to adapt and modify these concepts to fit differing circumstances. Their socialism, therefore, was an agrarian socialism, which took the peasantry and its institutions as the basis of the new order.

The object of the present study is to give a brief outline of the theories of these *émigré* Polish socialists.

I

At the outset a few words should be said about the political ideas of a man who, though he cannot properly be classed as a socialist himself, exercised a great influence on the socialists as on the whole Polish left. The historian Joachim Lelewel (1786–1861) [2] was the leading figure among the democrats both during the insurrection and afterwards in exile; in the late forties he worked closely with Karl Marx and became a well-known figure in left-wing circles throughout Western Europe. His historical researches had led Lelewel to the conclusion that in pagan times the Poles, like the other Slavs, had lived under a system of collective landownership organised on the basis of the commune (*gmina*) rather in the manner of the modern Russian *mir* or the South Slav *zadruga*. In the course of time, alongside the peasantry with their communal lands, there arose

[1] This question is dealt with in a valuable essay by G. Missalowa, 'Francuski socjalizm utopijny i jego wpływ na polską myśl rewolucyjną w latach 1830–1848', Pt. II, *Wiosna Ludów*, iii (Warsaw, 1951).

[2] The standard edition of Lelewel's writings on Poland was published in twenty volumes under the title *Polska, dzieje i rzeczy jej* (Poznań, 1853–64). Selections from his works, including some not in the standard edition, have recently been published: *Wybór pism historycznych*, ed. H. Więckowska (Wrocław, 1949), and *Wybór pism politycznych*, ed. M. H. Serejski (Warsaw, 1954). Both volumes contain select bibliographies.

a warrior class which held its estates as private property. At first, so Lelewel claimed, the two groups were politically on an equal footing. But later the warrior nobility succeeded in destroying the people's liberties and imposing an alien way of life on the nation. The peasants sunk to the status of serfs deprived of all political rights. The nobility, however, succeeded in taking over many of the features characteristic of the primitive democratic communities and incorporating them in their traditions; it was this that accounted for the creation under the old Polish Commonwealth of a gentry democracy. But in fact the people had never abandoned the struggle to regain their rights. The task of Polish democracy, therefore, was to aid them in this by working for complete political equality and for the restoration of full property rights over the land to those who tilled it, and the abolition of all remaining feudal privileges.

Lelewel himself was opposed to proposals for the introduction of some form of common ownership among the peasants; and many of those, whether of left or right, who were influenced in their political thinking by his theories concerning the primitive communes (*gminowladztwo*), tended to regard them as patterns of democratic decentralisation rather than models for a socialist society.[1] But clearly for those Poles

---

[1] The historical theories of Lelewel provided the main inspiration for a school of thought among the Poles that arose around the middle of the century and may perhaps be considered as the counterpart in an agrarian society of the 'conservative' socialism existing in Germany about this time. The ideas of this group, whose members are to be found both in exile and in the home country, also bear some resemblance, on the one hand, to those of the reactionary slavophils in contemporary Russia who wished to preserve the communal institutions of the Russian village as a bulwark against revolution and, on the other, to the land nationalisation proposals of the Decembrist Pestel. The Poles wished to make use of socialist measures for the preservation of the existing order which, in their view, was otherwise threatened with collapse. Their main proposal was the introduction of collective ownership among the peasantry based upon the village commune, with the retention at the same time of private proprietorship for the estates of the gentry. Their advocacy of a limited socialism was conceived, therefore, as a protection against violent change. The former landlords were to receive compensation for giving up their rights over the peasants' holdings, and either the state or the individual communes, which were to administer the peasants' lands as a common concern of the whole village, would be responsible for its payment. This, together with the fact that the lord of the manor was usually assigned a deciding voice in

who were looking for a native root, an indigenous tradition for the socialism they had learnt in Paris or in London, Lelewel's theories provided what they were seeking ; and thus it is that the commune figures so prominently in the schemes of the Polish Utopians. What the *mir* was to be for Herzen and the Russian *narodniki*, the *gmina* was for the Polish Utopian socialists. It was at the same time a pattern for the future and a battle cry for the present.

The first *émigré* group which came out with a fully fledged socialist programme was formed as a break-away group from the Democratic Society. The Society's first manifesto (known as the Little Manifesto), which was issued on 17 March 1832 immediately after its formation, had called for the abolition of all forms of privilege and for the solidarity of the peoples in the struggle to establish on an international scale a new social order in which Poland would take its place as a free nation. This new order — and here the influence of the Saint-Simonians is obvious — was seen as the final goal of historical development after society had evolved through a series of stages each with its specific characteristics. The manifesto too speaks in one place of 'the land and its fruits common to all'[1] ; and this phrase seems to have been understood by some members as a pronouncement in favour of land nationalisation. That it was in fact no more than a rhetorical flourish is probable ; at any rate only a month later, in an appeal to former Polish soldiers, the Society interprets it to mean merely that 'the peasants have a right to the land they cultivate as their own property'.[2] This was in fact the position taken up by the Society throughout the next two decades.

---

the administration of the commune, gave such schemes — despite their socialistic colouring — a decided advantage, in the eyes of most landowners, over the proposals of the democrats, since the latter, while retaining private ownership in land, excluded the gentry from village life and deprived them of compensation. Most of the prominent representatives of this 'socialist' school (*e.g.* the philosopher Trentowski) belonged to the extreme conservative camp ; though there were several liberals (*e.g.* the historian Jędrzej Moraczewski and the political theorist Karol Libelt) who held very similar views. See H. Mogilska, *Wspólna własność ziemi w polskiej publicystyce lat 1835–1860* (Warsaw, 1949), pp. 58-67, 69, 70.

[1] *Towarzystwo Demokratyczne Polskie: Dokumenty i pisma*, p. 6.
[2] *Ibid.* pp. 15, 20.

The Socialists of the Polish 'Great Emigration'

Among the members of the Society at this time, as well as outside its ranks, the doctrines of the French Utopians had found a number of sympathisers. The left-wing *émigrés* worked closely with the communist elements among the *carbonari*, led until his death in 1837 by Babeuf's old associate Buonarroti;[1] and *babouvisme*, with its egalitarianism and its appeal — in contrast to the attitude of most of the Utopians — to violent revolution, was to exert a great influence on early Polish socialism.

The arrival in Portsmouth at the beginning of 1834 of 212 soldiers and non-commissioned officers, veterans of the uprising against the Russians, who had been released after over two years' captivity by the Prussians, provided suitable ground for propagating socialism. The soldiers were all of peasant or artisan origin. The humiliations of serfdom still rankled in their minds; in addition disillusionment with the conduct in captivity of most of the officers, who had enjoyed comforts and privileges denied the common soldiers, increased their discontent and made them susceptible to radical slogans. Thus when several of the socialist-minded *émigré* intellectuals, then most strongly represented in the Society's group on the island of Jersey, settled among the largely illiterate soldiers, they found ready converts. Neither the expulsion of the Jersey socialists from the Democratic Society, nor the almost universal condemnation with which their views were greeted by the rest of the membership, was effective in deterring the Portsmouth soldiers from following their example. On 30 October 1835 they announced the setting-up of an independent organisation under the name *Lud Polski* (The Polish People), and called for the abolition of private property in the means of production and distribution.[2]

[1] See W. Łukaszewicz, 'Wpływ masonerii, karbonaryzmu i Józefa Mazziniego na polską myśl rewolucyjną w latach poprzedzających Wiosnę Ludów', Pt. I (3-5), in *Wiosna Ludów*, iii.
[2] I have dealt in some detail with the events leading up to the founding of the Polish People in my article 'The Birth of Polish Socialism', *Journal of Central European Affairs*, xiii (1953), no. 3. There is no adequate up-to-date monograph on the Polish People. Almost the only source for their history is to be found in the documents published by Świętosławski in Jersey in 1854, *Lud Polski w emigracji, 1835–1846*. The more important of

The Polish People was to be divided into sections known as communes. The Portsmouth commune was called after Grudziąż, the town where the soldiers had been interned: the small Jersey group, all members of the gentry, took the name of Humań, the scene of a peasant *jacquerie* in the eighteenth century, as a symbol of vicarious penitence for the wrongs done to the peasantry by their class. It was three members of the original Jersey group who were mainly responsible for shaping the ideology of the Polish People: Stanisław Worcell (1799–1857), a former count and deputy to the Diet in 1831;[1] Tadeusz Krępowiecki (1798–1847), of middle-class origin and possibly the most consistently radical of the three;[2] and Zeno Świętosławski (1811–75), who came from a well-to-do gentry family.[3]

The Polish People considered themselves in a special sense the disciples of Buonarroti, 'the first . . . publicly to accept his teaching as their own'.[4] The ideas of Buchez were also particularly close to them. They studied his works, especially the history of the French Revolution which he compiled with Roux-Lavergne, subscribed to his paper *L'Européen*, and frequently corresponded with him.[5] The theories of the Saint-Simonians, Fourier, Lamennais, Owen, Laponnaraye, and later of Cabet and Proudhon, were expounded by the leaders and eagerly discussed among the members, who also knew the writings of such Polish political thinkers in the progressive tradition as Frycz Modrzewski.[6]

None of the leaders at this period attempted to create a finished system. The Polish People's ideology can only be pieced together from fragmentary references scattered among a number of manifestos, open letters, and other polemical

these have been reprinted in *Lud Polski: Wybór dokumentów*, ed. H. Temkinowa (Warsaw, 1957).

[1] Bolesław Limanowski's biography originally published in 1910 remains the best.

[2] See W. Łukaszewicz, *Tadeusz Krępowiecki: żołnierz-rewolucjonista* (Warsaw, 1954).

[3] See my article 'Zeno Świętosławski, a Forerunner of the Russian *Narodniki*', *American Slavic and East European Review*, xiii (1954), no. 4.

[4] *Lud Polski: Wybór dokumentów*, p. 227. They may also have known something of Pestel's scheme for partial nationalisation of the land.

[5] *Ibid.* pp. 350, 375.   [6] Missalowa, *op. cit.* p. 115.

writings. All documents were put out in the name of the organisation and had to be presented to the whole group first for discussion. Nevertheless it was undoubtedly the leaders' views which predominated among the peasant soldiers.

The most bitter attacks were directed not towards the Polish conservatives, but against the rival Democratic Society accused of betraying the principle of common ownership of the land, which the Portsmouth socialists claimed to find expressed in the Little Manifesto of 1832. The Society's advocacy of small peasant proprietorship was due, in their opinion, to the predominance within it of the gentry and bourgeoisie. Such a position would lead to the development in Poland of the evils of industrial and commercial capitalism.

The Society [they went on] wishes to see in Poland instead of the small number of proprietors there today a much larger number. In this way tyranny and exploitation will be multiplied and Poland will be transformed from an agricultural to an industrial country. A caste of monied men will be created . . . lords of workshops and stores, avaricious and vile, men without feeling whom Christ flayed in His holy wrath.

If after emancipation the peasantry were made owners of the land they cultivated, then political democracy (*wszechwładztwo ludu*) would become a farce, a façade. They would continue to elect the gentry as their representatives, since the latter would still have the real power in their hands. And this would mean a new form of serfdom. Why, too, did the Society advocate leaving the landowners with their estates intact? 'The peasant cottager and other wretched inhabitants of Poland, through the preservation for the lords of extensive acres, are condemned without pity to misery or death from hunger.'[1] In time a new class of village rich would grow up.

In all their documents the Polish People stressed the social origins of the rank and file and bitterly denounced the oppression of the peasantry in the home country.

Coming all of us from the plough, we best of all can feel the poverty of the countryman, his needs and his hopes; we would wish therefore in the name of our suffering brethren to tell society

[1] *Lud Polski: Wybór dokumentów*, pp. 55, 57, 71, 116-17, 123, 195.

the tale of oppression. . . . Hunger, cold, sickness, the lash, stunted intellectual growth : these are the afflictions of the Polish people. The possessors create poverty ; the propertyless suffer it. In order to establish equality, it is necessary to struggle so that mankind is not divided into two camps : those who have property, and the landless, a race of demigods and a race of animal-like beings with human features.

Their country's past was seen as a story of war between classes, the exploiting gentry and the oppressed peasantry :

Our fatherland, that of the Polish people, was always separate from the fatherland of the gentry, and if there was contact between the two, it resembled that between a murderer and his victim. Throughout the whole world a sea of blood divides the gentry from the people.

Justice could only come by force, by a violent revolution which would overthrow the old order. With the help of a few 'penitent' gentry come over to the people's side, the ruling class would be defeated and destroyed. A 'dictatorship of the people' would then take over and exercise power during the transition period. It would be armed with drastic powers — though no clear picture is given of the nature of the state which would be created after the revolution. 'Terrorism, the use of the sword to bring principle into effect, intolerance of all that either now or at any time harms this principle or can endanger our aims . . . there is our faith, here are our methods.'[1] The Jacobin example obviously influenced the Polish People's revolutionary strategy. A justification of terrorism was also found in the Gospels: their conception of Christ the avenger of social wrong is indeed reminiscent of the medieval chiliasts.[2]

There was, they held, no alternative between slavery, veiled or open, and absolute equality, the principle expressed by Voyer d'Argenson in the phrase — 'l'égalité des conditions

---

[1] *Lud Polski : Wybór dokumentów*, pp. 54, 58, 61, 69, 93, 96.
[2] *Ibid.* pp. 93, 96. The Polish People held that the Christian church had advocated communism until it was corrupted by the ruling caste and its tools, the priests. Primitive Christianity had been revived by Robespierre and his cult of the Supreme Being. Paris had then become 'the capital of a new papacy', Rome the seat of Antichrist. (See *ibid.* pp. 92, 112, 206-7.) The influence of Lamennais's anti-clerical version of Christianity is apparent here as in the writings of many other Polish left-wing 'Catholics' of this period.

sociales'. These words, which are constantly repeated by the Polish People, could in their view only mean collective ownership of a country's resources.[1]

In order not to gather in the hands of individuals the means by which they could make their influence predominate and their will all powerful, the community will proclaim itself the sole legal owner and distributor of the instruments of labour. The main instrument is the land, which is destined to maintain the life of every member of the community. The right to life is the only undeniable human right and in no way can it depend on individuals. Hence the right to life comes before the right to property.

No able-bodied person should become a burden on the community. Inherited wealth, which arose from privilege and resulted in inequality, was to disappear. The obligation to work at socially useful tasks was incumbent on all; but there was apparently to be no direction of labour. The necessary tools would be supplied by the state through the local communes as being in closest touch with the citizens. The commune would exercise supervision over agricultural production — something in the manner of the contemporary Russian repartitional commune — alloting holdings to its members and reassigning them if any were unable to fulfil his tasks properly or in the case of death. Their policy is very similar to that of Proudhon in the next decade: 'Everyone [they write] will receive for life an equal portion [of land] properly equipped with livestock, buildings, and implements; from such a holding each individual may draw a profit for himself, provided this in no way injures the welfare of the whole community.' In this fashion it was hoped Poland would be shielded 'from the capitalist vultures circling around her'.[2]

Industry, to which in fact little attention was paid by the Polish People, was to be run on a co-operative basis. The credit system was to be nationalised and, following the pro-

[1] *Ibid.* pp. 60, 63, 69, 89.
[2] *Ibid.* pp. 79, 82, 84, 125, 127, 202. The contrast between the decadent, capitalist West and the 'young' Slav world preserving intact elements of a primitive socialism is to be found in the thought of the Polish People and some of the other Polish Utopians. But it is much less pronounced than, for instance, with Herzen and the Russian *Narodniki* — due to the strength of anti-Russian feeling among the Poles.

posals of Saint-Simon, the banks were to be in charge of the country's economy. A system of social security was to be set up to care for the aged and the sick. The arts and sciences were to receive public support — provided they were directed toward social ends.[1] Defence was to be entrusted to a citizen militia. 'One and the same moral feeling will infuse people and army.'[2]

Special attention was to be paid to the education of the community's children. They were to be regarded as wards of the state and not exclusively the concern of their parents. (This was quite a revolutionary proposal even in early Victorian England.) The manors of the landowners were to be taken over as schools and homes for children. After passing through the educational system even the offspring of former class enemies would be transformed into good citizens of the socialist state; and when this had been accomplished, the danger of counter-revolution would have passed away and the Kingdom of God on earth be established for ever.[3]

The members of the Polish People were not theoreticians, as they constantly reiterate. But their leader, Worcell, did try to set down a reasoned apologia for his organisation's thesis that property is theft.[4] In an essay entitled *On Property*,[5] Worcell regards property as a social product, whose form is subject to the laws of change which regulate society and which are different from those governing the natural world. Human history is progressive and not cyclic, and has evolved through a number of epochs with different needs and ends. While in earlier 'pagan' ages private property was an element of progress and civilisation, helping to bind society more closely together, in the present epoch, which should give expression to 'the word of Christ, the gospel of brotherhood',[6] other forms

[1] *Lud Polski : Wybór dokumentów*, pp. 82-4.   [2] *Ibid.* pp. 168-70.
[3] *Ibid.* pp. 82, 125, 202-5.
[4] 'The property of today was born simply of plunder (*Własność dzisiejsza urodziła się po prostu z grabieży*)': *ibid.* p. 201. This statement, which was probably Worcell's, occurs several years before Proudhon's famous maxim appeared in print. The idea in almost identical phrasing also occurs in France at the end of the eighteenth century.
[5] Reprinted *ibid.* pp. 135-59. The essay was completed in 1836.
[6] A. G. Duker, 'Polish Émigré Christian Socialists on the Jewish Problem', *Jewish Social Studies*, xiv (1952), pp. 322-3, detects an anti-

are needed. Private ownership must yield to collective, since equality is impossible with differences in property rights, liberty impossible when some citizens are dependent on others for their livelihood, and brotherhood cannot flourish where society is based on the principle of egoism. Rejecting, therefore, the eighteenth-century view which defended socialism on the basis of natural rights,[1] Worcell adopts and develops the Saint-Simonian theory of socialism as the final outcome of human progress.

Despite attempts to gain converts among the *émigrés* and to spread their doctrines in the homeland, where they optimistically believed 'the spirit of Christian sociality which the peasant preserves in his heart' would make their ideas welcome among the peasantry, the Polish People failed to make much impact on their fellow countrymen.[2] They lacked the money which the bigger *émigré* societies had at their disposal for large-scale propaganda missions to Poland — and anyhow the hostility of the manor house would in fact have made work among the peasantry extremely difficult.[3] Among the *émigrés* they were naturally the objects of bitter attacks from the conservative and centrist groups. That the ideas of the Polish People, however, had supporters among the rank and file of the Democratic Society is shown by some of the comments sent in from its sections in 1836 on the draft of a fresh manifesto which had been prepared by the new leadership. While right-wing members

semitic element in Worcell's writings. He does in fact attack Jewish finance capital in his essay on property. Describing the effects of the rapid spread of capitalism in Poland, which he alleges would result from carrying out the Democratic Society's policy, he exclaims: 'Fertile Poland suddenly condemned to eternal hunger! Christian Poland suddenly given over into the hands of the Jews to be beaten . . . and crucified by them' (*Lud Polski: Wybór dokumentów*, pp. 149-50). Such sentiments, however, do not necessarily have a racial connotation and similar passages may be found, for instance, in the editorials of Ernest Jones's *People's Paper* or, as a series of articles in *Jewish Social Studies* has recently brought out, in the writings of many west European socialists of the period.

[1] This argument had been used earlier by the Portsmouth socialists to support collective ownership (see *ibid.* p. 411). It was also frequently employed by the Democratic Society in defence of private property.

[2] See pp. 156-7 below. For their contacts with the British left, see my article 'Polish Democrats and English Radicals, 1832-1862: A Chapter in the History of Anglo-Polish Relations', *Journal of Modern History*, xxv (1953), pp. 142-4.

[3] *Lud Polski: Wybór dokumentów*, pp. 20 (intro.), 84, 127.

of the Society had wanted the authors of the draft to tone down their criticism of the role played by the nobility in Polish history, in order to leave the door open for collaboration with other *émigré* groups, the extreme left urged that the Society should come out squarely in favour of collective ownership of the land — or at least for its equal division among the whole peasantry. Both points of view represented minority positions within the Society ; the bulk of the membership was solidly behind the leaders.[1]

Typical of the left critics were the two anonymous members of the Reims section who based their case for collectivisation on the Society's own Little Manifesto of 1832. This document had stated that all forms of privilege were a negation of equality.

What is property [they demand angrily] if it is not [a form of] privilege ; the enrichment of one person while leaving another in poverty ; the bestowal of an exclusive right to profit from a portion of the land ? This, as its fruits increase, providing more than suffices for the satisfaction of mere physical needs, brings with it the desire for luxury at a time when others deprived of their material livelihood are likewise unable to support a moral life. . . . [Thus] one section of the people will have been granted the rights which belong to them, while the rest of the people — much greater in numbers — will have been left in the same position as they are in today.

The Prussian government in granting the peasantry the ownership of the land they cultivated at the time of emancipation had not bettered the general condition of the country folk, since the dwarf holders and the landless labourers had reaped no benefit from the reform. 'That majority, which had no share in it, remains in great poverty, in terrible distress.' The same phenomenon, they claimed, might be seen in the case of France where the land reforms of the revolutionary era had transformed those peasants, who had come into full possession of the land, into 'enemies of humanity and pillars of despotism'.

Timidity on the part of those responsible for drawing up the draft must, the Reims members thought, have been the cause of their failure to advocate collective ownership of the

[1] *Towarzystwo Demokratyczne Polskie: Dokumenty i pisma*, pp. 98-108, 124-5. See also *ibid.* pp. 59-60.

land. Such a solution of the social question was the only one compatible with the Christian gospel.¹

Similar views were voiced by the Society's London section, which came out as a whole in favour of socialism. 'In theory you condemn inequality; in practice you uphold it [they tell the leaders of the Society]. . . . We are profoundly convinced that this question of property is the question of the century . . . that private property must inevitably be transformed into common property.' ²

Less radical but also differing on essentials from the position taken up by the authors of the draft, was the statement emanating from three nameless members of the Avignon section. Emancipation and the abolition of the remnants of feudal rights were, they were prepared to grant, an enormous step forward. But was it sufficient? What of the great mass of working people — 'the landless labourers, the servant class, the poor townsfolk, the tenant gentleman farmer [*czynszowa szlachta*] ?' ³

These millions, are they to be deprived of the benefits of the Fatherland and the privileges of that country where they were born, which they have more than once defended, where through want they have [till now] been forced to serve the great ones, who have trampled upon their human dignity and often treated them with the cruellest disdain? Are they political bastards to be cast aside and condemned for eternity to misery and ignorance, outrage and contumely, persecution and everlasting servitude, and to support the indolence and lawlessness of others?

Industrialisation, it was true, would help but it could not provide a solution. In the circumstances, therefore, the proposals embodied in the draft manifesto would only mean a new variety of serfdom for countless persons.

The rich — that is, the landlords — who constitute only a small proportion of the total number of those possessing land, will have in addition to their fortunes in money as much land as the whole peasantry put together. . . . In time, through the conditions under

---
¹ *Ibid.* pp. 99-102.   ² *Ibid.* pp. 107-8.
³ *Ibid.* p. 103. In using this last phrase the writers show themselves nearer in spirit to the main body of opinion in the Society, which regarded the minor gentry as one of the mainstays of Polish democracy, than to the anti-gentry class consciousness of the Polish People.

which the latter are employed, they will bind them to themselves in an iron servitude. . . . The great ones, having enslaved some, will find ways to expropriate the rest. This will not be at all difficult. It may be achieved either as a result of the preponderance which comes through great inequalities in landed property or by means of various . . . frauds, which may easily take place so long as education and culture have not become widespread. . . . [Thus] equality, freedom, and the sovereignty of the people are nothing if they are not founded on peasant proprietorship [*własność gruntowa*] and laws to secure it for all time. If we want to abolish trading in human beings let us do away with the buying and selling of the land.

The land should be 'parcelled fairly among all' in exactly equal lots. Jews and foreigners long resident in the country were to be included in the reform. Differences in the quality of land, apart from wastes and mountainous and inaccessible places, were not to be taken into account, in order to speed the process and win support for the insurrectionary movement, which would initiate the reform. Some forms of industry, such as the mines, would be nationalised. The land, as in the rather similar proposals put forward later by Proudhon, was entailed in the family of its 'owner-cultivator' and would pass down from generation to generation as the common property of the whole family. If the family died out, their farm would revert to the community for reallotment.[1]

The influence of the Polish People, which comes out clearly in the comments of the Society's left-wing dissidents, found a determined opponent in Wiktor Heltman,[2] the leading spirit in drawing up the new manifesto and perhaps the most influential figure in the Society at this period. Heltman, fervent democrat as he was, was strongly opposed to any hint of collectivism in the Society's programme. Common ownership, in his opinion, was nothing but 'universal theft'. Work should indeed be rewarded according to its social utility. But man had a natural right to dispose of the products of his labour as he pleased, to regard them as his private property — provided this was not to the detriment of his fellow-citizens. The community had a right to demand contributions from him in

[1] *Towarzystwo Demokratyczne Polskie: Dokumenty i pisma*, pp. 102-7.
[2] See H. Łuczakówna, *Wiktor Heltman, 1796–1874* (Poznań, 1935).

the form of taxes in order to finance schemes of public utility and to support those incapable of working. Though Heltman was prepared to grant that land nationalisation might be a feasible solution in the far distant future, and that rural producers' co-operatives on a voluntary basis were beneficial, he was convinced that the peasant masses could only be won over as a whole for the revolution by granting them the land they cultivated in unrestricted ownership. Therefore the Great Manifesto,[1] as the document became known, despite socialistic phraseology in places — for instance in its demand that the profits of society should be divided 'according to work and capabilities' — and its plea for the democratic freedoms and for unconditional equality and the abolition of all privilege, comes down in practice in favour of small peasant proprietorship. Emancipation was to be carried out without compensation to the landowners; but the latter, on whom to a large extent the Society relied in its conspiratorial work in the home country,[2] were by implication to be left with their estates. This was indeed in clear contradiction to the Saint-Simonian doctrine stated in the Manifesto that 'the right of owning land and every other form of property is assigned only to labour'. No mention was made of the landless labourer: the problem of land hunger among the rural proletariat was one that dogged the Society to the end.

The debate between the Polish democrats and their socialist rivals died down after a few years. The Polish People, whose theoretical writings were mostly composed within the first two years of its existence, drew in upon itself, ceased in practice to try to convert the emigration and the nation to its creed, and became a closed group of visionaries mapping out blueprints of imaginary Utopias. Without ceasing to be socialists both

[1] The Manifesto is reprinted in *Towarzystwo Dem. Polskie: Dokumenty i pisma*, pp. 87-96. (See also pp. 120-3.) It made a deep impression in left-wing circles at the time, and an English translation was published in 1837. Extracts from the Manifesto may be found in *The Democratic Heritage of Poland*, ed. M. Kridl, J. Wittlin, W. Malinowski (London, 1944), pp. 49-54. A most useful introduction by Czesław Leśniewski is to be found in the Polish edition of the Manifesto published in Warsaw in 1936.

[2] The position is well brought out in R. F. Leslie, 'Left-wing Political Tactics in Poland, 1831-1846', *Slavonic and East European Review*, xxxiii (1954), pp. 132-3.

Krępowiecki and Worcell, ambitious to exert more influence on their contemporaries, now left the organisation. Only the mystic Świętosławski was left to guide the peasant soldiers of Portsmouth from his island home in Jersey.

II

Among the *émigrés*, as has been seen, socialist ideas enjoyed quite a wide circulation, even though only a very small number had thrown in their lot with the one organisation with an avowedly socialist programme. In the home country circumstances were much more unfavourable to the spread of socialism. Censorship, except under Prussia during the more liberal era which opened with King Frederick William IV's accession in 1840, made any open propaganda virtually impossible. The backwardness of the peasant masses and the weakness of the middle class forced the emissaries of the democrats abroad to rely on the support of the gentry who, however liberal, shied away from any talk of nationalisation of the land. The consequences of this dependence are illustrated, for instance, in the story of Szymon Konarski (1808–39),[1] who was sent into Poland in 1835 to prepare the ground for an uprising and perished on the gallows in Wilno in 1839. In exile Konarski had inclined towards socialism, collaborating with the future Fourierist Jan Czyński in producing a radical journal, *The North* (*Północ*). 'Let us set up,' he wrote there, 'a society based on the principle of love and fraternal equality, so that each with a moderate amount of labour may maintain himself freely and be lacking in nothing essential. Let us diffuse knowledge and education among all — and then delinquency and crime will disappear from the earth.'[2] After his arrival in the home country in 1835, Konarski soon became convinced that the success of his mission depended on basing conspiratorial action on the gentry — and in these circumstances the propagation of any form of socialism was, of course, out of the

[1] There are biographies of Konarski by W. Łukaszewicz (1948) and H. Mościcki (1949). Both were published in Warsaw.

[2] 'Zbrodnie ludu są skutkiem źle urządzonego społeczeństwa', quoted by Mościcki, *op. cit.* p. 34.

The Socialists of the Polish 'Great Emigration'

question. Nevertheless, that socialism by the early forties had come to have its adherents in the home country, even though they were severely hampered in giving it expression, is shown by the examples of Father Piotr Ściegienny and his peasant conspiracy in the Congress Kingdom; the Poznań bookseller, Walenty Stefański, and his Union of Plebeians and the little-known Woykowski circle in the territories under Prussian rule; the aristocratic socialist, Count Leon Rzewuski, in Austrian Galicia; and, perhaps most important of all, the theoretician Edward Dembowski, who was killed during the brief Cracow uprising in 1846 in his twenty-fourth year.[1]

Dembowski's socialism was not based on Christian principles, however broadly conceived. Though Ściegienny and Stefański, as well as Rzewuski a little later, drew inspiration for their social doctrines from religious sources, none of them were in any sense mystics; they were more concerned with practical issues than with building Utopias. Even the Polish People at the beginning were most interested in analysing the defects of the existing order and devising means to overthrow it. But by the eighteen-forties we find the Utopia builders and the mystics dominant among the *émigré* socialists. The influence of writers such as Cabet, and even more of the doctrines of Polish Messianism, according to which Poland was the Christ of the nations whose resurrection would usher in a new golden age for mankind, were partly responsible for this development. Most decisive perhaps was the disillusionment resulting from the realisation that the overwhelming mass of the *émigrés* remained impervious to socialist propaganda and that in the home country only the promise of property rights to the land they tilled would attract the peasantry to the national cause.

The most finished of the Polish Utopias came from the pen of Świętosławski, the leading figure now in the Polish People. His Statutes of the Universal Church [2] were the fruit of several years' labour. The Universal Church is Świętosławski's name

[1] I hope to deal elsewhere with the spread of Utopian socialism in Poland itself during the eighteen-forties.
[2] The statutes (*Ustawy Kościoła Powszechnego*) are reprinted in full in *Lud Polski: Wybór dokumentów*, pp. 230-315.

for the socialist world federation of his dreams, which was to be established after the existing order had been overthrown; the statutes the constitution which was to govern it. With its capital on the isthmus of Suez (an echo of the Saint-Simonians) and Polish as its official language, the Church was eventually to embrace all men in a single creed, the religion of socialism and human brotherhood, the unorthodox version of Christianity propounded by Świętosławski and the Polish People. 'Neither the earth, nor its produce, neither the buildings, nor the fruits of your toil, nor the implements of labour, nothing shall you call your property, for everything that you possess or can possess is God's.' The whole economy, therefore, was to be in the hands of the Church, which would create a special central planning department to direct it. Minute regulations were laid down for the organisation of the machinery of government. Some fourteen 'ministries' were to be set up in charge of the various branches of the community's life — and Świętosławski goes into considerable detail in describing their functions. These 'ministries' bear some resemblance to the corporations of later syndicalist theory, since every citizen was enrolled in one or other of them, according to his occupation. The officers of the Church, from Christ's Viceroy (*Namiestnik*) at the top down through an elaborate hierarchy of lower officials, were all to be elected by the people, in whom sovereignty was to lie, according to a complex system of elections; and they were to be responsible for their administration to the people. Citizenship was confined to the 'faithful'; there was, however, to be complete equality between the sexes. The arts and sciences would be subsidised by the Church. A free health service and research into the prevention of disease were to be instituted. The care of the children was to be the special concern of the Church. Mothers with pre-school children would be freed from other duties in order to devote themselves to their education. For older children there was to be a system of universal, free state education. The type of training given to a child was to be adapted to its capabilities and inclinations. Secondary education would be open to all; and the upper ranks of the bureaucracy would be chosen from the most talented pupils. For infractions of the law only penalties which were not degrading to man's dignity should be imposed. Corporal punishment would be abolished and the death penalty used as a last resort for crimes against the state. Prisons were to aim at the reform of the criminal as much as the protection of the public, and proper health standards were to be maintained in all penal institutions.

The Church, like Cabet's Icaria, was conceived on totalitarian lines. No opposition was to be allowed; no unorthodox opinions voiced. 'Like a guardian angel, it was to watch over all the thoughts and feelings' of its citizens from early childhood. The clergy, who combined the functions of political commissar and party theoretician, were to see that the purity of the Church's doctrine was maintained and that the public observances of the faith were properly followed. To them persons with doubts were to come in order to receive instruction; and they were to exercise a general supervision over the educational system.

Once installed throughout the world the Church would continue for ever. There would be an end to wars and hatred. But until its role was acknowledged by all nations, until the old competitive order based on private property was not completely wiped out, it was to consider itself in a state of war, of permanent revolution. Selective service for the citizen army would be obligatory during this period for all able-bodied males — provided they were not opponents of the régime. As each new country was taken over, the poor and the oppressed would be placed under the Church's special protection and the exploiters liquidated as a class. Land and industry would be socialised. Should any nation later revolt, 'the Church will put an end to its existence, will divide its territories among the nations . . . expunge its name, suppress its language, scatter its people'.

The statutes, setting forth a *Nouveau Christianisme* filled with a communist content, were completed in 1844 and issued in the name of the Polish People — and then virtually forgotten for over a century. Despite the apocalyptic, half-prophetic language in which they were written, the moralistic and religious terminology which cloaks their essentially social content, their obscurity in many places, the statutes form an interesting document in the history of socialist thought.

III

Until the dissolution of the Polish People in March 1846 on news of the outbreak of the revolution in Cracow, which was expected to lead to the unification behind its programme of the whole democratic emigration, Polish socialism had been concentrated mainly on English soil. But in France, the centre of *émigré* activities, the socialist 'sects' from the outset had had their adherents among the Poles, and a series of minute and ephemeral socialist groups arose among the exiles there. Most of them made little or no contribution to the development of socialist ideas. But the attempts made by Fourier's disciple, Jan Czyński,[1] and Cabet's close collaborator, Ludwik Królikowski (1799–1878),[2] to apply the theories of their masters to Polish conditions, deserve some attention; especially since in works devoted to the two famous Utopians their Polish followers receive scant mention.

Królikowski's was an original, if somewhat naïve, mind. His works, written in a prophetic style and crammed with biblical texts, repelled his contemporaries, and make them today exceedingly tiresome to read. At first a Saint-Simonian, in the early forties he became an ardent supporter of the communist doctrines of Cabet and the personal friend and co-worker of the latter, who entrusted him with the editorship of his paper, *Le Populaire*, when he departed at the end of 1848 to found his Icarian colony in the United States. During his absence Królikowski, as the 'mandataire du citoyen Cabet',[3]

[1] See *Polski Słownik Biograficzny*, iv (Cracow, 1938), pp. 375-8; K. Świerczewska, 'Jan Czyński — działacz polityczny, literat i publicysta czasów Wielkiej Emigracji (1801–1867)', Pt. I, *Prace Polonistyczne* (Łódź, 1950), pp. 111-36. Only the biographical section of Świerczewska's study has been published; a second part, which is to deal with Czyński's political and social ideas, has not appeared so far.

[2] See the essays by J. Ujejski in *Wiek XIX. Sto lat myśli polskiej*, vii (Warsaw, 1913), pp. 429-47, and by K. Lubecki in *Polska filozofia narodowa*, ed. M. Straszewski (Cracow, 1921), pp. 429-59. See also Missalowa, *op. cit.* pp. 135-46.   [3] *Système de fraternité*, no. 4 (Paris, 1850), p. 114.

The Socialists of the Polish 'Great Emigration'

defended his master and his system against attacks from right and left in a series of articles later reprinted in pamphlet form; and he continued in charge of the paper until it ceased publication in the autumn of 1851. In the previous decade he had gathered around him a handful of fellow-exiles to whom he interpreted Cabet's doctrines in the pages of his own journal: at first, *Poland for Christ* (*Polska Chrystusowa*) (1842–6) and then *Brotherhood* (*Zbratnienie*) (1847–8).[1] In the process of adapting Cabet's ideas for his countrymen Królikowski added a number of new elements not to be found in the original creed. Indeed Królikowski's approach to social problems is in many respects more akin to libertarian socialism than to the totalitarian communism of Cabet; and after the latter's return from America a serious disagreement developed between the two men concerning the relationship between communism and individual liberty. Though Królikowski continued to propagate his own version of communism till his death, the breach with the Icarians was never repaired.

The source of Królikowski's communism lay in his understanding of the Gospels, though he derived much, of course, from Cabet as well as from the Saint-Simonians and the other Utopians. Christ, in his view, had set aside the Old Testament law, which justified private property, commerce, and nationalism; calling his followers to a higher way of life, he instituted for them a community of goods. The early Christians therefore had held all things in common; but later the official church, the object of bitter attack from the extremely theologically unorthodox Królikowski, had betrayed its trust by sanctioning private property, the oppression of the state and class privilege, all of which resulted from Satan's machinations. From them flowed wars and discord. God had given the earth to all men; there was no need for private possessions since man's wants could be supplied by the community. The second coming of Christ, however, was approaching, when the rule of brotherhood and love in social as in personal relationships

[1] I am much indebted to Dr. Józef Żmigrodzki for allowing me to make use of his notes on articles from these two journals, which were inaccessible to me during the preparation of this study.

would be restored. Królikowski's was indeed a vision reminiscent of the Waldenses and the other apocalyptic sects of the Middle Ages.

The Polish people in his view, having suffered most from the existing unjust international order, had a special mission to lead humanity towards the brave new world. He was strongly opposed to the Polish democrats' policy of granting the peasants after emancipation property rights to their land. Not only would this be morally wrong; it would also, he believed, be economically unsound, socially retrogressive and would inevitably lead to the creation of a class of poverty-stricken and land-hungry labourers.

Królikowski's Utopia [1] was similar in many respects to Świętosławski's Universal Church, though he never described it in such detail and with such precision.[2] For both, man was essentially good; evil, the product of bad social institutions of which private property was the most harmful, would disappear as soon as society was run on truly Christian principles. While Świętosławski envisaged a highly centralised state as necessary to achieve this, Królikowski on the other hand wished to see the devolution of powers. Parliamentary institutions were, in his opinion, a fraud. Central government would virtually be abolished; each community would govern itself on the model of the early Christians. All decisions were to be unanimous; there was to be complete freedom of speech; and the only sanction enforcing the will of society would be the compulsion of brotherly love exercised towards the wrongdoer. The most virtuous and devoted would be chosen to perform the few administrative tasks still necessary. Class differences and racial prejudice would disappear. Women would enjoy full equality with men, and the children of the community would be educated in a spirit of service. Most important of

[1] See especially 'O zjednoczeniu', *Polska Chrystusowa*, ii (Paris, 1843), pp. 209-383; 'Ojczyzna matka do swoich dzieci', *Zbratnienie* (Paris, 1847), pp. 16-64.

[2] In a letter to *Zbratnienie* (12 April 1847) Świętosławski takes Królikowski to task for his neglect of all forms of political organisation above the level of the commune. Królikowski, on the other hand, criticised Świętosławski for attempting in his statutes to provide a too rigid political framework.

all, property would be held in common and distributed on the basis of need — only private ownership in consumption goods would be allowed. In contrast to the more militant Świętosławski, Królikowski hoped that the transition to communism could be achieved through peaceful propaganda. But he was ready to admit that it might be necessary to use the sword to extirpate the most dangerous oppressors of the people: the landowners and the bourgeoisie.

This conditional justification of revolutionary violence, combined with Królikowski's egalitarian communism, brought forth a reply from his friend Czyński, which was published in *Poland for Christ*.[1] Czyński, who came of an assimilated Jewish family and throughout his life was to be active on behalf of Polish-Jewish conciliation and the social emancipation of the townspeople in Poland, was at this period an ardent Fourierist. During the forties he published a number of books and pamphlets, mainly in French, expounding the Fourierist doctrine.[2] Like his master, Czyński wished to introduce a better social order by the force of example and by the gradual conversion of the ruling class. The reorganisation of property not its abolition, he writes, not equality but variety, was what was needed. In Poland Czyński hoped that model phalansteries (he uses the Polish word *gmina*) might be established on the estates of benevolent landowners ready to act as patrons and to join together manor lands and peasants holdings for this purpose. The phalansteries so formed would be run on Fourierist principles. Talent and capital, presumably provided by the lord of the manor, would be rewarded along with labour, presumably given by the peasants.[3]

Neither Królikowski nor Czyński made much impression on their fellow-exiles. A much more prominent figure among the *émigrés*, who was also active for a short period during the

[1] 'Urządzenie gminy', *Polska Chrystusowa*, ii, pp. 393-415.
[2] See the list of his writings in Świerczewska, *op. cit.* p. 133. For Fourier's influence in Russia at this period, see F. I. Kaplan, 'Russian Fourierism of the 1840's: A Contrast to Herzen's Westernism', *American Slavic and East European Review*, xvii (1958), no. 2.
[3] Królikowski strongly objected to this proposal, which he considered would help prolong the existing social order, the rule of Satan ('Zbawienie tylko w Chrystusie', *Polska Chrystusowa*, ii, pp. 415-33).

late forties in the international socialist movement, was the famous romantic poet, Adam Mickiewicz (1798-1855). As a recent writer has pointed out,[1] the poet's views on politics are often contradictory, at one period conservative and nationalist, at another socialist and internationalist. He has therefore been claimed by both left and right in Poland as their own. 'One can understand Mickiewicz the politician only if one keeps in mind his position as a mystic desperately trying to model his political action and thought on his mystical ideas.' His naïvety in regard to practical politics and the fact that he often wrote as the result of temporary emotional impulses accounts for the frequent contradictions and seeming *volte-face* in his writings.

During the thirties and most of the forties the exiled Mickiewicz was not formally associated with any party. His idealisation of Poland's past brought him near to the conservative wing of the emigration, and indeed throughout his life he remained on terms of friendship with its leader, Prince Adam Czartoryski. With most of the radicals, on the other hand, his relations were bad — with the exception of Lelewel, whose theories concerning the ancient Slav commune he incorporated into the framework of his own political thinking. To the French Utopians, with some of whose works he was acquainted, he was at first hostile. He criticised them for their nationalist and materialist approach to social problems, for their belief in the possibility of peaceful evolution towards a juster social and international order, and for their neglect of patriotism as a primary factor in political life. Indeed a romantic, mystical nationalism was basic in Mickiewicz's political thinking. It drove him to becoming for a time a devotee of the extreme form of Polish Messianism which is connected with the name of the half-mad mystic Towiański; and it led him to associate, as did most Polish radicals, the introduction of social change in his native land with the overthrow of the old order by means of a revolutionary war of liberation on behalf of the oppressed peoples.

[1] W. Weintraub, 'Adam Mickiewicz, the Mystic Politician', *Harvard Slavic Studies*, i (Cambridge (Mass.), 1953), pp. 137-78. Much of what I have written in this section is based on this penetrating study, which is also most useful on account of its extensive bibliographical data.

The Socialists of the Polish 'Great Emigration'

After the outbreak of revolution in 1848, Mickiewicz's political opinions moved very rapidly towards the left. For this the strong support given by the socialist sections of the French working class and their leaders to the idea of a war on behalf of Poland and the other subject nationalities against the autocrats of Europe, coupled with the hostility or indifference with which such plans were regarded in conservative circles, was largely responsible. 'As he was a man of strong passions rushing headlong in one direction or another [Professor Weintraub writes of the poet] he could not stop halfway. He became a passionate advocate of the workers and their cause.'

His recent faith in the European left found practical expression in two undertakings for which Mickiewicz was largely responsible. The first was his formation in March 1848 of a Polish legion to fight in Italy beside the republicans against Austria. The venture, however, was supported neither by the Polish democrats nor by the conservatives, and it finally ended in failure.

For his legion Mickiewicz issued a 'Set of Principles' (*Skład zasad*), a short document of only fifteen paragraphs consisting of brief phrases or slogans.[1] As regards social problems, in paragraphs 13 and 14 Mickiewicz advocated a vaguely conceived agrarian socialism.

12. To each family the family farm under the protection of the commune. To each commune the communal lands under the protection of the nation.

13. All property to be respected and held inviolate under the guardianship of the national office.[2]

What Mickiewicz meant exactly by these words has been a matter of controversy. Most probably he was thinking of some form of the peasant commune along the lines advocated earlier by the socialists of the Polish People. But an agrarian structure under which the country would be divided up

[1] See S. Kieniewicz, *Legion Mickiewicza, 1848–1849* (Warsaw, 1955), pp. 73-9. The Principles were translated into French as *Symbole politique de la Pologne renaissante*.
[2] A. Mickiewicz, *Dzieła*, ed. J. Krzyżanowski *et al.*, xii (Warsaw, 1955), pp. 7, 8, 323-4. Cf. Weintraub, *op. cit.* pp. 167-9

between the estates of the gentry, the individual holdings of the peasantry — including those who had previously been landless — and property held by the villagers in common, would also not be inconsistent with Mickiewicz's wording.[1]

After the collapse of his Italian legion Mickiewicz returned to Paris still anxious to do what he could to further the cause of the international revolutionary movement. He soon became convinced that this might best be done through the setting-up of a daily paper in its support which, while published in French, would at the same time be international in its editorial staff and the range of its contributors. On 15 March 1849 the first number of *La Tribune des peuples*[2] appeared with Mickiewicz as chief editor. The necessary funds had been supplied by a liberal-minded Polish aristocrat, Count Ksawery Branicki;[3] and, although a number of French left-wingers of various shades of opinion as well as radicals from Belgium, Germany, Russia, Spain, Italy, and the Danubian lands collaborated on the paper and the Polish issue was not stressed in its policy, it was the Poles who played the leading role until forced out by the reaction.[4] The name of Mickiewicz's journal harks back to Babeuf's organ, *La Tribune du peuple*. The journal sought to strengthen the international solidarity of the peoples and the national liberation movements throughout Europe. France under the influence of the industrial proletariat would lead in this work of liberation. Though Mickiewicz regarded the most pressing task to be the establishment of national independence and of political democracy, he also pleaded for a

---

[1] This is Professor Weintraub's interpretation. He writes: 'The cake was to be preserved for the landlord and eaten by the peasants. The Manifesto reveals an embarrassing inability to think in terms of concrete social conditions' (*op. cit.* p. 169).

[2] Mickiewicz's contributions have been reprinted in a French edition edited by his son Władysław, *La Tribune des peuples* (Paris, 1907). See also W. Łukaszewicz, 'Trybuna Ludów', *Prace Polonistyczne*, xi (Wrocław, 1953), especially pp. 255-74; Weintraub, *op. cit.* pp. 169-73.

[3] See *P.S.B.*, ii (1936), pp. 408-9. In addition to helping *La Tribune des peuples* Branicki gave financial support at this period for Proudhon's publications.

[4] Among these the most important was the Proudhonist Karol Edmund Chojecki (pseudonym: Charles Edmond). See *P.S.B.*, iii (1937), pp. 391-2. The paper's collaborators also included several conservatives, followers of Prince Czartoryski.

social revolution, for 'un état social conforme aux besoins nouveaux du peuple'.[1]

In his articles in *La Tribune des peuples* Mickiewicz declared himself a socialist. What did he mean by this? For the poet socialism has primarily an ethical and spiritual content; it is more an attitude of mind than a rounded political or economic doctrine. Socialism, he writes,[2] is a factor of unknown potentiality, terrifying to the defenders of the old order who seek therefore to destroy it. But, he goes on:

> Effacer n'est pas détruire. On n'efface pas les mots qui sont reproduits un million de fois chaque jour dans les feuilles publiques, et qui sont devenus des mots d'ordre de partis politiques. On ne détruit pas un parti politique en l'empêchant de proclamer son mot d'ordre, son principe.

Socialism, he admits, is still only half formed, not entirely conscious of its aims and methods; but it is no mere negation, as its enemies declare. At its roots lie love of country and the Christian religion — despite the fact that the Pope and the Catholic Church have become a bulwark of reaction and thereby lost their moral authority. As a working journalist, however, it was not his business to give a considered judgment on the socialist systems which had been put forward as universal panaceas, but rather to deal with the events of the moment. The main task of socialists was to help the oppressed nations — the socialists of tomorrow — to regain their freedom and not to engage in controversy over purely theoretical issues.

In his view it was impossible to achieve socialism by peaceful means. Not class war, however, but a war of the peoples was the means advocated by Mickiewicz. 'Every scheme ... will be purely Utopian so long as it tries to solve a world problem [*i.e.* like socialism] by peaceful means and to hurt no one. ... In order to achieve [a social revolution] war is a necessity, not peace. One must first liberate Italy, help Germany free herself from her past, and support the peoples in destroying Austria. ... A free and independent Poland must be established.'[3] Thus a successful conclusion to the

---

[1] 'Notre Programme', *La Tribune des peuples*, p. 58.
[2] 'Le Socialisme', *ibid.* pp. 162-75.
[3] Mickiewicz, *Dzieła*, xii, pp. 116-20.

struggle for national liberation was an essential preliminary to the introduction of social democracy.

Assorting strangely with Mickiewicz's socialist and republican views, and bringing him at times into serious conflict with his colleagues, was his cult of the Napoleons, which he shared with many of his fellow-countrymen, with their memories of 1812, and which eventually led him to make his peace with the Third Empire. For Mickiewicz, however, there was no inconsistency. He distinguishes between the Napoleonic idea, which stood for the use of French military might to support the rights of the oppressed nationalities, and Bonapartism, which represented the exploitation for dynastic ends of the Napoleonic legend. What was needed was a fusion of the Napoleonic idea with the social radicalism of the Utopian sectaries who had mistakenly wished to impose their theories regardless of national differences.[1] Undoubtedly Mickiewicz was also taken in by the future Emperor's use of democratic and even socialistic phraseology before his achievement of power — but his admiration for him survived the persecution of the French radicals and socialists led by Blanc and Ledru-Rollin, to whose party *La Tribune des peuples* had given its support, and finally the suppression of the paper itself in the autumn of 1849. Thereafter, while still remaining nominally a socialist, Mickiewicz was to centre his efforts, until his death during the Crimean War, on trying to gain the support of the French Government for the Polish cause.

For all the confusion of his ideas, and the contradictions in thought and behaviour, Mickiewicz by his editorship of *La Tribune des peuples* had made the one important Polish contribution to European socialism during the Springtime of the Nations.[2]

IV

The eighteen-thirties and forties had been the period when socialism was most strongly represented in Polish left-wing

[1] 'De l'idée napoléonienne', *La Tribune des peuples*, pp. 274-6.

[2] Mickiewicz's importance in the development of European radicalism is also shown in his influence on Lamennais. See M. Kridl, 'Two Champions of a New Christianity: Lamennais and Mickiewicz', *Comparative Literature*, iv (1952), no. 3.

The Socialists of the Polish 'Great Emigration'

thought. After the successive failures of the revolutionary movement in Poland in 1846 and 1848–9 there was little chance of socialism finding adherents in the home country. Though it was still represented among the left-wing *émigrés*, the 'Great Emigration' was itself only a shadow of its former self; weak in numbers and increasingly out of touch with the home country, the *émigrés* no longer played the important role they had formerly had in the political and intellectual life of the nation.

After reaction developed in France, the Democratic Society transferred its headquarters to London. The leading figure in the Society was now Stanisław Worcell, who had helped to found the Polish People in the mid-thirties. Under his influence and that of the talented but little-known publicist, Jan Kanty Podolecki (1800–55)[1] — though not without protest from some members — the democrats abandoned their rigid defence of private property and wrote socialism into the programme of their Society. An attempt was even made to prove that the Society had never been opposed to socialism. Worcell and his colleagues now argued that socialism was the natural fulfilment of democracy and republicanism and the realisation of the Christian ideal. The winning of national independence was to be accompanied by the bestowal of full property rights on the peasants, which should, however, be regarded as only a temporary measure, the first step towards a juster social order. Once genuine parliamentary government and civil liberties had been introduced, socialism would come gradually through piecemeal reforms; there would be no need of a violent overthrow of the old order; those who stood to lose through reform would be compensated by the state.

Today [its leaders state in a passage typical of their public pronouncements at this period] the Society believes ... that socialism must and will bring its influence to bear on the changes taking place in industry, science, government, religion, the family, property relations, and capital. These changes ... however will come about not by coercion or violence, annihilation or confiscations, or

[1] See J. K. Podolecki, *Wybór pism lat 1846–1856*, ed. A. Grodek (Warsaw, 1955). Podolecki was a member of the Society's central committee (*Centralizacja*) in London between 1849 and 1851.

by tyranny; but by seeking out and adapting . . . the principles and means appropriate for the general need and for universal brotherhood, and by putting justice, education, and truth in the place of oppression, ignorance, and falsehood. . . . Where the nation is itself both legislature and executive, there the tyranny and despotism of one section [of the nation] over another cannot exist. Let us suppose for a moment that the community, as a result of that unawareness of which some accuse it, errs in enacting or enforcing a law . . . with harm to a minority. Will not the wrong done to a part of its members react on all ? . . . Will it not become a wrong done to the whole community ? . . . In such a case the people will easily recognise its mistake and, without any violent upheavals, enter upon a more proper course, giving compensation for any loss it may temporarily have caused.[1]

No attempt was made to work out in detail how land and industry were to be managed in a socialist state; but the Society seems to have envisaged private enterprise in industry and the landed estates of the gentry existing at least for a time side by side with voluntary associations of the industrial proletariat and the communal working of the land by the peasantry. In an article, unsigned but probably from Podolecki's pen, praise was given to Buchez, an old friend too of Worcell's from the period of his membership of the Polish People, for his proposals to establish co-operative workers' associations, which might also provide a model for the village commune. 'Although associations will not transform the earth . . . into an El Dorado. . . . At any rate they will exercise a great influence towards bettering the lot of the working class. To them belongs the future.'[2]

The Democratic Society's socialism, therefore, differed

[1] 'Towarzystwo Demokratyczne Polskie i kwestie socjalne', *Demokrata Polski* (1852), reprinted in *Towarzystwo Demokratyczne Polskie: Dokumenty i pisma*, pp. 324-36. See also Baczko, *op. cit.* pp. 395-404; K. Groniowski, *Problem rewolucji agrarnej w ideologii obozów politycznych w latach 1846-1870* (Warsaw, 1957), p. 69.

[2] 'Znaczenie rewolucji socjalnej w Europie i w Polscie', *Demokrata Polski* (1851), quoted in Podolecki, *op. cit.* p. 292. I have not been able to trace any contacts between the Polish Democratic Society and the contemporary English Christian socialists, also disciples of Buchez. Podolecki had been a member in the early forties of a short-lived organisation, Polish Democracy of the Nineteenth Century, which was founded by Józef Ordęga with a programme based on Buchez's social and religious principles. See E. Kostołowski, *Studia nad kwestią włościańską w latach 1846-1864 ze szczególnym uwzględnieniem literatury politycznej* (Lwów, 1938), p. 29 ff.

The Socialists of the Polish 'Great Emigration'

little from the vaguely socialist radicalism of the school of Ledru-Rollin and his fellow-exiles from France, with whom Worcell and the Polish democrats collaborated closely at this time. Its moderate and reformist character did not satisfy some of the extremer spirits among the Polish *émigrés*. As a result, a rival organisation under the leadership of Worcell's old colleague, Świętosławski, was formed out of several small groups in London, which took the name of the London Revolutionary Commune of the Polish People.[1] As this name implies, the Commune harked back to the tradition of the Polish People of the thirties and early forties. Socialism, they state, means:

Community of work and produce, and the division of labour in proportion to physical strength and intellectual capacity. Individual capitalism . . . produces cupidity, exploitation, and deception, because it forms society into masters and slaves, sanctions plunder and misery. In a society so organised, notwithstanding democratic forms of government — and the words inscribed everywhere, 'Liberty, Equality, and Fraternity' — servility and fractricide . . . executioners and victims, will exist. We condemn idleness as the source of corruption and immorality. . . . To labour we accord the right of participation in social institutions. . . . Public instruction . . . we consider as an obligatory law for all. For the base of the edifice, and the model for future social reform, we adopt the commune as restoring the patriarchal life of the Slavonian and suiting the desires of the people.[2]

The abolition of private property and the establishment of collectivism based upon a revival of the primitive Slav commune, complete political equality, a transition period after the revolution of the dictatorship of the people, the establishment of a Slav federation within a world-wide socialist republic: the London Commune's programme follows in the footsteps

---

[1] See W. Knapowska, 'Lud Polski — Gromada Rewolucyjna Londyn', *Kwartalnik Historyczny*, lxii (1955), no. 2 ; A. Wojtkowski, 'Plany powstańcze komunistów polskich w r. 1859', *Przegląd Narodowy* (1921), no. 5 ; and my article 'The Polish Revolutionary Commune in London', *Slavonic and East European Review*, xxxv (1956), no. 84. For the doctrines of the Revolutionary Commune's Paris sympathiser, Fr. Ks. Zawadzki, see C. Bobińska, *Marks i Engels a sprawy polskie od osiemdziesiątych lat XIX wieku* (Warsaw, 2nd edn., 1955), pp. 143-4 ; Groniowski, *op. cit.* pp. 74-6.

[2] *People's Paper*, 17 March 1855. I have slightly corrected the English of the original.

of the earlier organisation. What was new, however, was a greater emphasis on industry and labour and less stress on the problems of an agrarian economy. This may undoubtedly be attributed to the influence of English industrial conditions, and of the British working-class movement, on the ideology of the Polish socialists.

By the beginning of the next decade both the Revolutionary Commune and the Democratic Society had virtually ceased to function. The failure of the new insurrection against the Russians which broke out in January 1863 brought a fresh wave of exiles to join those already in the West. But neither in numbers nor in influence was the new emigration to equal its predecessor, the 'Great Emigration'. Socialist ideas indeed still found a number of adherents, and the traditions of the communes of the Polish People in the earlier decades were still alive. Proudhon, among the Utopians, was particularly influential as were also the Russians, Herzen, who had worked closely with Worcell in the fifties, Bakunin and Chernishevsky. Several Poles were prominent as co-workers with Marx in the First International; a number participated in the Paris Commune of 1871. The Utopian period in the history of the Polish socialist movement, however, had passed. The ideas of Marx and of Lassalle were spreading; and within a dozen years the modern working-class movement, based on the industrial proletariat, makes its first appearance on the Polish political scene. A new age had begun.

The Polish socialists of the 'Great Emigration' had drawn for their ideas upon every contemporary school of socialist thought. *Babouvisme* and Saint-Simonism; the Christian socialism of Buchez and the Christian democracy of Lamennais; Fourierism, Owenism, and the communism of Cabet; the anarchist mutualism of Proudhon; and the democratic socialism of Louis Blanc: all had their disciples among the Poles.[1] But Polish socialism of this period is not purely derivative. It produced, it is true, no outstanding theorist, no

[1] The writings of the Utopian socialists in the West also influenced the thinking of some of the right-wing *émigrés*. For instance, the former Saint-Simonian turned conservative, Stanisław Bratkowski, who advocated collective working of the peasants' land in his book *Gmina i szkoła wiejska w*

major work; it made little impact outside the ranks of its own nationals and in Poland itself, owing to political conditions, its influence was sporadic and impermanent. None the less in several respects its contribution was an original one. This originality stemmed from the differing circumstances in which Poland found herself when compared with Western Europe, from her agrarian economic structure and her loss of political independence.

Almost without exception the *émigré* socialists were primarily 'peasant' socialists. Like the later Russian populists, from Herzen down to the socialist revolutionaries, they wished to base socialism on the village and its institutions; they wished — and they believed it was in their power — to preserve their country from the evils of capitalism and the domination of the *bourgeoisie* by avoiding the kind of industrial development that was taking place in the West. Secondly they were all, to a greater or less degree, involved in the struggle to regain national independence. Their socialism, therefore, was strongly tinged with nationalism — however much the ultimate ideal of a world society might figure in their programmes. And it was the fact of foreign domination, combined with the backward social structure of the country and the lack of parliamentary government, that made a double revolution — to overthrow both the foreign and the domestic oppressor — seem essential. It was this that drove almost all the Polish *émigré* socialists, in contrast to the apolitical gradualism of the other Utopians in the West, to advocate not peaceful means but violence in order to bring in the new socialist order. Often disguising their thought in religious and mystical language the more radical, following in the *babouviste* tradition, put forward a doctrine of class-struggle: the war not, however, of proletarian against capitalist, but of serf peasant against his lord. National independence, the social revolution and the village commune: these three ideas were fundamental to the thinking of the socialists of the Polish 'Great Emigration'.

Polsce (Paris, 1866) (quoted in Mogilska, *op. cit.* pp. 65-6), was inspired by his reading of the works of Owen and Fourier to urge also the setting up of communal institutions in the villages. But at the same time, of course, the estates of the gentry were to remain untouched. See above, p. 143, n. 1.

5

STEPHEN COLTHAM

THE *BEE-HIVE* NEWSPAPER: ITS ORIGIN AND EARLY STRUGGLES

THE *Bee-Hive*, founded by George Potter 'in the interest of the working classes' in October 1861, appeared weekly under its original title until the end of 1876. It was then renamed the *Industrial Review*, and survived for exactly two more years before it was finally closed down. During that time — an extraordinary length of life for a working-class paper of those days — it was adopted as the organ of some of the most important bodies in the labour movement. While this did not necessarily imply any control over the paper, it did mean mutual support, as well as columns open to contributions from these bodies. Until September 1865 it was the organ of the London Trades Council; and for the last ten months of this period, of the First International as well. (It was not in fact until 1870 that the International formally severed all connection with the paper.) During the eighteen-sixties, individual unions that adopted the *Bee-Hive* in this way included Macdonald's National Association of Mineworkers, while other bodies included the Labour Representation League. Throughout the labour laws campaign of 1871–5, it was the organ of the T.U.C. and its Parliamentary Committee. It was also, of course, the organ of the London Working Men's Association during the industrial and political struggles of 1866–8; but here the relationship was of a different kind, since the main purpose of the L.W.M.A. was to provide the conductors of the *Bee-Hive* with the backing of a permanent organisation.

Although the highest recorded circulation of the *Bee-Hive* was only 'upwards of 8000', which was reached in the early

The 'Bee-Hive' Newspaper: its Origin and Early Struggles

months of 1865,[1] there can be no doubt that it exercised an influence out of all proportion to its circulation. The Webbs, writing in 1894, described it as 'the best labour newspaper which has yet appeared'; and they retained this judgment in their revised edition of 1920, in spite of changing other statements in the footnote that included it.[2] It must be admitted that the Webbs had not worked very thoroughly on the *Bee-Hive*, and in some of its many phases it fell far below this level. Nevertheless, the *Bee-Hive* during its best periods was by any standard a remarkably good paper, combining effective journalism with a range of news and comment that was of the utmost value to the labour movement. The *Bee-Hive*'s own development is thus an important aspect of nineteenth-century working-class history. Moreover, the way in which the paper was founded and conducted, the changes in ownership, editorship, and policy, help to explain developments in the wider movement which would otherwise remain obscure. Of outstanding importance, both for the *Bee-Hive*'s history and for that of the labour movement as a whole, are the circumstances of its origin, which not only conditioned its development for years to come, but also prepared the way for some of the subsequent conflicts within the movement. This makes it all the more unfortunate that the first fifty issues can no longer be consulted, since no copies of these issues are now known to exist.[3] However, the story of the founding of the *Bee-Hive*, as well as much of its early history, can be reconstructed from other records and from later issues.

Like the London Trades Council, the Amalgamated Society of Carpenters and Joiners, the Operative Bricklayers' Society, and Potter's own reputation as a working-class leader, the *Bee-Hive* had its origin in the nine-hours movement in the London building trades. It was July 1859 when this agitation sparked off what was to become one of the most famous industrial

---

[1] *Bee-Hive*, 27 May 1865.
[2] *History of Trade Unionism* (1920 edn.), p. 298 n.
[3] As a result of the acquisition of John Burns's files, the set in the British Museum Newspaper Library is now complete from No. 51 to the end of the *Industrial Review*. But much diligent searching in recent years by labour movement historians has failed to unearth any of the first fifty.

disputes of the nineteenth century. The Building Trades Conference, which represented the organised workers in the main building trades, had sent deputations to selected firms. The leader of one deputation was sacked, his workmates came out on strike, and the Conference decided that they would not return until that firm had granted the nine hours. The employers retaliated — first with a general lock-out, and then by introducing the Document, which made renunciation of trade-union membership a condition of employment. The Conference at first stood firm 'for the nine hours and against the Document'; but in November they dropped the nine-hours demand and concentrated on fighting the Document. In the following February, the employers gave way, and the Document was unconditionally withdrawn. It was at least a partial victory. But it had cost immense suffering; and it was only the financial support from sympathisers outside their own ranks that had enabled the building operatives to hold out.

One result of this struggle was that Potter, who was secretary to the Building Trades Conference, received his first great object-lesson in the power of the press. In the effort to whip up support from workers in other trades, and sympathisers among the general public, he spent much of his time organising publicity on behalf of the Conference. He met with very varying degrees of success. *Reynolds's Newspaper* supported the Conference wholeheartedly, the *Morning Advertiser* published everything Potter submitted; at the other extreme, the *Daily Telegraph* rejected all his letters and statements, and constantly abused the Conference in its leader-columns. When Potter came to write his report on the dispute, a surprisingly large section was devoted to the press. 'It has enabled us', he wrote, 'to distinguish our friends from our enemies amongst the daily and weekly press of the country'; and then followed a commentary on the main London dailies and weeklies, with the attitude of each one assessed in some detail.[1] Potter had obviously been made acutely aware both of the difficulty of countering misrepresentation in a hostile newspaper, and of

---

[1] Building Trades Conference, *Balance Sheet of the Late Strike and Lock-out in the London Building Trades* (May 1860).

the value of favourable press comment.

In other ways, his experiences at this time had a still more profound effect upon Potter. In January 1858 he had been no more than the chairman of one of the small carpenters' unions that abounded in London at that time — the Progressive Society of Carpenters and Joiners. His success during the next few months in reviving the nine-hours movement among the carpenters, and then his work as secretary to the Building Trades Conference from its formation until the eve of the lockout, had made him known in the building trades, and to a limited extent among other London trade unionists. But this had naturally made very little impact on the outside world. Then quite suddenly, within a matter of days from the beginning of the lock-out, he had acquired a national reputation. The chorus of praise from his supporters, and equally flattering abuse from his opponents, the general assumption that he wielded immense power, would have been enough to turn the head of a far more mature and experienced man. Potter was only twenty-seven, with no previous experience of public life. His connection with the trade-union movement had lasted scarcely six years ; and for the greater part of that time he had been concerned only with trade unionism on the smallest possible scale. But everything conspired to thrust him into prominence. To begin with, there were few outstanding leaders among the London working men. The best-known figures were William Allan, who had been secretary to the Amalgamated Society of Engineers since the amalgamation in 1851, and Thomas Dunning, secretary since 1840 to the far smaller but very firmly established London Consolidated Society of Bookbinders. But Allan was primarily an administrator, more at home in his office than on the platform, Dunning was a quiet, scholarly man ; and although both were well known and respected in trade-union circles, neither had made much impression on the wider public — who were in any case very ill-informed on trade-union matters. Potter then burst on the scene as the working men's leader in a dispute which aroused great public interest. Standing head and shoulders above the other members of the Conference, kept constantly in the limelight by his own flair for publicity, he dominated the supporting meetings attended not only by building operatives but by representatives of all the main London unions, and was also supported, and sometimes welcomed in person, by other unions throughout the country. While his prestige among trade unionists was deservedly very high by the time the Document was withdrawn, other sections of the community were already regarding him as the acknowledged leader of the whole trade-union movement. It is hardly surprising that Potter, suddenly subjected to such pressures, soon developed a boundless confidence in his own powers of leadership.

It was unfortunate for Potter that these powers had not yet been fully tested. As chief spokesman for the Conference, he had played his part admirably; and his energy and determination had been invaluable assets. But the policy of the Conference had been very largely dictated by circumstances. Potter was no policy-maker — throughout his career, the policies he advocated with such vigour were to be almost invariably policies formulated by others — and his weaknesses were clearly shown by a series of misjudgments in the months that followed the withdrawal of the Document. Apart from the Operative Stonemasons' Society, which was the one national union involved, the builders' unions in London were exhausted by the struggle, and their most responsible members were preoccupied with the glaring need to reorganise on a sounder basis. It was at this time, in the summer of 1860, that some of the small carpenters' societies came together to form the A.S.C.J., the London Order of Bricklayers was reorganised as the Operative Bricklayers' Society, and the London Trades Council was established as a result of the joint meetings that had been held in support of the building operatives. But Potter was determined to maintain the movement with which he had become identified; and he pursued this object to the exclusion of all other considerations. Although he at first welcomed the idea of a carpenters' amalgamation,[1] the Progressive Society soon withdrew from the negotiations, and Potter remained with them — thereby missing his chance of

[1] *Reynolds's Newspaper*, 11 December 1859.

becoming the first secretary to the new union. He made no attempt to obtain a seat on the Trades Council, leaving it to a fellow-member of the Progressive to represent his views. To address one of his meetings he brought in a tory M.P. who, although prepared to sympathise with the nine-hours demand, had shown himself a fanatical opponent of any extension of the franchise; and Potter was both hurt and amazed when *Reynolds's* and some of the old Chartists expressed their disgust.[1] Eventually, at the beginning of 1861, Potter attempted with very slender resources to establish the nine-hours movement on a national basis, and announced that a new approach would be made to the London employers in March. This was bound to provoke counter-measures which the workers were in no state to resist, and the Operative Bricklayers in particular protested strongly.[2] Thus, by the time the master builders reacted by introducing the hour system, Potter, although still immensely popular among rank-and-file trade unionists, was already becoming alienated from some of the other leaders — particularly the newer men whose rise dated from the 1859 strike and lock-out.

On the face of it, the introduction of payment by the hour seemed reasonable, and even generous. In fact, it was a very clever attempt to undermine the operatives' position.[3] But the subsequent dispute followed a very different course from that of 1859–60. There was far less unity on either side; and a very confused situation resolved itself after a few weeks into

[1] *Reynolds's Newspaper*, 8 July to 5 August 1860; *Morning Star*, 2, 12, and 16 July 1860; *Weekly Times*, 22 and 29 July 1860.

[2] A report of the Derby Conference, at which the United Kingdom Association for Shortening the Hours of Labour in the Building Trades was founded, was issued by Potter under the title *The Nine Hours Movement in the Building Trades* (January 1861). For the Operative Bricklayers' views, see the Society's *Report and Balance Sheet of the Dispute Relating to the Attempt to Introduce a System of Hiring and Paying by the Hour* (November 1861).

[3] The 'hour-firms' paid 7d. an hour instead of 5s. 6d. for a 10-hour day (8½ hours on Saturday) — an increase of 1s. 1¼d. for the 58½-hour week. Their workmen, they stated, could work nine hours or more according to their own choice. But in the absence of any general agreement on the length of the working day, it was difficult for an individual workman to knock off after nine hours; while the new system meant the loss of extra pay for overtime, and the acceptance of dismissal at an hour's notice. [For a further discussion of this issue, see p. 211 ff.—Editors.]

a strike of stonemasons and bricklayers against the new system, while members of the other trades had returned to work 'under protest'. Potter was no longer the strike-leader, since by this time he represented only the delegate meetings of carpenters and joiners; but he did try to collect subscriptions for the strikers, and he made some attempt to publicise their views. In this, he was very seriously hampered by the attitude of the press. With the basic disagreement so much more difficult for outsiders to grasp, and the whole course of events so much more confused and less dramatic than the events of 1859–60, far less public interest was aroused. Most newspapers simply condemned the strike, and for nearly four months there was scarcely a suggestion in any except *Reynolds's* that the men even had a case. It was this that brought about the intervention of the Christian Socialists and the Positivists, whose famous joint letter, explaining the objections to the hour system, appeared in most of the national newspapers in mid-July. The same set of circumstances also led Potter to make the most important decision of his career. He had already shown, in his 1860 report, how much attention he paid to the press. His reaction to the situation of 1861 was summed up in a leaflet which he issued on 26 April. This was headed 'Strikes, Trade Unions, "Demagogue Leaders", and the Hireling Press', and in it Potter accused the press in general of being 'in the hands of the capitalist, who pays well for any denunciations against labour'.[1] By July he had made up his mind that the only answer was to launch a national trade-union newspaper; and for the next three months he was primarily concerned with making the necessary preparations. On 16 September he registered the paper at Stationers' Hall, under the name that was to become famous — the *Bee-Hive*. It was a more striking title than those of the general run of working-class papers, and a very appropriate one at a time when the industrial life of Britain was so often compared to that of a beehive, and the workers to 'working bees'. This was not in

---

[1] A copy of this leaflet is in Thomas Dunning's scrap-book, in the office of the London Bookbinders' Branch, National Union of Printing, Bookbinding and Paper Workers.

fact the first time that it had been proposed as a newspaper title — the Christian Socialists had intended to replace their *Journal of Association* with a paper to be called the *Bee-Hive* in 1852 — but Potter may not have known about this earlier attempt.

The circumstances of the time were in many ways favourable to the establishment of a well-run national trade-union newspaper. Together with increased activity, and some measure of concerted action, the events of the past two years had also brought a widespread awareness of the need for such a paper. *Reynolds's*, the one survivor of the newspapers started under the direct stimulus of Chartism, had of course supported the London building operatives consistently during their recent struggles. But *Reynolds's* was not under the control of working men; and George Reynolds had built up its circulation of some 300,000 by concentrating on the more sensational items of general news, and the expression of extreme Radical views in politics. While at times of crisis he could generally be relied upon to give outspoken support to the men, at other times weeks might pass with no mention of the unions at all. *Lloyd's*, the one weekly newspaper with a circulation among working men which approached that of *Reynolds's*, was far more capricious in its treatment of trade-union affairs, and sometimes even opposed trade unionism. In the rest of the national press, such papers as the *Morning Advertiser*, or the *Weekly Mail*, might in particular disputes give some support to the unions; but there was no regular coverage of trade-union news, and certainly no consistent advocacy for trade-union policies.

Outside the ranks of those that could justly be called national newspapers, there was one newcomer to the London press which had made a special appeal for the support of trade unionists. This was the *Workingman*, a penny weekly paper first published on 21 June 1861. Founded and edited by Joseph Collet, a French political refugee, it had some pretensions to being a general organ of the working classes, the early subtitle of 'Co-operative Newspaper' having been changed to that of 'Political and Social Advocate of the Rights of Labour'.

A Committee of Management had been set up, including some trade unionists, and from time to time the paper carried scraps of London trade-union news. But the *Workingman* was a struggling and rather ineffectual paper, which had been launched with insufficient capital ; and although there was talk of raising funds through the establishment of a limited liability company, this plan was never carried out. Among provincial papers, those that included trade-union news were mainly concerned with their local unions. There was one interesting new venture, with a broader outlook, in Manchester — *Weekly Wages*, which first appeared on 1 August 1861, as a four-page penny monthly. The founders, a group of Manchester building operatives, stated that it was the attitude of the national press towards their fellow-workers' struggle in London that had induced them to make the attempt ; and in their first issue they devoted more than five columns to an article by Potter on the London dispute. However, *Weekly Wages* had even less chance of becoming firmly established than had the *Workingman*. Although in this case a company had been formed, less than a hundred 5s. shares were taken up, and the paper expired, after three monthly issues, as soon as the *Bee-Hive* appeared in competition with it. There were also journals (as well as reports) published by individual unions. But even when these were sold to non-members of those unions — as were the *Flint Glass Makers' Magazine*, the *Bookbinders' Trade Circular*, and the new *Operative Bricklayers' Trade Circular*, which was started by one of their rising young men, George Howell, in September — they were far too limited in scope and possible circulation to meet the need.

Another important factor in the situation, and one which had already helped to bring into being the newcomers among these publications, was the impending disappearance of the last of the 'taxes on knowledge'. The advertisement tax had gone in 1853, followed by the stamp duty in 1855, and the paper duty was now about to be abolished. The removal of this duty, announced in Gladstone's Budget in April, was to take effect from 1 October ; and this naturally seemed to Potter to improve the *Bee-Hive*'s prospects considerably.

Nevertheless, the removal of this last restriction was not an unmixed advantage. It was this relaxation which encouraged the spate of new journals of the early eighteen-sixties, and made possible the reduction in price of established papers. *Reynolds's Newspaper* and *Lloyd's Weekly*, already with large circulations among working men, were reduced in price at the earliest possible moment, both coming down from 2d. to 1d. on 22 September — 'surrendering to the public all the immediate advantages that can possibly be derived from the abolition', as George Reynolds announced to his readers in the first penny issue. The *Bee-Hive*, if it were to reach the standard Potter intended to set, could not at the start be produced at less than 2d.; and in an editorial just over a year later 'the war of the weeklies', when new ventures were being started and 'contemporaries reduced their price to a penny', was put forward as one of the difficulties that kept down the *Bee-Hive* circulation in its early stages.[1]

Potter's first problem was, of course, the raising of the necessary capital. The *Bee-Hive*'s own editorial account of the financing of the paper at its commencement appeared in 1865, thrown out as a retort in the controversy between Potter and the men the Webbs called the Junta:

> The *Bee-Hive* was brought out in October 1861 by Mr. George Potter, who formed a company on the principle of limited liability, with certain sums of money subscribed for shares by a few societies connected with the building trades, and a voluntary loan made by Mr. W. Dell, to assist in establishing a paper in the interest of the working classes.[2]

Some statements appearing in the *Bee-Hive* at that time were questionable; but this one was strictly correct. Mr. W. Dell was William Dell — an upholsterer by trade, but also, according to George Howell, 'possessed of independent means'[3] — who gave generous assistance to working-class movements in the eighteen-sixties. He became Treasurer to the General Council of the International in 1865, and Joint Treasurer to the Reform League in 1866; and he was, says Howell, 'a good business-

---

[1] *Bee-Hive*, 1 November 1862.   [2] *Ibid.* 8 April 1865.
[3] George Howell's MS. notes for an autobiography.

man to have in any movement'. On 5 September, Dell lent Potter £120. Potter then brought in seven of his friends from among the building trades workers, and proceeded to form a limited liability company. Seven was the minimum number of prospective shareholders required by law at the formation of such a company.

The company was registered on 23 September, as the Trades Newspaper Co., Ltd., with a nominal capital of £1250 in 5000 shares at 5s. each. The Memorandum of Association, which included the objects for which it was formed, summarised the *Bee-Hive* prospectus which Potter had already circulated. He was obviously aiming at a wide appeal, since this section read:

> To print and publish newspapers advocating the principles set forth in the Prospectus of the Journal registered under the title of the *Bee-Hive*, viz.: the claims of the working classes for a complete reform in Parliament: a reduction in the present hours of Labour: the co-operative system: sanatory reform; and educational measures on non-sectarian principles in reference to religion.

The Articles of Association, giving the regulations under which the Trades Newspaper Co. was to operate, laid it down that 'the company shall be under the management of a Board of Directors consisting of seven persons, who shall be shareholders, with power to add to their number up to twelve'. 'Societies or associated bodies', as well as individuals, were to be allowed to take up any number of shares. But no shareholder was to have more than five votes — 'Every shareholder shall have one vote up to ten shares, and he shall have an additional vote for every ten shares held by him up to fifty shares'.[1] On the same day that these documents were deposited with the Registrar, Potter was made manager to the company, at a salary of 33s. a week.[2] This sum appears to have been deliberately chosen as the equivalent of his earnings if he had remained at the bench.

That the trade-union support came mainly from building workers' unions is confirmed by the first list of shareholders

---

[1] The Memorandum and Articles of Association are in the company's file, now in the Public Record Office.
[2] *Bee-Hive*, 29 April and 24 June 1865.

The 'Bee-Hive' Newspaper: its Origin and Early Struggles

sent in to the Registrar, dated 19 October 1863.[1] The names are arranged in order of subscribing, not alphabetically; and the first seven unions in the list — possibly the only ones that took out shares before the *Bee-Hive* had actually appeared — all represent branches of the building trades:

>   Old Lambeth Carpenters: 20 shares.
>   Maidenhead Society of Carpenters [2]: 20 shares.
>   Painters' Society [3]: 20 shares.
>   Silver Cup Carpenters: 20 shares.
>   Barley Mow Carpenters: 20 shares.
>   Green Man Carpenters: 12 shares.
>   Operative Bricklayers, Hull: 50 shares.

The Flint Glass Cutters of Manchester were the first non-building union to subscribe. The next ten names of unions include five more from the building trades, four of them outside London; and thereafter the union entries are very mixed, the building workers ceasing to predominate. Interspersed with these entries are the names of individual shareholders, averaging out in the early stages at some seven to each union entry, the majority holding only one share, and again including a large proportion of carpenters and painters. The thirty-fifth entry on the return — and, with the exception of one licensed victualler, the first name which is neither that of a trade union nor that of an individual trade unionist — is 'E. S. Beesly, Gentleman: 4 shares'; but it is an interesting fact that Frederic Harrison, in spite of the literary assistance he was to give the *Bee-Hive*, does not appear as a shareholder on this or either of the later lists. Apart from the earliest entries, the first one that can be dated with any certainty is that of 40 shares in the name of the London Consolidated Bookbinders, who decided to subscribe on 3 March 1862.[4] With this entry, the total of shares taken up came to 666. It thus seems very likely

---

[1] In the file of the Trades Newspaper Co. These returns should have been sent in annually, but the file contains only three — dated 1863, 1864, and 1866, each one made up to 19 October.

[2] This was a London society, not one located in Maidenhead.

[3] Since other painters' societies later in the list are given their local names, this was presumably the London Amalgamated Society of Operative House Painters — another (though less successful) product of the period of reorganisation in 1860.

[4] *Bookbinders' Trade Circular*, 27 March 1862.

indeed that Dell's £120 had provided more than half the capital with which the *Bee-Hive* was started on its career.

Once he was assured of some financial support, Potter's most urgent problem was to find a suitable editorial staff. Since Potter was widely regarded in the early eighteen-sixties as a kind of embodiment of the very spirit of trade unionism, and was from time to time described, in *The Times* and even in the House of Commons, as 'Secretary to the Trade Unions', it was perhaps natural that he should also be occasionally credited with the editorship of the *Bee-Hive*, in spite of published disclaimers. This was perpetuated by the Webbs, who said in their footnote on the *Bee-Hive* : 'The editor and virtual proprietor during its whole life appears to have been George Potter'. But Potter did not make the mistake of undertaking a task which at that time would have been completely beyond his powers. To edit the *Bee-Hive*, he obtained the services of two men with far more experience than himself — George Troup and Robert Hartwell.

George Troup, who became the first editor, was a professional journalist who had moved the vote of thanks to Potter at a meeting in Edinburgh in the previous February.[1] Born in 1811, Troup had been associated with the press for nearly thirty years. He had edited several Liberal and Free Church papers in Scotland, including the *North British Daily Mail*, the first Scottish daily newspaper ; and after some twenty-five years' editorial experience, he had the reputation of being a first-rate editor but a poor businessman. From 1849 he had been editor-proprietor of *Tait's Edinburgh Magazine*, a political and literary monthly published in Edinburgh and London, which ceased publication in July 1861. Troup had been greatly impressed by Potter, and in an article in the May issue of *Tait's*, in which he praised the efforts of the London and Edinburgh building operatives, described him as a workman who 'came from his labour, and at once asserted a place as one of the few men in this country who can rivet the attention of

---

[1] *Scottish Press*, 22 February 1861. This was a public meeting in support of the Edinburgh building operatives, who had launched their own agitation for the nine-hour day.

an audience for hours, without the slightest effort to act a dramatic part, but by a calm, clear and cool enunciation of facts'. After the failure of *Tait's*, Troup apparently settled down for a time to free-lance journalism in London. There was nothing to hinder him from accepting Potter's proposal that he should edit the *Bee-Hive*, and he met the directors, and accepted their terms, on 27 September.[1]

Troup's sub-editor on the *Bee-Hive*, Robert Hartwell, was an old stalwart of the labour movement. He was only a year or two younger than Troup, and his record of activity in the movement stretched back to the early eighteen-thirties. He had been a member of the National Union of the Working Classes, held the office of secretary to the Dorchester Labourers' Committee, and attended the Chartist Convention. He had also taken part in the agitation for the unstamped press, and in 1839-40 had been publisher of the *Charter*, the organ of Lovett's London Working Men's Association. A compositor by trade, and at one time an active member of the London Society of Compositors, Hartwell had been for the past fifteen years employed by the *Daily News*, in a post which he described as that of 'foreman and managing printer'.[2] He also acted as occasional reporter for some of the London morning papers, and apparently met Potter when reporting meetings during the 1859 lock-out. There is no record of the salaries paid to Troup and Hartwell by the Trades Newspaper Co. ; but it was often remarked during the next few years that the *Bee-Hive*'s editor received 'little remuneration'. Both had other sources of income. Troup was 'correspondent' to papers in Scotland and Canada, while Hartwell continued his occasional reporting, and set up a small-scale printing establishment, which for the next three years he advertised in the *Bee-Hive*.

In the formation of the company, and the arrangements for the editorship, Potter's methods show some resemblance to those used by John Gast and his Metropolitan Trades Com-

[1] *Bee-Hive*, 24 June 1865. Troup's earlier career (though not, in any detail, his work in London in the eighteen-sixties) is described in a biography by his son — George Elmslie Troup, *Life of George Troup, Journalist* (Edinburgh, 1881).
[2] *Bee-Hive*, 16 March 1867 and 4 January 1868.

mittee in establishing their *Trades' Newspaper*, the first journal owned and conducted by an organised body of trade unionists, in 1825. They too had set up a joint-stock company, the Trades' Newspaper Association. It is true that their shares were £5 each, and that only trade societies, not individuals, were allowed to subscribe; while the Committee of Management was composed of representatives of the shareholding unions. But they had also anticipated Potter by insisting upon having a professional journalist as their first editor.[1] The Metropolitan Trades Committee had made a lasting impression on London trade unionists. It may well be that Potter was adapting Gast's methods, with the advantage (made possible by the 1856 Companies Act) of limited liability for the shareholders, and deliberately using almost the same name for his company.

But whatever model Potter was following, he was not doing what William Dell had expected. Dell's part in the launching of the *Bee-Hive* was much discussed when the quarrel between Potter and the Junta flared up in 1865. The chairman of the *Bee-Hive* directors was even reported to have said at one meeting that it was Dell who gave the name to the paper;[2] and it was generally agreed that the *Bee-Hive* could hardly have been started without his assistance. In a letter which appeared in the *Bee-Hive* on 15 April 1865, Dell gave his own account of the matter. He first met Potter, he said, 'in his capacity of secretary to the lock-out movement, to whom I was in the habit of taking subscriptions to support the men'. They had a number of discussions on the need for a working-class newspaper, and the problem of financing it, and Dell eventually made his loan for this purpose. But the loan was not, Dell claimed, an unconditional one.

I advanced to Mr. Potter £120, upon the condition that he should consult with the London Trades Council and the leading representative men who had conducted the dispute in the London building trade; and . . . if they thought it would not succeed, Mr. Potter was to return me the money. I need not say Mr. Potter

[1] The first editor of the *Trades' Newspaper* was J. C. Robertson, founder and editor of the *Mechanics' Magazine*.
[2] *Workman's Advocate*, 14 October 1865.

deceived me at the outset, for in looking over the first eight Directors' names, not one of the several representative men, upon the faith of whose energy and ability I entrusted my first £120 to Mr. Potter, are there represented.

The charge that Potter deceived Dell had already been made by George Odger, at a Trades Council meeting held just over a week before Dell's letter was published.

He neither consulted the Trades Council or Bricklayers' Society; neither was any public meeting called of the trades for their advice or sanction to bring out the *Bee-Hive*, and appoint Directors; but, on the contrary, Mr. Potter collected men together who made themselves Directors. . . . Mr. Potter's desire was not to do business legitimately, but to arrogate to himself all power and all control.[1]

When Odger's charges were investigated by an independent committee headed by Edmond Beales, Potter was able to produce letters promising support from trade unions in 'both London and other towns in England, Scotland and Ireland'; and the deception of Dell was considered unproven, since it depended merely on his word against that of Potter, who flatly denied any such conditions.[2] But there can be no doubt that Potter had tried to ensure that control was in his own hands. The letters promising support were obviously written in response to the prospectus which he had sent out in August. Whether Dell had made it a condition or not, it is clear that there was no official consultation, during the preparatory stages, with either the Trades Council or any 'leading representative men'.

Odger probably specified the Bricklayers' Society, in his Trades Council speech, because they were particularly annoyed by Potter's attitude. Relations between Potter and the Bricklayers' officers had in any case been strained ever since the policy disagreement at the beginning of 1861. Presumably they received a copy of the prospectus; and certainly, before the end of September, they knew that the paper was coming

[1] Report of London Trades Council Delegate Meeting, 6 April 1865; published by the Trades Council, with other reports, under the title *Mr. Potter and the London Trades Council*.
[2] *Bee-Hive*, 24 June 1865.

out. But although the second issue of the *Operative Bricklayers' Trade Circular*, dated 1 October, included a note on the abolition of the paper duty which gave the names of three new papers of interest to working men, there was no mention of the *Bee-Hive*. Their reaction to the establishment of the *Bee-Hive* is still more forcibly suggested by a letter in *Reynolds's Newspaper* of 10 November, signed by the Operative Bricklayers' strike committee, and ending with an assurance of continued support for *Reynolds's*, 'whatever candidates may come forward claiming our support'. The Executive Council of the society did eventually decide to become shareholders in the Trades Newspaper Co., but it was May 1862 before they reached this decision.[1]

As for the London Trades Council, by 1865 it was exercising that authority which made it the forerunner of the T.U.C. as a central organisation for the national trade-union movement. But it must be remembered that in 1861 it had not yet attained the position that was to be built up during succeeding years. Scarcely more than a year old, the Council was still struggling to establish itself, with comparatively little in the way of positive achievement to offset the failure of its first important action — the publication of a Trade Union Directory which had proved unsaleable. The Progressive Carpenters instructed their representative to bring the *Bee-Hive* to the notice of the Council; and that was apparently the only approach that Potter considered either necessary or desirable before the *Bee-Hive* had made its appearance. The Minutes for 21 August contain the only recorded reference to the *Bee-Hive* at a Trades Council meeting until a month after the paper was first published:

Mr. Hayes (Ropemaker) informed the Council that his Society had received a prospectus of a paper called the *Bee-Hive*, he wanted to know if it came recommended by the Council as he thought it best for the Council to take up such matters and then if satisfactory recommend them to the Societies.

Mr. Tremlett (Progressive Carpenters) said that he was instructed to bring the subject before the Council.

---

[1] O.B.S. Report and Balance Sheet, April-July 1862.

The 'Bee-Hive' Newspaper: its Origin and Early Struggles

The Secretary said that he had received no information concerning the paper in question. He had been written to in relation to another called the *Workman*. He attended a meeting of its supporters where he was requested to assist in working the paper up.

The Council considered it inadvisable to assist any private speculation of this kind, believing that in order to have a paper at once powerful and thoroughly devoted to Trades Unions it should be brought out by an influential body connected with those Unions and understanding them.

The secretary at this time was George Howell, of the Operative Bricklayers, who had taken office at the beginning of June. The concluding paragraphs of the Minutes show Tremlett attempting to rebuke Howell for 'an unmanly attack on Mr. Potter's integrity'. The attack, which had apparently taken place before the meeting, may not have been directly connected with the launching of the *Bee-Hive*; but it could hardly have been dissociated from any consideration of whether the paper was worthy of trade-union support.

The *Workman*, referred to by Howell at this meeting, was the paper which became better known as the *Workingman*, the title having been changed after the third issue. The conductors of this paper, who were also ignored by Potter, felt that they too had a grievance. On 19 October, the day the *Bee-Hive* first appeared, the *Workingman* carried a rather pained editorial regretting that members of the working classes should sponsor 'a new weekly newspaper purporting to be started for the same object . . . instead of rallying round us'. The same editorial announced that the *Workingman* would in future appear monthly instead of weekly. A long letter from William Glazier, a building operative, also expressed regret that the *Bee-Hive* had entered into competition with the *Workingman*, and inquired whether Potter was becoming one of those men 'in whom self predominates'. In a footnote to this letter, the editor complained that Potter had made no attempt to communicate with them about his plans, adding: 'We repeatedly invited him to attend our committee meetings, but he has thought proper to keep aloof'. The next issue, which came out on 1 November, expressed editorial disappointment that there had been no explanation from the *Bee-Hive* as to its 'principles and intentions'.[1]

It was characteristic of Potter that he should have started the *Bee-Hive* in this way, in spite of the disadvantage of having the paper regarded as a 'private speculation'. The compensating advantage, from Potter's point of view, was the opportunity of establishing the paper under his own control, with a Board of Directors composed of reliable supporters. Gast's Trades' Newspaper Association had started with a Committee of Management representing the shareholding unions, and elaborate regulations governing the annual retirement of a proportion of the committee, and the election of their successors.[2] The Articles of Association of the Trades Newspaper Co. included nothing on the appointment of future directors, except the right of the original seven to co-opt up to five more of the shareholders on to the Board. These Articles of Association were signed on 23 September by the same seven men who, as prospective shareholders, signed the application for the company to be incorporated; and since the first meeting of the Board recorded in the Directors' Minute Book was also dated 23 September, it is safe to assume that these were the men who, in Odger's words, were 'collected together' by Potter, and 'made themselves Directors'.[3] Their respective occupations were an exact reflection of Potter's main sources of support among the trades. Four were carpenters — William Reynolds, William Nightingale, Thomas Bevan, and Frederick John Burgess; while the remaining three were painters — James Tapper, Aldred Vickery, and William Sibly. James Tapper became the first chairman.[4] Not one of these names figures at all prominently in the trade-union records of the period. Dell's letter, with its reference to 'the first eight Directors' names', suggests that the first

[1] The *Workingman* continued as a monthly until May 1863, when it was closed down. It was restarted by Collet in January 1866, and appeared at somewhat erratic intervals until August 1867.
[2] *Laws and Regulations of the Trades' Newspaper Association* (1825).
[3] Potter produced the Directors' Minute Book for Beales's investigating committee (*Bee-Hive*, 24 June 1865).
[4] See obituary (where his name is misspelt Capper) in *Bee-Hive*, 8 April 1871.

co-opted director was equally obscure.

However, although Potter's methods were storing up trouble for the future, the *Bee-Hive* duly made its first appearance on 19 October, and obviously impressed readers from the start as being a great advance on such a paper as the *Workingman*. It was warmly greeted by at least two important unions. Richard Harnott, the Operative Stonemasons' General Secretary, enclosed a copy of the prospectus with each copy of his next *Fortnightly Return*, and his Central Committee recommended the *Bee-Hive* to their members as an advocate of 'the interests of the working classes' which would without doubt 'become a valuable desideratum on the rights of labour'.[1] Thomas Dunning, writing in the *Bookbinders' Trade Circular* of 21 November, was still more enthusiastic. The *Bee-Hive*, declared Dunning, was 'by a great deal, the best trades newspaper that has yet appeared. . . . It is first-class in every respect — good paper, good print, and good matter'. He also explained how the paper was being run, in a note which throws light on Potter's share in compiling the contents:

> It is under the able editorship of Mr. G. Troup, of *Tait's Magazine*, whose well-known ability renders any remark from us superfluous. The sub-editor is a gentleman long connected with the *Daily News*, and consequently 'well up' in that department. The collecting of the various matters of trade interest, relating to trade societies and their movements, is under the direction of Mr. George Potter, who, however opinions may differ in other respects, must be allowed — even by the most adverse critics — to be admirably adapted for that department. . . .

As soon as the *Bee-Hive* had been safely launched, Potter was quite willing to make an official approach to the Trades Council. At a meeting held on 19 November — the next one to be held after the *Bee-Hive*'s first publication date — the Council received a deputation from the Trades Newspaper Co.'s directors. This was led by William Petherbridge, a member of the Silver Cup Carpenters, who by then had been co-opted on to the Board. No doubt on the strength of the impression made by the early numbers, the deputation was

---

[1] *Operative Stonemasons' Fortnightly Return*, 24 October 1861.

favourably received. The Trades Council Minutes for 19 November include the following passage :

> Deputation admitted from *Bee-Hive* soliciting the support of the Council — Mr. Petherbridge &c. They stated that it was progressing though slowly, their circulation had reached about 5000 but they must nearly double that number to make it secure.
>
> Proposed by Mr. Butler sec. by Mr. Burn 'that it is the opinion of the Trades Council of London, that the *Bee-Hive* is worthy of the support of the members of the various Trades'. Carried.

This was followed up at later meetings. On 9 January 1862, at a delegate meeting called by the Trades Council in support of the stonemasons, 'The Painters' Delegate proposed a vote of thanks to the chairman, and coupled therewith a motion on the necessity of supporting the *Bee-Hive* Paper'. The motion was put to the meeting, and carried. At the next Council meeting, on 17 February, it was agreed that 'the Minutes should be sent to the *Bee-Hive* for insertion'; and during the first three years of Odger's secretaryship (which commenced in July 1862) the Minutes are often the printed reports cut out from the *Bee-Hive* and pasted into the Minute Book. Until 4 September 1865, when it was decided that the resolution of support should be 'expunged from the Minutes', the *Bee-Hive* was regarded as the official organ of the Trades Council.

To all appearances, Potter was overcoming the prejudice against his methods; and when the fifty-first *Bee-Hive* came out in an 'enlarged and improved form', it must have seemed to most of its readers that the paper was becoming very firmly established. The *Bee-Hive*'s conductors had already laid down the pattern to which, with only minor variations, it was to conform until the end of the decade. The most striking characteristic of the paper — and no doubt one of the main reasons for its survival during the eighteen-sixties — was the combination of all the features of a popular weekly newspaper with the more specialised features of a trade union and working-class journal. In these issues of autumn 1862, sometimes as much as half the space was devoted to general news, particularly the more lurid details of police-court cases, rapes, murders, suicides, accidents, and the like.[1] The *Bee-Hive* was in fact described in the sub-title which it carried at this time as 'A Weekly Newspaper of General Intelligence ; and Trades, Friendly Society, and Co-operative Journal'. The second half of this description was justified by the columns of Trades Intelligence, and occasional reports of Co-operative and Friendly Society activities ; while the editorials and the correspondence columns were likewise devoted to matters which would be of interest primarily to members of the working-class movement. Although few concessions were made to the hasty reader, the lay-out, judged by the standards of the time, fully deserved the verdict of 'first-class' which Dunning had pronounced on the earlier issues. The whole paper gave the impression of professional competence which Potter had hoped to achieve when he secured the services of Troup and Hartwell.

There had also been drastic changes in the composition of the Board of Directors, which had produced a stronger and more representative Board. A half-yearly shareholders' meeting was held in April or May 1862, and at least one special meeting, in the following August ; and the Board of Directors was probably reconstructed at one of these meetings. At all events, during the first fifty weeks of the *Bee-Hive*'s existence Reynolds, Nightingale, and Bevan ceased to be directors, while ten newcomers (including Petherbridge) joined the Board, bringing the total up to fourteen. The fifty-first issue gives a list of the names and occupations of the men who were directors at that time. Remaining from the original seven were Tapper, Vickery, and Sibly, the three painters, and Burgess, who was one of the carpenters. Petherbridge was also a carpenter. The rest were : Henry Jarvis, plasterer ; Joseph Butler, tin-plate worker ; Thomas Jones, tin-plate worker ; Thomas W. Hughes, carpenter ; George Odger, shoemaker ; John Shave, plumber ; Thomas Vize, painter ; William Hamlyn, carpenter ; and Thomas Critchett, carpenter. Of the five carpenters, all except Hughes belonged to one or another of

[1] This had been the policy from the beginning. A correspondent in the far more austere *Workingman* complained, on 7 December 1861, that in spite of all its news about trade societies the *Bee-Hive* was 'more a regular newspaper than the advocate of the rights of working men'.

the small local societies. Hughes (who was sometimes embarrassed by finding his name mistaken for that of his more famous namesake) was a member of the A.S.C.J. The Board had thus come to represent a somewhat wider section of the trades, while it had been strengthened by the inclusion of two of the more prominent London trade unionists — George Odger, who after a slow start was now rapidly coming to the forefront,[1] and Thomas Jones, who was secretary to the Black Jack Society of Tin-plate Workers and had been the first secretary to the Trades Council.

But although the 'enlarged and improved' *Bee-Hive*, and the more representative Board of Directors, might seem evidence of some solid achievement, the Trades Newspaper Co. was in fact facing very serious difficulties. The first problem was that insufficient share capital was being subscribed. This was considered by a special meeting of shareholders on 4 August 1862, and three resolutions were passed — that shareholders should be urged to take up more shares, that share clubs should be started in shops and societies, and that district meetings should be held to explain the principles of the *Bee-Hive* and advertise the paper. From the report of the first Annual General Meeting at the end of October, when the chairman 'congratulated the shareholders that the directors met them with a more cheering prospect than on the last occasion', these measures seem to have had some effect.[2] However, during the first year only 1171 of the 5000 shares were taken up. The supporting unions were mainly the smaller ones, and few had taken more than a handful of shares. None had been taken by the A.S.E. — the wealthiest union of the time, and the one that had astonished everybody in 1859 with three successive donations of £1000 to the funds of the Building

---

[1] Although Odger was, of course, to become one of the most outstanding figures in the whole history of working-class radicalism, his career up to 1859 had been curiously undistinguished. He was born in 1813, and according to his own statement became a trade unionist in 1836 (*Bee-Hive*, 3 July 1869); but when he first attended the meetings called in support of the building operatives, as a delegate from the West End Ladies' Shoemakers, he was scarcely known outside his own society.

[2] *Bee-Hive*, 1 November 1862. A note on the three resolutions appeared on the editorial page throughout October 1862.

Trades Conference. Neither the A.S.C.J. nor the Ironfounders had subscribed; while even the Operative Stonemasons, although they did eventually take 100 shares, were at this stage still hesitating. The moral of all this was rubbed in by Dell in his letter of April 1865. The A.S.E., said Dell, 'would, I have no doubt, had proper representations been made, with an offer of a seat on the directory, have lent us, in common with many other trades, their powerful and wealthy assistance'.

Nor was this the only handicap that Potter's methods had imposed upon the *Bee-Hive*. In the early stages, his own book-keeping was very casual.[1] This attitude was typical of the old-fashioned unions, but very different from the scrupulously correct approach of the new Amalgamated Societies; and it left Potter open to charges of corruption which may not have been justified. Whatever the truth about these charges, the fact remains that at a time when every penny counted, the comparatively inexperienced Potter was left a free hand by the directors, and apparently advised only by Troup, whose record suggests an equally casual approach towards business matters. There can be little doubt that a lack of strict accountancy in the *Bee-Hive* office contributed to the financial difficulties.

To set against these drawbacks, the *Bee-Hive*'s main assets were expert journalism and Potter's vigorous salesmanship. If the circulation figure of 5000 in the Trades Council Minutes is reliable, the paper had made an unusually promising start. Potter was certainly making every effort to build up a national circulation. Still in great demand as a speaker at trade-union meetings, he made full use of these opportunities to advertise the *Bee-Hive*; and by October 1862 he was able to give readers the names and addresses of 130 well-placed 'country agents', together with those of 18 London newsagents who had undertaken to supply the paper. Nevertheless, in spite of all his efforts, the early circulation of 5000 could not even be maintained. Two years later (the next date for which any circulation figure is available) it was only 2700; and the

---

[1] For comments on Potter's unsatisfactory book-keeping — by the auditors as well as by Potter's opponents — see *Bee-Hive*, 19 November 1864 and 24 June 1865; and *Mr. Potter and the London Trades Council*.

indications are that in the meantime it had reached an even lower point.[1] Potter was also working hard — and using somewhat questionable methods, which were later quoted against him — to increase the income from advertisements; but only £112 came from this source in the first year. In December 1861, Dell had advanced another £20. In the following April, the copyright was mortgaged to George Troup. Altogether, over the first year, the company had accumulated debts amounting to £827.[2] The decision to enlarge the *Bee-Hive* to 'eight full-sized pages' was not a sign of success, but a desperate effort to retrieve the situation.

By the time this decision was taken, conflicting views on policy were adding further complications to the company's affairs. There had apparently been no serious complaints about the *Bee-Hive*'s industrial news and comment — much of which took the form of support for the stonemasons in their long-drawn-out strike against the hour system.[3] Nor had Hartwell aroused noticeable antagonism by his attempts to break down the old 'non-political' attitude among trade unionists.[4] Hartwell was in fact applauded for this by many of the newer men, particularly Odger, Howell, and Robert Applegarth, who came from Sheffield to take over the secretaryship of the A.S.C.J. in August 1862. But on one question — that of the American Civil War — Troup was advocating views which had already caused Beesly to stop writing for the *Bee-Hive*. Moreover, these views were completely opposed to those which soon came to be accepted by the vast majority of organised working men. Troup was a convinced supporter

[1] *Bee-Hive*, 27 May 1865.
[2] Advertisement revenue and details of the early debts were included in a financial statement presented to the third Annual General Meeting (*Bee-Hive*, 19 November 1864). For Dell's second loan and the mortgaging of the copyright, see *Bee-Hive*, 10 and 24 June 1865 ; and *Miner and Workman's Advocate*, 15 July 1865.
[3] Although the bricklayers had given up in November 1861, the stonemasons were still on strike until the following June. During these months, items from the *Bee-Hive* were frequently quoted in the *Operative Stonemasons' Fortnightly Return*.
[4] Hartwell constantly argued that trade unionists must become politically active, and even 'make use of their organisation' in the political struggle. Articles in the early extant issues show that he had been writing on this theme from the very beginning of the *Bee-Hive*.

of the South. He had made this clear in an article in the final issue of *Tait's Magazine*, an article which expressed a deep distrust of North American capitalism, sympathy with states struggling for independence, and the belief that an independent South (unlike a victorious North) would be forced to deal with the problem of slavery. In spite of the disappearance of the first fifty issues, some evidence has been preserved — in the form of pro-Southern statements later reprinted on a leaflet by Potter's opponents [1] — which shows Troup repeating in the *Bee-Hive* the arguments he had put forward in *Tait's*. Potter, who had not so far paid much attention to politics, seems to have accepted Troup's views unquestioningly. Hartwell did not; but Hartwell stayed with the *Bee-Hive*, even though he was unable to influence its policy on the Civil War.

The arguments used by Troup had some appeal during the early stages of the conflict. It is true that the contrast between 'the free North and the slave-owning South' was clear enough, and antagonism towards aristocracy naturally induced sympathy for the North. But at least until President Lincoln's declaration of October 1862, it could be plausibly argued that victory for the North did not inevitably mean freedom for the slaves; while pro-Northern agitation did mean an alliance with John Bright and the 'Manchester School' of Radicals, whose lack of sympathy for trade unionism had often been demonstrated. During the early stages there were Southern sympathisers, even among the London trade unionists. It was the fact that such views as Troup's could make some impression on working men that did so much to increase the bitterness with which Northern supporters regarded those who advocated them. This was especially true of such men as Odger and Howell, who had very soon become convinced that working-class interests were identified with the Northern cause.

That 'Mr. Potter allowed (as long as he could) the interests

[1] Copies were distributed outside the hall when Potter, who by then had changed sides, addressed a meeting called by the Working Men's Anti-Slavery Committee in 1865. The leaflet was quoted in full in the *Miner and Workman's Advocate*, 6 May 1865. [See also below, p. 218 ff.— Editors.]

of the Southern rebellion to be advocated by the *Bee-Hive*' was another of Odger's charges in 1865. Many years later, Howell, in one of the *Reynolds's* articles in which he reminisced about his early experiences in the labour movement, recalled the time when 'For years one test of a man in Liberalism was — What was he on the American question?' Howell then named some of the important 'Southerners', including Troup and Potter. 'The editor of the *Bee-Hive*, Mr. Troup, used the paper in support of the South'; and although Howell was, according to his own account, asked by the directors at some stage to write a series of articles supporting the North, he was defeated by the editorial scissors. This conflict of views, which certainly embittered relations between Potter and many of those who had previously worked with him, even seemed to Howell, as he looked back on it, to have been the original cause of the split. 'Mr. Potter sided with his editor, and a breach began which was never wholly healed between him and his colleagues in the Nine Hours Movement.'[1]

It was later stated, in a letter signed among others by Dell and Odger, that 'these opinions were found to be destructive of the *Bee-Hive*'s prosperity'.[2] They could not have made much difference during the early period of confusion; but as opinions hardened, the attempt to establish the paper on a firm footing was certainly hampered by its attitude to the Civil War. These interlocking problems of policy and finance resulted in the election, at the first Annual General Meeting, of a still stronger and far more independent Board of Directors. Odger and Jones retained their places; and among seven new members were William Dell, who had come to feel that he must take a more active part in the running of the paper, and Edwin Coulson, the Operative Bricklayers' General Secretary. Dell and Odger were soon leading a reforming party among the directors. Dealing first with the financial problems, they raised enough money in long-term loans (including another £100 from Dell) to pay off the mortgage and satisfy the most pressing creditors. The next problem was Troup, who,

[1] *Reynolds's Newspaper*, 29 November 1896.
[2] *Bee-Hive*, 12 March 1864.

although much more restrained, was still telling his readers that the *Bee-Hive* could not support either 'the claims or conduct' of the North. In January 1863 the directors decided, by a majority vote, that this policy must be reversed — a decision which marked a turning-point not only in the *Bee-Hive*'s history but also in the efforts of Northern supporters to swing the trade-union movement into pro-Northern agitation. Troup's resignation followed as a matter of course. The reforming party then turned their attention to Potter, and attempted to remove him from his post as manager. On this, the directors were evenly divided; and when they referred the matter to a special shareholders' meeting, Potter's friends rallied to his support, and gave him by a large majority the vote of confidence for which he appealed. The directors had reached a deadlock, and tempers were becoming increasingly frayed. At the next Annual General Meeting, in November 1863, the whole Board resigned. They were replaced by lesser men, again, with one insignificant exception, entirely from the building trades, and most of them known supporters of Potter.[1]

Thereafter, Potter had little trouble with the directors; and once his own position had been threatened, his supporters always came in strength to shareholders' meetings. In February 1864, Potter was even able to bring Troup back as a contributor to the *Bee-Hive*. It is true that the directors — prodded by Beesly — passed a resolution dissociating the paper from Troup's Southern sympathies; but although the *Bee-Hive* showed no further signs of wavering on the American question, Troup continued to write for it on other matters.[2] Meanwhile, Hartwell, who had been appointed editor, was making the *Bee-Hive* a still more lively and outspoken paper, and he and Potter settled down to a working partnership which soon brought an increasing circulation, proportionately increased advertisement revenue, and much support from provincial

[1] These developments of 1862–3 can be pieced together from a number of reports, statements, and published letters. See, in particular, *Bee-Hive*, 1 November 1862, 22 August and 7 November 1863, and 10 and 24 June 1865; *Miner and Workman's Advocate*, 15 July 1865; and *Workman's Advocate*, 9 September 1865.

[2] For Troup's return, and the controversy that followed, see *Bee-Hive*, 20 February to 2 April 1864.

unions. But the burden of debt, although it was eased, remained a problem; and the struggle for control, in one form or another, went on. By the end of 1864, Karl Marx had even started a share fund, with the aim of creating enough new shareholders to 'swamp the old majority', dismiss Potter ('this rat of a man'), and make the *Bee-Hive* in the fullest sense the organ of the International.[1] Before this attempt had been abandoned, relations between the *Bee-Hive* and the International had become inextricably entangled with the growing conflict between Potter and the Junta.

This is not the place for a full analysis of this conflict, which opened a new and most exciting chapter in the *Bee-Hive*'s history. What is important here is the fact that the dispute over industrial policy, which in 1865 split the London movement into two opposing camps, really came as the climax to these earlier developments. Long before the men who are now known as the Junta — Applegarth, Odger, Coulson, Allan, and Daniel Guile of the Ironfounders — had even begun to work together as a team, at least the first three named had already been deeply offended by Potter's claims to leadership, his preference for treating the *Bee-Hive* as though it were his own property, and more specifically his support for Troup. Potter, for his part, was well aware of their antagonism, and disinclined to make any concessions to them. The climax came, of course, when Potter persisted in supporting every group of men who decided to strike, whatever the circumstances. To responsible officials whose main aim was to build up stable and disciplined organisations which would win complete recognition, this was the last straw; and the result was the open warfare of the next few years. Since control of the *Bee-Hive* seemed unattainable, the Junta set out to diminish its influence, with the *Workman's Advocate* (later *Commonwealth*) as their rival paper.[2] It was 1868 when Potter began

[1] Marx to Engels, 2 December 1864 and 9 May 1865; Engels to Marx, 12 May 1865 (A. Bebel and E. Bernstein, *Briefwechsel zwischen Engels und Marx*, iii (Stuttgart, 1913), p. 201 and pp. 255-7). The *Bee-Hive* had been adopted as the organ of the International on 22 November 1864.

[2] The *Miner and Workman's Advocate* (founded in 1862 as the *British Miner*) was already on terms of rivalry with the *Bee-Hive* when it was acquired and renamed, in September 1865, by the Industrial Newspaper

The 'Bee-Hive' Newspaper: its Origin and Early Struggles

to come to terms with them — partly through the proved ineffectiveness of his own policies, and partly through the increasing financial difficulties of the *Bee-Hive* during a period of economic depression. Five years later — after the *Bee-Hive* had undergone many changes, and Potter himself had experienced several reversals of fortune — the *Bee-Hive* did eventually become his own paper.[1] But by that time, he had long given up his pretensions to leadership, and was working in some degree of harmony with most of his old enemies.

It is nowadays becoming recognised that Potter was not quite the malignant figure that the Webbs, under Applegarth's influence, made him out to be. Nor, in spite of his defeat, was he 'broken' by the Junta in the way described by Raymond Postgate in *The Builders' History*.[2] He had many weaknesses, as the events of the early eighteen-sixties show only too clearly. But it was his misfortune to have been thrust by circumstances, at the very beginning of his career, into a position of leadership which he was unable to sustain. In spite of the misjudgments and the early desire for personal aggrandisement, the fact remains that his immense energies were often devoted to causes in the best interests of the labour movement. The Reform agitation, the establishment of the T.U.C., the campaign against the Criminal Law Amendment Act, and the organisation of the agricultural labourers, are only the most outstanding examples of campaigns in which Potter (and also, inevitably, the *Bee-Hive*) played a useful part. Even his opposition to the Junta was not wholly destructive, since it did make them clarify their own ideas, and it brought about some modification of their over-exclusive attitude towards other unions. But Potter's most important contribution was, of course, the *Bee-Hive* itself. No doubt the paper would have been given a far better start, and much bitterness would have

Co. — a joint effort by members of the Junta group and others from the General Council of the International. With yet another change of name in February 1866, it continued to appear until July 1867.

[1] In 1868, Daniel Pratt, a Liberal Nonconformist publisher, became controlling shareholder — a position which soon changed to that of sole proprietor. The *Bee-Hive* became Potter's property after Pratt's death in 1873.

[2] *The Builders' History* (1923), pp. 286-9.

been avoided, if it could have been founded in the way that Dell had in mind. However, in the circumstances of the time, such an attempt might well have ended in failure; while Potter's methods at least gave the *Bee-Hive* the advantage of unified control, the lack of which proved a severe handicap to the *Workman's Advocate* and *Commonwealth*. Potter, for all his faults, did get the *Bee-Hive* established. Moreover, it was Potter who, as manager, later as editor, and finally as editor-proprietor, was mainly responsible for keeping the paper in existence, often against heavy odds, for more than seventeen years. There were certainly times when some aspects of its policy could justifiably be criticised. But on balance, these were far outweighed by its services to the labour movement during a great formative period.

6
ROYDEN HARRISON

PROFESSOR BEESLY AND THE WORKING-CLASS MOVEMENT

LIKE many other Victorian rationalists, Edward Spencer Beesly had an evangelical upbringing. He was born in 1831, in Feckenham, Worcestershire. His father was the Rev. James Beesly, a man of devout religious persuasions and severe moral standards.

At the age of 18, the young Beesly was admitted to Wadham College, Oxford, which was, at that time, the great stronghold of the evangelical party in the university.

Beesly soon distinguished himself among his contemporaries at Oxford. He had an impressive appearance. He was very tall, fair-haired, blue-eyed, and with prominent features. Already passionately interested in politics and religion, he had followed the revolutions of 1848 with profound interest and felt the deepest disappointment with the Parisian workers for their conduct during the 'Days of June' — an attitude for which he subsequently reproached himself.[1] In the Union his ultra-radicalism did not prevent him from attaining office, but he was suspected of atheism and republicanism. At Wadham, he began his lifelong friendship with Frederic Harrison and John Henry Bridges, and all three of them became equally subject to the influence of their tutor, Richard Congreve.[2] It was Congreve who was primarily responsible for showing Beesly the possibilities of a new faith; a faith which would allow him to retain the moral earnestness of his evangelical forebears while breaking irrevocably with their shallow theology and, indeed, with theology in general.

---

[1] E. S. Beesly, 'Strike Riots', *Positivist Review* (hereafter referred to as *Pos. Rev.*) (October 1911).
[2] F. Harrison, *Autobiographic Memoirs*, i (1911), pp. 83-8.

When, at the age of 28, Beesly was appointed Principal of University College Hall, London, he was to all intents and purposes a convert to Congreve's teachings. A few months later he was made Professor of History in the college. Thus, in 1859, when the struggle in the London building trades was to open a new era in the history of the British labour movement, Beesly was resident in London; a Positivist and a professor at the beginning of the great age of militant Positivists and fighting professors. However, his Positivism was not all of a piece with that of Huxley or Tyndall. If he fought every bit as courageously as they did, it was on a distinct, if neighbouring, battlefield. If they chose as their forum the British Association or the Metaphysical Society, he used the London Trades Council or the Trades Union Congress. If their main adversary was theological obscurantism, his was 'metaphysical' prejudice, by which he meant the worship of fashionable abstractions; of 'individual liberty' and 'majority rule'; the conversion of the dubious science of political economy into a code of morals.

In order to understand how Beesly came to be associated with the labour movement and to interpret correctly the character of his influence, it is essential to take account of the philosophy upon which his whole public life was based.

'What is Posivitism?' asked Guizot in his *Meditations*, and answered, 'a word: in language a barbarism, in philosophy a presumption'. However, this 'barbarism' — which enjoyed great currency in Victorian England — covered different degrees of 'presumptuousness'. It stood, first, for an influential tendency of mind which was common to many of the most distinguished literary and scientific men of the day. Thus J. S. Mill, T. H. Huxley, John Morley, and Herbert Spencer, were all Positivists in the sense that they respected the spirit of free inquiry and, while declining to entertain any belief which did not seem to be warranted by the available evidence, they adopted a sympathetic attitude towards theories of evolution and of progress.

In its second sense, the term was applied to a definite school which based itself upon the teachings of Auguste Comte. Beesly, Harrison, and Bridges held that the founder of sociology had provided a basis for social reconstruction. He had shown that a new society was both desirable and historically necessary, and by doing so had put morals and politics upon a scientific basis.

In its third sense, the term 'Positivism' was applied to the programme of those among the organised Positivists who were not content that the new faith should find its sole expression in a school, and who insisted that it had to become a Church. Comte had argued that with the triumph of sociology, religion and science could be reconciled. As men came to discern the 'real', 'human' providence which was at work in history, so their religious sentiments would come to be detached from God and directed towards their proper object, Humanity. To help this inevitable process along, the French philosopher devised an elaborate secular religion, a system of public worship complete with all the appropriate liturgical and devotional forms. Congreve, who apparently believed that his Master was infallible, eventually insisted on fully instituting this system of worship in England. Beesly and others feared that this would discredit Positivism as a school and cause it to be dismissed as so much 'superstitious mummery'.[1] It was partly in consequence of this difference of opinion that a formal division occurred among the organised Positivists in 1878–9.[2]

These three distinct varieties of Positivism — the broad tendency, the School, and the Church — were continually being confused with one another, to the great embarrassment and annoyance of Mill, Huxley, and Spencer. These 'incomplete' Positivists did their best to dispel the confusion by disowning much of Comte's work, denying the unity of his life and doctrine, and by trying, as Beesly sadly observed, to put him on the Index Expurgatorius.[3]

Comte's central principle, upon which the validity of all else depended, was his celebrated law of the three stages. According to this law, the mind has an inherent tendency to

[1] E. S. Beesly, 'Positivism and Comte', *Pos. Rev.* (February 1897), p. 40.
[2] J. E. McGee, *A Crusade for Humanity* (1931), pp. 103-12.
[3] E. S. Beesly to T. H. Huxley, 8 February 1869 (Huxley Papers, Imperial College of Science and Technology, London).

pass from theological interpretations of experience to abstract or metaphysical ones, until it finally progresses to the point of attaining positive or scientific understanding. This doctrine was, for Comte, at once a theory of knowledge, a philosophy of history, and a programme for social reconstruction. John Stuart Mill, who was heavily indebted to Comte, tried to sever the first two aspects of this law from its last. He argued that Comte's polity and secular religion bore no necessary relation to his earlier scientific work, but represented a pathetic aberration occasioned by the French philosopher's unrequited love for Madame Clotilde de Vaux.[1]

The organised or 'complete' Positivists, strongly resisted Mill's attempted distinction between Comte's earlier and later career, even if some of them were disposed to draw a discreet veil over some of their Master's latter-day extravagances. Thus, Beesly might show little interest in the pedantic detail of the new religion, its calendar, its saints, its new Trinity (in which Clotilde appeared as the new Virgin Mother despite the fact that she was neither a virgin nor a mother),[2] but he was profoundly persuaded of the authoritative and scientific character of Comte's social philosophy and, in principle, of his secular religion. He found it inconsistent of Mill or Huxley to allow that a secular religion was possible [3] or that a science of politics was eminently desirable [4] and then to refuse to assent to Comte's teachings which had effected these things. It suggested that these *savants* were not yet up to the level of the age, that they had not grasped the social and moral implications of modern Positivism, but preferred the positivism of David Hume which had no social consequences other than preparing its admirers for backgammon with their friends. It was clear to Beesly that the 'incomplete' Positivists still clung to the individualist ideals which corresponded to the 'metaphysical stage' of thought regarding political and social questions. They were too deeply imbued with a sense of the sanctity of individual

[1] J. S. Mill, *Auguste Comte and Positivism* (4th edn. 1891).
[2] N. Annan, *Leslie Stephen* (1951), p. 197.
[3] J. S. Mill, *op. cit.* pp. 132-7.
[4] T. H. Huxley, 'The Scientific Aspects of Positivism', *Fortnightly Review*, v (June 1869), p. 654.

rights and of individual judgment in matters of thought and conscience. These notions had done good work in their day, but they were now the condition of a fevered competition which left men with security neither in their livelihoods nor in their opinions.

Beesly, following Comte, saw the solution of the social and intellectual problems of his age in the creation of an organised and all-powerful public opinion which would be guided and directed by teachers who had a thorough understanding of the impersonal forces that shaped society. Until this spiritual power was established anarchy would continue to rule in most departments of life, and the struggle between the bourgeoisie and the proletariat would become more intense and unmanageable. Fortunately, Posivitism was destined to exercise an increasing attraction for the most hard-pressed groups; for women and for workmen. Sooner or later, the working class would see that the fundamental solution of its problems was a moral and social, rather than a political one. It would come to acknowledge that Positivism alone offered it hope for what it most needed: secure employment, a wage that was determined by moral criteria rather than by the law of the market, and, finally, the right to education. Positivists believed that the corrupting influences of Protestantism and mammon worship had made the least headway among workmen. Of all classes in modern society, the workmen were best prepared to receive large principles and to grasp the truth of the proposition that wealth, which was social in its origins, ought to be used in socially beneficial ways. Their trade unions were the elementary schools of a higher morality and they would, in close conjunction with the Positivist teachers, help to 'moralise' the capitalists and institute the new order in which private rights were subordinated to social duties.

According to Comte, this process of moralising the capitalists was not going to take too long, even if it was accompanied by very sharp class struggles and a period of provisional dictatorship in which all power became concentrated in the hands of a proletarian governor. Capital, he asserted, was becoming concentrated in fewer and fewer hands. The decline of competition would increase economic security and allow for an increasing degree of moral accountability by capitalists to society as a whole. Ultimately political units would become smaller even while the control of capital became more centralised. All the powers of government would be assumed by a triumvirate of moralised bankers, while spiritual power rested with the Positivist priesthood, sustained in its authority by the support of the proletariat.[1]

Such, in its barest outlines, was the social philosophy which Beesly tried to apply and develop within the British Labour Movement. It might be expected that the exponents of such a bizarre creed would be treated with impatience or laughed to shame in working-class circles; that Beesly and Harrison would at once be told, as John Burns did indeed tell them in the eighteen-eighties, that the moralisation of the capitalist was about as practicable as the moralisation of the tiger or the boa constrictor.[2] But this was not the mood of the labour movement in the sixties. Burns might scoff, but Applegarth and Odger were sympathetic to Positivism and were close friends and admirers of Beesly. The trade union leaders of the day were intent, not on overthrowing existing society, but on securing what Comte had called the 'incorporation' of the working class within it. To the extent that they abandoned any attempt to develop a distinctive working-class outlook, they embraced the encyclopædic ideal of education and culture which Comte represented so well. Their own practice corresponded to his teaching on the primary importance of social rather than political action. Their limited ambitions did not extend to projects for the nationalisation of the mines or the building industry, but they were well aware that mine-owners and master builders needed to be moralised, and were only too glad to find middle-class men who agreed with them, and who would work tirelessly to explain to the public where justice lay in trades disputes.

Despite his pedantry and many absurdities, Comte never-

[1] A. Comte, 'Le Prolétariat dans la société moderne' (*Textes choisis, avec une introduction de R. Paula Lopes*, Paris, 1946). This is the most convenient source for the study of Comte's teachings on the working class.
[2] *Report of the Industrial Remuneration Conference* (1885), p. 484.

theless had recognised some of the significant trends of the age — a fact that must be reckoned with if one is to understand how Beesly came to be in friendly association not only with Applegarth, but with Marx.[1] If he was the most trusted adviser of the Conference of Amalgamated Trades, he was also 'the friend and teacher' of H. M. Hyndman [2] and exercised a formative influence on the Labour Church Movement [3] and many of the early Fabians.[4]

I

Comte did not imagine that the proletariat would come to Positivism of its own accord. The teachers of the new religion would gain a hearing only if they proved themselves to be capable of rendering real service to the working class. The protracted struggle which took place in the London building trades between 1859–62 provided his English followers with an opportunity of which they readily availed themselves.

In the late fifties the London building workers had begun a campaign for the nine-hour day. The master builders had decided to put a stop to this nuisance. Explaining that they were 'being cruel only to be kind',[5] they locked out the men, and a bitter, but inconclusive, struggle followed. In 1861, the battle was resumed when a number of large contractors decided to introduce a system of payment by the hour. This arrangement, they said, would put a stop to all disputes about the length of the working day by leaving each workman free to decide for himself how many hours he chose to labour. This gambit received a favourable press. Journals which had shown some sympathy with labourers who were resisting the 'document' were at one in condemning the 'besotted' workmen who could strike against 'freedom'. The workers' leaders were unable to put a fair statement of their position before the public

[1] R. Harrison, 'E. S. Beesly and Karl Marx', *Internat. Review of Social History*, iv (1959), Pts. 1 and 2.
[2] H. M. Hyndman, *Justice*, 15 July 1915.
[3] C. H. Hereford, *P. H. Wicksteed: His Life and Work* (1931), pp. 43-4. (A 'Labour Church' was a term first coined by Positivists. Beesly influenced Wicksteed, who in turn influenced John Trevor.)
[4] E. R. Pease, *History of the Fabian Society* (2nd edn. 1925), pp. 18-19.
[5] 'Manifesto of the Central Association of Master Builders', *Reynolds's Newspaper*, 9 August 1859.

or to explain clearly why the freedom which was being conferred upon them bore such a delusory character.[1]

In this situation, a joint committee of Christian Socialists and Positivists was established with the object of securing a hearing for the strikers. In long letters to the press,[2] the committee explained that the employers' plan would substitute an elastic for a regular, working day, and that it would result in pecuniary loss to the men and increased profit to the employers through the abolition of overtime rates. In view of the social character of the labour process, it was quite sophistical to talk of each man making his own terms with his employers. These letters did something to modify public opinion and earned for the members of the committee the gratitude and confidence of many of the new working-class leaders.

However, within the committee a certain tension existed. Although Positivist and Christian Socialist were united in their hostility to individualism and unregulated competition, they were far apart on other matters. Beesly was inspired by a boundless enthusiasm for the workers' cause and held that the struggle of the London builders might prove to have consequences of as far-reaching a kind as the establishment of Christianity itself.[3] He spent much of his time visiting the homes of workers' leaders and attending their committee meetings, where he found that business was conducted — as he did not fail to tell his academic colleagues — far more efficiently than it was in University College.[4] Like Harrison, he was tremendously impressed by the justice of the men's case and their orderly proceedings in contrast with the 'incredible falsehoods' and 'malignant and wilful misrepresentation' indulged in by their employers.[5] He grew impatient with the Christians who wished to preserve an air of impartiality about the committee's pronouncements. He began to produce

[1] S. and B. Webb, *History of Trade Unionism* (1894 edn.), pp. 228-9.
[2] *The Times, Daily News*, and other national papers, 15 and 22 July 1861.
[3] E. S. Beesly, 'Trade Unions', *Westminster Review*, xx (October 1861), p. 510.
[4] Henry Crabb Robinson, *Diary*, ii (3rd edn. 1872), entry for 15 October 1861, p. 376.
[5] F. Harrison, *Autobiographic Memoirs*, i (1911), p. 254.

letters and articles of his own in which he attempted to show the economic and moral validity of trades unions and strikes. Finally, he lost all patience with the Christian Socialists after J. M. Ludlow produced a 'Tract for Priests and People' in which it was asserted that Auguste Comte had taken and dried the arms of the late and much-lamented Clotilde de Vaux, and worshipped them.[1] Such irresponsible allegations, coming from men who elsewhere insisted on the value of objectivity, were not to be borne. Beesly laid about him with vigour; he had already thumped Charles Kingsley for denying the possibilities of historical science;[2] he now warned the bricklayers against listening to socialists in 'white ties'[3] and, dissociating himself from the Christian Socialists as a whole, declared: 'We are not angling for the sympathies of generous, but half-educated working men in order to win a favourable hearing when we advocate a return to worn-out ideas either spiritual or temporal. If priests and people are "as vinegar upon nitre" it is no affair of ours. . . .'[4]

While the Christian Socialists were far from being discredited among workmen — they had, at this time, a much longer record of service than the Positivists — it must be acknowledged that Beesly and Harrison did emerge, in the eighteen-sixties, as quite the closest and most influential advisers of the trade-union movement. They owed their pre-eminence to the fact that they displayed more energy, both during and after the builders' strike, than did Tom Hughes or Ludlow. Unlike the Christian Socialists, Beesly at once associated himself with the new institutions that had been called into being by the struggle in the building trades. He became an important contributor to the *Bee-Hive* newspaper, attended meetings of the newly established London Trades Council, on whose premises the Positivists were, at one time, to establish their headquarters, and entered into close relations

---

[1] J. M. Ludlow, *Tracts for Priests and People*, No. vii (1861); discussed in R. Congreve, *Essays: Political, Social and Religious* (1874), pp. 258-61.
[2] E. S. Beesly, 'Mr. Kingsley and the Study of History', *Westminster Review*, xix (April 1861), pp. 305-36. The article was unsigned.
[3] *Operative Bricklayers Society Trade Circular*, November 1862.
[4] E. S. Beesly, 'Trade Unions', loc. cit. p. 511.

with Applegarth, Coulson, Howell, and others who were promoting the principles of the new model unionism. Applegarth regularly consulted Beesly about problems of union policy and administration and repeatedly acknowledged his debt to the professor's counsel.[1] He was pleased to accept Beesly as the first honorary member of the Amalgamated Society of Carpenters and Joiners and declared that he regarded the friendship and mutual confidence which distinguished their relationship as the highest honour of his life.[2] Not only the carpenters, but the bookbinders and bricklayers acknowledged Beesly's services.[3] If his influence was most marked upon the new model unions which had their seats of government in London, he had already, by the early sixties, been of considerable service to the miners whose cause he had publicly recommended during a trade dispute.[4] While Alexander Macdonald was struggling to establish his new National Association of Miners, Beesly worked on a sub-committee in London which helped Macdonald to secure a parliamentary inquiry into conditions in the mines [5] and which assisted the miners' leader in his battle with the disruptive tendencies inside the union which were being exploited by a journal called the *British Miner*.[6]

If the Positivists displayed more energy in the labour movement than the Christian Socialists, this was partly due to the fact that Beesly's and Harrison's philosophy allowed them to co-operate more wholeheartedly with the new labour leaders. In the first place, such men as Odger and Applegarth were fair representatives of that 'unconscious secularism' which official inquiry showed to be very prevalent among 'the classes which are most in need of the restraints and consolations of religion'.[7]

[1] *Amalgamated Society of Carpenters and Joiners Monthly Report*, July 1869. And see the interview with R. Applegarth, Col. E. Section A, Folio 393, Webb T.U. Coll. (British Library of Political and Economic Science).
[2] Commemoration of Edward Spencer Beesly. Note of Address by Mr. Applegarth. *Pos. Rev.* (November 1915), pp. 243-4.
[3] *Bookbinders Trade Circular*, 21 November 1861.
[4] E. S. Beesly, 'The Coal Strike', *Spectator*, 12 December 1863.
[5] T. Shepperson : letter in *Bee-Hive*, 2 December 1865.
[6] E. S. Beesly, 'The Defence of the Committee for the Benefit of Miners', *Bee-Hive*, 27 August 1864.
[7] H. Mann, *Religious Worship in England and Wales* (1854), p. 93.

Of still more importance, the Positivists did not regard co-operative production as the highest and most helpful form of working-class association. On the contrary, they were inclined to regard it as a breeding-ground for bourgeois values and self-help morality.[1] They were not afraid, as the Christian Socialists were suspected of being afraid, of the combative element in trades unionism. The unions were the basic and most important form of working-class organisation.[2]

Beesly was essentially a partisan of the new model unions as against the old-fashioned, local strike societies. These unions with their national organisations, their high contributions and benefits, their moderate and practical trade policies, aimed at securing an improvement in the material security and cultural opportunities of their members; and Beesly thought all this was eminently desirable. If his friendship with Applegarth and Odger did not stop him writing numerous articles for the *Bee-Hive*, he was ready to make his opinion of Potter quite clear when occasion required. Thus, in what was described as 'the most complete and faithful account of the life of a trade society ever written',[3] Beesly dismissed Potter in a sentence and held up the Amalgamated Carpenters' government, policy, and leadership as an example.[4] In the pages of the *Bee-Hive* itself he severely criticised the policies with which Potter was associated. When Potter appeared to be making a particularly damaging attack on Applegarth for his 'weakness' during a strike on the 'discharge note' in Birmingham,[5] Beesly pointed to the virtues of a conciliatory policy based on the principle of 'the hand of iron in the glove of silk'.[6] When the *Bee-Hive* denounced the leaders of the great amalgamated societies as the 'filthy pack' or 'the clique', Beesly observed that only the larger societies had a career of

[1] F. Harrison, 'Industrial Co-operation', *Fortnightly Review*, iii (January 1866), pp. 477-503.
[2] E. S. Beesly, 'Trade Unions', *loc. cit.* pp. 510-42.
[3] *Amalgamated Society of Carpenters and Joiners Monthly Report*, March 1867.
[4] E. S. Beesly, 'The Amalgamated Society of Carpenters', *Fortnightly Review*, i (March 1867), pp. 319-34.
[5] R. Postgate, *The Builders History* (1923), pp. 214-16.
[6] E. S. Beesly, 'The Discharge Note. Mr. Benfield and Mr. Applegarth', *Bee-Hive*, 11 February 1865.

usefulness before them.[1] If the leaders of these societies used unfair means to control the London Trades Council, as Potter alleged they did, then he suggested that the rules should be changed so as to allow this control to continue without need of resorting to these means.[2] Beesly ridiculed the idea that Allan and Applegarth were members of an unrepresentative oligarchy. He was inclined to think that the rules of the unions which they led allowed too much scope for dissident elements.

However, as a general principle, Beesly tried to avoid being publicly involved in working-class quarrels, and, if he defended the 'Junta', this did not imply that he was an uncritical admirer of its policies. He knew that the new model unionists were inclined to regard a hefty bank balance as an end in itself and that they sometimes carried their opposition to state intervention to extravagant lengths. His association with the miners had taught him that reliance upon industrial action, to the exclusion of any demand for state regulation and control, was not an appropriate policy for every section of the labour movement. As for the popular slogan of the new model unionists, 'Defence not Defiance', he could not bring himself to applaud it. He agreed that strikes ought not to be called so long as there remained a possibility of successful negotiations, but he believed that most strikes were, in fact, justified.[3] To suppose that aggressive policies were inherently evil was, he maintained, 'a very irrational, though eminently British, way of looking at the matter. The question is, not which party introduced an innovation, but whether an innovation is an improvement or the contrary. For my part I hope to see many innovations introduced into the relation of master and workman before very long.'[4]

He took a similar view of industrial arbitration. It failed to impress him, despite the fact that a fellow Positivist, Henry Crompton, became one of its principal popularisers.[5] It might

[1] E. S. Beesly letters, *Bee-Hive*, 2 August and 9 September 1865.
[2] E. S. Beesly, 'Trades Councils and Delegate Representation', *Bee-Hive*, 23 September 1865.
[3] E. S. Beesly, 'The Strike in the Building Trades', *Bee-Hive*, 21 January 1865.
[4] *Ibid.*
[5] H. Crompton, *Industrial Conciliation* (1876).

be useful in the settlement of secondary differences, but it was a great mistake to imagine that it signalled the triumph of reason over force. When arbitrators succeeded in preventing a conflict it was usually because they had made an intelligent assessment of the relative strengths of the contending parties and had split the difference accordingly. To look for arbitrators who would be impartial in some higher sense than this was a waste of time. If someone suggested that a lofty-minded minister of religion might qualify for the office, Beesly replied that such people usually lacked the technical knowledge and added, 'besides, he might be in favour of eking out insufficient wages by celestial compensations'.[1]

However, Beesly considered that the most serious weakness of the great craft unions of his day was their narrowness. Too often their vision failed to reach beyond the horizons of their own particular trade. They ought to see that they had responsibilities towards the unskilled labourers; they ought to acquaint themselves with social and political conditions in other countries; they ought to make themselves into a political force capable of promoting progress at home and stopping the pursuit of predatory and imperialist policies abroad. Beesly never supposed that Comte's teachings on the primary importance of social issues could justify indifference to politics. To induce the trade unionists to accept political commitments was one of Beesly's major preoccupations and the ruling idea of all his work in the labour movement.

II

The London Trades Council was only a few weeks old when Beesly visited the secretary to discuss 'the steps likely to be taken by the Council with reference to politics'.[2] During the following months the Positivists put all the pressure they could upon the London labour leaders in the interests of associating them with progressive and working-class movements in other countries. Their efforts helped to prepare the

[1] E. S. Beesly, 'The Railway Commission', *Pos. Rev.* (December 1911), p. 368.
[2] Minutes of the London Trades Council, 17 December 1861.

ground for the founding of the International and it was appropriate that Beesly was in the chair at its inaugural meeting.[1]

While Beesly encouraged fraternal relations between British and Continental workmen, his main effort was directed to showing them their responsibility in relation to the Civil War in America. He argued that the principle of the international solidarity of labour was involved and that it was the highest duty of workmen to oppose any attempt by the British Government to bring aid or comfort to the Southern Confederacy. While John Bright was complaining that 'the working men have no leaders of their own class and little faith in any others',[2] Beesly was trying to persuade them that, on the American question, they ought to join hands with capitalist manufacturers and accept the leadership of Bright himself.[3]

This was no easy task. He had to fight against the tradition that unions ought to steer clear of politics, and he was confronted with the determined resistance of a small, but influential, group of Southern sympathisers within the labour movement itself.[4] The long-standing hostility towards Bright had to be broken down and the possibility of following the lead of the great Radical without supporting the doctrines of the Manchester School had to be established. Matters were not made easier by the conduct of the middle-class relief committees in the cotton towns. At first, Beesly dismissed stories about the victimisation of Lancashire unionists and co-operators as so much vicious gossip put about by 'Tory Democrats', 'Socialists in white ties', and other Southern sympathisers.[5] In the end he had to admit his mistake and recommend John Bright, not as the representative of his class,

[1] L. E. Mins (ed.), *The Founding of the First International* (New York, 1937), pp. 1-2.
[2] John Bright to R. Cobden, 6 August 1862 (Bright Papers, British Museum ; Add. MSS. 43,384, Folio 296).
[3] E. S. Beesly, *Operative Bricklayers Society Trade Circular*, November 1862.
[4] R. Harrison, 'British Labour and the Confederacy', *International Review of Social History* (Amsterdam), ii (1957), Part I, pp. 78-105. [See also above, p. 198 ff.—Editors.]
[5] E. S. Beesly, 'The Rev. Verity and the Cotton Famine', *Bee-Hive*, 20 December 1862.

but as one who had heroically risen above its limitations.[1]

On 26 March 1863, the leaders of London trades unionism shared the platform with Bright at a great 'Emancipation' meeting in St. James Hall. It was an historic occasion, not only because it was the greatest single demonstration of British working-class sympathies in the American war, but because it foreshadowed new departures for democracy at home. Henry Adams described the meeting in a despatch to the State Department and noted that its organisation was largely due to the 'patient efforts' of Professor Beesly [2] — a statement which is confirmed by other evidence.[3]

In his own speech at the meeting, Beesly expressly referred to its larger significance and declared that they were met to champion Reform in England as well as to denounce slavery in America.[4] He worked incessantly to consolidate the new alliance with Bright and to keep workmen 'sound' on the American War.[5] When, at last, the Federals emerged victorious he summed up its social and political implications for Britain. 'America', he wrote, 'is a standing rebuke to England. Her free institutions, her prosperity, the education of her people, the absence of a privileged class, are in too glaring contrast with our own position to be forgiven. . . . Our opponents told us Republicanism was on its trial. They insisted on us watching what they called its break-down. They told us that it was for ever discredited in England. Well, we accepted the challenge. We forced them to keep their hands off when they wanted to break into the ring. . . . It is now we who call upon the privileged classes to mark the result. They may rely upon it that a vast impetus has been given to Republican sentiments in England, and that they will have to

[1] E. S. Beesly, 'Lancashire Discontent', *Bee-Hive*, 28 February 1863.
[2] C. I. Glicksberg, 'Henry Adams Reports on a Trade Union Meeting', *New England Quarterly* (1942), pp. 724-8.
[3] Beesly attended a preparatory meeting of London trade union officers on 6 February 1863 (*Bee-Hive*, 7 February 1863) ; on 17 February the London Trades Council passed a vote of thanks to him for his advice that they protest against slavery (*Bee-Hive*, 28 February 1863) ; he audited the meeting's accounts (*Bee-Hive*, 9 May 1863).
[4] *Bee-Hive*, 28 March 1863.
[5] E. S. Beesly : articles in *Bee-Hive* between 18 April 1863 and 12 March 1864.

reckon with it before long. That sentiment may not take exactly the shape that most people expect. The tottering edifice of English society may be shaken by other engines than the six pound franchise.'[1]

Beesly's work in the early sixties, his efforts to induce the trade unionists to commit themselves on great international issues, was distinguished by its paradoxes as well as by its successes. He helped to persuade them to associate not only with John Bright, but with Karl Marx. Having participated in the founding of the International, he declined an invitation to become a member of its General Council.[2] Similarly, he heralded the new Reform movement at the meeting with Bright in St. James Hall, but two years later refused to be actively associated with that movement in its organised form. When the secretary of the newly established Reform League asked him for his support, Beesly told him that the working class was not interested in the League's programme and that the upper classes would resolutely oppose it. 'So fast increasing', he wrote, 'is the divergence between the aims and (apparent) interests of the working class and the classes that have more or less wealth, that one of two things must happen before long — either the latter class will have to modify their present pretensions and adopt an entirely new attitude towards labour, or a vast convulsion will upturn society, in the course of which I should expect, and hope, to see political changes effected of a far more fundamental description than those put forward in your programme.

'I believe the crisis, though not far distant, may be several years coming. In the meanwhile, I do not expect to see the people moved by any of the old cries.'[3]

Palmerston died on the day these words were written, but his departure, although welcome, did not persuade the professor that the prospects for a substantial measure of Reform

[1] E. S. Beesly, 'The Republican Triumph', *Bee-Hive*, 29 April 1865.
[2] Minutes of the General Council of the International Working Men's Association, 8 November 1864. (International Institute of Social History, Amsterdam; hereafter referred to as I.I.S.H.)
[3] E. S. Beesly to George Howell, 18 October 1865. (Howell Collection; Bishopsgate Institute, London; hereafter referred to as H.C.B.I.)

were much brighter. He feared that a shallow, democratic ideology should take hold of working-class leaders. They were too inclined, so all the Positivists thought, to state the case for Reform in 'metaphysical' terms, presenting it as a matter of abstract right instead of seeing it, at best, as a mere means to an end. They ought to urge the need for Reform by showing that there were great tasks which could not be accomplished without it.[1] Even if they regarded Parliamentary reform solely as a means, they ought to realise that Parliament was not the centre of power, which always resided in the hands of the wealthy classes. Only under the most exceptional circumstances could Parliament be anything but their instrument.[2] Because they still failed to recognise these truths, the Positivists feared that a group of workmen in the House of Commons would be liable to 'catch the tone of the House' and to render themselves utterly useless to their constituents.[3]

Working-class naïvety was not confined, in Beesly's view, to what they hoped from Reform; it extended to their conception of how it might be carried. They tended, in their innocence, to assume that the working and middle classes had a great common interest in political progress. In fact, unlike the position in 1832, the masses in 1866 had two classes against them. Beesly observed: 'To talk as Mr. Bright did at Manchester . . . about the reform discussion "more firmly uniting the middle and working classes on the question" is to ignore our real difficulty. The grievances working men complain of, are, for the most part, perpetuated in the interests of the very class to which Mr. Bright belongs.'[4] He continued to regard Bright as the greatest of British political leaders, but he was firmly convinced that 'the bulk of the middle class is inaccessible to any argument drawn from reason or morality. It will yield only when it can no longer resist.'[5]

[1] F. Harrison, 'Parliamentary Reform', *Bee-Hive*, 1 July 1865.
[2] J. H. Bridges, 'Republicanism', *Commonwealth*, 24 March 1866.
[3] F. Harrison, 'The Workmen's Representatives', *Bee-Hive*, 26 October 1867.
[4] E. S. Beesly, 'The Middle Class and the Reform Bill', *Commonwealth*, 12 May 1866.
[5] *Ibid.*

However, by March 1866, Beesly was satisfied that the agitation for reform was reaching serious proportions and that it was impossible to stand aloof from it. He asked to be kept informed of developments within the Council of the Reform League and volunteered to address meetings.[1] John Bright had decided to support Russell and Gladstone despite the fact that he did not think much of their limited proposals. Similarly, the Positivists thought it important to support Bright in the hope that the movement would gather momentum and pass out of the control of the slippery parliamentarians who were interested in nothing but preserving the *status quo*, and in calculations of party advantage. Beesly explained that two things had induced him to join the agitation ; the first was the amount of opposition it had aroused ; the second was that 'as a humble soldier in the ranks of the Liberal army, he considered it right to follow his general ; but he wished them particularly not to imagine that, when he spoke of his general, he alluded to Lord Russell, or any other Lord — he spoke of that great and good man, John Bright. (Enthusiastic cheers.) Since Oliver Cromwell was laid in his grave, they had not seen a leader so worthy, and therefore, when he led, it was time for all to follow.'[2]

In private, Congreve was urging Bright on to Cromwellian audacity :

In the present state of affairs so much depends on you — on your not merely working with others, but leading them. . . . We, for I am sure I speak the language of many, would wish to see you oust by a direct act the present ministers, put aside the feebler men whom you have hitherto consented to support — put them aside while you accept their support, and work with them in so far as they are available — by virtue of your superior courage (excuse my speaking so freely), your superior intelligence of the national requirements, your greater honesty, and your greater eloquence, assume the direct lead in the great movement now visible — nor hesitate to place in an openly subordinate position to yourself such men as Gladstone and Lord Russell.[3]

---

[1] Beesly to Howell, 15 March 1866 (H.C.B.I.).
[2] *Buckinghamshire Advertiser and Uxbridge Journal*, 31 March 1866.
[3] R. Congreve to J. Bright, 27 September 1866 (Bright Papers, British Museum ; Add. MSS. 43,389).

Professor Beesly and the Working-class Movement

It was because of his high estimate of Bright's moral and political qualities, that Beesly endorsed the decision of the Reform League to follow Bright in supporting the Liberal Government's Bill. Ernest Jones temporarily broke with the League on this question,[1] but the position taken up by Jones and Beesly was much closer than this circumstance might suggest. Karl Marx had been in the audience at the great St. James Hall meeting of 1863 and had confessed that on that occasion old Father Bright had appeared 'quite like an Independent';[2] and Beesly always tended to see the great radical in that light. But support for Bright did not stop the professor from making the opposition of interests between the working and 'non-working' classes the starting-point of his analysis of the entire political situation. He saw all political and social divisions being reduced — as Comte had taught they would be — to this final form. He paid little heed to nice distinctions such as those between the manufacturing middle class of the North and the commercial middle class of the South. He saw the forces of property as a whole closing their ranks and told workmen that if they wanted to judge the middle class correctly they should look at those who passed round the hat for Governor Eyre or who rewarded 'the faithful policemen, who, for twenty shillings a week, knocked around men of their own order in the cause of the swells'.[3]

Thus it was not surprising to find members of the Reform Union lumping Marxists and Positivists together and denouncing them as very bad counsellors for working men to listen to; and as people who were endangering the class alliance upon which the success of the agitation depended.[4]

With the treachery of the Adullamites, the onset of trade depression, and the beginnings of mass demonstrations for Reform, Beesly and the Positivists called upon the workers to exert their utmost force upon what they called 'this palpable

---

[1] E. Jones to E. Beales, 11 and 22 May 1866 (H.C.B.I.).
[2] K. Marx and F. Engels. *Selected Correspondence, 1846–1895* (1934), p. 147.
[3] E. S. Beesly, 'The Trial of Mr. Eyre', *Bee-Hive*, 18 August 1866.
[4] S. C. Kell, 'An English Radical's Protests Against the Political Doctrines of the Comtists', *Commonwealth*, 12, 19, 26 May 1866.

mockery of popular government'.[1] Beesly did not believe in the likelihood of revolution, but he did consider it possible that John Bright might go the way of the Jamaican leader, G. W. Gordon, who had so recently died at the hands of Governor Eyre.[2]

At the end of 1866 he was suggesting a course of action which Bright himself thought working men might easily follow but which, if taken, would imperil the peace of the country.[3] Beesly openly recommended that they should be prepared to organise themselves on a physical force basis. They had been told by the First Commissioner of Police that 'a grave responsibility rests on those who call together large masses of people in the public places and streets of a crowded city without possessing the power of influencing and controlling disorderly and ill-disposed persons . . .'.[4] Very well, replied Beesly, if Sir Richard Mayne wants to devolve the duty of keeping roughs in order, workmen will have to accept it. 'It seems to me, therefore, that the wisest course would be to organise at once a body of, say, 5000 volunteer police, or Reform Constables, distinguished by a badge, acting under sergeants, inspectors, and superintendents, and provided with useful sticks. . . .

'Even if time is short now to make these arrangements, yet something might be done, and the experience acquired might be turned to good account another time. I, for one, shall be ready to serve as a Reform Constable.'[5]

III

By the beginning of 1867 Beesly was rejoicing that the Tories, by waiting until thousands were starving, had ensured the complete triumph of the agitation for Reform. Early in the year he spoke at a great mass meeting in London, and in seconding a resolution put by Ernest Jones, he advised work-

[1] F. Harrison, 'The Government Defeat', *Bee-Hive*, 23 June 1866.
[2] E. S. Beesly, 'The Trial of Mr. Eyre', *Bee-Hive*, 18 August 1866.
[3] G. M. Trevelyan, *Life of John Bright* (1913), p. 364.
[4] Alfred Austin's reply, on behalf of the First Commissioner, to R. Hartwell's letter of 17 November 1866 (Home Office Papers, 45/7854/4).
[5] E. S. Beesly, 'Reform Constables', *Bee-Hive*, 25 November 1866.

men to be in no hurry to see matters settled and to take care that they were not cheated as their fathers had been in 1832.[1]

Beesly now turned his attention to other matters which seemed to him to equal, if not to exceed, in their importance the question of an extension of the franchise.

On 22 March 1867, John Bright presented a petition to the House of Commons which had been circulated and signed by Beesly and the other Positivists, calling for lenient and civilised treatment for the Fenian prisoners. The last paragraph of this petition, which recalled the crimes of the British Army in 1798, during the Indian Mutiny, and recently in Jamaica, so infuriated a number of Honourable and gallant members that they took the unusual course of defying the advice of Disraeli and dividing the House on the question of whether or not the petition should be allowed to lie upon the table. In the eyes of 'respectable society' it was a staggering piece of impudence to suggest that British conduct in Ireland was no better than that of the Hapsburgs or Romanovs. It was evident that the petitioners were bent on encouraging murder and rebellion.[2]

The storm raised by this affair had barely subsided before Beesly provided his more unscrupulous opponents with another opportunity to present him as an apologist for assassination and terror. This time the occasion was a meeting of trades unionists in Exeter Hall, called in order to express horror and indignation at the crimes to which William Broadhead, of the Sheffield Sawgrinders' Union, had just confessed. Before the disclosure of Broadhead's activities, the position of the trade-union movement had already been difficult, but now it seemed desperate. As a result of the ruling of the Queen's Bench Division in the case of *Hornby* v. *Close*, the unions had in effect been denied a legal status and consequently had no redress against officials who defrauded them. Moreover, under the law of conspiracy as interpreted by Baron Bramwell

---

[1] *Standard*, 12 February 1867.
[2] *Hansard*, 3rd Ser., clxxxvi, 1929–33 (3 May 1867). See also debate of 14 June 1867, clxxxvii, 1886–1906.

in a recent case involving a strike of some London tailors, those who engaged in normal trade-union activities were liable to criminal penalties. The activities of the unions were already being investigated by the Royal Commission announced in the Queen's Speech of February 1867, and public opinion was now running strongly against them. The union leaders were tending to adopt an apologetic and defensive attitude. At the Exeter Hall Beesly delivered a speech which transformed the situation.

He began by approving the sentiments of the earlier speakers who had expressed their abhorrence of Broadhead's methods. 'He was no apologist for murder. During the last twelve months he had subscribed his money and given what other assistance he could to bring a greater murderer to justice — a murderer whose hands were red with the blood not of two or three victims, but of more than four hundred.' The middle class were in a great hurry to condemn the Sheffield outrages; but what about the Jamaican outrages which were committed in the interests, not of wage-earners, but of property and wealth? Did the middle class hold meetings in the Exeter Hall to repudiate Governor Eyre? 'No: but they offered him banquets; they loaded him with honours; they made his deed their own.' The middle class repudiated crime; but by refusing protection to union funds they invited thieves to do what they feared to do themselves. The middle class denounced outrages; but they allowed the magistrate who tried the strikers in the tailoring trade to 'commit more outrages in a week than Broadhead had for twelve months'.

The existing state of the law in relation to trade unions meant that workmen had 'monstrous grievances, and the middle class would try, by raising a dust about Sheffield, to prevent workmen from getting redress from them. They would make a great mistake if they assumed a more humble tone or confined themselves to a defensive attitude. A defensive attitude was always a weak attitude.' They should make themselves felt at the next election. They should get Bills drawn up to remedy their grievances and 'every popular constituency should pledge candidates not to such rotten tests of radicalism as were now proposed, but to these . . . bills'.[1]

The next morning Beesly found himself the best-abused man in England. Steps were taken to try to have him removed from his chair at University College since he had shown himself to be 'unfit to be entrusted with the instruction of young men in History'.[2] There were attempts to expel him from the Reform Club. *Punch* proposed that a wax effigy of this precious professor of rattening should be placed next to one of Broadhead in Madame Tussauds, and that he should change his name to BEESTLY.[3] Virtually the entire press joined in the hunt. He was described as 'a perfectly unique specimen of the human race'.[4] No more scandalous and unpardonable statement had ever been made than his insinuation 'that a dastardly murderer is as good as a lawful magistrate'.[5] He made a habit of defending murderers and was always 'foaming at the mouth', and sneering 'against the class to which he naturally belongs'.[6] Did he want to be 'the Marat of an English Revolution?'[7]

The principal motive for this hysterical outcry was disclosed by the *Spectator*: 'A single word coming from a man whom artisans admire and respect, of a kind which they could take for extenuation, will do more to deaden their sense of guilt of what has been done, than all the denunciations of the middle-class press can do to deepen that sense of guilt'.[8]

Beesly was made to suffer for his speech at the Exeter Hall. The plan to dismiss him from University College looked for some time as if it would succeed and he told Congreve, 'I am afraid it is all up with me'.[9] But as his friends rallied round him his confidence grew. 'If they turn me out of the College',

---

[1] J. B. Jefferys, *Labour's Formative Years* (1948), pp. 101-4.
[2] Minutes of the Council of University College, London, Special meeting, 27 July 1867. (See also Minutes of meetings held on 6 and 13 July 1867.) (Records Office, University College.)
[3] *Punch*, 13 and 20 July 1867.   [4] *Globe*, 3 July 1867.
[5] *The Times*, 4 July 1867.   [6] *Pall Mall Gazette*, 8 July 1867.
[7] *Globe, op. cit.*
[8] *Spectator*, as cited in the *Globe*, 6 July 1867.
[9] E. S. Beesly to R. Congreve, 5 July 1867. ('A Positivist Archive', British Museum; Add. MSS. 45 227-64, vol. 1; hereafter referred to as P.A.B.M.)

he wrote, 'I shall be free and I shall placard London.'[1] It was some weeks before he saw that he was going to 'emerge from the tempest, if not without damage, yet afloat'.[2] The ordeal had been worthwhile, for Beesly's speech did as much as Harrison's able cross-examination at the Royal Commission[3] to wrest the initiative from the enemies of trade unionism and prepare the way for a radical change in the tone of the press and of public opinion.

Karl Marx was among those who saluted Beesly for his performance in the Exeter Hall. In his reply to Marx, Beesly observed 'the combat is only adjourned. In some shape or other it must sooner or later be renewed. . . .'[4] Indeed, the Positivist was already at work formulating a political strategy for labour which, in the conditions of the day, bore a most advanced and daring character. The central principle of this strategy was to pass beyond middle-class radicalism to the formation of an independent labour party which would be based on and supported by the trade unions and which would make unionist demands for a satisfactory legal settlement the main planks in its programme. Beesly agreed to a request from a group of workers in Bradford to put his ideas together in a printed document which could be widely circulated. As he dryly observed to Congreve, 'There will be little harmony between Bright and us henceforth, I fear'.[5]

In his 'Programme for Trade Unions', Beesly suggested six main planks.[6] A law to protect union funds; laws to prevent workmen who entered into combination for trade purposes being subject to the law of conspiracy; juries in trials for trade offences to be drawn from the electoral register;

[1] E. S. Beesly to R. Congreve, 11 July 1867 (P.A.B.M.).
[2] *Ibid.*, 20 July 1867 (P.A.B.M.).
[3] S. and B. Webb, *History of Trade Unionism* (1894 edn.), p. 250.
[4] E. S. Beesly to K. Marx, 24 July 1867. (Microfilm from Marx-Engels-Lenin Institute, Moscow; hereafter referred to as M.E.L.I.)
[5] E. S. Beesly to R. Congreve, 28 August 1867 (P.A.B.M.). [For a parallel attempt by John Hales to develop an independent Labour Party, see the essay by H. Collins in this volume, and especially p. 262 ff.; and p. 271, note 1.—Editors.]
[6] 'The General Election of 1869: Programme for Trade Unions.' In Beesly's hand, 'written by E. S. Beesly'. Coll. E. Section. B. vol. cxx, item 41, Webb T.U. Coll. (British Library of Political and Economic Science).

a large and progressive extension of the Acts restricting the employment of women and children; a reduction in regressive indirect taxes with the deficit in the revenue met from a property tax and a cut in military expenditure; a system of primary education which would be national, secular, and compulsory.

There were, Beesly observed, other very valuable demands that might be made, such as 'Justice for Ireland', reform of the land laws, manhood suffrage and equal electoral districts. But what workmen had, at all costs, to guard against was an attempt by middle-class radicals to put slogans of a merely democratic or ultra-democratic character on a par with, or in front of, specifically working-class demands. Workmen had to realise that candidates who accepted his programme would certainly accept the merely political proposals of radicalism as well, but that the converse was not the case.

Beesly suggested that all the trade unionists in every borough should meet without delay, and that wherever they formed more than half of a Liberal constituency they should tolerate no candidate who did not pledge himself to 'all or most' of this programme; an exception would have to be made for really outstanding men such as Bright or Mill. They should put forward their own working-class candidates and undertake, if they were elected, to pay them the average wage of their trade plus a small amount for expenses. In such candidates, strength of character and tried honesty were more important qualities to look for than fluency or education.

From 1867 until the period of his close association with the labour movement ended in the early eighties, Beesly continued, under a variety of forms and in varying circumstances, to recommend this political programme and strategy to workmen. Ultimately it brought the twenty-year-old association of Positivist and trade unionist to a close, but before that happened it made an important contribution to securing for trade unionism the privileged legal status which it still requires and enjoys.

For a brief moment, it looked as if Beesly's programme was going to be widely taken up and endorsed. The working-class reformers of Bradford, to the intense anger of the local capitalist who was an old antagonist of Beesly and Ernest Jones, acclaimed it. Beesly and Bridges were able to expound its principles in the local press. They announced that Tory democracy and middle-class radicalism were perishing species and that they had come under challenge from a third party which saw 'social questions' and the control of capital as the crucial issue. They prevented the middle-class reformers from side-stepping the claims of trade unionism and exposed the thoroughly unsatisfactory attitude they took up towards them.[1]

However, the power of middle-class catch-cries — and even more of middle-class purses — was too great to allow the success of Beesly's project, whether in Bradford or at a national level. As Beesly subsequently learnt, certain working-class leaders were getting money or money's worth out of the approaching election. George Howell and W. R. Cremer had entered into a secret agreement with Samuel Morley and the Liberal Whips whereby the machinery of the Reform League was placed at the disposal of the Liberal Party.[2] George Potter was pledging the full support of 'his' paper to the Liberal cause in exchange for financial help from wealthy employers and politicians. The London Working Men's Association put forward a 'platform' which was without benefit of class analysis and which simply tagged working-class demands on to the tail of the radical ticket. As for the full-time officials of the national unions who were organised in their newly established Conference of Amalgamated Trades, they were too timid, exclusive, and conservative to accept Beesly's proposals.

Since trade unionists were not ready to be their own party, Beesly resolved to do what he could to ensure that they at least functioned as an independent pressure group in relation

[1] *Bradford Review*: Letters by J. H. Bridges, 7 and 14 September 1867, and 5 October 1867. Letters by E. S. Beesly, 14 September, 9 November, and 7 and 21 December 1867.

[2] R. Harrison, 'Practical, Capable Men', *New Reasoner*, No. 6 (Autumn 1958), pp. 105-19. For a detailed discussion of this and related topics, see R. Harrison, 'The English Positivists and the Labour Movement, 1859–1885' (D.Phil. thesis, Oxford, 1955).

to their own demands for a secure legal status. With his fellow Positivist, Henry Crompton, he drew up a Bill which he entitled the 'Trades Societies Act, 1868' around which he hoped unionists might unite. But even this proved stronger medicine than some members of the Junta could stomach. Referring to Beesly's proposal that juries in cases involving trades disputes should be drawn from the electoral register, William Allan observed that he would rather be tried by middle-class men than by his fellow-workers.[1] Although Beesly's Bill was eventually endorsed by the conference, Potter continued to oppose it, and for a long time declined to take the professor's advice and put his 'pride in his pocket'.[2]

Under these circumstances Beesly was not surprised that unionists failed to make themselves felt at the election. The professor took little direct part in the proceedings, although he did go to Blackburn to speak with his friend John Morley. He found the town on the verge of civil war, with numerous cases of victimisation, aggravated assault, manslaughter, and an alleged murder. The Home Office felt obliged to despatch a troop of cavalry from Preston to maintain order.[3] At the meeting which Beesly addressed, the Tories put out all the lights and panic was narrowly averted. However, the professor refused to allow the partisan atmosphere to sway him. He told the citizens of Blackburn that the Liberals were too interested in stale issues and that if the Tories would really do more for workmen he would have no hesitation in advising electors to vote for them. As it was the working class was beginning to aim at bigger changes than could be accomplished by 'the frothy excitement of election contests'.[4]

IV

In 1869 Beesly married the sister of his co-religionist, Henry Crompton. He explained to Marx that his wife fully

[1] Howell's rough notes on the proof of Beesly's Bill (H.C.B.I. 331,88. 340).   [2] *Bee-Hive*, 17 October 1868.
[3] J. M. Benthall, Captain of the King's Dragoon Guards, to the Military Secretary of the Horse Guards, 3 November 1868 (Home Office Papers, 45/8111/1).   [4] *Blackburn Times*, 7 November 1868.

shared his political and social views and that there was no fear that he would have to become respectable.[1] He soon provided adequate assurances on this point. No sooner were trade unionists united round the Bill, which Frederic Harrison had prepared on the basis of the Minority Report of the Royal Commission on trade unions, than he began to insist that the Liberal majority in the Commons was made up, in large part, of dishonest procrastinators and that workmen must force a division on the Bill at the earliest date. He illustrated his theme of middle-class perfidy by references to 'the Days of June', at which Frederic Harrison observed that 'Karl Marx grinned a ghastly grin and Samuel Morley smiled a sickly smile'.

However, for some months before the outbreak of the Franco-Prussian war, Beesly felt that the labour laws agitation was assuming less importance than political developments in France.[2] He always regarded France as his second country [3] and Paris as the sacred city. France was not only the home of the new religion, but of the Left Republican political tradition, personified by such men as Raspail and Rochefort, with which Beesly was as closely identified as he was with the English tradition of radical-philosophic ginger groups which runs from the Utilitarians to the Fabians.

With the proclamation of the Republic in France in September 1870, police reports began to record the appearance of Professor Beesly in the pro-French and Republican agitation. The reports observed that his 'quasi-respectability' ought to have saved him from association with men who referred to her Majesty's First Minister as 'Coercion Bill' and Her Majesty herself as 'Mrs. Brown' or in other terms which would 'befit a brothel'.[4] But Beesly was not interested in the exuberant but shallow creed of the English Republicans;[5] his interest

[1] E. S. Beesly to K. Marx, 21 May 1869 (M.E.L.I.).
[2] E. S. Beesly, 'Rochefort', *Birmingham Weekly Post*, 22 January 1870.
[3] E. S. Beesly to Dr. Hillemand, 12 October 1903. (Le Musée d'Auguste Comte, Paris.)
[4] Summary of Police Reports Registered in the Home Office with reference to Political Meetings held in the Metropolis during the years 1867 to 1870 inclusive; Gladstone Papers, British Museum 44617.f.95.
[5] E. S. Beesly, 'London Republicans', *Bee-Hive*, 24 June 1871.

was in securing recognition for the new Republic across the Channel and in preventing her suffering territorial spoliation at the hands of Prussia. Marx declared that Beesly and his friends were the most energetic organisers of this campaign,[1] although Engels subsequently charged the Positivists with dividing the working class by introducing unrealistic slogans calling for military intervention by Britain on behalf of France.[2]

During the Commune, Beesly identified himself with the cause of the Parisian workers while dissociating himself from Communism and Socialism, to which he held Positivism to be the only alternative.[3] Once again he and his fellow Positivists showed that what distinguished them from other middle-class 'friends' of labour was that they regarded the proletariat, not merely as the most hard-pressed and suffering class in modern society, but as the one which carried the most progressive potentialities. Week after week Beesly supplied readers of the *Bee-Hive* with a brilliant and passionate vindication of the Revolution. As the battle raged about the walls of Paris, he observed that there was one thing which respectable society had desired more earnestly than a working-class defeat; and that was the dishonour of that class. 'It desired that they should discredit themselves and their class before the world and be taught not only that they were slaves, but that they deserved to be slaves — of which the labouring class of other countries might take note. This idiotic cackle has died away into blank and chopfallen dismay. . . .'[4]

As the Commune went down, Beesly told English workmen that they were witnessing 'the first act of the most momentous historical drama of modern times'. As a Positivist he had a deep religious reverence for the historic buildings of Paris, her palaces and monuments, the legacy of past to future generations of humanity. But he now declared, 'There is something in Paris nobler than her palaces, more precious than

---

[1] Minutes of the General Council of the I.W.M.A., 3 January 1871 (I.I.S.H.).
[2] *Ibid.* 31 January 1871.
[3] E. S. Beesly, 'The Communists', *Bee-Hive*, 29 April 1871.
[4] E. S. Beesly, 'Professor Beesly on the "Poltroons of Belleville"', *Bee-Hive*, 15 April 1871.

her monuments, it is her breed of men, which even the National Assembly cannot utterly exterminate. . . . I know the howl which is going up today from the class in this country who think that not Paris alone, but all creation, exists simply for their pleasure and amusement. But I am writing for workmen with whom life is very far from being a pleasure, and I think that they will distribute praise and blame with a more even hand.'[1]

By defending the Commune, the Positivists once more incurred the wrath of that part of society which Beesly described as 'the friends of order', people with 'shiny silk hats and delicately gloved hands'.[2] Lord Arthur Russell declared that 'everybody' regarded Beesly as 'an absolute fool'.[3] The *Pall Mall Gazette* likened the 'Comtist agitators' to the most desperate revolutionaries ever known in any age or nation.[4] The most advanced Liberals were declared to be classing the Positivists with Odger and Bradlaugh and 'would fain have hanged the whole lot'.[5] Even in the pages of the *Bee-Hive*, Beesly's articles were described as 'pestilential heresies' and the professor was repeatedly recommended to try 'forty days of humility and silence'[6] — an invitation which he quietly declined to accept. Nor did the Positivists' defence of the Commune enhance their standing with the ruling oligarchy in the trade-union movement. It did not please the labour leaders to be told that the Criminal Law Amendment Act, a measure which imposed new penalties upon peaceful picketing and which the Liberal Government introduced to balance the concessions contained in its Trade Union Act, was what came of their profane indifference to the fate of working-class Paris.[7] It pleased some of them still less to have Professor

[1] E. S. Beesly, 'Professor Beesly on the Fall of Paris', *Bee-Hive*, 27 May 1871.
[2] E. S. Beesly, 'Professor Beesly on the Paris Revolution', *Bee-Hive*, 25 March 1871.
[3] B. and P. Russell, *The Amberley Papers*, ii (1937), p. 462.
[4] *Pall Mall Gazette*, 15 April 1871.
[5] J. S. Storr, 'English Workmen and their Friends', *Bee-Hive*, 14 October 1871.
[6] *Bee-Hive*, 3, 10, and 17 June 1871 (articles by J. S. Storr).
[7] Beesly, E. S., 'The Division on the Trades Union Bill', *Bee-Hive*, 29 July 1871.

Beesly publicly describing them as bought men; men who converted politics into a trade and pursued with mean calculation the course they originally entered on with high purpose or who, mistaking their own ambition for public spirit, persuaded themselves that they were jealous for a good cause when all the time they were feeding a grudge or scheming against a personal rival.[1] In particular, George Howell recognised that he was the object of some of this criticism and he denounced the professor for his 'dastardly' and 'unmanly' attack.[2]

By 1871 Howell was secretary of the Parliamentary Committee of the T.U.C. and one of the most powerful men in the trade-union movement. It was not surprising that Beesly and Harrison were not consulted about trade-union affairs as continuously as they had been in the days when Applegarth and the Conference of Amalgamated Trades were directing policy at a national level. Their fellow Positivist, Henry Crompton, who had not publicly defended the Commune now tended to take their place as the principal adviser to the ruling circle of the trade-union world, but he was in poor health and was frequently out of the country. Under these circumstances Howell and Alexander Macdonald, who was Chairman of the Parliamentary Committee, kept as much power in their own hands as possible and ran trade-union affairs as they saw fit.[3] Although they had been instructed to secure the repeal of the Criminal Law Amendment Act, they decided that the only practicable policy was to try and get a useful amendment.

In the middle of 1872 Beesly and Harrison launched a joint attack on the officers of the Parliamentary Committee. Howell was charged with sponsoring a Bill which would put the trade-union movement in a thoroughly false position. In order to get rid of certain clauses in the Criminal Law Amendment Act which had been introduced in the House of Lords,

---

[1] *Ibid.* See also E. S. Beesly, 'A Rallying Point', *Eastern Post*, 26 August 1871.
[2] G. Howell, 'Professor Beesly and the Pall Mall Gazette', *Bee-Hive*, 4 November 1871.
[3] Minutes of the Parliamentary Committee of the T.U.C., 1872 (H.C.B.I.). See also G. Howell to A. Macdonald, 24 August 1872 (H.C.B.I.).

he had accepted a Bill which re-enacted all the other clauses.[1] Beesly had long since exposed the arguments of such Liberal apologists as A. J. Mundella that it was only the Lords' amendments which could rise to legitimate grievances among unionists.[2]

Beesly went on to argue that if Howell's links with the Liberal party caused him to prefer private negotiations in the Lobby of the House of Commons to a mass agitation in the country, then Alexander Macdonald's relations with his 'patron', the great coal-owner Lord Elcho, were responsible for certain damaging amendments to the Mines Regulations Bill.[3]

The Positivists' exposure of the way trade-union affairs were being mismanaged led to a great wave of dissatisfaction with the Parliamentary Committee, and this, in conjunction with a series of harsh decisions in the courts, put paid to all further attempts to arrive at a settlement by compromise and concession.

The sentence of twelve months imprisonment upon four London gas stokers in 1872 who were charged under the Master and Servant Acts, the Criminal Law Amendment Act, and the Law of Conspiracy;[4] the prosecution of the seventeen women of Chipping Norton;[5] the prosecution and repeated imprisonment of William Cutler for the same offence under the Master and Servant Act;[6] and finally the imprisonment of the London cabinet-makers under the Criminal Law Amendment Act for what was universally admitted to have amounted to no more than peaceful persuasion,[7] helped to persuade thousands of workmen that Professor Beesly had been right all along and that only unremitting mass pressure upon the

[1] E. S. Beesly, 'The Criminal Law Amendment Act', and F. Harrison, 'The New Criminal Law Amendment Act', *Bee-Hive*, 31 May 1872.
[2] E. S. Beesly, 'The Criminal Law Amendment Act', *Bee-Hive*, 13 January 1872.
[3] E. S. Beesly, 'The Mines Regulation Bill', *Bee-Hive*, 6 and 20 July, and 3 and 24 August 1872.
[4] H. Crompton, 'The Gas Stokers Prosecution', *Bee-Hive*, 21 December 1872.
[5] F. Harrison, 'The Chipping Norton Case', *Bee-Hive*, 7 June 1873.
[6] *Hague and Another* v. *Cutler*, *Bee-Hive*, 27 June 1874.
[7] E. S. Beesly to the London Trades Council, *Bee-Hive*, 15 May 1875.

government would be of any avail. They gradually came to agree with Frederic Harrison that if this agitation broke up the 'Great Liberal Party' then the 'Great Liberal Party' would just have to break up.[1] Throughout the last years of the labour laws agitation Beesly and his friends taught that the defeat of Gladstone and Bruce was 'a religious duty'.[2]

Beesly rejoiced in every fresh evidence of working-class independence and strength. He ridiculed Liberal explanations that it was simply a 'mistake' when working-class intervention in by-elections cost them seats;[3] he gave a cautious welcome to the numerous political projects and gestures which both Radicals and Tories began to bring forth in recognition of the new political importance of the working class. In particular, the Positivists were impressed by Chamberlain's 'firmly drawn quadrilateral': "Free Church; Free Land; Free Schools; Free Labour". However, Beesly warned that 'the danger about a coalition to agitate about any number of points more than one, is that when some of them are carried the coalition dissolves and one section finds itself duped'.[4] Chamberlain's programme ought only to satisfy workmen if the section on labour was sharpened up and expressly given priority over the claims of the dissenters. The Positivists wanted Chamberlain invited to the next T.U.C. so that he could be pinned down to the workman's demands,[5] but in the Parliamentary Committee George Howell put a stop to this by condemning the quadrilateral as 'Broadheadism'.[6]

Howell's action was a portent of things to come. The trade-union triumph on the Labour Laws question — a triumph to which Positivist advice and counsel had powerfully contributed — removed the one obstacle that stood in the way of the complete subservience of the organised labour movement

[1] F. Harrison, 'Address to the Working Men's Congress at Leeds', *Bee-Hive*, 25 January 1873.
[2] H. Crompton, 'The Government and the Working Classes', *Bee-Hive*, 5 July 1873.
[3] E. S. Beesly, 'The Greenwich Election', *Bee-Hive*, 9 August 1873.
[4] E. S. Beesly, 'The Middle and Working Classes', *Bee-Hive*, 13 September 1873.
[5] H. Crompton to G. Howell, 30 December 1873 (H.C.B.I.).
[6] G. Howell, Diary, 10 January 1874 (H.C.B.I.).

to the Liberal Party. In the early eighties Beesly and his friends appealed in vain to the trade-union leaders to take a stand against Gladstone's policy of coercion in Ireland. They could not get Henry Broadhurst and his friends to see that working men made a mistake 'in allowing themselves to be the supporters of a political party, instead of being independent and their own party — the Labour Party'.[1] A few old stalwarts in the London Trades Council stood by the Positivists,[2] but basically their trade-union support was gone. Beesly was reduced to trying to organise sympathy for the Irish Land League among the workers in the Radical Clubs, and he participated in the formation of Hyndman's Democratic Federation in the hope that it would provide a centre in the campaign for 'Justice for Ireland'.[3] But from 1881 until his death in 1915, he ceased to exercise much direct influence upon the labour movement.

V

In the early seventies, Frederic Harrison believed that Beesly did much to make the power of organised labour felt and he described his friend as 'a great leader'. John Morley objected to this description. 'There is no nourishment', he observed, 'in broth that is all made of pepper and salt. It is all very well to talk of a man being a great party leader — but the truth is that the great party leader *makes* a party to lead and if he cannot do this, either from excessive *roideur*, or from contempt for the men he has to use, why I don't see any proof in your correspondent that he deserves your title. He [Beesly] and Congreve are not politicians, but clergymen gone wrong, or rather, gone right.'[4]

Beesly himself would have laid no claim to the title which Harrison sought to bestow upon him. He possessed great political and journalistic talents, but he was inhibited from employing them to full advantage because Positivism taught

[1] H. Crompton, 'Despotism in Ireland', *Labour Standard*, 22 October 1881.
[2] Minutes of the London Trades Council, 8 March 1881, and of Delegate Meeting, 24 March 1881.
[3] *Newcastle Weekly Chronicle*, 12 March 1881.
[4] F. W. Hirst, *Early Life and Letters of John Morley*, i (1927), p. 192.

that neither journalism nor politics were altogether morally respectable vocations. Comte believed that Positivist teachers would diminish their authority by involving themselves in polemics or the amenities of the hustings. Thus Beesly generally allowed opportunities to acquire positions of direct power or control to pass him by. He recognised that party discipline and the exigencies of the political struggle required men to act on other grounds than personal conviction. He drew the conclusion that it was all the more important that some of those who sought to influence public affairs should be free from any concern for majorities or party interests.[1]

Beesly was never able to give much body to his conception of an independent political life for labour, because Positivism looked to social and moral, rather than to political, solutions. Its principles did not possess the sort of fecundity that supplies and replenishes party programmes. Once the labour laws question was settled and power no longer resided in the hands of the small knot of trade-union leaders in London with whom Beesly had been on close terms in the sixties, his influence necessarily diminished. If the trade-union oligarchy did not like being pressed to act independently in politics, then the advanced thinkers in the labour movement were more attracted to land nationalisation or socialism than to Positivism. The Great Depression presented workmen with problems to which Beesly and his friends did not appear to have any convincing answer. Instead of socialism preparing the way for Positivism, as Beesly believed it would,[2] rather the converse of this tended to occur — a circumstance which never stopped the professor from expressing his fraternal feelings towards militant left-wingers.[3]

Beesly was not 'a great party leader', but he was a leading precursor of a great party. He was more closely identified with the labour movement and exerted more influence upon it than

---

[1] *Bee-Hive*, 16 January 1875. Report: 'Labour Representation in Parliament'.
[2] E. S. Beesly, 'Positivists and Workmen', *Fortnightly Review*, xviii (July 1875), pp. 64-74.
[3] E. S. Beesly, 'Positivists and Social-Democrats', *Pos. Rev.* (June 1900), pp. 107-10.

any other university teacher before G. D. H. Cole. He played an important part in inducing the new model unions to engage in political action and he was the first architect of the political strategy that secured the unions in their present 'privileged' legal status.

If the extent and character of Beesly's achievement has been misunderstood or neglected, this is partly due to the brilliant, but one-sided, estimate which the Webbs made of the labour laws agitation and its consequences. They paid tribute to the Positivists for their gratuitous legal services,[1] but suggested that the agitation retarded the 'theoretic progress' of the movement both by bringing its leaders into contact with 'fertile thinkers of the middle class' and by encouraging them to adopt the slogan of 'no class legislation' which expressed the intellectual position of their opponents.[2]

In fact, Beesly laboured to prevent workmen from accepting the 'Liberal Shibboleth' of 'no state interference'.[3] He pressed the trade-union case for a satisfactory settlement not 'metaphysically', in terms of abstract principles, but in class terms; the unionist demands were legitimate because they corresponded to the interests of the working class. Unfortunately, the Webbs made a characteristic error in that they directed attention to a *form* which was given to the working-class demand to the exclusion of any detailed investigation into the conditions and experience of the *struggle* which was required to carry it. Had they looked at the question in this light they would have seen how Beesly and his friends tried, in practice as well as in theory, to encourage trade unionists to go beyond the 'worn out denominations of English Liberalism'.[4]

Since the Webbs' own 'theoretic progress' owed a good deal to the Positivists, there is less excuse for them lumping them together with other 'fertile thinkers of the middle class'. It was a Positivist who first taught Beatrice 'the economic

---

[1] S. and B. Webb, *History of Trade Unionism*, p. 254.
[2] *Ibid.* pp. 276-83.
[3] E. S. Beesly, 'The Ministry and the Workmen', *Bee-Hive*, 16 August 1873.
[4] E. S. Beesly, 'George Odger and French Workmen', *Weekly Despatch*, 2 July 1877.

validity of trade unionism and factory legislation',[1] and in the early days of the Fabian Society Sydney considered that Positivists certainly ought to be classed as socialists.[2] Such facts reinforce the view that Beesly should be remembered not only for his great moral courage, but as a representative of a school which exerted a significant influence on many of the diverse tendencies that went into the shaping of the modern labour movement. Karl Marx — who was not in the habit of flattering his contemporaries — rightly described him as 'a very capable and courageous man'.[3]

[1] B. Webb, *My Apprenticeship* (1926), p. 145.
[2] S. Webb, 'What Socialism Means', *Practical Socialist* (June 1886). See also: Summary of a discussion of the Economics of a Positivist Community, *Practical Socialist* (February 1886).
[3] K. Marx, *Letters to Dr. Kugelmann* (n.d., ? 1934), p. 114.

7

HENRY COLLINS

THE ENGLISH BRANCHES OF THE FIRST INTERNATIONAL

'THERE is a bookseller's shop in High Holborn. It is in every sense an unpretending establishment. . . . An inscription above it calls it "The Reformers' Library". . . . There are sights more hunted after by mere sightseers. There are edifices linked with many an historic narrative or fable. Yet we would venture to set that undistinguished shop above more than one palace and monument. For there are the headquarters of a society whose behests are obeyed by countless thousands from Moscow to Madrid, and in the New World as in the Old, whose disciples have already waged desperate war against one government, and whose proclamations pledge it to wage that war against every government — the ominous, the ubiquitous International Association of Workmen.' [1]

When these lines appeared in the *Tablet*, a few weeks after the fall of the Commune, they expressed the view of the International widely held in conservative circles. Yet there were, at that time, no branches of the International in Britain; at the most, there were a few hundred individual members, and the affiliated societies, mainly trade unions, made use of the International but took no notice of its politics. Some members of the General Council refused to accept this situation and called for the establishment of an English section of the International, a Federal Council with its own branches of the kind that existed in all the other countries to which the International

---

[1] *Tablet*, 15 July 1871. Note: All MS. sources quoted in this essay are in the International Institute of Social History, Amsterdam; and all letters from Marx and Engels that have been quoted are in the Russian *Sochinenia*, vols. 21-9.

had spread. In September 1871 they got their way and an English — later British — Federal Council was duly constituted. It soon had more than twenty branches and, under more favourable conditions, it might have developed into a labour party with a federal structure, much like the Labour Representation Committee which emerged in 1900. The times were unfavourable to the experiment and, in fact, it failed. What made its failure more certain was the split in the international movement which, starting with attacks on the General Council by anarchist sections in Switzerland, spread rapidly, at last reaching England, though in an altered form.

The anarchists constituted, in the view of Marx and Engels, the biggest threat that the International had faced since its formation in 1864. Marx had never tried to impose doctrinal uniformity on members or on sections of the International. He had co-operated with Proudhonists from France, Mazzini's followers from Italy, and English trade unionists who regarded the International as a useful auxiliary during strikes and whose political outlook went little beyond left radicalism. While there had been, at annual congresses, innumerable political arguments on the national question, trade-union strategy and, most recently, at Basle in 1869, on land nationalisation, there had been no attempt to dictate internal policy to the constituent sections. With Bakunin's entry into the Association, however, the situation changed drastically. The task of the workers, according to Bakunin, was not to challenge the control over the state by established classes or parties but to destroy the state itself, as the source of all oppression and exploitation. It followed from this that political activity by working-class parties, with a view to capturing the state, was a diversion. The task of a revolutionary international was to stimulate the spontaneous resistance of the workers until this culminated in an uprising which overthrew the state and replaced it by voluntary associations of producers.

The International, though seriously weakened by the defeat of the Commune, had become a legend, a banner symbolising the aspirations of labour. Marx's greatest fear was that, in its weakened condition, it might pass under the control of the anarchists, whose policies of political abstention and revolutionary adventure would render it futile and ineffective. To avoid this he was prepared to use the most drastic means, including the expulsion of individuals and sections. These tactics alienated a good many people, especially in England, who had no ideological sympathy for the Bakuninists but who did believe strongly in the freedom and autonomy of national sections. In the ensuing controversy the Bakuninists acquired strange allies and the International was wrecked. The English section, becoming involved in the fight without fully realising what was happening, went down with the wreck, yet, though the organisation vanished, a tradition remained which was to have some consequences for the later development of the socialist movement.

I

The anarchist, Michael Bakunin, had joined the International in 1868 and had immediately organised inside it the Alliance of Socialist Democracy, through which he meant to control the whole organisation. Ordered by the General Council to disband his Alliance, Bakunin had nominally complied while maintaining his underground society intact. Marx knew this and was desperately trying to stop the spread of Bakunin's influence before it dominated the International. But for the socialists of Geneva, Le Locle, Naples, and Barcelona — centres of handicraft production in which mechanised production had made little headway and where the Bakuninists had their own organs — Bakunin's revolutionary *élan* and destructive zeal had more attraction than Marx's scientific approach, with its insistence on the painstaking development of working-class political organisation.

Marx could always rely on solid support from Germany, where his ideas were rapidly gaining ground, but in the Europe of the eighteen-seventies, Geneva and Le Locle were more typical than Hamburg and Bremen, and Marx could not maintain control of the International through Germany alone. Always in the past, and most notably in the fight against

Proudhon, Marx had relied on the English members of the General Council to weigh in heavily and decisively on his side. Little as they might understand of Dialectical Materialism or Surplus Value, the English had found Marx's support for trade unionism, the strike weapon, the eight-hour day, and even land nationalisation more to their taste than what seemed to them the bizarre ultra-individualism of the French Proudhonists. Surveying the International after the crushing defeat of the Paris Commune, Marx could reasonably expect support from the English when confronted with the even more alien and much less rational individualism of Bakunin. Socialism, Marx knew, would survive the defeat of the Commune and the massacre of its supporters. When it revived in France and grew further in Germany, and when it developed, as it would, to become the leading idea of the European proletariat, it seemed to Marx of the utmost importance that socialist ideas should be organised within a centralised, disciplined, scientifically led party, and not as the spasmodic, incoherent, and ineffectual movement that Bakunin would make of it.

As long as the General Council remained in London, Marx believed that he and the English could hold Bakuninism at bay. In September 1871 a conference was held in London to discuss the organisation of the International, pending a full congress in the following year. Though on this occasion the English took little part, Marx could count on the support of the French Blanquists, led by Vaillant and, more precariously, of the Belgians, led by de Paepe. France was heavily represented on the General Council and at the London Conference by Communard refugees, most of them Blanquists. On the crucial question of political action versus abstention the Blanquists were in agreement with Marx although they were critical of his revolutionary tactics. The Belgians also, in the matter of political action, sided in general with Marx, though on industrial policy they tended to share the syndicalist approach of the Bakuninists. More important, however, was the fact that the anarchist centres were further from London than Brussels, so that Bakunin's followers were weakly represented at the conference. Despite their protests the London

Conference decided in favour of political action and, in particular, for strengthening the powers of the General Council relative to the Federal Councils of the various countries. A syndicalist resolution on trade-union organisation, supported by de Paepe, was defeated. All these decisions strengthened Marx's position in preparation for the final clash with Bakunin which was to take place a year later at The Hague. Another decision, attracting little attention and adopted on the proposal of Marx himself, was to have the opposite effect. This was the resolution establishing a Federal Council in England which, alone among the countries represented in the International, had up to then been without one.

As long as London was the headquarters of the International, Marx always insisted that the General Council could perform the double role of leading the International and functioning as its English section. He explained his reasons very frankly in a confidential circular to the sections of the International which he drew up for the General Council and which it endorsed on 16 January 1870. The Bakuninists, through their Geneva paper, *Égalité*, had started a comprehensive attack against the conduct of affairs by the General Council. Among other things, *Égalité* wanted to know why 'the General Council submits to this burdensome accumulation of functions'. Marx felt that he could not reply in public, but in the confidential circular he explained that 'Although the revolutionary initiative will probably come from France, England alone can serve as the lever of a serious economic revolution'. England alone had abolished its peasantry, through the penetration of capitalism into agriculture. England alone had an absolute majority of wage-earners and, as such, she was 'the only country where the class struggle and the organisation of the working class through the trade unions has acquired a certain degree of maturity and universality'. Since, besides all this, England dominated the world market, it was essential that she participate fully in the next round of European revolutions, which, Marx was convinced, could not be far off.

But though the English, through their economic development and working-class organisation, had 'all the material requisites necessary for the social revolution', they notoriously lacked 'the spirit of generalisation and revolutionary ardour'. This deficiency could only be supplied by the General Council, which found itself, through the International, 'in the happy position of having its hand directly on this great lever of the proletarian revolution. . . '. If a Federal, or Regional, Council were formed in England it could only have one result. 'Placed between the General Council of the International and the General Council of the trade unions, the Regional Council would lose its control of the great lever.'[1]

From its foundation, the General Council of the International had maintained close and friendly relations with the London Trades Council, on which one of its members, George Odger, served as secretary. In mobilising financial support in England for Continental strikes and in alerting the European workers' organisations to dissuade their members from taking the jobs of English workers on strike, the General Council had established an important niche for itself in the British labour movement. A large number of trade unions had affiliated, including the Bricklayers', Carpenters', and London Tailors' Societies. Even the Engineers and Ironfounders, which did not affiliate, had been persuaded through the medium of the Council to send financial help to the Paris Bronzeworkers, during their strike in 1867. Nor was the relationship between the General Council and the unions confined to industrial matters. In 1865 the English members of the General Council had taken a prominent part in the foundation of the Reform League, which led the agitation culminating in the Reform Act of 1867. In 1869, Applegarth and Lucraft, attending the Basle Congress of the International as delegates, had voted for the resolution demanding land nationalisation, and in doing so had scandalised a large part of the English press. Soon after Basle, the Land and Labour League had been established, with Marx's friend, J. George Eccarius and the O'Brienite, Martin J. Boon, as joint secretaries, and the Owenite, John Weston, as treasurer — all three being active members of the

[1] The confidential circular is reproduced in K. Marx, *Letters to Dr. Kugelmann* (n.d., ? 1934), pp. 102-9.

General Council. It seemed to Marx that through such connections the theory of socialism and the spirit of revolution could be imparted to the English trade unions so that, in time of crisis, he could manipulate 'this great lever' in the interests of the Revolution.

How mistaken he was became apparent in the days of the Paris Commune, from March to May 1871. While a section of the working class 'did sympathise with the Commune, though not upon strictly Communistic grounds',[1] not one trade union came out in its support, or looked remotely like doing so. The General Council itself refrained, during the period of the Commune, from issuing a single call for solidarity from the British working class, despite appeals from Paris, Brussels, and from at least one member of the General Council itself.[2] No doubt Marx realised that there would be no response from the trade unions, though Engels later complained bitterly that 'the working men of England had made no effort to show sympathy' with or to 'assist' the Commune.[3] While Marx conducted a vigorous private correspondence in support of the Commune, his first public pronouncement, the *Civil War in France*, was a brilliant and spirited obituary, issued after its fall.

Whatever his illusions may have been about the possibility of revolutionising the British working class, Marx had no doubt about the magnitude of the defeat which the international labour movement had suffered after the overthrow of the Commune. By the time of the London Conference in September he had withdrawn his objections to the establishment of an English Federal Council and John Hales, by trade an elastic web-weaver who had been expelled from his union in 1870 for supporting the employment of female labour, and who had consistently demanded an autonomous English section since joining the General Council in 1866, became its first

[1] Thomas Wright, *Our New Masters* (1873), pp. 194-9. The essay on the Commune first appeared as an article in *Frasers Magazine* (July 1871) by 'Journeyman Engineer', Wright's *nom-de-plume*.

[2] The member was the O'Brienite, George Milner (General Council Minutes — hereafter referred to as G.C. Minutes — 18 April 1871). See also *Pervy International vdni Parishkoi Kommuny* (Moscow, 1941), pp. 192-5.

[3] G.C. Minutes, 8 August 1871.

secretary. Having replaced Eccarius as secretary to the General Council on 16 May 1871, Hales for a time concentrated considerable power in his own hands. At first Marx saw no objection to this, since Hales had been his consistent follower, allowing Marx to draft public statements which Hales, as General Secretary, duly signed. Trouble was not far ahead.

II

At the first meeting of the General Council following the London Conference, it was Marx himself who re-nominated Hales as General Secretary, and there was now no controversy over the resolution announcing the formation of 'a Federal Committee for England, so that the influence of the Association might be brought to bear more directly upon English politics, than it had hitherto done. . .'[1]. Since Marx had issued his uncompromising defence of the Commune he had been subjected to severe criticism in the press, where he was widely accused of dictating the policy of the International and of involving innocent British trade unionists in his revolutionary plans. In reply to such an attack in the *Eastern Post*, Hales insisted that the International in England, with 8000 paid up members,[2] was fully democratic and controlled by no dictator, English or foreign.[3]

With branches already existing in Bethnal Green and Middlesbrough, the English Federal Council was formally constituted at a 'numerously attended meeting of the London members' in Holborn in October. The enigmatic figure of Maltman Barry made his first appearance in the International, taking the chair, and being elected provisional chairman — with Hales as provisional secretary — at the conclusion of the

[1] *Ibid.* 26 September; and *Eastern Post*, 30 September 1871.
[2] The Alliance Cabinet Makers, Cigar Makers, London Tailors, Day Working Bookbinders, West-End Boot Closers, and West-End Bootmakers paid affiliation fees on the basis of 3d. per member. In the case of the Amalgamated Society of Carpenters and Joiners and the Operative Bricklayers Society, only the executives were affiliated, leaving it to branches to join if they wished. Of the 33 trade unions affiliated in 1867, most or all others had discontinued their subscriptions by 1871. (G.C. Minutes, 31 October 1871; MS. by C. Keen.)
[3] *Eastern Post*, 7 October 1871.

meeting.[1] A news item appearing in *The Times* [2] alleged that since the Commune, and the International's declaration of support, English trade unionists, finding themselves outvoted through the 'great preponderance of foreign and political influence', and refusing 'to find the sinews of war for foreign agitations', had withdrawn their support. The English Federal Council had been launched, said the report, at a large meeting in Holborn of 'members of this secret society'. Hales at once replied,[3] denying that the International was a 'secret society in any sense'. All its meetings, he claimed, were open, and of the 'many thousands of members we have in England only two have withdrawn their names or entered a protest'. Hales thought that both Odger and Lucraft, who had resigned rather publicly from the General Council after the appearance of the *Civil War in France*, now regretted their decision.[4]

The accusation that the International was a secret society was repeated by Charles Bradlaugh, among others, and there followed an acrimonious controversy, in which Marx, Hales, and Longuet participated enthusiastically.[5]

A more dangerous threat to the International, however, resulted from the machinations of Maltman Barry, a correspondent of the *Standard* and a tory agent who, for the next thirty years, intrigued tirelessly to bring about an alliance between the labour movement and the Conservative Party. Almost universally distrusted in the labour movement, then and later, Barry maintained a strange friendship with Marx, who provided him with material for articles and who also used him as his agent at international congresses.[6] Soon after

---

[1] *Eastern Post*, 28 October 1871. [2] *The Times*, 23 October 1871.
[3] *Ibid.* 28 October 1871.
[4] Cf. the four-and-a-half-column history of the International — the author of which was probably Eccarius — in *The Times*, 27 October 1871. Of all the unions affiliating, 'only three have seceded on account of the Council meddling with politics; none since the fall of the Commune'. The three were the Amalgamated Cordwainers, the Birmingham House Painters, and the Curriers — the last because of the Council's support for the Fenians.
[5] *Eastern Post*, 2, 16, 23 December 1871; 20 January, 3 February 1872. *National Reformer*, 7 January 1872.
[6] See W. Collison, *The Apostle of Free Labour* (1913), pp. 235-42; J. Burgess, *Will Lloyd George Supplant Ramsay MacDonald* (n.d., ? 1930), pp. 59-100; H. M. Hyndman, *The Record of an Adventurous Life* (1911),

joining the Federal Council, on 2 December, Barry wrote to Marx complaining that Hales was trying to strengthen the Federal at the expense of the General Council.[1] When the General Council met, three days later, Barry succeeded in bringing about the first important clash between Marx and Hales.[2]

On the day the General Council met, the *Standard* reported a meeting of the Federal Council at St. Luke's which had taken place a few days earlier. The report was clearly written by someone present at the meeting. It referred to a speech by 'the elastic Hales . . . full of mystery'. Though well informed on all other details, the report described Barry himself as 'Citizen Barry, who is called a barrister . . .' and described him as speaking in support of Gladstone and liberalism. Barry was a journalist, not a barrister, detested liberalism and was a conservative agent. It seems only too likely that he wrote the report, though he himself drew attention to it at the General Council meeting on 5 December, in an attempt to discredit Hales. Barry's attack was followed by a demand from Marx that Hales resign as secretary of the Federal Council, on the grounds that one man should not be secretary of both Councils. Hales was forced to comply, and almost at once his relations with the General Council deteriorated.

Though Marx had allowed himself to be used in Barry's intrigues, he was not prepared at this stage to accept all of Barry's allegations. Barry seems to have written to Marx some weeks later warning him against a party led by Hales on the General Council, to which Marx replied on 7 January 1872, denying the existence of a Hales party. 'If we ever came out against Hales', he wrote, 'when we considered him wrong, then we carried out our duties as members of the Council. The same would apply to any other member. Why then a party? There are no parties in the Council. Amongst Hales's friends there are many who have worked for long for our aims.'

For his part, Hales was still Marx's loyal supporter. He wrote in the *Eastern Post*, on 3 February 1872, replying to

p. 285; Max Nettlau in Grunberg's *Archiv für die Geschichte des Sozialismus und der Arbeiterbewegung*, ix (1921), p. 140, n. 2.

[1] K. Marx, *Chronik Seines Lebens* (Moscow, 1933), p. 320.
[2] G.C. Minutes, 5 December 1871.

Bradlaugh: 'There are no official subordinates to Dr. Marx on our Council. He is secretary for Germany, and would as little dream of interfering in English affairs, as I should in German. The only position he occupies in the Council is an equal one with the rest of the members, and he would — as he has been — (*sic*) the first man to resent an assumption that he held a superior position.'

At some time in January, Maltman Barry was expelled from the British Federal Council — either for reporting on private meetings or for trouble-making, or both. He maintained, however, his friendship with Marx, who, presumably, took him to be a useful source of information. Some resentment was expressed by the branch in St. Luke's (where the meeting reported in the *Standard* had been held) at the fact 'that Maltman Barry was still received by the Association in face of his expulsion by the British Federal Council', and the branch 'respectfully drew the attention of the London branches' to the anomaly.[1]

At the beginning of 1872, however, though there was already friction between the two Councils, it did not appear serious. The Federal Council had been energetic and reasonably successful in forming branches, and Charles Keen, who had succeeded Hales as secretary, presented a report on 9 January which contained a list of provincial branches consisting of Manchester, Middlesbrough, Loughborough, Liverpool, and Nottingham.[2] J. P. McDonnell, an active Fenian, had begun to form Irish branches in London, the provinces, and Ireland itself. Two active branches in London, Bethnal Green and St. Luke's — which had a membership of fifty — were reporting considerable progress at about the same time.[3]

The Manchester branch, destined to be one of the most successful, was addressed by Harriet Law[4] on behalf of the Communard refugees at one of its earliest meetings. Eugene Dupont, French musical instrument maker and an old friend of Engels, kept him informed about developments in the branch

[1] *Eastern Post*, 3 February 1872.   [2] MS. Report.
[3] *Eastern Post*, 6 January 1872. The Irish branches seem to have had little success; few, if any, survived The Hague Congress.
[4] She later edited the *Secular Chronicle* in Birmingham from 1872-9.

and constantly sought his advice on policy. They had, he told Engels, leased 'a *respectable* room' for their meetings, which were lively. Manchester's delegate to the General Council was Dr. Sexton, who had, somewhat to Dupont's surprise, declared himself a Communist.[1]

On 12 November 1871 the anarchist Jurassian Federation had issued a circular denouncing the decisions of the London Conference and repudiating the authority of the General Council. Though the circular had gained some support internationally, notably in Italy, it caused no ripples in England, where the new Federal Council pointedly passed a unanimous resolution supporting the London Conference decisions 'in their integrity'. 'Every member', the resolution stressed, 'was in favour of combining political and social action, and thoroughly endorsed the policy of the General Council'.[2] Besides preserving a broad unity of outlook, in a period when the International was deeply split, the English section was about to possess a journal of its own, for the first time since the *Commonwealth* had ceased to appear in 1867.

On 2 March 1872 the first number of the *International Herald* appeared, published by W. Harrison Riley. In a letter to Engels on 9 February Riley asked him to write for the journal, and on the following day he wrote again, asking for assistance and promising to print full reports of the International's activities. Appearing fortnightly at first, the paper became a weekly from 11 May. Its statement of objects covered all the demands of contemporary working-class radicalism, ranging from shorter working hours and universal suffrage to 'the nationalisation of land and currency', and the liquidation of the National Debt. Though not solely an organ of the International, the *Herald* aspired to be 'the special organ of such societies as are not already specially represented by the *Bee-Hive* or the *National Reformer*'.

[1] Dupont to Engels, 11 January 1872. Sexton had, up to that time, written a number of rationalist tracts. Later, in 1872, he announced his conversion to spiritualism, thereby disconcerting some of his new friends in Manchester. Nevertheless, he attended The Hague Congress in September 1872 as a staunch supporter of Marx.
[2] *Eastern Post*, 17 February 1872.

The first anniversary of the Commune, in March, was celebrated by two small meetings in London. An attempt to do the same in Cork met with disaster, and John De Morgan, an elocution teacher and a powerful if somewhat vacuous orator, who tried to address the meeting, was thrown out of the hall by a largely working-class audience, many of whose members had seen service in the Fenian movement.[1] The Carpenters' and Coach Makers' Societies were, for a short time, affiliated to the Cork branch, but the Carpenters were soon forced to withdraw by a combination of Catholic propaganda, police pressure, and economic victimisation. De Morgan, no longer able to earn a living in Cork, left for England where he became a professional lecturer in the service of radical organisations. Marx, Milner, and McDonnell drew up an address for the General Council called *Police Terrorism in Ireland*, which was issued as a leaflet on 12 April. Repression which had the support of the mass of the people was, however, bound to succeed, and McDonnell tacitly admitted that both branches in Ireland were dead when the General Council met on 7 May.

In England the atmosphere was very different. When, on 12 April, Alexander Baillie-Cochrane introduced a motion in the House of Commons calling for the suppression of the International, his speech fell flat. The Home Secretary, Bruce, while not underrating 'the dangers of this society', was convinced that 'Education with some religious teaching was not only the best, but the only way of resisting the propagation of such doctrines.'[2] In its report of the debate on 15 April, *The Times* expressed some fear that honest British trade unionists might be infected with the 'strange theories . . . respecting the constitution of society in general' — which the artisans of Paris had brought into the International.[3] Still, *The Times* agreed with the Home Secretary.[4] 'We cannot', it insisted, 'take arbitrary measures for the suppression of a

[1] *Express*, 25 March 1872; *Freeman*, 25 and 26 March 1872.
[2] *Parl. Deb.* 3rd Ser. ccx, 1183-1210 (12 April 1872).
[3] French commentators, on the other hand, deplored the trade unionism and the strikes which they feared the French workers might learn from the English. Cf. Louis Reybaud in *Revue des Deux Mondes* (1 November 1866).
[4] For other discussions of the International in the House of Commons in 1872, see *Parl. Deb.* 3rd Ser. ccix, 1025-6; ccx, 244-5, 401, 1268.

Society which, so far as we know, is within the pale of our law.'[1]

Secure from legal interference, the International went its way, with a growing number of branches, two of which — Manchester and Nottingham — showed a fair amount of stability and vigour. Both branches were meeting regularly to discuss their political programmes. In Manchester, opinion was divided on the land question. 'Some suggested that the government should lease the land to the peasants, others that it should be divided out, as in France.' Dupont, who wrote to Engels for advice, set out his own views as follows : 'Common ownership of land is a social necessity. . . . Sharing, fragmentation would run contrary to modern ideas and means of production, which require large-scale exploitation. . . . To hand over the exploitation of the land to a single category of producers would be to put society at the mercy of that category. . . . Nationalisation of the land will only be genuine when the people . . . is itself the government.' Dupont added that he would have written to Marx, but knew he would be too busy to reply. 'The little I know I have learned from him', he added.[2]

The Nottingham branch, which met weekly at Lester's Coffee House in Houndsgate, issued its own programme calling for 'political and social revolution'. Its five-point programme, differing in emphasis from that of the International, called for freedom of expression and education, the abolition of privileges based on class and sex, 'emancipation of the land', including 'the right and duty of men to enjoy the fruit of their own labour', and 'capital the servant of labour, and not labour the servant of capital' — a vague provision, as compatible with the views of J. S. Mill as with those of Marx — universal suffrage, national and racial equality and, unique among the British branches of the International, 'the protection of the rights of minorities by the principle of federalism and by

[1] See also Lord Granville's reply to the Spanish Government circular demanding the suppression of the International, *Correspondence between the British and Spanish Governments respecting the International Society* (1872, 4 pp.).
[2] Dupont to Engels, 3 March 1872. It is doubtful whether a single English worker understood Marx's theories in 1872.

decentralisation of power — so as to take away the temptation of the central government to trample on the rights of its opponents'.[1] The statement was signed by Thomas Smith, the branch secretary, and probably the most original thinker among the English members of the International.[2]

Alongside these developments there were the beginnings of a campaign against Marx and the General Council. A section of the French Republicans, who had quarrelled violently with the French Proudhonists and had been expelled from the International in 1868,[3] had been reinforced by Communard refugees and a small number of Englishmen. On 15 April *The Times* reported a 'large meeting of the seceding members of the International' at the Black Swan, in Leicester Square, with English, French, and German speakers. Soon after, the secretary of the meeting, Richard Dennis Butler,[4] issued a statement denying that the participants were seceders from the International. They considered themselves members of the Association, but had set up a Universal Federalist Council to combat the General Council, which had 'constituted itself into a centralising and despotic power', expelling individuals and sections without appeal, and generally tyrannising over the membership.[5]

Few, if any, of the members of the Universal Federalist Council sympathised with the Bakuninists. Most of them, however, had grievances of one sort or another against the General Council and the disciplinary powers which it exercised. All, therefore, were prepared to make common cause with the Bakuninists in support of federal autonomy. All joined, too, in attacking the powers of a General Council elected as long ago as the Basle Congress in 1869.[6] While the Englishmen

[1] *International Herald*, 13 April 1872.
[2] For Smith's political philosophy, see below, pp. 265-6.
[3] Marx at first tried to compose the quarrel. When this proved impossible he sided with the Proudhonists as representatives of the French working class.
[4] Richard Dennis Butler was a compositor. As delegate from the London Trades Council he had proposed Professor Beesly as chairman at the foundation meeting of the International on 28 September 1864.
[5] *The Times*, 23 April 1872.
[6] No Congress had been held in 1870 because of the Franco-Prussian war, or in 1871 because of the Paris Commune.

participating in the 'secession' were few in number and would, in themselves, have constituted no threat to the General Council, there were now on that body itself members who were, for a variety of reasons, in revolt against Marx.

For some months Marx had been aware of a correspondence between some members of the Council and the dissident, anarchist Section 12 of New York. 'There is no doubt . . .', he wrote to Frederick Bolte, on 23 November 1871, 'that G. Harris and perhaps Boon — two English members of the General Council — are carrying on private correspondence with Internationalists in New York, etc. Both of them belong to the sect of the late Bronterre O'Brien, and are full of follies and crotchets, such as currency quackery, false emancipation of women, and the like. They are thus by nature allies of Section 12 in New York and its kindred souls.' The O'Brienites had, however, important redeeming qualities, constituting 'in spite of their follies' a 'necessary counterweight to trade unionists in the Council. They are more revolutionary, firmer on the land question, less nationalistic, and not susceptible to bourgeois bribery in one form or another. Otherwise they would have been kicked out long ago.'

More disturbing for Marx than the contacts of Harris and Boon with Section 12 was the behaviour of Eccarius. After resigning as General Secretary in May 1871 with the plea — which Marx regarded as an excuse — that he had too much other work, Eccarius had been appointed corresponding secretary for America. There was soon reason to believe that, in this capacity, he was also intriguing with Section 12 against the 'official' New York section led by Marx's friend, Sorge.[1] When Marx proposed, on 28 May, that the General Council should recognise only the Sorge section his motion was carried against opposition not only from Eccarius but also from Hales, still secretary to the General Council. Perhaps it was then that Marx took his strange decision to transfer the General Council from London to New York. Having broken irreparably with Eccarius, one of his oldest friends who had collaborated with him since the days of the Communist League

[1] G.C. Minutes, 23 April 1872.

in the 1840s, and with a growing strain in his relations with Hales, for long one of his few reliable English followers, Marx had had enough. 'I am terribly overworked', he wrote to Danielson on 28 May 1872, 'and meet so many obstacles in my theoretical studies that after September, I am determined to leave the General Council, all the work of which lies on my shoulders'. But if Marx left the General Council, into whose hands would it fall?

Had his differences with Eccarius and Hales been entirely personal, Marx would have taken energetic steps to compose them. But now political differences had appeared, similar to those which had come to divide Marx from Ernest Jones in the late eighteen-fifties. Eccarius was becoming convinced of the need to develop working-class political action in collaboration with — and even under the leadership of — the liberal bourgeoisie. Hales, who had parliamentary ambitions, and who was to stand, unsuccessfully, for the Borough of Hackney in 1874, was coming to favour a labour party with trade-union affiliations, with the loosest of international ties and free from compromising revolutionary objectives.

To the strains developing in the General Council there was added, as a minor irritant, a broadside in the shape of a sixteen-page pamphlet, issued by the Universal Federalist Council, accusing the General Council of every crime in the political calendar and in particular of postponing Congresses, manipulating elections, failing to account for the management of its finances, ignoring Congress decisions, and behaving in a despotic manner towards affiliated sections.[1] It was easy for the General Council, in replying, to make clear the circumstances in which it had had to postpone Congresses since 1869 and to point to the unrepresentative character of the Universal Federalist Council. But the accusations of this tiny group were soon to be taken up, without acknowledgment, by a majority in the British Federal Council itself.

In a muted form the antagonisms within the Federal

[1] *Universal Federalist Council of the International Working Men's Association and of Republican and Socialist Societies Adhering* (May 1872), 16 pp.

The English Branches of the First International

Council were expressed at the first Congress of that body in July 1872. By the time of the Congress the Council could claim twenty-five branches, of which the most active were Manchester, Nottingham, Liverpool, Birkenhead, Sunderland, Dundee, Hinckley, Loughborough, Middlesbrough, Glasgow, and, in London, the West End, Bethnal Green, Woolwich, Stratford, and St. Luke's. Manchester was still the most successful, with regular open-air meetings on Sundays of four to five hundred. It had enrolled seventeen new members at its meeting on 24 April and fifteen at a meeting on 8 May. Besides its individual members, it secured the affiliation of the Shoemakers' No. 1 Branch with 150 members and, perhaps, of the Bricklayers. (This was later disputed.) [1] Nottingham had been strengthened by the affiliation of the International Labour Protection League, which had developed out of the local Nine Hour League, and had for its object the co-ordination of trade-union action during strikes.[2] The West End branch, to which Charles Murray's Society of Boot Closers was affiliated, had twenty-nine members and St. Luke's — perhaps the largest London branch — had more than fifty.

Unlike the General Council, the local branches of the International inevitably became socialist propaganda bodies and equally inevitably the ideas propagated — the only socialist ideas in the field — were those of Bronterre O'Brien. The main O'Brienite propaganda society, the National Reform League, was affiliated to the International. Of its seven-point programme issued in 1850, soon after its formation, land nationalisation and currency reform had become the items most commonly stressed. Nationalisation of industry had never been part of the O'Brienite policy, and even 'the expropriation of railways, canals, bridges, docks, gas-works, waterworks, etc.', though considered desirable, were regarded as of secondary importance, 'easy of accomplishment', once the more fundamental problems of land, currency, and credit had been solved.[3]

[1] *International Herald*, 27 April, 11 and 18 May 1872.
[2] See the prospectus of the League, June 1872, Amsterdam.
[3] *Propositions of the National Reform League for the Peaceful Regeneration of Society* (1850), 4 pp.

Presiding at a meeting of the 'Mutual Land Emigration and Colonization Company' at the Eclectic Institute in Denmark St., Soho, at the end of May 1872, Charles Murray, veteran Chartist and later a member of the Social Democratic Federation, described 'the Company' as having been 'founded by a number of advanced Social Reformers, disciples of the late Bronterre O'Brien, who finding they could not put into practice just laws on land, credit, currency, and exchange in England, were determined to go to America' where the conditions 'would enable them to put into operation those principles which were identical with those upon which the "International" is based'. The 'crowded audience' was then addressed by John Hales on 'Nationalisation of the Land'.[1] The West End branch of the International, in which Charles Murray and George Milner were leading members, was addressed by Martin J. Boon — like Milner, a member of the National Reform League — on the theme 'That the land and currency laws are of vital importance to the people'.[2] And in Manchester, one of the earliest meetings, addressed by Walker, had as its subject, 'Land, Currency, and Credit'.[3]

Besides the National Reform League and the Colonisation Company, the *International Herald* also preached the O'Brienite gospel, with, characteristically enough, the occasional anti-semitic embellishment. In the issue of 13 April 1872 Disraeli had been attacked on racial grounds. The idea that finance was the common enemy of capital and labour, and the identification of finance with the Jews, forms a strand which runs, perhaps without interruption, from Cobbett to the Social Credit propaganda of the twentieth century. In its issue of 18 May 1872 the *Herald*, commenting on a recent increase in the bank rate, remarked that:

> The members of the 'Ring' are sure to profit by every change in the rate, for they *make the change for that purpose*. What matters it to them if a thousand working tradesmen are ruined and a hundred thousand more are distressed ? They are the dispensers of the only money of the nation and they obtain their wealth by keeping the supply insufficient to meet the natural demand. We must have

[1] *International Herald*, 1 June 1872.   [2] *Ibid.* 25 May 1872.
[3] *Ibid.* 11 May 1872.

national bank notes and not leave our only mediums of exchange to the control of Jews.

Not economic theory, however, but politics in the narrowest sense, was the cause of the split rapidly developing in the English section of the International. And there can be little doubt that the speed with which the conflict grew was intensified by the intrigues with which John Hales was now occupying himself, while still secretary of the General Council. In a speech to the Federal Council on 20 June 1872 he referred scathingly to 'those who, with democracy on their lips and jesuitry in their hearts, tried to sow discord in the ranks of the International';[1] and in a letter to Sorge on 2 July he affirmed that 'No one would be more determined than I am to maintain the principles of the Association inviolate but I would make almost any concessions upon questions of policy rather than see the Association dissolved'. On 19 July, however, on the eve of the Nottingham Congress of the British Federal Council, Hales was suspended as secretary by the General Council, pending an inquiry into his correspondence with the dissident section in America. Cournet, who moved the suspension, explained that 'he is accused by the American secretary of having abused his powers', while Marx added more forcefully: 'we have evidence given that the secretary works against the Council while he is paid by the Council'.[2]

These accusations of double-dealing were never, apparently, either denied or effectively explained by Hales. He appeared at the Nottingham Congress, however, with a number of resolutions designed to weaken the General Council, two of which were carried. Both were designed to strengthen the autonomy of the national sections, a cause with which he was now openly identified. The first authorised the British Federal Council to 'place themselves in communication with all Federal Councils, and exchange organs of information with a view to greater solidarity'. That this would give maximum freedom to all opposition elements to organise against the General

---

[1] *Eastern Post*, 22 June 1872.
[2] G.C. Minutes, 23 July 1872. The secretary's salary was fifteen shillings a week.

Council was recognised by Thomas Smith of Nottingham who, despite his strongly federalist views on politics, was a centralist on matters of organisation. He insisted that the 'plan would be tantamount to doing away with the General Council altogether'. The resolution was carried, and Dupont, who kept Engels informed on developments at Nottingham, was furious. 'I have no need', he wrote from the Congress, 'to draw your attention to this resolution which coming from Hales is neither more nor less than treason'.[1]

Hales's second resolution, while more subtle, was equally directed against the General Council. Edward Jones, who had succeeded Dupont as Manchester secretary when the latter went to live in London, moved that the time had arrived 'for the formation of a third political party in this country, based upon the claims of the labourer. . . . The rule that they must keep in view was that laid down by the International Association, that the freedom of the working classes must be worked out by the working classes themselves.'[2] After the motion had been seconded by another Manchester delegate, Hales moved a curious amendment. After claiming that 'Never had there been such an opportunity of building up a real Liberal party, not a sham one, under the patronage of the philanthropy mongers' he proposed that 'while we recognise the fact that the social emancipation of the working classes is the greatest end to which our efforts should be directed, we also recognise the fact that it is necessary to take political action to work out that social emancipation, and we hereby pledge ourselves to establish a distinct Labour Party, based upon the principles of the International . . .'. Read literally, Hales's amendment was quite compatible with the motion, but the emphasis was very different, and the words 'while' and 'we also' suggested the difference. Jones had asked for the International to set up a third party, 'based upon the claims of the labourer', and in the spirit of the International's *General Rules*, though organisationally distinct from the Association. The Inter-

[1] Dupont to Engels, 21 July 1872.
[2] Cf. 'The emancipation of the working classes must be conquered by the working classes themselves'. General Rules of the I.W.M.A., drafted by Marx in 1864.

national, however, would continue to work for its long-term social revolutionary aims. Hales wanted a liberal-labour party, 'based upon the principles of the International', but working for immediate political reforms, with the long-term social aims, if not formally abandoned, very much in the background. This, at least, was the interpretation of Dupont, who told Engels in his letter of 21 July that Hales had modified his amendment before it was put to the vote. What Hales wanted, explained Dupont, was 'that a workers' party be formed and that it should be recognised that only *through political action*, etc. (that is the spirit, if not the letter of his proposal)'. In a final series of resolutions the Nottingham Congress dealt with trade unionism, and among other things called on the unions to take 'immediate action by joining the new Labour party'. Neither Hales's amendment nor the trade-union resolutions could be successfully operated in the conditions of 1872. Had they been, the International would have sponsored a party which, with its trade-union affiliations, would have anticipated politically and structurally the Labour Representation Committee, with the O'Brienite National Reform League providing inspiration for its political wing. Significantly enough, the only economic demands adopted by the Nottingham Congress were for the nationalisation of land and banking.[1]

III

The decisions of the Fifth Congress of the International, which opened at The Hague on 2 September 1872, are perhaps sufficiently well known. It is noteworthy, however, that while Marx, in his confidential communication on the Bakuninists in January 1870, had confidently looked forward to the revolutionising of the British trade unions by the International, his only English supporters at The Hague were the tory journalist, Maltman Barry, and the rationalist turned spiritualist, Dr. Sexton. The days when Odger, Howell, Cremer, Lucraft, and the like could work harmoniously with Marx on the General Council were gone, and though Applegarth attended a meeting

[1] For the Nottingham Congress, see *Eastern Post*, 27 July 1872.

of the Council as late as 13 August 1872, he was no longer an active trade unionist. Marx acknowledged the change when, in reply to Thomas Mottershead's challenge as to how Maltman Barry came to be at The Hague, he explained that Barry had a mandate from the Chicago Germans. 'As to the accusation,' he went on, 'that Barry was not a recognised leader of English working men, that was an honour, for almost every recognised leader of English working men was sold to Gladstone, Morley, Dilke, and others.'

Marx and Engels were successful on every issue at The Hague, including the endorsement of political action, the expulsion of Bakunin and his chief lieutenants and, most sensational of all, the removal of the General Council from London to New York. 'This', said the *Manchester Guardian* on 7 September, 'was at first sight almost as strange as if the Pope had proposed to send the Holy Congregation and the College of Cardinals away from Rome.' The explanation, thought the *Guardian*'s correspondent — very possibly Eccarius — was that 'all the English members of the General Council but two are dissatisfied; that Jung has revolted from Marx, and that there is open war among the French members', the older members, Dupont, Serraillier, and Johannard, being at loggerheads with 'the new members who have been admitted to the Council since the fall of the Commune' — chiefly Blanquists. With the General Council in this state, and with the Bakuninist advance in Switzerland, Spain, Italy, and France, the Bakuninists and their allies in Belgium and England might well have secured a majority at the next Congress. Neither Marx nor Engels was prepared any longer to expend the enormous amount of energy that would have been needed to keep control. Both were preparing, as in the period after 1848, to retire from active politics, at least for a time. Rather than see the Council fall to the Bakuninists, they moved it out of reach. The U.S.A., in Marx's view, was destined to become an important centre of international labour, and in the meantime the General Council would be safe in the hands of Sorge and his supporters. That the formation of a British Federal Council under the control of Hales played an important

part in this decision was hinted at by Barry when he wrote:
'During the last year or so, since the accession to the Council
of a number of "representative' Englishmen, it has taxed all
his [Marx's. H.C.] efforts (and these have sometimes failed)
to keep the Council to its legitimate work. If he retired from
the Council, and it still remained in London, it would be in
great danger of falling into the hands of men who would make
it either a pothouse forum or an electioneering machine.'[1]

To all appearances, the English branches of the International continued with their normal activity when the delegates returned from The Hague. Manchester, which was now a Federation, with a foreign section and a branch in Hulme, besides the original Central branch, held a public meeting addressed by Odger on 'Capital and Labour'. Odger confined his remarks to an advocacy of trade unions and arbitration, but when questions were asked about his relations with the International he defended it as 'one of the original founders'. Its support for the Commune had been 'a great mistake' but it had done splendid work in promoting international labour solidarity.[2]

Nottingham, like Manchester, was a Federation having, besides its Central branch, the Labour Protection League and a local French branch, presumably based on the silk workers. Thomas Smith, secretary of the Central branch, had written at the time of the Commune a series of letters to the *Nottingham Daily Express*. The letters, with dates ranging from 25 March to 13 July 1871, were collected and published as a pamphlet: *Letters on the Commune. The Law of the Revolution ; or the Logical Development of Human Society* (20 pp., March 1872). In the preface Smith wrote that 'all phenomena are the results of laws eternal in their operation. . . . Each period of history — ancient, mediaeval, and modern — had its own distinctive tendencies and laws of development. The modern period — "the era of the revolution" — had started with the Reformation. Its inherent principles included universal suffrage and political

[1] Maltman Barry, *Report of the Fifth Annual General Congress of the I.W.M.A. held at The Hague, Holland, September 2-9, 1872* (44 pp.). First printed in the *Standard*.
[2] *International Herald*, 5 October 1872.

decentralisation. The Commune was an expression of this tendency, and social upheavals, accompanied by bloodshed, would continue until those principles were recognised and applied.' The pamphlet was sent in October to a number of prominent people including John Stuart Mill, who, in a long and friendly reply, expressed general agreement with its contents, objecting only to the use of such abstract terms, inadequately defined, as 'The Revolution'.[1]

Other branches of the International were developing regular public activity. The Birkenhead branch was selling the *International Herald* in the docks, while Liverpool was publicising the appeal of the local dockers against the attempt to impose non-unionism by importing Belgians.[2] It was some weeks before the effects of the split began to be felt in the branches. When they were, the result was devastating.

On 16 November Engels wrote to Sorge in some concern. Hales and Mottershead, he complained, had captured the Federal Council with the votes of 'delegates from non-existent sections . . .'. Foreseeing that it was only a matter of time before the Federal Council repudiated New York, Engels asked Sorge for authority to act in England on behalf of the General Council. Important in the struggle would be the control of the *International Herald*. Riley, its editor, was 'an honest man . . . but he is weak and depends to a certain extent on the Federal Council in connection with his paper'.

Riley's political views, like those of almost all his socialist contemporaries, were O'Brienite, with the characteristic blend of physical-force Chartism, producers' co-operation, and land and currency reform. The enemy of the worker was the monopolist of land and money, not the employer. In his pamphlet, *Strikes. Their Cause and Remedy*,[3] he wrote: 'The

[1] *International Herald*, 26 October 1872. See also *Daily News* and *Daily Telegraph* of 28 October 1872. Reprinted in *Letters of J. S. Mill*, ii (ed. H. Elliott, 1910), pp. 346-8.

[2] *Ibid.* and letters from W. Dodd to Vickery, 29 September 1872.

[3] Probably 1873 (Leeds, 16 pp.); and see also Riley's pamphlet, issued by the same publishers at about the same time, *British Slavery. A Tract Dedicated to All Working Men* (8 pp.). For a favourable account of Riley, see Edward Carpenter, *Sketches from Life in Town and Country*,

active employer who organises and superintends labour, and buys, and sells, is really a working man, and, as such, his interests are identical with those of his employees'. By contrast: 'No man has any more right to make a profit upon the mere use of money than he has by letting land'. After some initial hesitation, Riley, like his fellow O'Brienites, Murray and Milner, and like Thomas Smith in Nottingham, sided with the General Council against Hales. On the British Federal Council, the opposition to Hales was led by Vickery and two Germans from the Arbeiterbildungsverein (the German Workers' Educational Society), Frederick Lessner and Adam Weiler. They were joined at the end of November, and not accidentally, by Charles Murray, representing Normanby, George Milner, from the National Reform League, and Eugene Dupont, with a mandate from Manchester.[1] This still left Hales with a substantial majority on the Federal Council, though Engels was right in describing it as largely fictitious. Two provincial branches, Liverpool and Hulme, were Halesite, though in East London, where Hales's personal influence was strong, he had overwhelming support. The mainly Irish branch in Middlesbrough was divided, each side claiming to represent the majority. Elsewhere in the provinces the branches either sided with the General against the Federal Council or waited on developments.

Hales might have founded a labour party, based on the Federal Council. There would have been little trade-union support, but as a party fighting for independent working-class representation it could, just conceivably, have influenced developments in the labour movement. He ruined his chances, however, by a precipitate action which may have been forced on him by his international affiliations. At the beginning of September 1872 he visited The Hague and made contact with

pp. 205-7; and for a less favourable picture, W. H. T. Armytage, 'Ruskin as Utopist', *Notes and Queries* (May 1956). For Riley's praise of O'Connor and advocacy of 'an Industrial Parliament', see *International Herald*, 2 November 1872.

[1] *International Herald*, 7 December 1872; and Engels to Sorge of the same date. See also Hale's circular, December 1872, and J. Guillaume, *L'Internationale. Documents et Souvenirs, 1864–78*, iii (Paris, 1905), pp. 24-7.

the anarchists of the Juras Federation. The *Manchester Guardian*, which knew a good deal about what went on in the inner counsels of the International, wrote on 7 September: 'Citizen Hales, of London, came to the Congress at his own expense simply to see the leaders of the anti-Marx party, and to exchange addresses, so as to be able to co-operate with them in the schism which was to follow the triumph of Marx'. In the few days he spent at The Hague, Hales seems to have reached an understanding with the anarchists by which their various sections would hold national Congresses of their own as soon as possible after The Hague and set up their own international organisation based on a repudiation of The Hague decisions. Obsessed with the need for quick action, Hales withdrew from the Federal Council's premises at 7 Red Lion Court at the beginning of December and, at a private meeting of his followers, arranged for a conference of the English section to be held on the first Sunday in January.

There followed a war of leaflets, in which the Hales party denounced the tyranny of the General Council and called for a new International based on the federal autonomy of national sections. A reply drafted by Engels, in the name of the Manchester foreign section, explained the reason for Hales overhasty action. 'Hitherto', it pointed out, '*minorities* have seceded often enough. This is the first instance of a *majority* seceding.' The reasons for this unusual procedure, explained Engels, was the private agreement reached at The Hague 'to call all sorts of congresses in all countries about Christmas and to get them to confirm their secessionist action'.

In the event, Hales had to postpone his Congress for three weeks. 'Secession is a foregone conclusion in *such* a Congress as can be held in London', wrote Riley in the *Herald* on 4 January 1873, blaming Hales's inordinate ambition for the approaching split. Presenting his own case in the same issue, Hales laid the main blame on Engels. Replying to a letter signed by Marx and Engels which had appeared in the *Herald* on 21 December, Hales wrote: 'I do not for one moment believe that Citizen Marx had anything to do with such a miserable production except to father it, the same as he has

The English Branches of the First International

done with other effusions from the same pen'. In a passage which is striking in the light of some later history, Hales accused Engels of trying 'to turn the Association into a secret one, with an infallible pontiff at the head of it, who shall thunder excommunication against all who shall dare to enquire or doubt. I decline to be a party to such a degradation of the Labour struggle.'[1]

Hales's precipitate withdrawal from the Federal Council proved to be a fatal mistake. It enabled the minority to appeal successfully to the loyalty of the provincial branches by appearing as the official council confronted with a breakaway. So essential did it seem to the 'official' council to maintain the appearance of continuity that when it could no longer afford the rent of 7 Red Lion Court it continued to meet 'ten strong at the Red Lion public-house in the same court'.[2] The impression so created during the first few critical weeks following the split was probably decisive in rallying the support of the provincial branches.

As a result, the London Congress of Hales's Federal Council which opened on 26 January 1873 was a miserable affair. Only eleven delegates were present, but they included Eccarius, Jung, and Weston, who had been members since 1864. The Congress was notable only for the speeches of Jung and Eccarius. Jung said that ill-feeling on the General Council had developed since Engels arrived in London in 1870. From then on, Marx ceased to consult his former friends and decided policy jointly with Engels. Jung had been disgusted by Engels's tactics in packing The Hague delegations so as to ensure a favourable decision. Eccarius, who made the last formal speech

[1] The view that Engels was Marx's evil genius was also expressed by Jung at the London Congress which assembled on 26 January 1873, and later by Hyndman, *op. cit.* p. 279, and, to some extent, by Belfort Bax, *Reminiscences and Reflections of a Mid and Late Victorian* (1918), pp. 52-3. Townsend, the old O'Brienite, told Max Beer early in the spring of 1895 that Marx, despite political disagreements, 'always behaved like a gentleman', while Engels was a 'domineering German'. *Fifty Years of International Socialism* (2nd edn., 1937), p. 133.

[2] Letter from Hales, Jung, and de Paepe in *Eastern Post*, 15 February 1873. Vickery admitted the charge, *ibid.* 22 February. The 'official' B.F.C. Minutes for 23 January to 1 February 1873 describe the place of meeting as merely 'Red Lion Court'. From 20 February 1873 they moved to the premises of the Arbeiterbildungsverein at the Eclectic Hall in Denmark St.

to Congress, believed in political action, but it should not, he added, be applied in all countries, irrespective of local conditions. In three countries, England, America, and Switzerland, 'the next great step in the labour movement must be to get working men into the legislature, and this, in the first instance, requires combinations and alliances with the advanced men of the middle classes'.[1] The resolutions of the London Congress inevitably denounced The Hague Congress and called for a British section based on the Nottingham resolutions.

The 'official' Federal Council held its Congress in Manchester on 1 June 1873, by which time it was virtually dead. The story of the British section of the International divided between the two rival Congresses is one of almost uninterrupted decline. For one thing, it is clear that the branches simply did not know what to do and either became or remained discussion groups. The Nottingham branch was exceptional in having a clear-cut outlook and programme which it owed to Thomas Smith. More typical was the Hull branch, which had a programme headed by free education, government control of gin palaces and pawnshops, extension of the franchise, and which concluded with the nationalisation of 'all great commercial undertakings' and the punishment of drunkenness other than by fines.[2] While the General Council remained in London the International had an obvious value to British trade unions, even though their interest and support might not long survive a dispute. But apart from the Liverpool dockers already referred to, there seems no record of British workers approaching the International for aid after The Hague, though the Federal Councils occasionally transmitted information from

---

[1] *Eastern Post*, 8 February 1873. In 1872 Eccarius gave a lecture to the Labour Representation League, with which he had become closely associated. Chairman at the meeting was Thomas Brassey, M.P. Eccarius's address was published as a pamphlet, *The Hours of Labour* (1872), 29 pp. The statistics used and general argument of the pamphlet followed closely the treatment by Marx in *Capital*, i. What Brassey — one of the 'advanced men of the middle classes' — thought of Marx and the International can be seen in his book, *On Work and Wages* (1873), p. 283, where he writes: 'The vague theory of the International Society, founded on atheism and in a narrow and contemptible spirit, acknowledging the existence of only one section of society. . . .'

[2] *International Herald*, 11 January 1873.

Continental workers on strike. Hales wanted to turn the Association into a political party with trade-union affiliations, but the unions were not nearly ready for such commitments. The International might have survived in England as a small political party, conducting propaganda for socialism of the O'Brienite brand. Even for this modest aim, however, the Association would have needed a clear and energetic political leadership which the mutually warring Federal Councils were incapable of providing.[1]

One by one the branches withered and died. Aberdeen, after some initial uncertainty, wrote a declaration of support to the Federal Council for its meeting of 6 February 1873.[2] But by the time of the Manchester Congress it was nearly extinct,[3] and many of its members had turned to Bradlaugh's republicanism as an alternative. The story of the Nottingham branches was more complex. As early as February the Central branch found difficulty in obtaining premises, though it assumed a variety of names. It had forty-two members and its associated Labour Protection League, appealing for trade-union support, had fifty. This, thought the branch secretary, was disappointingly low, due to the 'employers not attempting to either reduce wages or alter the working hours'. Then the Amalgamated Society of Engineers, of which the writer, S. L. Parker, was a member had forbidden its members to affiliate, despite the services of the League 'in the Nine Hours struggle as well as in the wage question'.[4] The branch further suffered competition, like a number elsewhere, including Aberdeen, from the National Republican Brotherhood, an eccentric and ephemeral body set up as a rival to Bradlaugh's republican

[1] For the very similar attempt by Professor Beesly to lay the foundations of an independent working-class party in the early 1870s, see the essay by R. Harrison in this volume, especially pp. 228-30. At least on this important matter there seems to be no evidence of political contact between Beesly and the Hales group. [Editors.]

[2] *International Herald*, 15 February 1873. The Aberdeen secretary at this time was William Stephen, author of a pamphlet entitled *Communism*, which advocated the 'Communism of Christ'.

[3] See the letter to Aberdeen from the B.F.C., probably by Alfred Days, no date, but almost certainly May 1873.

[4] S. L. Parker to S. Vickery, 28 February 1873. Parker was referring to the assistance given by the General Council to the A.S.E. in August 1871 during the Nine Hours strike in Newcastle.

movement by John De Morgan and Thomas Smith.[1] On 21 May Parker wrote again to say that the Labour Protection League had collapsed, its surviving strength, in the silk hose trade, having been sapped by a wage increase extracted from Samuel Morley. The Central branch survived the collapse of the Labour Protection League, and still existed at the time of the Manchester Congress, but it seems to have been sickly. The Nottingham French branch went through a crisis in April when a former member of its committee, Leuliette, formed a rival French section which established contact with the Juras Federation and Hales's Federal Council.[2] This was, no doubt, connected with the expulsion of seventeen members a few weeks later, which left the 'official' Nottingham French branch with twenty members.[3]

The developments at Leicester illustrate the way in which the split at the centre was affecting the local branches. In Leicester the Internationalists established close relations with the republican club, which was said to have five hundred members, and its secretary wrote to the Federal Council to ask for conditions of affiliation.[4] Randle, secretary of the International branch, wrote enthusiastic letters to the Council on 12 March and 9 April, when he reported that the decision to affiliate had been taken, and emphasised the possibilities this opened up of links with Loughborough and Nottingham and a resulting propaganda drive in the villages of the East Midlands. Abruptly the Republicans' decision to affiliate was reversed. Following a visit by Thomas Mottershead (an active trade unionist and member of the B.F.C., who had also been responsible for the decision of Liverpool to side with Hales) their secretary, Hill, became extremely hostile and successfully opposed the affiliation to what he described as a 'secret society'.[5]

Manchester also suffered in the same way, though the

[1] *National Reformer*, 8, 15, 22 December 1872 and 26 January 1873.
[2] Letter in French from Leuliette to the 'official' B.F.C. dated 27 March, and the Council's reply, B.F.C. Minutes, 13 April 1873. See also *Eastern Post*, 12 April 1873.
[3] Charles Hazard to B.F.C., 21 April 1873.
[4] Joseph Hill to B.F.C., 9 February 1873.
[5] Randle to Vickery, 23 May 1873.

foreign section was able to keep going, with a membership of eighteen, until after the Manchester Congress in June, for the organisation of which it was largely responsible. The story was very different in Manchester's Central branch. Jones wrote to say that despite weekly meetings, 'we have been in a state of lethargy for some months'. 'The unfortunate quarrel that you had in London had a very detrimental effect on our work in Manchester.'[1] On 27 May, on the eve of the Manchester Congress, Jones's successor, McDermott, sent in the affiliation fees for only twelve members of the once-flourishing Manchester Central section.

A momentary exception to the general tendency towards disintegration and collapse was provided by the Woolwich branch, which flickered briefly into activity when the workers at the Siemens plant in Charlton went on strike for the payment of special night rates. H. G. Maddox, secretary of the branch, wrote to the Federal Council on 6 February 1873, to report that eight to ten Germans had been introduced into the works, with more expected. The branch established friendly relations with the Germans, who refused to work overtime and sent a message to Berlin warning others not to follow. But on 30 March Maddox had to report that while the strike had been completely successful, the branch had almost collapsed, as 'in this town of Government Hacks anything in advance of what is termed Liberalism has no favour with the men'. On 3 April Maddox, together with a friend, attended the Federal Council to explain that 'owing to the fear of Government pressure the men would not take any active part in the I.W.A.'.[2]

The Manchester Congress in June was a pathetic affair, representing an organisation that had largely ceased to exist.[3] The *International Herald* published its last issue on 18 October 1873. Members of the Council continued to meet in 1874, but Marx wrote to Sorge on 4 August that the British section of the International was 'as good as dead for the present. The

---

[1] Undated, but probably late February 1873.
[2] B.F.C. Minutes. James T. Brownlie, first President of the A.E.U., once told G. D. H. Cole that the Woolwich branch of the Social Democratic Federation claimed descent from the local branch of the International.
[3] *Manchester Guardian*, 3 June 1873.

Federal Council exists as such only in name, although some of its members are active individually.'

Hales's Federal Council achieved, for a short time, a network of branches in East London — City Road, Hackney, Bethnal Green, Limehouse, and Stratford — while in the provinces they had Liverpool, and may have established branches in Greenock and Leicester,[1] but little was heard of them after the middle of the year. In August 1873 Hales and Eccarius attended the Geneva anarchist Congress, both representing their Federal Council, though Hales, in addition, claimed a mandate from Liverpool. Though agreeing with their hosts on federalism, they could agree on nothing else, and when Eccarius alone attended the anarchist Congress in Brussels in the following year, he attacked anarchism as a scheme to restore the Middle Ages, 'where the corporations fought each other'.[2] There was no English delegate at the Berne anarchist Congress of 1876.

Marx and Engels watched the decline of the International in England with indifference. After The Hague they had taken no part in its work, except to attack the Hales secession. So far as they were concerned, the International was over for the moment. One day it would revive, purer and stronger. Until that day came, it could remain in suspended animation in New York, where it would escape the Bakuninist contagion. In England, the trade unions could be written off as a political force and without them the O'Brienites were pointless. For the rest, Marx and Engels would endorse Barry's view of them as tiresome cranks.

Abandoned by their leaders and isolated from international contact except for an occasional letter from New York or the Juras Federation, the English socialists in both camps had fought on for a brief spell. With booming trade, politically neutral trade unions, and with Bradlaugh's republican agitation competing successfully for what radical energy there was, the

---

[1] *Eastern Post*, 11 January, 1 and 29 March, 18 and 25 May 1873.

[2] *Daily News*, 18 August 1873. *Compte-Rendu officiel du Sixième Congrès Général de l'Association Internationale des Travailleurs* (Geneva, 1873), p. 30 ; *Compte-Rendu . . . du VIIe Congrès . . . Bruxelles, septembre 7-13, 1874*, p. 180.

cause was hopeless. But their work was not lost. In his essay on Riley, Edward Carpenter was to write of him as one of the small band 'whose names are now unknown or forgotten' but who 'did a great work in their time, bridging over the interval between the old Chartism of '48 and the Socialism of the early eighties'.[1] James MacDonald, later secretary of the London Trades Council, was introduced to socialism by Adam Weiler. E. Belfort Bax, a leading member of the Socialist League and the Social Democratic Federation, attributed his conversion to Weiler and Hermann Jung.[2] Writing in the time of the Second International, George Lansbury affirmed: 'My adviser and friend was John Hales. . . . Hales told me about the International and taught me the need of working-class solidarity . . . most of these men lived the latter part of their lives in the odour of sanctity of the Liberalism of Mr. Gladstone and died therein; nevertheless, they deserve honour because they helped establish the First International, and by so doing made the present International possible.'[3]

[1] *Op. cit.* pp. 205-9.
[2] *How I Became a Socialist*, published by the Social Democratic Federation (1896).
[3] George Lansbury, *My Life* (1928), pp. 31-2.

8

E. P. THOMPSON

HOMAGE TO TOM MAGUIRE *

As the writing of labour history becomes more professionalised, so the centre of interest shifts from front-line engagements to the disputes and strategical plans of G.H.Q. In the Colindale Library, the Public Record Office, the national archives of trade unions, the Place or Webb Collections, the techniques proper to a constitutional or economic historian can be employed. The dubious reminiscences of local worthies can be disregarded (unless required for 'colour'), the regional skirmishes can be dismissed with an irritable footnote, and the historian can get down in earnest to national minute-books, Congress proceedings, intrigues among the leadership, and underhand political agreements.

And yet — how far are the techniques of the political or constitutional historian adequate to deal with the tensions and lines of growth in movements which (until the highly bureaucratised post-1945 era) have always been exceptionally responsive to problems of local social and industrial context — local splits and breakaways — ground-swells of opinion at the rank-and-file level?

The national historian still tends to have a curiously distorted view of goings-on 'in the provinces'. Provincial events are seen as shadowy incidents or unaccountable spontaneous upheavals on the periphery of the national scene, which the London wire-pullers try to cope with and put into their

* In collecting material for this essay I am indebted to Mrs. Florence Mattison (the widow of Alf Mattison), Miss Norah Turner (daughter of Sir Ben Turner), and Mr. A. T. Marles, first secretary of the Leeds Fabian Society, for help, information, and the loan of documents. Among other debts I must mention the kindness of the librarians or officials of the Brotherton Library, Leeds; the Bradford Trades Council; the Bradford Independent Labour Party; and the Colne Valley Labour Party.

correct historical pattern. And provincial leaders are commonly denied full historical citizenship ; if mentioned at all, they are generally credited with various worthy second-class abilities, but rarely regarded as men with their own problems, their own capacity for initiative, and on occasions a particular genius without which national programmes and new political philosophies can never be wedded to movements of men. Hence labour historians tend to fall into a double-vision ; on the one hand, there are the mass movements which grow blindly and spontaneously under economic and social pressures : on the other, the leaders and manipulators — the Places, the Chartist journalists, the Juntas and parliamentarians — who direct these elemental forces into political channels. And where this superficial national approach is beginning to give way to a more mature school of local history, employing sociological techniques, nevertheless we still find that the national and local pictures are rarely put together.

The early years of the I.L.P. provide a striking example of this. The I.L.P. grew from the bottom up : its birthplaces were in those shadowy parts known as 'the provinces'. It 'was created by the fusing of local elements into one national whole. From the circumference its members came to establish the centre. . . .'[1] Its first council seat was won in the Colne Valley : its first authentic parliamentary challenges came in Bradford and Halifax : its first conference showed an overwhelming preponderance of strength in the North of England :[2] its early directories show this strength consolidated.[3] When the two-party political structure began to crack, and a third party with a distinctively socialist character emerged, this event occurred neither in Westminster nor in the offices of Champion's *Labour Elector* but amongst the mills, brickyards, and gasworks of the West Riding.

[1] J. Clayton, *The Rise and Decline of Socialism in Great Britain* (1926), p. 82.
[2] Of 115 delegates, 24 came from Bradford, 8 from Leeds, 6 from Huddersfield, 3 from Halifax, and 8 from other parts of West Yorkshire. *Report of the First General Conference, I.L.P.* (1893).
[3] Of 305 branches listed in the 1895 Directory, 102 were in Yorkshire, followed by Lancashire (73), Scotland (41), London (29). Of Yorkshire's share we find Bradford (29), Colne Valley (11), Spen Valley (9), Leeds (8), Halifax (8), Huddersfield (8), Dewsbury (5). *I.L.P. Directory* (Manchester, 1895).

Unless we register this fact, it is futile to speculate on the true origins of the I.L.P. Certainly Hardie and Burgess and Blatchford were the foremost propagandists for an independent party of labour. Certainly Champion worked for it, and so did Mahon, the Avelings, and the Hoxton Labour League : so — for that matter — did Hyndman when he first founded the Democratic Federation, and Engels in his *Labour Standard* articles of 1881, and the pedigree is a great deal longer than that.[1] Indeed, there was no lack of prophets. The problem was to translate prophecy into stable organisation and mass enthusiasm. Moreover, local grievances, severe industrial disputes, mass disaffection amongst Liberal voters — these in themselves were not sufficient to bring the thing about. The 1880s saw more than one false dawn — the crofters' struggle, the socialist propaganda among the Northumberland miners during the strike of 1887, the municipal revolt at Bolton in 1887.[2] In every case the socialist pioneers threw their hats in the air ; in every case they retired disappointed and puzzled, as the electorate swung back to old allegiances, the new organisations crumbled, the councillors were re-absorbed by the Great Liberal Party.

The customary national picture of the West Riding breakthrough attributes the emergence of the I.L.P. to one event — the great strike at Manningham Mills, Bradford. Pressed forward blindly by economic hardship and the effect of President McKinley's tariffs, the good-hearted Nonconformist Yorkshire workers turned instinctively to the arms of 'Nunquam' and Keir Hardie. But this will not do at all. It does not explain why a strike at one firm could have become the focus for the discontent of a whole Riding. It does not explain

---

[1] For Champion, see especially H. Pelling, *The Origins of the Labour Party 1880-1900* (1954), pp. 59-64. For Mahon, see E. P. Thompson, *William Morris, Romantic to Revolutionary* (1955), pp. 614-16, where, however, the direct influence of Mahon's 'Labour Union' model upon the Yorkshire labour unions is under-estimated. For forerunners of the 'independent labour' pattern, see above, p. 271, note 1, and his 'Land and Labour League', *Bulletin of the International Institute of Social History, Amsterdam*, 1953.

[2] For Northumberland, see Thompson, *op. cit.* pp. 517 ff. For Bolton, see Dona Torr, *Tom Mann and His Times* (1956), i, pp. 251 ff.

the nature of this discontent. It does not explain why the Yorkshire I.L.P. was so deeply rooted, so stubborn in face of Liberal blandishments, so competently led. It passes over incidents of equal importance to the Manningham strike. It implies an appalling attitude of condescension towards these provincial folk who are credited with every virtue except the capital human virtue of conscious action in a conscious historical role.

If we must counter-pose to this legend our own propositions, then they are these : the two-party system cracked in Yorkshire because a very large number of Yorkshire working men and women took a conscious decision to form a socialist party. The fertilisation of the masses with socialist ideas was not spontaneous but was the result of the work, over many years, of a group of exceptionally gifted propagandists and trade unionists. This work did not begin with street-corner oratory and end with the singing of the 'Marseillaise' in a socialist clubroom, although both of these activities played their part ; it required also tenacity and foresight, qualities of mass leadership and the rare ability to relate theory to practice without losing sight of theory in the press of events. And if we must have one man who played an outstanding role in opening the way for the I.L.P., that man was a semi-employed Leeds-Irish photographer in his late twenties — Tom Maguire.

I

Of course, an individual does not create a movement of thousands : this must be the product of a community. And the West Riding woollen district, in the 1880s, was a distinctive community, with common characteristics imposed by its staple industries, geographical isolation, and historical traditions. Although the population was rapidly swelling and absorbing immigrants,[1] Yorkshire traditions were vigorous, local dialect almanacs still thrived, the *Yorkshire Factory Times* made a feature of dialect stories and verses, and in the more isolated

[1] Census figures : Leeds (1851) 172,000, (1901) 429,000 ; Bradford (1851) 104,000, (1901) 280,000.

areas, like the Colne and Calder and Holme Valleys, memories were long. In such communities, an 'alien agitator' from outside would make little headway ; but once the local leaders moved, the whole community might follow. Leeds, on the western edge of the woollen district, was a more cosmopolitan city, with more diverse industry, a larger professional and clerical population, and a recent influx of Jewish workers into the ready-made clothing trade.[1] New ideas, new national movements, tended to extend their influence to the woollen districts, not directly from London but by way of Leeds ; the textile workers' leaders learnt their socialism from the Leeds and Bradford Socialist Leagues ; Ben Turner, the dialect poet from Huddersfield, was initiated into the movement when he 'flitted' for two years to Leeds.[2]

It is important to recall how far 'independent labour' was already, in the mid-1880s, part of the structure of this community. In one sense, the I.L.P. gave political expression to the various forms of independent or semi-independent working-class organisation which had been built and consolidated in the West Riding in the previous thirty years — co-operatives, trade unions, friendly societies, various forms of chapel or educational or economic 'self-help'. Among these, the co-operative societies were strongest '[3] George Garside, who won the first I.L.P. seat in the Colne Valley was a prominent co-operator.[4] The trade unions were the weakest. In the late sixties or early seventies trades councils existed in Leeds, Bradford, Halifax, Huddersfield, and Dewsbury ; but by the early eighties all had disappeared except for those at Leeds and

[1] See Joan Thomas, *History of the Leeds Clothing Industry* (Yorkshire Bulletin of Economic and Social Research, 1955), Chapter Two.
[2] Ben Turner, *About Myself* (1930), pp. 78-9. Turner had made contact earlier with the S.D.F. and had been attached to a London branch.
[3] Amongst the voluminous local literature, the following are of value in marking the 'independent' tradition : G. J. Holyoake, *History of Co-operation in Halifax* (1864) ; Owen Balmforth, *Huddersfield Industrial Society* (Manchester, 1910) ; and the reminiscences of John Hartley (*Todmorden & District News*, July 1903) and Joseph Greenwood (*Co-Partnership*, September 1909) — both of the strong Hebden Bridge Society.
[4] Garside, born 1843, had a long record in the A.S.E., radical politics, and co-operative productive ventures, before his election to the County Council for Slaithwaite in March 1892 : *Yorkshire Factory Times* (hereafter referred to as *Y.F.T.*), 26 February 1904.

Homage to Tom Maguire

Bradford, and these survived in attenuated form through the support of skilled and craft unions.[1] When the Bradford Trades Council invited the T.U.C. to meet in their home town in 1888, one of the reasons given was 'the fact that the workpeople engaged in the staple industries of the district are in a very disorganised state';[2] a Bradford Congress would boost local morale — as indeed it did, although in unexpected directions. Ben Turner's history of the early years of the textile union is a record of erratic spurts of organising, followed by dissolution and apathy; 'We were all poor folks with poor incomes and poor trade and hadn't the vision that we ought to have had'.[3]

If the 'independence of labour' found expression in some parts of the community's life, there was little evidence of this in the early eighties in the political complexion of the West Riding. It required a new generation, and the new militant unionism, to twist 'self-help' into socialist campaigning. The prevalent tone of the earlier years is one of surfeited, self-satisfied Liberalism. Local papers were busy celebrating the improvements in standards of life since the hungry forties, and recalling for the hundredth time the wisdom of the repeal of the Corn Laws. Local historians, with genuine feeling, commended the passing of the sanded floors and cellar-dwellings and oatmeal diet of the days of the 'poverty-knockers'; and some looked back, almost with nostalgia, to the fiery woolcombers and the Chartist weavers with their torchlight meetings.[4] In March 1885 a gathering of Chartist veterans took

---

[1] Shaftoe, secretary to the Bradford Trades Council, was a skep and basket-maker; Bune, the Leeds secretary, was a brush-maker. In 1880 the Bradford T.C. represented Warpdressers, Stonemasons, Joiners, Plumbers, Lithographers, Engineers, Letterpress Printers, Tailors, Moulders, Hammermen, Dyers, Brush-makers, Skep & Basket-makers, Coach-makers, and Coopers. But six monthly meetings in 1881 were abandoned with 'no quorum' or 'desultory conversation'. (Bradford T. C. Minutes, 24 September 1880 *et seq.*) The Leeds T.C. had 33 societies affiliated in 1883; 25 in 1887. (*Annual Report*, 1894, p. 3.)

[2] Circular, dated 1887, in Shaftoe Cutting-book (in possession of the Bradford T.C.).

[3] Turner, *op. cit.* p. 93.

[4] J. Lawson, *Letters to the Young on Progress in Pudsey* (Stanningley, 1887); F. Peel, 'Old Cleckheaton' in *Cleckheaton Guardian*, 25 January to 4 April 1884.

place in a Halifax temperance hotel; after an 'excellent repast' and an address reviewing the progress of the people since 1844, the best thanks of the meeting were moved 'to Mr. Gladstone and his government for passing into law those principles which we have endeavoured during a long life to enjoy'. The motion was seconded by George Webber, at one time the most intransigent of physical force leaders. 'The majority of those attending the meeting', the report concludes, 'have become men of business and in some cases employers of labour'; and the reporter could not pass over the opportunity for taking their lives as a text for a small piece on the rewards of 'economy, industry, and temperance'.[1] Even Ernest Jones's Chartist stalwarts had found their place in Smiles's Valhalla.

Indeed, it is difficult to recognise the Bradford of Jowett's recollections — squalid back-to-backs, open privy middens, an infant mortality rate (in some districts) of over one in four [2] — in the complacent compilations of a committee originated by Sir Jacob Behrens to inquire into the Condition of the Industrial Classes in 1887.[3] Here the statistics are carefully compiled, the rise in the wages of the skilled workers abundantly proved, the abolition of some of the worst abuses of the forties noted. And yet, less than three years later, not only the *Yorkshire Factory Times*, but also local Liberal and Conservative papers carried exposures of decaying slums, insanitary conditions, appalling social evils.[4] What made the difference?

It is true that a new generation was arising which demanded more of life than had contented their parents. In the 1850s the cramped blocks of back-to-backs were at least a step forward from the cellars, and the warren-like 'folds' of earlier days; in the nineties the ending of all back-to-back building

[1] B. Wilson, *The Struggles of an Old Chartist* (Halifax, 1887), 40 pp., p. 40.
[2] See Jowett's foreword to F. Brockway, *Socialism over Sixty Years* (1946), pp. 13-24.
[3] W. Cudworth, *Condition of the Industrial Classes of Bradford & District* (Bradford, 1887).
[4] See, *e.g.*, *Halifax Guardian* for 12 articles on 'The Slums of Halifax' commencing 17 August 1889. Tom Maguire contributed a series of articles on 'Insanitary Leeds' to the *Leeds Weekly Express*, and see also Maguire and other contributors to *Hypnotic Leeds* (Leeds, 1893), edited by A. Marles.

was to be a leading point in I.L.P. municipal campaigns.[1] But too much influence in this change of outlook should not be attributed to the Education Act of 1870. The I.L.P. strongholds, Bradford and Halifax, were also the strongholds of half-time working; children went into the mills at the age of 10, on passing Standard III, and in Halifax, by a little-known local exemption clause, they could commence work when barely literate.[2] Moreover, in the previous twenty years the enforcement of the Factory Acts in the West Riding had been notorious for its laxity.[3] 12 per cent of those married at Bradford Parish Church in 1887 still signed their names with a cross.[4]

Nor should too much weight be placed upon the argument that the general improvement in trade in the later eighties emboldened the textile workers and placed them in a strong position for strike action and organisation. This was certainly a factor in the success of the Leeds unskilled agitation among the bricklayers' labourers and others. But the textile industry presents a very different picture. The West Riding woollen trade provides a notoriously dangerous field for generalisation, owing to its manifold subdivisions, local variants, and specialised markets; where American tariffs might create chaos in the fine worsted industry of Bradford they would leave Batley, the new 'shoddyopolis', unaffected.[5] Nevertheless, certain

[1] Turner's election address for Batley in 1893 in Turner, *op. cit.* p. 171; 1893 Manifesto of Leeds I.L.P. in T. Paylor, *Leeds for Labour* (Leeds, 1905), etc.

[2] In 1885, 18,312 half-timers worked in the worsted industry alone, 92 per cent in Bradford district (Cudworth, *op. cit.* p. 10); in 1898, 6887 half-timers were employed within the Bradford borough boundaries, and 4086 within Halifax (*The Trade Unionist*, November 1898). On the question of the local exemption standard see the evidence of R. Waddington, secretary of the Half Time Committee of the N.U.T. before the *R.C. on Labour*, 1892, xxxv, Group C, 3662 *et seq.*; and of G. D. Jones, 3855 *et seq.*

[3] An old Birstall lady recalled: 'The mill-owners were very cute in dodging factory inspectors. . . . They had a big whisket handy in the sheds, and when they expected the inspector, we young girls were popped underneath the baskets until he had gone.' *Heckmondwike District News*, 14 August 1926.

[4] Cudworth, *op. cit.* p. 20.

[5] In 1885 North America did not feature among Batley's markets but was the second export market for Bradford's worsteds. *R.C. on Depression of Trade and Industry* (1886) I, pp. 75, 78.

common features may be indicated. (1) Yorkshire employers had been 'spoiled' by the abnormal boom years, 1870-4, a boom to which they looked back, even in the nineties, with nostalgia ; during this period there was a spate of mill-building, inflated valuations, and profits were admitted to be 'inordinately large'.[1] (2) In the ensuing ten years, tariffs (especially in Germany and U.S.A.), keener world competition, and the onset of the 'great depression', led to a marked decline in profits, sharp local competition, and readjustments within the industry ;[2] but despite a falling-off in overtime, and the onset of periods of short time, the volume of trade continued to expand and (as a Leeds observer noted) 'in many trades the *sum of profits* has been to some extent kept up by the *increased volume* of trade'.[3] Between 1886 and 1890 (the year of the McKinley tariff) problems of competition and readjustment were intensified. (3) Throughout these fifteen years (1875-90) we have nothing approaching a depression of the kind met by the cotton industry in the inter-war years of this century. Vast fortunes continued to be amassed, and the brunt of the crisis was borne by the textile workers whose wages declined throughout the period.[4] This decline was effected through direct wage reductions ; increased mechanisation and intensification of labour ; and the increasing proportion of women to male workers in the industry. (4) Thus we have in the wool textile industry of the late eighties an extreme example of the gulf which opened between the labour aristocracy and the

---

[1] Evidence of Mark Oldroyd of the Dewsbury and Batley Chambers of Commerce, *ibid.*, iii, 14,105-7.

[2] Evidence of H. Mitchell of the Bradford Chamber of Commerce, *ibid.*, ii, 3764 *et seq.* The export of raw material and semi-raw material (tops) was compensating for the decline in worsted stuffs.

[3] *Ibid.*, ii, 6494 *et seq.*

[4] The amount of the decline was an endless source of controversy ; but friendly and unfriendly sources agree upon the fact. Cudworth, *op. cit.* p. 41 : 'During the past ten years deductions have been made in wages and quietly submitted to by the workpeople'. See *Y.F.T.*, 20 September 1889 (Leeds wage tables, 1872-89) ; 10 July 1891. *R.C. on Labour*, 1892, xxxv, C, evidence of Gee, Turner and Drew, *passim*, especially 5092, 5124, 5389-5411, 5675 ; 5554 (family wage) ; 5469, 5548-9 (Manningham Mills). For a summary of evidence presented by the weavers' leaders before the Royal Commission, see Tom Mann, *An Appeal to the Yorkshire Textile Workers* (Huddersfield, n.d., ? 1893).

unskilled workers at this time in other industries. Despite a few pockets of organised male aristocrats — power-loom overlookers, card setters, warp dressers, and the like [1] — the bulk of the labour force endured a stationary or declining standard of living. The high proportion of women and juvenile workers, and the variations and jealousies between town and town, mill and mill, and even shed and shed, placed almost insuperable difficulties in the way of trade-union organisation.[2] Men's wages were continually forced down to the level of the women, and throughout the district the custom of the 'family wage' prevailed. (5) In these conditions, general trade unionism could scarcely 'get off the ground' unless backed by exceptional resources. The skilled trade unionists cannot be blamed for indifference ; in 1876 the Bradford Trades Council made a sustained attempt to organise the dyers, but only ten workers attended a well-advertised meeting.[3] The Weavers' Union, consolidated after the Huddersfield strike of 1883, hung on for several years only by the skin of its teeth.[4] It was the enormous publicity provided by the *Yorkshire Factory Times*, founded in 1889, by the successful struggles of the unskilled workers in London and (above all) in Leeds, and the indefatigable activity of socialist and new unionist propagandists which provided the catalyst for the movement of 1890-3.

Even so, a paradox must be noted : it was not the success, but the partial failure — the impossibility of complete success

[1] Minutes of power-loom overlookers in possession of Bradford Trades Council ; Minutes of Card Setters and Machine Tenters in possession of existing union.

[2] It is important to note that even on the crest of the new union wave, with the assistance of the *Yorkshire Factory Times*, only 2 in 9 of the Huddersfield weavers were organised ; 1 in 13 in the heavy woollen district ; and 1 in 16 in the Bradford district. *R.C. on Labour*, 1892, xxxv, C ; evidence of Gee (4790) ; Drew (5455-8) ; Turner (5682-3) ; see Drew's comment (5499) 'when people get down to the pitch to which the textile operatives are in the W. Riding, they have very little heart for anything [and] . . . cannot afford even . . . the subscription.'

[3] Bradford T.C. Minutes, 29 November 1876. See also Walter Bateson, *The Way We Came* (Bradford, 1928) for the assistance given to the dyers by Shaftoe, who 'worked alongside of them as if he was a dye-house worker himself, and not a member of . . . an exceptionally skilled trade — skep-making'.

[4] B. Turner, *Heavy Woollen Textile Workers Union* (Y.F.T., 1917), pp. 61-3.

— in the trade-union field, which turned the textile workers into the channels of independent political action. Had the Manningham Mills strike ended in victory, like the struggles of dockers, gasworkers, and building workers, then Bradford might not have been the birthplace of the I.L.P. Defeat at Manningham, and the precarious nature of the partial organisation achieved elsewhere, were a spur to political action — and for three leading reasons: First, the bitter indignation aroused by economic oppression and social injustice, against which industrial action appeared to provide no effective remedy, was bound to break out in the demand for an independent class party opposed to the parties of the employers. Second, if the causes of poverty could not be removed, its *effects* could be tackled by resolute independent action in the field of local government: hence the great importance of the early campaigns of the I.L.P. in the West Riding on unemployment, against the half-time system, for 'fair contracts', school milk and medical services, on sanitary problems and artisan's dwellings, nursery schools and slum clearance.[1] Third, the complexity and subdivisions of the textile industry, and the preponderance of women and juvenile workers, together with the sub-contracting and 'sweat-shops' in the Leeds tailoring industry — all these gave overwhelming point to the demand for the Legal Eight Hour Day. Political action was seen as the only effective remedy for industrial grievances.[2]

The appeal of the Legal Eight Hour Day had a massive simplicity; it appeared to offer at one blow results which trade-union action could only hope to achieve after many years of hazard and sacrifice; it might go some way towards relieving unemployment as well. Moreover, the demand was in the direct line of the strongest West Riding traditions: Oastler and the Ten Hours Movement: the more recent campaign of the Factory Acts Reform Association, whose efforts to win

[1] The best accounts are in Brockway, *op. cit.* Chapter Two, and M. McMillan, *The Life of Rachel McMillan* (1927), *passim*.
[2] The comparison with the cotton industry, with its strong unionism among the male spinners, and the union leaders' opposition to the Legal Eight Hour Day, is instructive.

the nine-hours day resulted in the 56½ hour week in 1874. The experience of half a century had led Yorkshire workers to believe that arguments that a shorter working day would lead to lower wages and loss of trade to foreign competitors, were no more than employers' propaganda points.[1]

Here we have some of the ingredients from which the West Yorkshire I.L.P. was made. A close-knit community, in which the independence of labour found social, economic, religious expression. An industry facing readjustment and competition. Declining wages and appalling social evils. Tremendous problems in the way of effective trade-union organisation. A strong tradition of campaigning for legal protection in industry and limitation of hours. And to this tradition, another must be added : the tradition of the *political* independence of labour. The Chartist organisation had survived in West Yorkshire as long as in any part of the country. Halifax was Ernest Jones's 'constituency', and while Chartist sentiments were appeased by the adoption of Stansfeld, the friend of Mazzini, as one of the two members in 1859, the flame broke out afresh during the Reform League agitation. Jones stumped the West Riding, addressing enormous crowds ; he was invited to stand both in Dewsbury and Halifax, and although he preferred Manchester, the Halifax men revolted against one of their sitting members, the local mill-owner Akroyd, and sponsored the independent candidature of E. O. Greening, the Co-operator, who achieved the very respectable poll of 2802.[2] This was in 1868 : lads in their 'teens at the time would be scarcely 40 years of age when the I.L.P. was formed. When John Lister contested Halifax for the I.L.P. in 1893 his election manifesto appealed to 'RADICAL HALIFAX', and his supporters recalled the traditions of Greening, Jones, and (local veterans) Ben Rushton and John Snowden, and demanded indignantly

[1] See the evidence of J. H. Beever, secretary of the Halifax Trades Council, when questioned by Mundella at the Royal Commission : 'Well supposing you lost the trade ? — Which I do not think probable. Suppose you did and you had passed an Act of Parliament, what would you do then ? — Past experience does not send us in that direction.' *R.C. on Labour*, 1892, xxxv, C, 10,040-10,047.

[2] Minutes of the Election Committee for Messrs. Greening and Stansfeld, 1868 (in our possession).

whether a 'Whig' should be allowed to sit for such a borough.[1]

All the same, we should not seek for an unbroken independent labour tradition, from Chartism into I.L.P. On its dissolution Greening's election committee handed on its funds to the Halifax Liberal Electoral Association; and were not those man-eating tigers, Geo. Webber and Ben Wilson, toasting Gladstone in lemonade in 1885? In 1884 19-year-old Tom Maguire was writing to the *Christian Socialist*, warning that land nationalisation might prove a diversion from the main assault on the bastions of capitalism, as Corn Law Repeal had proved before:

> Do you not remember, good folk, the Bright and Cobden cry of 'Free Trade and Corn Law Repeal', which along with capitalistic combination, annihilated Chartism, the only genuine political movement of modern times in favour of the people? . . . Ernest Jones and Bronterre O'Brien are forgotten, ridiculed, out of history. John Bright and Richard Cobden are household words.[2]

The surviving Chartists, and many of their sons, had come to terms with Liberal Radicalism; they were (as Engels said) the grandchildren of the old Chartists who were now 'entering the line of battle',[3] rediscovering Chartist traditions from family or local folk-lore or published reminiscences.[4] A quite remarkable proportion of the young men and women prominent in the early Yorkshire I.L.P. claimed Chartist forebears or the influence of Chartist traditions in their childhood.[5] 'Eh, love, you cannot understand now', one Chartist great grandfather

---

[1] John Lister, 'The Early History of the I.L.P. Movement in Halifax', MSS. in the Mattison Collection, Brotherton Library; and Election Manifesto and copy of *Halifax Free Press* in the same collection.

[2] *Christian Socialist*, September 1884.

[3] K. Marx and F. Engels, *Selected Correspondence* (1943 edn.), p. 469.

[4] Ben Wilson, *op. cit.* was published in 1887; J. Burnley's Chartist novel, *Looking for the Dawn* (Bradford, 1874); Frank Peel, *Risings of the Luddites, Chartists and Plugdrawers* (Heckmondwike, 1888). A gentleman named Aurelius Basilio Wakefield, one-time secretary to the Leeds committee of the Labour Representation League, was indefatigable in the 1870s and 1880s, delivering lectures on Ernest Jones.

[5] C. L. Robinson, first I.L.P. councillor in Bradford, had imbibed Chartist principles as a boy, was an admirer of Ernest Jones, and founder of a Republican Club in Bradford in 1870 (*Y.F.T.*, 15 January 1904). See also Tattersall, *Y.F.T.*, 22 July 1892; Ben Riley, *Y.F.T.*, 17 June 1904; Ben Turner, *About Myself*, pp. 28-9, 66; Philip Snowden, *An Autobiography* (1934), i, pp. 18-19.

said to a little girl who was to become a leader of the Bradford textile workers, 'but when you get to be a big girl I want you always to think for the people, and live for the people, for it will be a long time before they can do it for themselves.' [1]

One further ingredient must not be overlooked: Radical Nonconformity. We may leave on one side the futile and unhistorical argument that goes by the name, 'Methodism or Marxism?' The attempt to suggest that the I.L.P. was founded by a slate of Methodist parsons and local preachers is even more wildly inaccurate than the attempt to attribute it to the single-handed efforts of Engels and Aveling. Of those prominent in its formation in Yorkshire, Tom Maguire was an atheist with an Irish-Catholic background; Isabella Ford a Quaker; Ben Turner and Allan Gee (a late convert from Liberalism) were secularists; [2] Alf Mattison was a disciple of Edward Carpenter; John Lister a Catholic; Walt Wood, the gasworkers' leader, would appear to have been a happy pagan — as may have been Paul Bland and Tom Paylor; [3] only Jowett, W. H. Drew, and perhaps Balmforth of Huddersfield, among the initiators of the movement, suggest themselves as active Nonconformists. In truth, Radical Nonconformity had become a retarding social and political influence in the eighties, its face set in a perpetual grimace at the Established Church and the Anglican landed aristocracy; the face was, only too often, the face of a mill-owner, like Alfred Illingworth, the Nonconformist worsted-spinner, whom Tillett fought in West Bradford. The Bradford textile workers owed their socialism no more to the Methodist Church than the peasants of South Italy owe their communism to the Catholic; and if the socialists succeeded in sweeping whole chapel-fulls of the former into the movement, by their broad, unsectarian, ethical appeal, the credit is due to them and not to the Nonconformist 'Establishment' which fought the I.L.P. every inch of the way.

---

[1] *Y.F.T.*, 22 July 1904.
[2] Ben Turner came to regard himself as an undenominational (or perhaps Benturnerite?) Christian, but he never 'belonged' to any Church (information from Miss Norah Turner). For Gee, see *Y.F.T.*, 15 July 1892.
[3] *Y.F.T.*, 5 February 1904, and *Labour Leader*, 20 April 1901, for biographies of Wood and Bland.

Once the break-through had been made, it is true that the movement gained a moral dimension; that Radical Christian tradition, which had been seen before on a Luddite scaffold and in Chartist chapels and camp meetings, swept the West Riding like a revivalist campaign; we meet again the full-toned moral periods, the Biblical echoes, the references to the Sermon on the Mount.[1] It is not a question of creed, belief, or church, but a question of language, a question of moral texture. It was as much a revolt *against* organised Christianity as a form of Christian expression. The Yorkshire I.L.P. was a sturdy cross-bred. Its leaders owed much of their theory to Marxist propagandists; but they preferred the moral exhortations of William Morris to the doctrinaire tones of Hyndman, and they were happier with 'Nunquam' than with Quelch. When they found out that Tillett was a Congregationalist, it made a fine propaganda point with the electorate.[2] But this was not among their reasons for their choice of him as candidate; he was selected as a prominent new unionist and a socialist.[3] Nonconformity — 'Radical' Nonconformity — was outraged. The Bradford and District Nonconformist Association passed a unanimous resolution of confidence in Alfred Illingworth, M.P., the 'widely-esteemed Nonconformist', and a correspondent to the *Bradford Observer* wrote of the I.L.P.'s intervention in terms that suggest they were guilty of sacrilege:

A humble but ardent supporter of a politician whom I regard as a constant and sagacious servant of God and the people, how could I see without sorrow, and I may say horror, the entrance of Mr. Ben Tillett to fasten like a viper on his throat?[4]

Mr. Illingworth's throat now and, the implication runs, God's throat next. The Nonconformist Association called a public

[1] At the mass execution of Luddites in 1813, the prisoners sang Methodist hymns on the scaffold. The outstanding West Yorkshire Chartist leader, Ben Rushton, was an expelled local preacher.
[2] See *Y.F.T.*, 17 July 1891: 'Ben is a deep Christian — an earnest, everyday Christian. . . . He is at home teaching trades unionism or preaching the religion of Christ.'
[3] When Tillett at first refused to stand, J. Bedford (of the General Railway Workers), E. D. Girdlestone, and G. B. Shaw were each invited to stand. *Y.F.T.*, 15, 22, and 29 May 1891.
[4] *Bradford Observer*, 9 and 13 June 1892.

meeting in support of both, with a pride of reverends on the platform. Tillett's followers packed the meeting, and Drew and Pickles intercepted Jowett — on his way to a Co-operative meeting — with the cry: 'You are just the man we want'. At the public meeting, Briggs Priestley, M.P., presided, fresh from an unpopular piece of parliamentary sabotage against a Factory Bill. One after the other, two reverends were shouted down; then the audience stormed the platform, pushing up Jowett, Minty, and Pickles (dubious 'nonconformists', these last two), and remaining in uproar until Jowett was allowed to move an amendment. Impressively he warned the clergy: 'If you persist in opposing the labour movement there will soon be more reason than ever to complain of the absence of working men from your chapels':

The labourers would establish a Labour Church (cheers and 'Bravo Jowett') and there they would cheer for Jesus Christ, the working man of Nazareth (cheers).[1]

The Labour Churches in Bradford and Leeds, when they were established, were not only undenominational; it is also difficult to describe them as Christian or religious in any sense except that of the broad ethical appeal of the 'religion of socialism' whose text was Morris's 'Fellowship is Life'. They retained sufficient ceremonial forms, and a sufficient admixture of Christian speakers, for the Nonconformist members to feel at home; but the 'hymn' might be Maguire's 'Hey for the Day!' and the 'sermon' might be by Edward Carpenter from a text from Whitman. Carpenter's friend and disciple, Alf Mattison, was first secretary of the Leeds Labour Church, while the 'sermon' at the Bradford Labour Church, on the occasion of the foundation conference of the I.L.P., was preached by George Bernard Shaw — a tactful but uncompromising address which ended with the avowal that he was an atheist.[2] We must not under-estimate the importance of the religious associations drawn upon in the speeches of Hardie or Tillett; these reverberated in the hearts of a generation who had picked up their little education in Sunday school or chapel. But these owed

[1] *Ibid.* 14 June 1892; Brockway, *op. cit.* pp. 40-1.
[2] *Bradford Observer*, 16 January 1893.

little to any doctrine of personal salvation or personal sin; the sin was the sin of the capitalist class, and salvation must come through the efforts of the working class itself, expressed through solidarity and brotherhood, and aspiring towards a co-operative commonwealth. Tom Mann, when he stumped Yorkshire, had little Christian charity to spare for non-union men or blacklegs, even though he was willing enough to employ the parable of the Good Samaritan as a scourge on the back of the Ossett Corporation which had let out its scavenging by contract.[1] The broad ethical appeal was the same, whether it was voiced by the Quaker Isabella Ford, or Margaret McMillan ('Educate every child as if it were your own'), or by the free-thinker Charles Glyde: 'I wish to treat all poor as I would my own father, mother, sister, or brother'.[2] In the early nineties this ethical appeal gave fervour, self-confidence, and stamina to the movement; later, when it was taken out of its direct social context and transformed into platform rhetoric by such men as Snowden and Grayson, it was to smudge political understanding and weaken the movement. But in 1892 this authentic moral revolt was one of the first indications to a close observer that the I.L.P. had come to stay: 'it is of the people — such will be the secret of its success'. The letter is from Tom Maguire to Edward Carpenter:

Now the mountain, so long in labour, has been delivered of its mouse — a bright active cheery little mouse with just a touch of venom in its sharp little teeth. . . . Our mouse though young in the flesh is old in the spirit, since to my own knowledge this is its third reincarnation. . . .

You will find in your travels that this new party lifts its head all over the North. It has caught the people as I imagine the Chartist movement did. And it is of the people — such will be the secret of its success. Everywhere its bent is Socialist because Socialists are the only people who have any message for it.[3]

II

No man had worked harder for this than Maguire. Of poor Irish-Catholic parentage, singled out by the priests for his

[1] *Dewsbury Reporter*, 8 June 1895.   [2] *Y.F.T.*, 14 October 1904.
[3] Isabella Ford (ed.), *Tom Maguire, A Remembrance* (Manchester, 1895), p. xii.

intelligence, he had found his own way to secularism at the age of 16, joined the Democratic Federation at 17, was finding his feet as an open-air propagandist and a lecturer in the debating clubs and coffee taverns in his 18th year.[1] J. L. Mahon was in Leeds for a period in 1884, and struck up a friendship with him. When the split in the S.D.F. took place, Maguire sided with Morris and was placed on the Provisional Council of the League. He commenced the work of building a small Leeds branch, while also giving aid to Bland, Minty, and Pickles in Bradford.[2] By October 1885 there were sixteen Leeds socialists in good standing : most were young industrial workers, unemployed or on short time.[3]

He went through the whole gamut of experiences which made up the lives of the 'pioneers'; the open-air work, the occasional big meeting for Morris or Annie Besant, the attacks — especially from his old Catholic associates ('we shall live their narrow fury down', he wrote to Mahon [4]), the week-end outings when propaganda and pleasure were combined,[5] the excitement when the first premises were opened, the songs and cameraderie of the fervent sect.[6] A poet, and a man of great intellectual vigour and curiosity, he was naturally drawn to William Morris's side of the movement. But more than most Socialist Leaguers, he knew that the early propaganda was too abstract to achieve a wide popular appeal. As early as 1884 he singled out the Eight Hours' Day demand as of prime importance;[7] although — as a photographer's assistant — he was not a trade unionist himself, he was directing the Socialist League, in 1885, towards work among the miners and the

[1] *Ibid.* pp. ix-x, xiii : Mattison Letterbook.
[2] For the early history of the Leeds and Bradford Leagues, see also Thompson, *op. cit.* pp. 488, 491-4, 496.
[3] Correspondence of the secretary, Socialist League, in the International Institute of Social History, Amsterdam ; Maguire to Mahon, October and November 1885.
[4] *Ibid.* September 1885.
[5] See E. Carpenter, *My Days and Dreams* (1916), pp. 134-5 ; Mattison Notebooks.
[6] 'The Socialist League stood definitely for a brotherhood built on pure comradeship. . . . The Paris Commune and Chicago Martyrs anniversaries we used to look forward to. . . . Songs and speeches were a feature of those gatherings.' W. Hill to A. Mattison, n.d. in Mattison Letterbook.
[7] *Christian Socialist*, September 1884.

A.S.E.[1] From the maturity of his late twenties he looked back tolerantly upon these years. 'We were kindly, well-disposed young chaps,' he wrote, whose object was 'the Internationalisation of the entire world.' As time went by, and no progress was made (after four years' propaganda the League branch was only 30 strong), the socialists began to divide:

Some thought that we might advantageously limit the scope of our ideal to the five continents, while directing our operations more immediately to our own locality. Others were strongly of the opinion that our ideal was too narrow, and they proposed as the object of the society the internationalisation of the known and undiscovered world, with a view to the eventual inter-solarisation of the planets. . . . They entirely ignored the locality to which, for the most part, they were comparative strangers. . . .[2]

The division so parodied followed closely the division between the anarchists and parliamentarians in the national Socialist League. In the wrangles of 1887 and 1888, the Leeds branch sided with the parliamentarians; after 1888, while the Leeds and Bradford Leagues maintained their link with the national body, sold their quota of *Commonweal*, and regarded William Morris with undiminished affection, they took less and less notice of London goings-on. They subscribed now to Keir Hardie's *Miner*; 2s. 6d. was scraped together for the Mid-Lothian election fund; and while Maguire still contributed poems and articles to *Commonweal*, he also maintained a link with Mahon, who had now broken with the League and who produced in 1888 his blueprint for a labour party, *The Labour Programme*.[3] After the Bradford T.U.C. of the same year, the Yorkshire Socialist Leaguers directed their energies towards the two main objectives: the conversion of the trade unions, and propaganda for an independent party of labour. 'A definite step is now being taken towards the formation of a Socialist Labor Party in Leeds', declared a handbill of autumn 1888, which announced lectures by Maguire on 'The Need of a Labor Party', and by Tom Paylor on 'The Lesson of the

[1] See Maguire, 'The Yorkshire Miners', *Commonweal*, November 1885.
[2] *Y.F.T.*, 4 November 1892.
[3] *Commonweal*, 28 April 1888; Thompson, *op. cit.* pp. 614-15. Jowett was advocating an independent Labour Party in 1887 (*Bradford Observer*, 8 February 1887).

Trades Congress'.[1] When Mahon and H. A. Barker launched their Labour Union, Maguire and Pickles (of Bradford) were among the signatories.[2] After Maguire's death, a correspondent in the *Yorkshire Factory Times* commented on the breadth of his reading and the volume of propaganda work which he undertook in these years — 'Three lectures each Sunday, and two, and occasionally three, in the course of the week, in addition to articles, poems, and letters to the press'.

The propaganda gained growing audiences in the coffee taverns, Radical clubs, and at the 'open-air spouting place' — Vicar's Croft. But the Leeds Trades Council was a stronghold of the Liberal skilled unionists, and — except in the A.S.E. — no headway could be made. The break-through, when it came, came in spectacular fashion. Some bricklayers' labourers, attending an open-air meeting, stayed on to discuss their grievances ('rather aimlessly') with Paylor and Sweeney. The Leaguers offered their clubroom for a committee meeting of the men on the next Sunday. On 30 June 1889 3000 labourers attended a meeting at which they were addressed by Maguire, Paylor, and other socialists; 200 names were handed in for the new union; a committee elected; within a week several thousand labourers were on strike for a ½d. an hour (from 5d. to 5½d.); within five weeks the union was 800 strong, and the strike had ended in victory.[3] A week later the great Dock Strike in London began.

It is a comment upon the divorce between the skilled unionists and the unskilled that the labourers turned to the socialists rather than to the Leeds Trades Council, on which the skilled building unions had long been represented. From the outset the skilled unionists in Leeds regarded the socialist intervention with undisguised hostility, while even the *Yorkshire Factory Times* published a grumbling, suspicious editorial.[4]

---

[1] Handbill in Mattison Collection. [2] Thompson, *op. cit.* pp. 615-16.
[3] Maguire's notes in *Commonweal*, 10 August and 16 November 1889; Thompson, *op. cit.* pp. 618-20; *Y.F.T.*, 2 August 1889. Tom Paylor was at this time an insurance agent; Sweeney a boot and shoe worker.
[4] It complained at the new unions which accepted as leaders 'outsiders who may have some other object in view than the sole interest of the workers. Joined by a few malcontents from other associations these are organizing attacks on the old and tried officials of the Congress.' *Y.F.T.*, 30 August 1889.

The socialists for their part were elated, and were not above rubbing salt in the wound: 'We are endeavouring to organise the unskilled labourers in all branches of industry in the town, since the aristocrats of labour take no steps in organising them'.[1] But no one anticipated the nearly incredible surge of unskilled agitation which engulfed the West Riding in the next twelve months. Trade was brisk, and Maguire repeatedly urged the workers to seize their opportunity; in December he was addressing a demonstration of the newly formed Leeds section of the Gasworkers and General Labourers Union (embracing already gasworkers, maltsters, draymen, general labourers, dyers, and claiming a membership of 3000) and urging them to press home their advantage while the employers 'could not afford to tarry';[2] a month later he was exhorting a meeting of clayworkers and brickyard labourers 'to go with the flowing tide'.[3] Mattison, the young skilled engineer, helped out the Gasworkers as secretary; he recalled later the shock of surprise when Will Thorne came up to help, with his heavy navvy's boots and knotted red handkerchief.[4] Week after week, Maguire, Paylor, Sweeney, Cockayne, and Turner attended demonstrations, assisted strikes, presided at the formation of new unions: tramway workers, blue dyers, corporation workers, plasterer's labourers, paviour's labourers, mechanic's labourers, axle workers. In October 1889 900 girls struck at Messrs. Arthur's tailoring works, against the deduction of 1d. out of every 1s. earned in payment for motive power on their sewing-machines; despite the selfless assistance of Isabella Ford[5] and Maguire, and the ambiguous support of the Trades Council,[6] the strike ended after the sixth week

---

[1] *Commonweal*, 6 July 1889.   [2] *Y.F.T.*, 13 December 1889.
[3] *Ibid.* 20 December 1890.
[4] *Leeds Weekly Citizen*, May 1931.
[5] I. O. Ford came from a wealthy Quaker family at Adel Grange, near Leeds. She had helped Miss Paterson with the Women's Provident League. In the summer of 1888 she assisted the Weavers' Union during a strike in Leeds, and from that time forward was associated with all the new union struggles involving women. *Report and Balance Sheet of the West Riding Power Loom Weavers Association*, September 1888; and *Y.F.T.*, 1 November 1889.
[6] *Y.F.T.*, 1 November 1889, and (for Sweeney's criticisms of the Trades Council officials) 10 January 1890.

in a sad collapse.¹ But the defeat scarcely checked the advancing wave of unionism. In late October 1889 the Leeds Tailors' Union (catering at first chiefly for Jewish workers) was formed, with Maguire in the chair.² The Tailoresses' Union continued to grow, with the particular assistance of Isabella Ford. When some 3000 tailoring workers went on strike, Maguire was adviser, organiser, and poet, writing for them 'The Song of the Sweater's Victim', 'the singing of which by several hundred Jews in their broken English may be better imagined than described':

> . . . every worker in every trade,
> In Britain and everywhere,
> Whether he labour by needle or spade,
> Shall gather in his rightful share.³

In March these new unions still remained outside the Trades Council, and had grouped in a new body called the 'Yorkshire Labour Council'.⁴ The first May Day in Leeds was celebrated by this Council, in association with the Gasworkers. The procession alone was estimated at 6000, headed by the banner of the Leeds Jewish Tailors, Pressers, and Machinists: a band playing the 'Marseillaise': 1100 Jewish tailors: 900 slipper-makers: 800 gasworkers: dyers, maltsters, teamsters, and labourers. Between the slipper-makers and the gasworkers there marched the smallest and proudest contingent — 40 members of the Leeds Socialist League. Maguire presided at the main platform, where the demonstration was swelled by several thousand, and a resolution passed endorsing the 'necessity of an Eight Hour Day . . . as the first step towards the abolition of national and industrial war; the overthrow of race hatred; and the ultimate emancipation of Labour'.⁵ The Annual Report of the Leeds Trades Council for 1890 mentions neither May Day nor the gas strike (!), but recorded the Council's resolution in October (on a small majority

---

¹ Y.F.T., 25 October 1889 to 27 December 1889.
² Ibid. 1 November 1889.
³ Tom Maguire, a Remembrance, p. xvi; slide of the song in Mrs. Mattison's possession.
⁴ Y.F.T., 7 and 28 March 1890.
⁵ Ibid. 9 May 1890; Leeds Weekly Citizen, May 1931.

vote) 'that a general Eight Hour's legislative measure is impracticable'.[1]

Maguire, Paylor, Mattison — all were in their early twenties when this sudden elevation from the status of a sect to that of leaders and advisers to the unskilled of half a populous county took place. They had no national advisers. Morris was retiring in disgust from the anarchist playground which the London League was becoming; anyway, he was writing 'News from Nowhere', which his Leeds followers read eagerly in the odd half-hours spared from union organising [2] — although he found time to deliver his last notable address for the League, on 'The Class Struggle', in Leeds in March 1890. It is a noble and far-seeing lecture, but its only practical proposal was that a General Strike for socialism might be the best next step — for which advice Maguire and Paylor moved a hearty vote of thanks.[3] Forty miles away, at Millthorpe, Edward Carpenter watched events with awe; he had no advice to offer, and his influence upon the Leeds socialists made itself felt in other ways.[4] Cunninghame Graham helped with a fleeting visit, as did Thorne. The only national figure who kept his finger on events in Leeds was Maguire's old friend, J. L. Mahon of the Labour Union; and his reputation was much tarnished by the failure of the London Postmen's Union.[5] The Leeds and Bradford socialists were virtually detached from London and thrown upon their own resources; in May 1889 they held a joint demonstration at the famous Chartist meeting-spot, Blackstone Edge, with the Lancashire branches of the S.D.F.;[6] in July of the same year a Yorkshire Socialist Federation was set up.[7] But their own resources were not

[1] Leeds T.C. *Annual Report* for year ending 31 May 1891, p. 6.
[2] It appeared in instalments in *Commonweal* throughout 1890.
[3] *Leeds Mercury*, 26 March 1890; Thompson, *op. cit.* pp. 632 ff.
[4] On 12 March 1890, in the midst of the new union struggles, Carpenter was writing to Mattison: 'An interesting book has turned up, by Havelock Ellis, called The New Spirit — on Whitman, Tolstoi, Ibsen, Heine, & others. Everything seems to be rushing on faster & faster. Where are we going? Niagara, or the Islands of the Blest?' Mattison Collection.
[5] See Thompson, *op. cit.* pp. 652-3. Mahon and Donald addressed the first demonstration of the Leeds gasworkers, *Y.F.T.*, 13 December 1889.
[6] *Commonweal*, 4 May 1889; *Leeds Weekly Citizen*, 29 April 1929.
[7] *Ibid.* 10 August 1889.

slender. The years of seemingly fruitless propaganda, when the joint forces of Leeds and Bradford socialism had tramped like a group of youth hostellers, spreading 'the gospel' in villages and singing Morris's songs in country lanes,[1] had not been wasted. Maguire and Jowett, in their very early twenties, both showed astonishing maturity; they had gained a fund of experience, a clear theory of politics, and a self-confidence and *élan*, which prepared them for those vintage years, 1889-92, when (in Ben Turner's words) 'it was not alone a labour of love, but a labour of joy, for the workers seemed awake'.[2]

The climax to Leeds new unionism, and the final proof of the ability of Maguire's small group, came in the gas strike (or lock-out) of June-July 1890. The rapid organisation of the previous winter had won, without a struggle, sweeping gains for the men, including the eight-hour day. In the summer of 1890, when the demand for gas fell off, the Gas Sub-Committee of the Liberal-dominated municipal council, determined to counter-attack with all the forces at its command, and to enforce the withdrawal of certain concessions.[3] A short, but violent and extremely ill-tempered, struggle ensued. The Gas Committee alienated general working-class and much middle-class sentiment by its stupid and high-handed tactics, particularly its elaborate attempts to displace local men by blacklegs imported (often under false pretences) from great distances and at great cost to the ratepayers. Worse, it made itself ridiculous in a hundred ways; the villain in the public eye was its chairman, Alderman Gilston, well known for his Radical Home Rule speeches and his claims to be a 'friend of the working classes'; another Liberal councillor set Leeds laughing by his renderings of 'Rule Britannia' for the entertainment of blacklegs temporarily housed in the Town Hall crypt. Ridicule grew as those few blacklegs who were transported to the gasworks turned out to be incapable of performing the work, or asked to be sent home at the town's expense. At

[1] See F. W. Jowett, *What Made Me a Socialist* (Bradford, n.d.).
[2] Turner, *About Myself*, p. 80.
[3] For the full case of the Gas Committee and the union's reply see the letters exchanged between Ald. Gilston and Tom Paylor in the *Leeds Mercury*, 27 and 28 June 1890.

the height of the struggle, a ludicrous procession moved through the surging crowds in the town centre; several hundred blacklegs, headed by cavalry, surrounded by a double file of police, and a file of military, and followed by the Mayor and magistrates. As they passed beneath the Wellington Road railway bridge, coal, sleepers, bricks, bottles, and assorted missiles were hurled down by pickets and sympathisers upon the civic procession. Arriving in the New Wortley gasworks in a 'very excited and exhausted state', the blacklegs at once held an indignation meeting in protest against their inadequate protection. Then — when pickets climbed on the walls to shout — they fled over the rear walls 'by the dozen' until only 76 remained inside. For several days the town was like an armed camp. On one side, Hussars with drawn swords patrolled the streets in defence of the Liberal Gas Committee; on the other, railwaymen, corporation workers, and even (it would seem) individual policemen, combined to give information to the pickets. When the strikers returned, with almost complete victory, it was estimated that the affray had cost the town £20,000.[1]

Maguire and Paylor, and their leading converts among the gasworkers, Walt Wood and Cockayne, bore the brunt of the struggle. They tried

to get the crowd into peaceful ways, but blood was shed nevertheless. In the morning after the first night of the riots, it was a sight to see the leaders of the union telling the members off to duty, arranging picketing work, and getting the men who had been deceived . . . off home.[2]

Maguire, rather than Thorne, deserved the copy of *Capital* which Engels gave to the victor of the struggle.[3] Moreover, in the height of the struggle he saw his political opportunity, and struck home hard. He addressed both of the mass demonstrations on the two Sundays of the strike, and drove home the lesson of the independence of labour. If the Leeds Gas Committee persisted in their course, he said, 'the Liberal party of

---

[1] The best accounts of the strike are to be found in the *Leeds Mercury*; *Commonweal* also carried (very strident) reports written by an anarchist.
[2] *Y.F.T.*, 5 February 1904; *Tom Maguire, a Remembrance*, p. xv.
[3] W. Thorne, *My Life's Battles* (1925), p. 131 f.

the town would get such a knockdown blow as they would never recover from. . . .' How long (he asked) are the working classes of this town 'going to return people to the Council who, when returned, use the forces of the town against the working classes?'[1] From this point on, many skilled unionists in Leeds began to turn away from Liberalism.[2]

If the first strong link in the chain which led to the I.L.P. was forged in the gas strike, it also led to the breaking of the last link which bound the Leeds socialists to the Socialist League. The occasion was a quarrel in the local club. 'Those of us who had to do with the gasworkers, in response to the men's wishes and in accordance with our ideas of policy, considered a Labour Electoral League should be formed', Maguire wrote to Carpenter. 'Our Anarchist friends, who were conspicuous by their absence in the gas fights', 'told the people that no policy should be entertained but physical force':

> I admit the Labour Electoral move is not all to be desired, but it seemed the next immediate step to take in order to keep the Labour unions militant, and to emphasise the conflict of the workers and the employers.

The incident disgusted him: 'as usual with Socialists when they fall out, all kinds of personal attacks and insinuations have been the order of the day'.[3]

The majority of the Leeds socialists went out with Maguire, to be followed, shortly after, by the Bradford Socialist League. Both groups formed socialist clubs, and soon, as a more stable form of organisation, these adopted a Fabian disguise; over the next year a rash of Fabian Societies spread across West Yorkshire, until the London Fabians became quite uneasy at

---

[1] *Leeds Mercury*, 30 June 1890.
[2] Arthur Shaw of the A.S.E., President of Leeds Trades Council in 1894 and 1896, relates how — before the gas strike — he 'worked with ardour and perseverance for the success of the Liberal Party'. During the strike he witnessed a Liberal Councillor and 'professed friend of Labour' entertain the blacklegs 'with "Britons never shall be slaves"'. Other Liberals provided them with beer and tobacco, while at the same time the Leeds gasworkers were provided with military, as another mark of Liberal friendship. This decided me. I vowed I would never again assist either of the Political Parties.' J. Clayton (ed.), *Why I Joined the Independent Labour Party* (Leeds, n.d.).
[3] *Tom Maguire, a Remembrance*, p. xi.

the threatened permeation.[1] But the Fabian Society offered no more prospect for turning the mass industrial unrest into political channels than had the Socialist League; and it was only with the formation of the Bradford Labour Union that the political wing of the movement got under way. 'I thought of a new move', recalled James Bartley, then a sub-editor on the *Workman's Times*, who initiated the first meeting :

On Sunday, April 26th, 1891, I took the first steps for putting it into operation. That particular Sunday . . . was a bright sunshiny day. I went to Shipley . . . in order to consult Mr. W. H. Drew. . . . He was attending anniversary services at Bethel Baptist Chapel, but during a lull in the proceedings I called him out to the chapel-yard. Here we talked over the situation. . . .[2]

When the Bradford Labour Union was finally founded in May it was under the heading Independent Labour Party. 'Suddenly a name was coined that hit off the genius of the English people', Maguire later said. From this moment it 'went like wildfire'.[3] Why was its birthplace Bradford and not Leeds?

III

Leeds was to provide a remarkable example of arrested development. Despite its early vigour, the movement met repeated barriers; the first authentic I.L.P. councillor in Leeds was not elected until 1906, when Jowett had already done fourteen magnificent years of service on the Bradford Council — eight miles away! But if we note the social and industrial contrasts, some of the reasons become apparent. Leeds was not as close-knit a community as other West Yorkshire towns : its industries were more diverse. The unskilled

[1] By the end of 1892 there were Fabian Societies at Batley, Bradford, Copley (near Halifax), Halifax, Holmfirth, Huddersfield, Leeds, and Sowerby Bridge; Castleford and Dewsbury were added before May 1893. *List of Members* (Fabian Society, October 1892) and *Tenth Annual Report* of Fabian Society, April 1893. A correspondent in the *Labour Leader*, 20 April 1901, notes that the Bradford Socialist League 'afterwards merged into the Bradford Socialist Society and finally became a branch of the Fabian Society'. The Halifax Fabian Society was especially effective in its propaganda; see Lister MSS. History.
[2] *Labour Leader*, 13 April 1901.
[3] *Dewsbury Reporter*, 13 October 1894.

male workers were in general successful in improving their conditions as a result of the new unionism, and some of their discontent was dispersed : the gas strike was short, sharp, and victorious where that at Manningham Mills was long, humiliating, and a defeat. Social antagonisms were modified by the interpolation of many intermediate strata between the mass of the workers and employers, including those skilled workers who owed a traditional allegiance to Lib-Labism.

It is this last fact, above all, which accounts for the failure of the Leeds I.L.P. to gather the momentum of Bradford. Although the new unions affiliated to the Trades Council after the gas strike, and the Yorkshire Labour Council was dissolved,[1] the old guard on the Trades Council maintained a controlling influence. In September 1891 they seemed to be drawing together, with a successful mass demonstration addressed by Mann and Tillett; and a Labour Electoral Union was sponsored by the Council, on independent lines.[2] But the Trades Council insisted on maintaining the right of veto over the Labour Union, and the old guard sought to exercise this in the Liberal interest; finally, in 1892, it severed its connection with the Union, which became the Leeds I.L.P.[3] Hence the impressive unity between Trades Council and I.L.P. which was the leading feature of developments in Bradford, Halifax, and the heavy woollen district was never to be found in Leeds.

This political friction was only to be expected in a centre where the Trades Council had a history covering a quarter-century, and the leaders of the skilled unions had a place in the Liberal firmament. But the problem was aggravated by socialist errors and accidents of person. In 1890 Maguire's old friend, J. L. Mahon, returned to Leeds. Maguire had defects as a political leader — he was without personal ambition

[1] At the same time the Leeds T.C. changed its name to the Trades and Labour Council.
[2] Leeds Trades Council, *Annual Report*, 1892, pp. 1-2, 6. This was the successor to the Labour Electoral Association which had been founded after the gas strike, with Maguire as secretary and the formidable old unionist, Judge, as treasurer. *Y.F.T.*, 18 July 1890, and for Judge, 1 July 1892.
[3] *Annual Report*, 1893, p. 5.

and incapable of political guile. In the intervals between storms (when necessity drove him to the front) he preferred to advise from the background.[1] He allowed Mahon — who shared none of his dislike of the limelight — to assume the leadership of the Leeds movement; perhaps he was glad to be relieved of the responsibility he had borne for so long.

Mahon was a man of great ability : the idea of Labour Unions was largely his. He had done stalwart service for the Socialist League in the past. But now his many defects were gaining on his virtues. He was vain, incurably quarrelsome, and given to intrigue, and he inspired neither loyalty nor trust. It would be tedious to recount the rows that gathered around him between 1890 and 1893. He wrangled inside the Gasworkers' Union :[2] he was prominent in a sensational row between the Gasworkers and the Trades Council over the School Board election of November 1891 :[3] he allowed himself to be drawn into a long and unsavoury public quarrel with John Judge, the leader of the old unionists.[4] Finally, he allied himself wholeheartedly with Champion's attempt to 'nobble' the I.L.P. in 1892. He flaunted Tory 'sympathies' in an attempt to shock Liberal working men from their allegiance.[5] With Champion's money, and under Champion's day-to-day direction, he stood as Independent Labour candidate for South Leeds in September 1892 — a by-election which ended in riot and anticlimax, but which did as much as anything to raise the well-justified taunt of 'Carlton Club money' which hung around the I.L.P. at its foundation conference.[6] 'What a cunning chap he is,' Carpenter wrote to Mattison, — 'I can't say I like him. I wonder how Maguire feels about it all.'[7]

[1] 'I'll retire into the corner and write poetry', he declared after the gas strike (*Tom Maguire, a Remembrance*, p. xii). See also letter quoted in Thompson, *op. cit.* p. 703 n. 1 : 'Tom . . . sinks his own individuality and allows other people to run away with his ideas', etc.

[2] Mahon was elected paid assistant secretary of the Yorkshire District of the Gasworkers on a slender majority vote in July 1891. *Y.F.T.*, 10 July 1891.

[3] *Y.F.T.*, 20 November 1891. [4] *Ibid.* 26 February 1892.
[5] Information from Mr. A. T. Marles.
[6] See Note on the South Leeds Election, pp. 315-6.
[7] Edward Carpenter to Alf Mattison, 2 October 1892, Mattison Collection.

But Maguire's opinions are not recorded. Mahon and Champion between them nearly succeeded in smashing the I.L.P. on the eve of its foundation; and yet Maguire's old friendship for Mahon, and his hatred for personal rancour and intrigue, led him to retreat into his shell.[1]

In the woollen districts the development was quite different. Here the origins were less spectacular: but when the movement began in earnest, the entire trade-union movement swung round behind it. In 1886 that other remarkable young Yorkshire socialist, Ben Turner, could only get two other members for a Huddersfield branch of the S.D.F.[2] The Bradford League, in its early years, depended a good deal upon speakers and guidance from Leeds; it paid serious attention to the trade unions only after the Bradford T.U.C. of September 1888.[3] The extant minute-books of the Bradford Trades Council have a hiatus between July 1889 and January 1893. As the former minute-book closes, the Trades Council claims to represent 3000 workers, mainly outside the textile industry. Its secretary, Sam Shaftoe, is a prominent unionist of the old Lib-Lab school, and the Council is still negotiating humbly with the Liberal Association for a member on their School Board Eight. When the latter minute-book commences, the Council claims 10,000 members, Drew of the weavers is on its executive, Shaftoe has disappeared, Cowgill — an I.L.P.er from the A.S.E. — is secretary, and the Council is functioning in close alliance with the I.L.P.[4]

Three events dictated this transformation; the publication of the *Yorkshire Factory Times*, the influence of the Leeds unskilled agitation, and the events surrounding the Manningham Mills strike. Andrews, the proprietor of the *Cotton Factory Times*, started the Yorkshire journal largely as a com-

---

[1] On the occasion of the first National Conference of the I.L.P. Carpenter wrote to Mattison (13 January 1893): '(I see that old fraud Mahon has got there — Champion too !) I am glad you didn't yield to Mahon about going, and Tom M. I think in his heart cannot be sorry that *you* were elected.' Mattison Collection.

[2] Article by Turner in *Yorkshire Evening News*, 1924, in Mattison Cutting-book.

[3] Obituary of Paul Bland, *Labour Leader*, 20 April 1901.

[4] Bradford T.C. Minutes, in possession of Bradford Trades Council.

mercial venture; it was his policy to employ the local union men as correspondents, and Drew, Bartley, Turner, and Gee were placed on the staff, with Burgess as the first editor. Its influence achieved in a few months what the painstaking efforts of organisers had failed to achieve in years. Its dramatic effect in the woollen districts, as propagandist for trade unionism, has been described in the vivid pages of Ben Turner's reminiscences.[1] Bad masters were exposed, grievances aired, successes advertised. With the textile workers on the move, the unskilled struggles in Leeds spilled over into the towns and villages to the West, swelling the tide. Maguire, Paylor, Turner, Mattison, organised the gasworkers and clayworkers at Halifax, where 9000 were claimed at a demonstration in the autumn of 1889.[2] Railwaymen were organised in other towns. In December 1890 the Manningham strike commenced.

This strike, which at its peak involved nearly 5000 workers and which dragged through a bitter winter until the end of April 1891 has often been described. Here we may select only certain features for comment. (1) Contrary to the general impression, it was not the most-depressed but the better-paid workers — velvet and plush weavers — who initiated the strike. The several thousand unskilled women and girls who later thronged the streets came out in sympathy or were forced out by the firm in order to embarrass the strike fund.[3] (2) Sympathy was aroused for the strikers, not only by their inexperience and pitiful plight, but also by the explanation of S. C. Lister that it was necessary to bring down their wages to continental standards, and peg them to the rate paid at his mills in Crefeld. This 'continental threat' the *Yorkshire Factory Times* took up as 'a distinct challenge to all the textile workers in the two counties of Lancashire and Yorkshire'.[4] (3) The outstanding

---

[1] Turner, *Heavy Woollen Textile Workers Union*, pp. 65-7 : 'The paper opened up a new vista. We scoured Yorkshire textile areas for members, and the Union grew from a few hundreds to a few thousands.' See also Paylor on its effect, in *Y.F.T.*, 25 December 1891.

[2] *Commonweal*, 19 October 1889 ; John Lister, a learned antiquarian, was later to write : 'I learned many useful, practical lessons from some of these "agitators" who . . . knew far more about the industrial history of our country than I'. Lister MSS. History.

[3] *Y.F.T.*, 19 December 1890, 16 January 1891.

[4] *Ibid.* 6 February 1891. But a German manufacturer wrote to the

organisers of the strike — Turner, Drew, and Isabella Ford — were proclaimed socialists ; Turner, living in Leeds, was in constant contact with the Leeds socialists, although his earlier experiences in West Yorkshire, where he had received generous assistance from Liberal unionists of the old school, led him to take up a mediating role. (4) It was the repeated attempts by chief constable, watch committee, town clerk, and Mayor to prevent the strikers and sympathisers from holding meetings, at first in halls, and then in customary open-air meeting-places (thus provoking the famous riots in Dockers' Square) which, willy-nilly, forced to the very forefront the question of independent political action. It was this struggle which induced the strikers to fetch up Ben Tillett for a great protest meeting ; and he voiced their sentiments when he declared that 'at election times the people can teach would-be Caesars — town clerks and Mayors and watch committees — a salutary lesson'.[1] After the strike was defeated, the *Factory Times* commented :

> The operatives have from the first been fought not only by their own employers at Manningham but by the whole of the monied class of Bradford. From the highest dignitary down to the lowest corporate official 'law and order' has been against them.[2]

'In future,' warned Drew, when presenting the balance sheet of the strike, 'capitalists will have to reckon with whole communities of labour rather than sections.'[3]

This, then, was the background to Bartley's discussion with Drew in the yard of the Bethel Baptist chapel. Even so, the formation of the Bradford Labour Union was only one in a chain of similar attempts, each of which had been re-absorbed within the Liberal Party ; [4] and at any time in the next year

Bradford Observer from Crefeld and claimed that their average wages were *higher* than those in Lister's mills.
  [1] *Ibid.* 24 April 1891.   [2] *Ibid.* 1 May 1891.   [3] *Ibid.* 17 July 1891.
  [4] The Bradford Trades Council was 'considering' contesting East Bradford with a Labour candidate in 1885 (T.C. Minutes, 10 February 1885). But in 1888 the Liberal Association could only be persuaded with great difficulty to admit a Trades Council nominee to the 'Liberal Eight' for the School Board. (Minutes, 6 November, and entries to 4 December 1889.) However, a Labour Electoral Association had been formed in 1888, and socialists like Bland, Cowgill, Conellan, and Bartley were making themselves felt on the Council. But the L.E.A. was hamstrung by Liberal-Socialist disagreements, and Jowett, who was secretary, let it die. *Labour Leader*, 20 April 1901 ; Brockway, *op. cit.* p. 31.

the Labour Union might have met with the same fate. Its programme, like that of the Colne Valley Labour Union, was largely a list of radical-democratic demands, adapted from Mahon's *Labour Programme* of 1888 which clearly provided the model.[1] Despite the admonition, 'WORKMEN, REMEMBER NOVEMBER' placarded in the streets from the time of the Manningham strike, only one Trades Council nominee was successful in the 1891 municipal elections, and he was the staunch old unionist, Shaftoe, who — when he had done his duty by securing guarantees from the Council for the right of public meeting — fell back into the Liberal Party, which rewarded him with nomination to the bench.[2] Moreover, the Bradford and Colne Valley Labour Unions had the utmost difficulty in finding suitable candidates to nurse the constituencies. Tillett and Mann were up to their necks holding the Dockers' Union together, and beating off an employers' counter-attack ; Shaw said the Bradford working men should choose one of their own number, and not run after the 'tall hats and frock coats'.[3]

At length Blatchford was persuaded to nurse East Bradford, only to withdraw, without an apology to the electors, when the launching of the *Clarion* absorbed all his time.[4] Tillett was persuaded to stand for Bradford West only when presented with 1000 electors' signatures, and after a deputation from the Labour Union had visited the Dockers' Annual Congress.[5] Mann, when invited by Colne Valley, held aloof longer ; he was wondering about permeating the Church ; he had his eye on the A.S.E. ; he was doubtful about parliamentary action ; he thought the Colne Valley men should get down to trade unionism and municipal action before they talked of Parliament.[6] The Yorkshire men had to solve their problems on their own.

[1] For Mahon's *Programme*, see Thompson, *op. cit.* p. 615, note 2. For the Bradford Labour Union programme, see *Labour Union Journal*, 30 June 1892. For Colne Valley, see Mann, *op. cit.*
[2] Bills and election leaflets in Shaftoe Cutting-book.
[3] *Y.F.T.*, 29 May 1891.   [4] *Ibid.* 15 and 22 January 1892.
[5] *Minutes of 2nd Annual Congress of Dockers &c.* (September 1891), pp. 25-6. The signatures have been bound and are preserved by the Bradford Trades Council.
[6] Minutes of Colne Valley Labour Union (in possession of C.V. Labour Party). For an example of Mann's views on the priority of trade union

Homage to Tom Maguire

In truth, it was a miracle that the Labour Unions survived into 1892, and multiplied so fast. This could not have been done without a resolute and capable local socialist leadership, aided by the inflexibility and stupidity of the local Liberal employers. It was a longer step than we realise from the running of occasional Labour candidates for council or school board, even against official Liberal nominees, to the formation of an independent party, pledged to a socialist programme. The Labour Union men were assisted by the uncompromising advocacy of Blatchford and Burgess; by the proportional representation system operating in local board elections, which enabled them to win spectacular and morale-building victories;[1] but above all, by the advance of the Trades Council movement.

The Trades Councils, even more than the Labour Unions, were the organisational unit upon which the West Yorkshire I.L.P. was based. Among Trades Councils re-formed or formed at this time were Halifax (1889), Huddersfield (1890), Keighley (1890), Brighouse (1892), Spen Valley (1891), the Heavy Woollen District (Dewsbury & Batley, 1891); the Yorkshire Federation of Trades Councils — the first county federation — was founded in 1893.[2] In almost every case, these were formed by socialists and new unionists with the direct aim of promoting independent political action; in some cases, the Trades Council formed the local I.L.P. as its political arm.[3] The socialists no longer sowed their propaganda broadcast or at thinly-attended meetings; they directed it first and foremost at the unionists, urging them to take political action, at first in the field of local politics.

Men of an antagonistic class [declared Maguire, addressing a demonstration of 2000 gasworkers and labourers at Dewsbury in

and municipal work over parliamentary, see the *Trade Unionist & Trades Council Record*, 5 September 1891; for an example of a reproof aimed at Mann, see editorial, 'Tom Mann and the Representation of Labour', *Y.F.T.*, 28 August 1891.

[1] *E.g.* at Huddersfield in February 1891, when Balmforth topped the poll in the School Board elections.

[2] *Y.F.T.*, 10 February 1893.

[3] The Heavy Woollen District Trades Council was formed in July 1891, with Ben Turner as secretary, and in only two months was intervening in local elections. Minutes, 15 September 1891 (in possession of Miss Nora Turner).

July 1891], were sent upon their various public bodies to manage their town's affairs. Men who polluted rivers and filled the air with smoke from their chimneys were sent to their Council chambers to carry out the Acts of Parliament to prevent the pollution of rivers and the air.[1]

Since the Trades Councils were young, the socialists encountered little opposition. At Bradford, Shaftoe was too good a trade unionist to stand aside from the tide of new unionism; he played his full part, speaking often alongside Paylor, Turner, and Drew, becoming secretary of the newly formed Woolcombers' Union, and although he was known to oppose the I.L.P. he held his silence during Tillett's 1892 candidature.[2] At Halifax the Liberals delivered themselves into the hands of the I.L.P. by an act of crass stupidity. Beever, the President of the Trades Council, had been converted to socialism and was taking an active part in the local Fabian propaganda in late 1891, but another prominent and influential member, Tattersall, was still a member of the Liberal executive. In 1892 both Beever and Tattersall were sacked, one after the other, by the same firm; the reason given, 'they did not want anyone in their employ who was engaged in setting labour against capital'.[3] It was well known in the town that the most influential partner in the firm was also a leading member of the local Liberal caucus, and the indignation in the town was so intense that testimonials were raised, demonstrations held, a Labour Union formed — the month after Tattersall's dismissal — on the initiative of the Trades Council, and a month later Keir Hardie was addressing a mass meeting which resolved that 'the time has come when a national and independent Labour Party must be formed'.[4] Two months later again, in November 1892, Beever, Tattersall, Lister, and one other I.L.P. candidate were swept on to the town council, while in January 1893, in the I.L.P.'s first parliamentary by-election, Lister, the local squire, mine-owner, and Fabian, who had come to socialism by way of Marx's *Capital* and Tom Maguire,

---

[1] *Y.F.T.*, 10 July 1891. [2] *Bradford Observer*, 14 June 1892.
[3] *Y.F.T.*, 1 July 1892. The firm was Clayton, Murgatroyd & Co.
[4] Lister MSS. History and cuttings in Mattison Collection, and *Y.F.T.*, 20 November 1891.

polled 3028 votes against the Liberal 4617 and the Tory 4219.

Indeed, this last incident points the pattern which can be seen throughout the West Riding. At Leeds the Liberal Gas Committee. At Colne Valley, the sitting Liberal member, Sir James Kitson — the 'Carnegie' of the West Riding, whose firm ex-Royal Commissioner of Labour Tom Mann described as having 'worse conditions . . . than could be found in any other engineering firm in . . . Leeds'.[1] At Halifax the Liberal employer, sacking the Trades Council leaders. In a dozen boroughs and urban districts Liberal councillors refusing trade-union demands for 'fair contracts' or artisan dwellings. In Holmfirth the Liberal Association which rejected the eight-hour day to the disgust of the miners' delegates who forthwith resigned.[2] In Shipley the Liberal caucus, where three men were 'ruling the roost', which held down Radical contendants.[3] In Bradford the worsted-spinning Liberal Nonconformist M.P. and the Liberal Watch Committee. In every case social and industrial agitation on questions in the immediate, everyday experience of the working people, confronted the face — sometimes complacent, sometimes oppressive, sometimes just plain stupid — of established Liberalism. As the people recoiled in confusion and anger, the socialists seized their opportunity and founded the I.L.P.

IV

How far was the Yorkshire I.L.P. an authentic socialist party ? How far was it a late product of Liberal-Radicalism, carried by a temporary tide of industrial and social unrest into independent political channels ? The evidence is conflicting. Lister, in his 1893 contest at Halifax, went out of his way to emphasise that he was a labour, and not a socialist, candidate.[4] Calculations at Halifax and Bradford suggest that a fair number of votes were drawn from former Conservative electors, but undoubtedly the majority came from Liberal

---

[1] *Trade Unionist & Trades Council Record*, 7 November 1891.
[2] *Y.F.T.*, 7 August 1891.   [3] *Ibid.* 14 August 1891.
[4] Election Manifesto and Lister MSS. History ; *Halifax Free Press*, January 1893.

electors or from young men voting for the first time.[1] In 1897 Tom Mann fought a by-election at Halifax, polling 2000 votes. In an after-the-poll speech he paid tactful and generous tribute to Lister, but —

most excellent man as he was ... his particular appreciation of Socialism, his method of advocating Socialism, his speaking of it as advanced Liberalism ... was one of the chief reasons he had succeeded in getting the number of votes he had. (Cheers.) In his judgement the Socialist movement generally, and the Independent Labour Party particularly, did not at the last fight reach that particular stage when the issues were sufficiently clearly defined. ... He contended that there were more Socialists in Halifax today than there were when Mr. Lister polled 3800. (Cheers.) [2]

The first years of the Halifax I.L.P. bear out this judgment; endless bickering and defections in the 600-strong branch called upon the time of Hardie, Mann, and even the Annual Conference and revealed how many disgruntled Liberals and even Tories had been swept into the movement in 1892.

No doubt this was true elsewhere, and helps to explain a certain decline in support in the late nineties. It is true also that socialist demands were sometimes tacked on to liberal-democratic demands in an almost ludicrous manner, to disarm opposition or as a casual afterthought.[3] But this is only half the truth, and the less important half. The Yorkshire I.L.P. was a party of youth; its leaders — Maguire, Ben Turner, Jowett — were young; the men and women who staffed the Labour unions and clubs, the Labour churches, the trade unions and Trades Councils, were often in their twenties. And the young people were socialists — ardent followers of Hardie, Morris, Blatchford, Tillett, Mann. When Blatchford accepted the East Bradford nomination he was uncompromising in his socialist advocacy: 'the earth and all that the earth produced — the tools they used, the land and all the capital belonged to

[1] Snowden, *op. cit.* i, p. 69: 'the I.L.P. was attracting in the main the young men who were not yet voters'.
[2] *Halifax Guardian*, 6 March 1897.
[3] In February 1894 a resolution was passed at the Yorkshire Federation of Trades Councils urging the government to 'take up at once the question of the nationalisation of the land, minerals, railways, and all the means of production and distribution, as a means of helping to solve the unemployed question'. *Y.F.T.*, 16 February 1894.

the people'. The *Yorkshire Factory Times* commended this doctrine in its editorial, as

> the foundation upon which the Independent Labour Party must be built. It is a rock, and is irremovable. It is as firmly fixed as the earth itself. It is a line of demarcation over which neither Liberal nor Tory may pass and retain his creed.[1]

It was this socialist conviction which prevented the Bradford men from surrendering to Liberal blandishments, when Tillett was offered a straight fight with the Tory in West Bradford.[2] The young socialist delegates gave an overwhelming rebuff to Mahon's attempt to draw the socialist teeth of the I.L.P. at its first conference. In October 1894 the delegates at the Yorkshire Federation of the I.L.P. were dissuaded from voting for a change of name to the 'Socialist Labour Party' only by the advocacy of Maguire who (at 29) was 'as old a Socialist as any in the room'.[3]

In private — it is true — Maguire had his doubts. There were troubles enough in the early I.L.P. — enough to make him wish to concentrate on his writing for the *Factory Times* and *Labour Leader*, or to prefer a part in the unemployed agitation to 'your damned party politics and silly quarrels'.

> People call themselves Socialists [he wrote to a friend], but what they really are is just ordinary men with Socialist opinions hung round, they haven't got it inside of them. . . . It's hard, very hard; we get mixed up in disputes among ourselves . . . and can't keep a straight line for the great thing, even if we all of us know what that is.[4]

No doubt, as a confirmed atheist, he distrusted the spellbinding 'Come to Jesus' appeal which the new men like Snowden were bringing into the movement.[5] His early maturity seemed to be giving way to a premature middle-age, hastened by illness and perhaps by the lurking awareness that he was soon to 'be eternally elbowed out of place after one small scrappy peep at the big show'. Not yet 30, he was to be

---

[1] *Y.F.T.*, 10 July 1892.
[2] See Burgess in the *Labour Leader*, 20 April 1901.
[3] *Dewsbury Reporter*, 13 October 1894.
[4] *Tom Maguire, a Remembrance*, p. vi.
[5] Snowden, *op. cit.* i, p. 82.

found more and more often drinking in the Leeds Central I.L.P. Club, telling stories of the 'old days' like an old-timer, and entertaining the company with anecdotes and songs. He continued his part in the unemployed agitation, 'concealing from everybody the fact that he was practically one of the unemployed himself'. Early in March 1895, in his thirtieth year, he collapsed with pneumonia; his comrades found him without food or fire in the house; he died on 8 March, refusing the services of a priest: 'I will stand or fall on the last twelve years of my life and not on the last five minutes'. His funeral was attended by a demonstration almost as large as those of 1889–90, in which Jewish tailoring workers and Irish labourers, gasworkers and I.L.P. councillors, all joined. With his death a phase of the movement comes to an end.[1]

The young men of the Yorkshire I.L.P. owed much to Maguire. He had been the point of junction between the theoretical understanding of the national leaders, the moral teaching of Morris and Carpenter, and the needs and aspirations of his own people. Nothing in history happens spontaneously, nothing worthwhile is achieved without the expense of intellect and spirit. Maguire had spent his energies without restraint. A poet of real talent, his feelings had been assaulted by the filth of Leeds; the rag, shoddy, and wool-combing industries, with their toll of disease and the dread anthrax. His bitter experiences while organising the tailoresses were recorded in his *Machine Room Chants*; sometimes in the moving tales of poverty:

> No, I wouldn't like to die, sir, for I think the good Lord's hard
> On us common workin' women; an' the like o' me's debarred
> From His high, uncertain heaven, where fine ladies all go to.
> So I try to keep on livin', though the Lord knows how I do.

sometimes in humorous sketches of the problems of the organiser:

> 'They say I am cutting the other girls out
> Who work for their bread and tea — no doubt;
> But, thank you! England's free,
>   Te-he!

[1] *Tom Maguire, a Remembrance*; T. Maguire, *Machine Room Chants* (1895); J. Clayton, *Before Sunrise* (Manchester, 1896); miscellaneous cuttings in Turner and Mattison Scrapbooks, and Mattison Notebook.

Homage to Tom Maguire

> I will do as I like as long as I dare,
> What's fair to me is my own affair,
> And I'll please myself anyhow — so there !'
>   Says the Duchess of Number Three.
>
> And the Number Three Department girls
> They copy her hat and the cut of her curls —
>   'Tis a touching sight to see,
>   Dear me !
> Her slightest word is their sacred law,
> They run her errands and stand her jaw,
> Content to find neither fault nor flaw
>   In the Duchess of Number Three.

If many of the Yorkshire young people had in fact got socialism 'inside of them', then something of its quality — the hostility to Grundyism, the warm espousal of sex equality, the rich internationalism — owed much to Maguire. It is time that this forgotten 'provincial' was admitted to first-class citizenship of history, and time also that we discarded the theory of the spontaneous combustion of the Yorkshire I.L.P.

NOTES ON THE SOUTH LEEDS ELECTION

On the resignation of the Liberal member for South Leeds in August 1892, J. L. Mahon at once wrote to Champion for his support in financing an Independent Labour Candidate in a three-cornered contest. 'I am rather sick of helping backboneless people into Parliament', Champion replied (27 August 1892). However, after various possible candidates had been approached without success (Mann, Hammill, Clem Edwards, Solly), Champion urged Mahon to stand himself. Champion saw his own part as that of an authoritative Parnell, and wrote to Mahon (5 September 1892) : 'If as I am rather inclined to do, I go in for taking hold of the I.L.P. and running it for all it is worth, I mean to have as lieutenants men who won't scuttle at the first shot and will agree with me that our only chance is to go for the Liberals all along the line without gloves. It is possible, given pluck to put out 50 Liberals at the next election by running men in 10 seats and voting Tory in the other 40. That will cause some little fuss, and will probably put in a Tory Govt. holding power at the sweet will of the I.L.P. But it will make the Labour question in general and 8 hours in particular what the Irish question has been made by similar tactics. . . .' While Champion scoured the London clubs for money, Mahon implemented this policy and mounted a campaign on aggressively anti-Gladstonian lines. From his letters Champion would appear to have been suffering from delusions of grandeur : he wrote of his conversations with Chamberlain ; his financial resources ; his 'personal adherents' in various towns ; his intention of sending the Liberals 'back to opposition' ; of buying control of the *Workman's Times* ; of 'exposing' all new union leaders who refused to speak for Mahon. He sent a strong-arm man from Liverpool (14 September 1892) : 'the handiest man with his fists of my acquaintance ... very good tempered doesn't drink and never hits anybody first. But he knows his business and will half kill the biggest Irishman in Leeds in two minutes.' Votes were not a serious consideration — 'the main thing is to stoke up the anti-liberal feeling for the future'. When Keir Hardie came up to help Mahon, Champion wrote (20 September 1892) 'please assure him from me, that if he will come and see me on his arrival in London, I shall be able, and willing, to render him independent of any attacks he may meet in his Constituency for helping you.'

Mahon's election manifesto was a long anti-Gladstonian harangue, culminating in a series of Radical (but not socialist) demands. The provocation offered to Liberal electors was only too successful. Mahon's main election meeting was packed with Gladstonian supporters — with the Irish most prominent ; neither the candidate, nor Tom Maguire (the Chairman), nor H. H. Champion himself, could gain a hearing ; and the meeting ended in violent riot (*Leeds Mercury*, *Sheffield Daily Telegraph*, 19 September 1892). Three days later Mahon was disqualified from standing owing to an error in his nomination papers, and the incident ended in general ill-will.

Champion and Mahon remained in correspondence and confidently expected to dominate the first I.L.P. Conference : on 4 November 1892 Champion was writing 'there will practically be none there — outside the local men — but my men.' Even Hardie was marked down as 'going on all right ... If he goes on as he is, I would help him and forgive him his "in-and-out running" just after the election.' Mahon, for his part, was advising Yorkshire audiences to support those in favour of Chamberlain's 'Labour Programme' unless the Liberals brought out a better one (*Keighley News*, 10 December 1892). His final action in the Yorkshire I.L.P. was to denounce John Lister's candidature at Halifax in February 1893. This curious combination of Parnellite tactics, Tory money, arbitrary intrigue, and apparently 'pro-Tory' interventions, helps to explain the set-back suffered by the Leeds I.L.P., the bitterness of feeling between old and new unionists on the Leeds Trades Council, and the profound suspicion with which some Socialists (who knew of Champion's and Mahon's strategy) regarded the first year of the I.L.P.

9

JOHN SAVILLE

TRADE UNIONS AND FREE LABOUR: THE BACKGROUND TO THE TAFF VALE DECISION

IT is a commonplace that public sympathy for the cause of the strikers was an important factor in the dockers' victory in the late summer of 1889.[1] What is not so well appreciated is that this sympathy was already beginning to waste away during the last weeks of the strike [2] and public opinion in general very quickly turned to outright opposition in the months that followed. Through all the decade of the nineties and well into the new century, a hostility developed towards trade unionism in general and new unionism in particular that bordered at times on the hysterical. It finds various expressions in the contemporary press, in the employment of large police and military forces during trade disputes, and in increasingly adverse judgments against the unions in the Courts. This whole period after 1889 is one of a developing counter-attack by the propertied classes against the industrial organisations of the working people. The final break-through is reached in 1901 when, as the result of the Taff Vale case and the decision in *Quinn* v. *Leathem*, the trade unions found themselves stripped

---

[1] See the cartoon in *Punch*, 7 September 1889, in which the docker is saying to the dock director: 'I don't want to be unreasonable, but if, in a general way, you would think less of your luxuries and more of my necessities it would be better for trade all round'. For a discussion by a hostile contemporary witness of the 'irrational sympathy, almost of blind infatuation' of the public towards the Dock Strike, see George Brooks, *Industry and Property*, i (Suffolk, n.d. ? 1892), pp. 47-9.

[2] H. Ll. Smith and V. Nash, *The Story of the Docker's Strike* (1889), p. 6; and see below, p. 322, for the attitude of *The Times*. *Punch* also changed its attitude (14 September).

of the legal rights that had been written into the Statute Book by the legislation of the 1870s.

It was the special characteristics of New Unionism that made it the immediate target of ruling-class fury. Recent research has modified the picture of New Unionism that has been generally accepted, and today it is recognised that 1889 was less of a break with the past than was formerly believed.[1] There were stirrings, and organisation, among the unskilled workers half a dozen years before 1889,[2] and, on the other hand, the old skilled unions were in some respects less conservative than is usually believed. Nevertheless, when all the necessary qualifications have been added to the traditional interpretation of old and new unionism, it is important not to under-estimate the climacteric of 1889. The economic problems of the unskilled and semi-skilled trade unionists were very different from those of the skilled workers, and their industrial methods and tactics were perforce also different. While the old unions were able to rely upon the skill of their members as a crucial bargaining weapon, the new unionists were at all times, even in the years of good trade, subject to the pressures of an overstocked labour market. Picketing, for instance, was rarely a major problem in the strike action of many sections of skilled workers. The Webbs noted that among the cotton spinners of Lancashire, or the boilermakers of the north-east coast, or the coal-miners in well-organised districts, both sides to an industrial dispute knew that when work was resumed the same men would have to be taken on.[3] The problem of scab labour did not, therefore, arise in the virulent form that occurred in the casual and semi-skilled trades. 'Picketing, in fact, is a mark not of Trade Unionism, but of its imperfection.' So the Webbs wrote in 1896.[4] The position was very different,

[1] See the important thesis by D. W. Crowley, *The Origins of the Revolt of the British Labour Movement from Liberalism, 1875–1906* (Ph.D. London, 1952), especially chapter xi. I am inclined to think that Dr. Crowley somewhat under-estimates the importance of 1889 in the history of the labour movement.

[2] Crowley, *op. cit.* p. 349 ff.; H. Pelling, 'The Knights of Labour in Britain, 1880–1901', *Econ. Hist. Review*, 2nd Ser. IX, No. 2 (1956), pp. 313-31; K. D. Buckley, *Trade Unionism in Aberdeen, 1878–1900* (Aberdeen, 1955).

[3] S. and B. Webb, *Industrial Democracy* (1911 ed.), p. 719, n. 1.

[4] *Ibid.* p. 857.

Unions and Free Labour: Background to Taff Vale Decision

for example, in the ports employing dock labour, where only a proportion of those applying for work on any one day would be accepted [1] and where much of the work could be performed by agricultural labour or casual labour drafted in from the outside. In such circumstances, and these were familiar in many other industries, it was immensely more difficult to make a strike solid or to achieve stable trade unions. Outside the highly skilled trades, to win even an approximation to the closed shop or to ensure that blackleg labour did not swamp a strike, militant tactics were demanded which the older unionists had pioneered decades before but which, by the end of the 1880s, they believed they no longer needed. The employers, too, in the semi- and unskilled trades were more uncompromising than their fellows in industries where unionism had been long established; and their first, and for men of property not unnatural, reaction was to smash these new upstart organisations rather than attempt to meet them on common ground.

Trade unionists in the newly organised trades like dockers and gasworkers were rarely more than a minority of the labour force, and to achieve their main objectives of higher wages, shorter hours, and union recognition, with or without a strike, brought them right up against the prejudice, ignorance, and apathy of important groups in their own class who were not prepared to accept the need for, or the decisions of, the unions. It was this clash between unionists and what was nicely called 'free' labour that provided much of the drama of the industrial struggles of the early 1890s, and it was this aspect of trade-union activity that public opinion mainly seized upon. The *Economist* noted in 1891 when commenting on the setting up of the *R.C. on Labour* that 'the general labour controversy is going largely to turn upon the respective rights and duties of free labourers and unionists' [2] — free labourers being defined as all those who wished to make their own independent contract with their employers regardless of the trade-union position.

---

[1] There is a useful summary of the employment position in the docks in P. de Rousiers, *The Labour Question in Britain* (1896), Pt. III, chapter iii.
[2] 28 February 1891.

If the union members came out on strike, that was not necessarily any concern to those who were not union members; and to insist that all shall stop work at the behest of a minority of trade unionists, was not this a new form of 'corporate tyranny' as oppressive as those forms of monopoly that Adam Smith, at the very beginning of the modern era, sought to destroy with the publication of *The Wealth of Nations*? Thus *The Times*,[1] never slow to recognise 'tyranny' in working-class dress.

Besides their industrial tactics, the attitude of the new unionists towards state intervention, symbolised by the slogan of the Eight-Hour Day, was a further cause for anxiety on the part of the propertied classes. Interventionism and socialism were for many indistinguishable terms, and the identification of New Unionism, state intervention and socialism was increasingly made. The opposition to the eight-hour day and to any increase in state intervention came from expected quarters: from business circles whose mouthpiece was the *Economist*; from social philosophers like Herbert Spencer; and from old-style trade unionists who had accepted much of middle-class ideology. For Herbert Spencer, in the introduction to a widely circulated volume of essays, published in 1891, whose title, significantly, was *A Plea for Liberty*, society has only the choice between freedom of contract and coercive status, and any infringement of the former can only lead to an extension of the latter.[2] George Howell, representing the lib-lab trade unionist, said the same things in more homely language.[3]

[1] 29 July 1895.
[2] T. Mackay (ed.), *A Plea for Liberty* (1891), pp. 1-26. Spencer's conclusion is worth quoting. The ultimate result of state intervention, he wrote, 'must be a society like that of ancient Peru, dreadful to contemplate, in which the mass of the people, elaborately regimented in groups of 10, 50, 100, 500, and 1000, ruled by officers of corresponding grades, and tied to their districts, were superintended in their private lives as well as in their industries, and toiled hopelessly for the support of the governmental organisation', p. 26.
[3] Essay on 'Liberty for Labour', *ibid.* especially p. 139; these comments by Howell are very similar to those of another lib-lab trade unionist, Henry Broadhurst, quoted in E. J. Hobsbawm, *Labour's Turning Point* (1948), pp. 96-7; and see also the amusing comment on these kind of arguments by Sidney Webb, quoted *ibid.* p. 45.

Unions and Free Labour: Background to Taff Vale Decision

It is difficult for the mid-twentieth century to appreciate fully the horror with which the middle and upper classes at this time regarded every new step towards a curtailment of *laissez-faire*. No doubt for those like Spencer, who regarded any intervention as a step along the road to serfdom, *laissez-faire* was still the only untried Utopia. What is relevant here is the way resistance was built up to some of the elementary demands of social justice. Against the background of Ireland, the growth of socialist movements on the Continent, and the dreadful example of labour legislation in Australia, the good bourgeois found that it was indeed time to cry halt.[1] When the demands of the new unionists found expression in the industrial militancy and the wave of disputes that followed the great Dock Strike, the stage was set for struggle. The old unions were reasonable; the new, impossible.

The older Unions, presided over by men having some knowledge of political economy and of the conditions of trade, have a defined policy. They desire, when it is possible, to improve the position of the working man; in times of commercial prosperity they will insist, using his obedience to them as a weapon, that he shall have what they consider his fair share of that prosperity; in times of commercial depression they will help him and, in effect, they perform many of the functions of a friendly society. Admission to such Unions is a privilege not lightly to be obtained. This policy is stigmatised as degenerate by the secretary of the new Union. His policy and that of his Union is that of the daughter of the horseleech[2]; it is a policy of continual importunity. The new Union

[1] The relationship between Irish politics and social movements in England is still insufficiently documented. The same is true, especially for labour matters and social legislation, of Australia in the two decades before 1914. For a typical comment which linked the Liberal Party's attitude towards the Irish Nationalists and the support that was thereby given to the tactics of the new unionists, see an article, 'The cause of the Epidemic of Strikes', in the *Economist*, 12 July 1890. George Brooks, *op. cit.* ii, pp. 131-2, believed that 'The new trade unionism . . . is the offspring of the Parnell movement in Ireland'; and he developed the argument at length in the first chapter of vol. i. For a hostile discussion of the results of much of Australia's social legislation, see Charles Fairfield, 'State Socialism in the Antipodes', in *A Plea for Liberty*, *op. cit.* pp. 145-98; Hon. J. W. Fortescue, 'State Socialism and the Collapse in Australia', T. Mackay (ed.), *A Policy of Free Exchange* (1894), pp. 103-41; and the widespread comment in the journalism of the 1890s.

[2] 'The horseleech hath two daughters, *crying*, Give, give', Proverbs, xxx. 15. I am indebted to my colleague, Margaret 'Espinasse, for this reference.

cares not whether men are ill or well paid; it is ever ready with a fresh demand. Concession does but whet its appetite; it claims for labour the whole of the profits made by labour and capital combined; it aims to be the absolute dictator of the conditions of toil; to say who shall work and how much he shall receive.

... The principle which underlies the militant Union is the principle of socialism. In the first place, the individual is subordinated to the class; in the second place, the class desires to obtain the whole of the profits which are derived from capital and labour combined. In other words, it desires to confiscate capital.[1]

There was, clearly, only one thing to be done with the offspring of the horse-leech.

I

The change in the temper of public opinion towards New Unionism is noticeable already in the closing stages of the 1889 Dock Strike from a reading of the editorial columns of *The Times*. Prior to 28 August the leader writers had been fairly sympathetic to the dock labourers; but on that day, in a tougher-minded editorial, *The Times* warned that 'evidence is accumulating that intimidation is playing an appreciable, if not an important, part in this strike'. Moreover, while it was no doubt 'natural' that the dockers should turn for leadership to the 'professional agitators', public sympathy was given 'not for the sake of, but in spite of such leaders. This sympathy is as yet a young and delicate plant. It may wither if they indulge in excesses or persist in immoderate demands.' By early September the leader writers had discovered that intimidation 'is playing a very definite part in the maintenance of the strike'.[2] If the strike continues, the editorial of 2 September went on, 'it must be conducted with a proper regard for personal freedom', by which *The Times* meant that blackleg labour must not be interfered with; and the police were warned that it was their elementary duty to see that 'the game was played fairly' and that men who wished to exercise their right to work must be 'thoroughly protected'. By the end of the strike, in mid-September, the 'sympathy' of *The Times* had been thoroughly dissipated; and thenceforward *The Times* was at

[1] Edmund Vincent, 'The Discontent of the Working Classes', in *A Plea for Liberty, op. cit.* pp. 213-14, 215.　　　　[2] 2 September 1889.

the head of all those who attacked New Unionism. In an extraordinary leader on Christmas Eve 1889 *The Times* exhorted employers to take the lead in encouraging and organising an anti-union labour force in their own industry, and once again reproved the police for their passivity in the face of mass picketing and intimidation. Referring to free labour, *The Times* wrote:

> Why should they suffer themselves to be intimidated by a set of loud-voiced bullies, whose skins, we venture to say, are quite as tender as those of the honest men they coerce? The difference lies, we believe, in discipline and organisation. The bullies organise themselves, having nothing else to do, while the workers feel themselves isolated and undisciplined. Surely there is a function here for employers to discharge. They ought to take the lead in organising, disciplining, and encouraging men who wish to work. If picketing is legal, as seems to be the theory of the police, then it must also be legal to picket the pickets. If a union can lawfully beset all the roads to a manufactory with paid bullies, why cannot employers take a leaf out of their book? Sauce for the goose is sauce for the gander, and if goose and gander came to blows at least the fight would be fair, and it might even expand the intelligence of the police authorities and enlarge their conceptions of duty.[1]

The employers were not slow to follow this advice. The famous strike at the South Metropolitan Gasworks, whose chairman was George Livesey, one of the best known of the union-baiters of the nineties, was already proceeding; and the strike was eventually broken by the large-scale importation of free labour under heavy police escort and protection. For once *The Times* was satisfied.[2] The most concerted effort on the part of the employers, and the beginning of a sustained

---

[1] 24 December 1889. The occasion for this outburst by *The Times* was the strike at the South Metropolitan Gasworks, and the news items in preceding issues of the mass picketing that the strikers were practising, and the report that the Seamen's and Firemen's Union was boycotting coal vessels destined for the South Metropolitan Gasworks.

[2] This strike of the South London gasworkers was recognised as of more than local interest. As *The Times* wrote on 14 December 1889, commenting on the safe arrival inside the works of a further batch of blackleg labour: 'The event showed how completely intimidation and illegitimate pressure may be nipped in the bud by a timely display of police'. The failure of the strike showed the way forward for those employers who wished to break the New Unions. For Will Thorne's account of the strike, see his autobiography, *My Life's Battles* (n.d.), p. 106 ff.

war against New Unionism on the waterfront, came exactly a year after the Dock Strike, when the shipping owners established the Shipping Federation.[1] 'From the first', wrote the author of the Federation's official history, 'the Federation was founded as a fighting machine to counter the strike weapon, and it made no secret of the fact'.[2] The Shipping Federation, which united seven-eights of all British tonnage, immediately began an offensive against the seamen's and dockers' unions, by establishing offices at all the main ports at which seamen must register before they could be employed; and then, early in 1891, it introduced its own ticket which pledged the holder to work with union and non-union men alike, and without which in many firms it was impossible to get work.

There was already in existence a United Labour Council of the Port of London which had been formed at the end of the Dock Strike and which embraced most of the waterside unions; and there were in addition a number of unions catering for seamen and firemen, of which the most important was that organised by J. Havelock Wilson. Faced with the opposition of the Shipping Federation all these bodies affiliated to a new Federation of Trade and Labour Unions connected with the Shipping, Carrying, and other Industries.[3] Its secretary was Clem Edwards,[4] and by the time Edwards gave evidence before

---

[1] The Shipping Federation was formally constituted on 2 September 1890 and incorporated on 30 September 1890. The official history of the Federation, which leaves out more than it includes, is by L. H. Powell, *The Shipping Federation* (1950). The most useful source for the early history of the Federation are the Docks, Wharves, and Shipping Volumes of the *R.C. on Labour* (1892).

[2] Powell, *op. cit.* p. 5; a statement fully corroborated by the testimony of G. A. Laws, first general manager of the Shipping Federation. See his evidence before the *R.C. on Labour, Minutes of Evidence*, Group B, vol. i (C. 6708), 1892, Qs. 4918-5471.

[3] For the history of these trade-union groupings in the docks, see Clem Edwards, 'Labour Federations', *Economic Journal*, iii (1893), pp. 205-17, 408-24, especially p. 419 ff.; and Clem Edwards's evidence before *R.C. on Labour*, Group B, vol. i, Q. 8614 ff. See Apps. 25 and 55 of the same volume for the rules of the Federation of Trade and Labour Unions; and App. 57 for a list of the unions affiliated to the Federation. For an account of the development of the Seamen's organisation, see the first part of the evidence of J. Havelock Wilson, *ibid*. Q. 9171 ff.; and his autobiography, *My Stormy Voyage Through Life* (n.d.).

[4] Clem Edwards (1869–1938) worked with Tillett and the Dockers' Union from the time of the 1889 strike. He started work as a farm labourer,

the *R.C. on Labour* in November 1891 some 25 or 26 unions were affiliated.[1]

The industrial war which now began between the employers' and workers' Federations was only a continuation on a larger scale of guerrilla actions that had been taking place ever since the Mansion House agreement brought the great strike of '89 to a close. Despite the fact that Tillett and others reported to the *R.C. on Labour* that for the first twelve months after the 1889 strike relations between capital and labour were fairly good,[2] strikes were in fact frequent in some of the docks.[3] Among the early strikes in the provinces that showed the emerging pattern were those at Southampton and Plymouth in the autumn of 1890. Port conditions at Southampton were said to be among the worst in the country.[4] The Dockers' Union had begun organisation among the labourers in the spring of 1890, and both wages and hours of work had somewhat improved by the late summer. The strike at Southampton began over the question of union recognition on Monday 7 September. Troops were called in on the second day and small sympathetic strikes began among other groups of labourers. The strike was solid, the spirit of the strikers good, but for reasons which are still unclear, the union executive were unwilling to recognise the strike and no strike pay was given. The strike ended five days later on the following Saturday. Will Sprow, a roving organiser of the Dockers' Union who led the strike, was later sentenced to three months'

---

did other casual jobs, and then studied law, being called to the Bar in 1889. Throughout the nineties he played an important part as trade-union organiser, publicist, and labour journalist. Edwards was Labour Editor of T. P. O'Connor's short-lived paper, the *Sun*. He entered Parliament in 1906 as Liberal M.P. for Denbigh Borough.

[1] Group B, vol. i, Q. 8618. By the time Edwards wrote his 1893 article on 'Labour Federations' for the *Economic Journal, op. cit.* p. 419, forty-one unions were affiliated with a total membership of 130,000.

[2] Tillett before *R.C. on Labour, Minutes of Evidence*, Group B, vol. i, Q. 3871.

[3] Including the well-known Hays Wharf strike over meal-time payments, for which see *ibid*. App. 38, which reprints a circular dated 21 May 1890 issued by the Dockers' Union explaining the issue, and which makes clear that the union executive had been pushed into the strike by the rank and file, most of whom belonged to the Tooley Street branch. See also *ibid.* Q. 65 (Frank Brien).

[4] *Ibid*. vol. ii, Q. 12,316 (Tom McCarthy).

imprisonment for intimidation and stated on his release that had the strike continued, the men would have won. The results of the strike were disastrous for dock unionism in Southampton. A Free Labour Association was formed in the month following this strike, the honorary secretary of which was also the vice-president of the Chamber of Commerce.[1] Tom McCarthy admitted in January 1892 that the present position of the union 'is very low indeed',[2] and he also admitted that in this case the union was not broken initially by the employers or the Free Labour Association but as a result of differences between the local branch and the national executive.[3]

In October 1890 a strike developed over the free labour issue in Plymouth. It was broken after nearly a fortnight and was the familiar story of heavy police protection for blackleg labour. A Free Labour Association was established, the honorary secretary this time being the secretary of the Coal Merchants' Association. Trade-union influence was 'most materially' diminished.[4]

With the establishment of the Shipping Federation in the autumn of 1890, strike-breaking along the waterfront became more organised. In the complicated strike in the London docks which originated with the Wade's Arms Manifesto on 5 December 1890 [5] and which lasted through until the end of February 1891, the Shipping Federation introduced free labour into the docks on a very extensive scale. A depot ship, the *Scotland*, was provided for accommodation for blacklegs who were given three months' agreements with food and lodgings. The metropolitan police were 'introduced' into the

[1] R.C. on *Labour, Minutes of Evidence*, Group B, vol, ii, Q. 12,159 ff. (Thomas Morgan, Vice-President of the Southampton Chamber of Commerce).
[2] *Ibid*. Q. 12,391. [3] *Ibid*. Qs. 12,392-6.
[4] *Ibid*. Q. 12,469 (A. H. Varnier, honorary secretary of the Coal Merchants' Association (12,501) and the Plymouth and District Free Labour Association (12,469-50).
[5] The Wade's Arms Manifesto, issued by the United Labour Council on 3 December 1890, is reprinted, *ibid*. vol. i, App. 13. Details of the strike were given in the evidence of Thomas Robb, Labour Superintendent of the Shipping Federation, *ibid*. Q. 5474 ff. ; and for the dock unions by Clem Edwards, Q. 8622 ff.

docks with most effective results. At the conclusion of the strike the Shipping Federation established a free labour office on the Albert Dock, and George Laws, the general manager of the Federation spoke of the strike as having been 'utterly defeated'.[1] His evidence before the *R.C. on Labour* on the organisation of strike-breaking is worth study.[2] Before this London strike had concluded another against the Shipping Federation had broken out at Cardiff. In the previous August (1890) a committee of the Cardiff Shipowners' Association had passed a resolution affirming 'the right of free labour' — a statement which all knew was a declaration of war on the unions. On 5 February 1891 a gang of coal-tippers, at the instance of the Amalgamated Seamen's and Firemen's Union, refused to service a boat whose crew were non-union; and a strike of port workers developed against the Shipping Federation which lasted five weeks. Free labour was introduced by the Bute Dock authorities and by the Shipping Federation, and a depot ship called the *Speedwell* was used for accommodation.[3] A similar strike took place at Aberdeen on the 24 February 1891 when the seamen struck work against the Federation ticket; and when blackleg labour was introduced, the dockers came out in sympathy. George Laws said that the Aberdeen strike 'was caused by the seamen refusing to accept what they perversely termed a "badge of slavery" and they came out'. He added that there 'was any amount of free labour in the country to be had . . . and good labour too',[4] and the strike collapsed within less than three weeks.

So the story could be continued. Before the end of 1891 there had been strikes against the Shipping Federation in

[1] *Ibid.* vol. i, Q. 4955. George Laws was very tough. When the Webbs wanted an example of 'a bitter and implacable enemy of Trade Unionism', to illustrate a point they were making about union politics in the 1870s, they introduced the name of Mr. Laws, as one which would be familiar to all their readers in 1894. *The History of Trade Unionism* (1894 ed.), p. 271.

[2] See especially the long answer to Q. 4954 in *Minutes of Evidence*, vol. i. Details of the main strikes in the years 1889–92 are summarised in *R.C. on Labour, Digest of the Evidence*, Group B, vol. i (C. 6708-11), 1892, Abstract No. 1.

[3] *Ibid.* pp. 51-2; *Minutes of Evidence*, vol. i, Qs. 9327, 9890, 9938, 10,105 ff. (J. Havelock Wilson); vol. ii, Q. 13,742 ff. (Captain R. Pomeroy, dock master at the Bute docks, Cardiff.)

[4] *Ibid.* vol. i, Q. 4956.

Liverpool, Shields, Newcastle, Leith, Hull, Glasgow, Hartlepool, Middlesbrough, and Swansea in addition to those mentioned above. The central issue was the introduction of free labour, and with only minor exceptions the strikes resulted in a marked weakening of unionism among the seamen and the waterside workers all round the country. Public opinion, led by *The Times*, was by now thoroughly aroused about the 'tyranny' involved in mass picketing, and there was a steadily increasing discussion in the press and in Parliament of the ways in which the law of conspiracy could be used to curb the activities of the New Unions. The last major battle between the Shipping Federation and port workers, thereby concluding the first main phase of New Unionism along the waterfronts of the United Kingdom, occurred in the spring of 1893 when, after a seven weeks' strike, the dock workers and seamen of Hull were forced to go back on the Federation's terms.

Hull had become the best-organised port in the whole country by the end of 1892. Almost every docker had joined the union and considerable improvement in conditions had resulted. A major reason for this satisfactory state of affairs was the sympathy shown towards the Dockers' Union by Charles Wilson, Liberal M.P. for East Hull, and head of the port's biggest shipping company. Thomas Wilson and Sons not only permitted their clerks and foremen to join a union but they co-operated in many ways with the dockers' organisation to ensure the smooth functioning of union affairs. The dockers had excellent relations with the stevedores, and in general both working conditions and productivity had improved along the quays.

The firm of Wilson had apparently left the Shipping Federation some time after its foundation but rejoined it early in 1893.[1] According to Clem Edwards, normally a reliable witness, considerable pressure had been brought to bear upon Wilsons by both shipowners and marine insurance companies in the Shipping Federation.[2] Certainly from the beginning of

[1] *The Times*, 20 May 1893.
[2] 'The Hull Shipping Dispute', *Economic Journal*, iii (1893), p. 347. I have used the files of the *Hull Daily News* for local details.

Unions and Free Labour: Background to Taff Vale Decision

1893 Wilsons' attitude towards the unions changed. By the middle of February they were refusing to co-operate with the union in the collection of arrears of dues, as had been their normal practice. This was followed by the firm insisting that all their clerks and foremen left the union. And then, on 20 March, a branch of the British Labour Exchange was opened, and the following notice issued:

To Working Men

The employers of labour in connection with the docks and shipping at Hull have determined, in order to facilitate the conduct of the business of the port, in employing labour in future, to give preference to men who are registered at the British Labour Exchange, which has been opened; and all respectable, steady workmen are invited to register their names free of expense, and thus secure preference of employment.

The matter that came into immediate dispute was the clause regarding preferential treatment; but the central issue, recognised on all sides, was that this was the beginning of an offensive by the employers against the waterside unions. The dockers' leaders — especially the national officials, Tillett and Mann — were anxious to avoid a strike, and throughout the conflict adopted a conciliatory position. There was already serious unemployment among the dock and shipping workers, and the general position of the union, after the grim history of the years since 1889, was highly vulnerable.[1]

After much preliminary skirmishing, and a clear indication from the employers that they were not interested in compromise, the strike began in the first days of April and lasted for seven weeks. Several thousand free labourers were introduced into the port under military and police protection. Two gunboats stood off in the Humber, and Hull for these seven weeks was an armed camp. There was much violence and some attempts, not all unsuccessful, at large-scale arson. The town became

---

[1] J. Havelock Wilson, M.P., the seamen's leader, was throughout more belligerent than the national spokesmen for the dockers. It is probable that Tillett was referring to Havelock Wilson in his curious comments on the Hull strike in *Memories and Reflections*, pp. 161-2. Whether this interpretation is correct or not, Tillett gives a wholly wrong account of the causes of the strike. Tom Mann does not mention the strike in his *Memoirs* (1923).

a battleground between most of the local property owners and the working class. Of thirty-eight magistrates, four were shipowners and nineteen others owned shares or were financially interested in shipping.[1] Five out of fifteen members of the Watch Committee were shipowners.[2] The Poor Law Guardians openly acted as recruiting sergeants for 'free labour' when able-bodied labourers applied for relief.

Hull had a strong Liberal tradition and not all the propertied class were hostile to the strikers. But the majority were, and the forces of law, order, and wealth were ranged against the men on the waterfront. The strike ended, inevitably, with defeat for the unions. It was the most spectacular victory the Shipping Federation had enjoyed. *The Times* exulted. In an editorial of 20 May 1893 it wrote that as a result of the counter-combination of the employers, 'at Hull, as elsewhere, the New Unionism has been defeated. But nowhere has the defeat been so decisive, or the surrender so abject.' The man who became secretary of a national strike-breaking organisation in 1893 noted later that as the main result of the strike, Hull became 'a stronghold of Free Labour'.[3]

II

The main problem for active strike-breaking employers like the Shipping Federation or George Livesey of the South Metropolitan Gas Company, was to find adequate substitute labour during periods of strike. A subsidiary problem, having found enough blackleg labour, was getting them safely into the works or docks and feeding and accommodating them. The supply problem naturally varied according to the degree of skill required. For much dock work, it was mainly physical strength and endurance that were required; and in general, for the unskilled and most of the semi-skilled trades, provided that adequate police protection was available, a strike could

---

[1] Answer from the Home Secretary (H. H. Asquith) to a question from Keir Hardie, *Parl. Debates*, 4th Series, xi (12 April 1893), 327.
[2] Statement by John Burns, *Parl. Debates*, 4th Series, xii (4 May 1893), 106.
[3] W. Collison, *The Apostle of Free Labour* (1913), p. 275.

Unions and Free Labour: Background to Taff Vale Decision

always be defeated by the importation of labour from outside.[1] The Shipping Federation formed a special Labour Department which undertook, as one of its main functions in the early nineties, the supply of blackleg labour to shipping and dock companies involved in trade disputes.[2]

Strike-breaking organisations were not new to the industrial scene in 1890. Especially in London there was an underworld of breakaway or independent unions as well as organisations with working-class names whose services were always for hire. In the 1880s such bodies had been active in both national and metropolitan politics and in their leadership were a group of men who quickly became notorious.

They first appear in the Fair Trade movement of the early eighties,[3] but their names reappear in half a dozen different political contexts during the course of the decade. Thomas Kelly had been expelled from the Bristol Trades Council at the end of the seventies; working with him in Bristol was Samuel Peters.[4] When they came to London early in the eighties they joined forces with other ex- and bogus trade unionists among whom were Patrick Kenny, expelled from the London Trades Council for conduct which was 'a disgrace to the principles of trade unionism',[5] and William Patterson Lind who, in the second half of the seventies, had been running a seamen's trade union, the main characteristic of which was the extraordinary high proportion of working expenses to

---

[1] George Livesey, in the South Metropolitan Gas Strike of 1890, advertised for unskilled labour as far away as Lincolnshire. Some of his blackleg stokers came from Manchester. In the Hull Dock Strike of 1893, some of the blacklegs were Roman Catholics and most of these, it is fair to assume, were Irish labourers. In the same Hull strike, a reporter in the *Westminster Gazette* wrote that 'a number of doss-houses in the East End and the Borough have been literally cleaned out' in the search for replacements for the striking dockers. (Quoted in *Hull Daily News*, 11 April 1893.) See also the evidence of John Polhill, an agricultural labourer formerly earning an irregular 15s. a week, who was offered 30s. a week and board and lodging if he would work as a free labourer in the London docks. *R.C. on Labour, Minutes of Evidence*, Group B, vol. i, Qs. 5973-6069.

[2] Evidence of George Laws and Thomas Robb, *ibid.* Qs. 4918-5627.

[3] B. H. Brown, *The Tariff Reform Movement in Great Britain, 1881–1895*. (Columbia University Press, 1943), chapter 2.

[4] *Ibid.* p. 31.

[5] London Trades Council MS., 7 November 1878, quoted *ibid.* p. 32, note 10.

total income.[1] At some point early in the eighties the group established their headquarters in the Trafalgar Temperance Hotel (a pleasant touch) to be found in Leman Street, Whitechapel. Their speciality was 'control' of a number of fictitious working-class organisations — including such apparently respectable bodies as the Dock Porters and Sugar Warehousemen, Docks and Riverside Labourers' Council, Thames Watermen and Lightermen, Delegate Meeting of Trades, British Seamen's Protection Society, East End Fair Trade League, Workingmen's Association for the Abolition of Foreign Sugar Bounties. In the next decade Clem Edwards could list fifty such organisations sponsored by, or associated with some members of, the Trafalgar Hotel group.[2] Some of these bodies had, in the past, been legitimate unions or associations, but by the time the Kelly-Peters gang obtained control it was only the scum of the East End who were represented.

Such were the working men's representatives with whom some Conservative politicians and businessmen, leading the Fair Trade agitation, associated themselves. Concurrently with the Fair Trade movement, and more important, were the activities of this political underworld in the great London municipal reform agitation which finally led to the establishment of the London County Council in 1889. The municipal reform movement began when John Lloyd, a barrister and son of a large landowner in Breconshire, inserted an advertisement in *The Times* in 1880 asking for support for a reform campaign.[3] From this beginning a vigorous agitation developed, and the Parliamentary Liberal Party found itself under increasing pressure from its own supporters and associations in

---

[1] See p. 335 below.

[2] *Free Labour Frauds. A Study in Dishonesty.* Reprinted from *The Critic* (1898), 24 pp., pp. 6-7. Elie Halévy, *A History of the English People, Epilogue*, vol. i, 1895–1905, p. 249, note 1, quotes Clem Edwards as the author of this pamphlet; and most contemporaries agreed. W. Collison, *The Apostle of Free Labour* (1913), p. 173 ff., says that Henry Hess was the author.

[3] John Lloyd, *London Municipal Government. History of a Great Reform, 1880–1888* (1910). See also Sir G. Gibbon and R. W. Bell, *History of the London County Council, 1889–1939* (1939), chapter 3. The most detailed material on most aspects of the reform movement is in *S.C. on London Corporation* (*Charges of Malversation*), 1887, x.

Unions and Free Labour: Background to Taff Vale Decision

London to expedite the democratisation of London's government. The City of London Corporation, the main target of the new movement, became increasingly alarmed at this growing threat to its monopolistic position and established a Special Committee to organise the opposition to the reformers. Considerable sums of money were placed at the disposal of the Committee [1] and by its lavish distribution a not wholly unsuccessful counter-reform movement was brought into action. Reform meetings were repeatedly broken up by hired thugs (leading to the establishment of a private police force by the municipal reformers to ensure order at indoor meetings); [2] audiences were hired by the score; [3] tickets were forged in order to swamp reform meetings with the opposition; [4] journalists were paid to write up the counter-reform movement; [5] separate Municipal Charter movements were promoted for different districts of London as a counter to the reformer's demand for centralised control.[6] For two years, 1883–4, what in effect was a general election raged throughout

---

[1] According to the *Report from S.C. on London Corporation*, between the years 1882–5 the Committee disbursed nearly £20,000, of which £14,000 alone was spent in the single year 1884.

[2] *Ibid.* Report and Qs. 128 ff.; 1631 ff. (J. B. Firth). A man employed as a sub-contractor to hire men for the purpose of breaking up meetings later made a statutory declaration of his activities in which, *inter alia*, he wrote: '... On the 23rd day of May last (1883) the said J. H. Johnson asked me if I knew anything about American political meetings. I informed him I did. He then asked me if I could get together a number of men at 2s. 6d. each to help break up a meeting at Kensington. . . . I met the men at the appointed time, and proceeded with them to Kensington where a disturbance was created ...' (Q. 130). From the side of the municipal reformers, a Liberal iron master brought his own workmen — 'smiths, ironhammerers, and foundrymen' — to act as a police force inside the reform meetings (Q. 1634).

[3] See especially the evidence of J. H. Johnson, *ibid*. Q. 2617 ff. Johnson was a journalist employed in many capacities by the City of London Corporation's solicitor, and among his duties was the hiring of audiences — which he did often through the help of the Trafalgar Hotel group. For an amusing account of the swindling methods of some of these 'subcontractors', see Q. 2836.

[4] *Ibid.* Report and Q. 167 ff. (J. B. Firth).

[5] *Ibid.* Q. 2868 ff. (J. H. Johnson). After admitting payments to journalists, Johnson added, 'You may take it that they took a pleasant view of my side of the question' (Q. 2892).

[6] *Ibid. Report*, p. xii, and 'Summary of Case handed in by Mr. Bradlaugh', App. No. 4, pp. 259-62, especially para. 9. Bradlaugh, together with a lawyer M.P. representing the City of London Corporation, sat on the Select Committee with powers of cross-examination but no voting rights.

the Metropolis; and the agitation only died down when the Liberal Government withdrew their Local Government Bill at the end of the 1884 session.

The detailed history of this extraordinary campaign was uncovered by a Select Committee of the House of Commons in 1887 following charges made in the House by George Howell.[1] From the evidence obtained by the Select Committee it became apparent that among those prominent in breaking up meetings, enrolling hired audiences, and enlisting 'stewards' (defined by one participant as 'persons engaged to prevent opposition'),[2] and generally acting as the shock troops against the municipal reformers were the Kelly-Peters group. For them it was gainful employment of a high order of gain.[3]

Kelly, Peters, and their associates were as lively, intelligent, and tough a bunch of scoundrels as any potential strike-breaker could wish for. Among the political campaigns they had actively worked for, in the 1880s, at the head of their bogus working-class associations, were the Fair Trade movement, the anti-municipal reform movement, the Sugar Bounties controversy, and the Coal and Wine Duties agitation. By the end of the 1880s their experience in the 'working-class movement' was unique; and they were indeed tailored-made for the Shipping Federation. W. P. Lind, who, in the Peters-Bradlaugh trial,[4] was mentioned as the proprietor of the

[1] *Parl. Debates*, 3rd Series, cccxi, 895 ff., 1089, 1224-6. Howell was supplied with the evidence for his charges against the City Corporation by the Liberal municipal reformers, into whose hands had fallen (*sic*) many of the account books belonging to the City Corporation (see evidence of J. B. Firth, *loc. cit.* Q. 114 ff.).

[2] *S.C. on London Corporation, op. cit. Report*, p. xi.

[3] Cf. the evidence of the Remembrancer of the City of London where he admitted that he paid Kelly between £150 and £200 during 1884. He further admitted that he was not aware that Kelly was being employed at the same time by other officials of the Corporation. *Ibid.* Q. 3724 ff. (G. P. Goldney). Kelly was also involved during these years in the Fair Trade agitation.

[4] *The Times*, 19 April 1888. Samuel Peters, who on this occasion was styled secretary of the 'Workingmen's National Association for the Abolition of Foreign Sugar Bounties', sued Bradlaugh for libel arising out of a letter printed in *The Times*, 3 December 1887. Bradlaugh's letter alleged that a number of leading Conservatives, including Lord Salisbury, were subsidising working men's Fair Trade meetings (including meetings on the sugar bounty question). The case for the prosecution was that monies sent by Lord Salisbury and others were in response to charitable appeals

Unions and Free Labour: Background to Taff Vale Decision

Trafalgar Temperance Hotel, became registry superintendent of the Shipping Federation for the whole Thames area. In his evidence to the *R.C. on Labour*, in addition to his job as registry superintendent, Lind also claimed to be secretary of the London United Riggers' Association.[1] He forgot to mention that he was also still secretary of the Amalgamated British Seamen's Protection Society, a union which the Shipping Federation encouraged by allowing joint membership with the Federation for all seamen who registered on the Federation ticket. This Protection Society was shown in evidence before the *R.C. on Labour* to be one more bogus union. It had been established in 1872, made regular returns to the Chief Registrar only until 1882, and the striking feature of its later years was the high proportion that expenses bore to total income. When total income, in 1881, was nearly £95, the working expenses were just over £90; when income fell in 1882 to £6 : 13s., working expenses took £6 : 2s. : 3d. At this point in the fortunes of the society membership was 42. No further returns were made to the Registrar in 1883 or in subsequent years, and this was the bogus union with which the Shipping Federation had allied itself in 1890.[2]

It was men trained in the Kelly-Peters tradition rather than the Deptford 'Eye-Ball Buster Gang'[3] (which the Shipping Federation also used) that were most useful along the water-

---

from T. M. Kelly, secretary to the Riverside Workmen's Council. All cheques received were handed to Mr. Lind, proprietor of the Trafalgar Temperance Hotel, 'where Mr. Kelly's work of charity was proceeding'. Bradlaugh, who conducted his own case, put up an unbelievably incompetent defence — considering that he was better informed than most about Kelly's 'charitable' propensities — and he was mulcted of £300 damages. See H. B. Bonner, *Charles Bradlaugh*, ii (1902), pp. 384-6, 392-7, whose account tells only a small part of the story. It may be noted in passing that Lord Salisbury maintained an interesting connection with the political underworld. He admitted in this libel trial knowing Peters and Kelly — 'for seven or eight years' — and he had contact with Collison of the National Free Labour Association in the nineties. See the latter's *Apostle of Free Labour* (1913), pp. 76-7, 202, 321-3. See below, p. 338.

[1] *R.C. on Labour, Minutes of Evidence*, Group B, vol. i, Q. 7651 ff.

[2] *Ibid.* Q. 7604 ff. (W. P. Lind); Q. 5127 ff. (G. A. Laws); Q. 9325 (J. H. Wilson); App. 65.

[3] *Ibid.* Q. 8915 (Clem Edwards). There is a further reference to 'Jimmy Wall's eye-ball busters' brigade from Deptford' in *Free Labour Frauds*, *op. cit.* p. 9.

fronts in the years immediately following 1889. Straight thuggery was not to be eschewed, but there must, as well, be other approaches to the problem. The Federation, in fact, experimented. Their first Labour Master, R. H. Armit, whose job it was to recruit free labour directly for the Shipping Federation soon left them in protest against the way the Federation broke the terms of agreement with a group of free labourers whom he had recruited.[1] Then the Federation began setting up free labour offices under their own control, and recruiting directly their own blackleg labour. Apparently there were considerable legal as well as other disadvantages in this kind of direct organisation,[2] and in 1893 they passed over some part of their problems to an independent association which they themselves subsidised. In May 1893 there assembled at 'Ye Olde Roebucke' in Duke Street, Aldgate, a general conference on Free Labour. The man responsible for calling the conference was William Collison, henceforth to be the leading figure in the development of the free labour movement for the next two decades.

Collison, the eldest child of a policeman, was born in Stepney in 1865. He started work when he was 10, went to the docks at 14, spent two years in the army, and from the age of 18 was a casual labourer in the East End. He became an omnibus driver at the end of the eighties and helped organise the transport workers, but was converted to anti-trade unionism by reading Charles Reade's novel, *Put Yourself in His Place*. From the time of the Dock Strike of 1889 Collison advocated typically *laissez-faire* ideas, the central principle of which was free labour, defined as 'the right possessed by every man to pursue his Trade or Employment without dictation, molestation or obstruction'.[3] Collison was a quite different type from the Kelly-Peters group. His intelligence as well as his courage were never in question, and while there is no doubt that in

---

[1] R.C. on Labour, Minutes of Evidence, Group B, vol. i, Qs. 7464-68.

[2] *Free Labour Frauds, op. cit.* p. 14.

[3] W. Collison, *The Apostle of Free Labour* (1913). The phrase in the text is taken from the programme of the National Free Labour Association which Collison drafted (p. 94).

material terms he prospered as a result of his advocacy of the employers' cause, he also believed that what he was doing was wholly right. His autobiography is a well-written document, interesting as much for the dark places which it fails to illuminate (such as the financial support he was receiving from the employers) as for the light that it sheds on the contemporary hostility to trade unionism. In some respects he can be compared with Maltman Barry, for an adequate study of whom we are also lacking.[1]

The National Free Labour Association (N.F.L.A.) was established for one main purpose — to supply employers with workmen in the place of trade unionists who withdrew their labour.[2] In each main area of the country there was set up a Free Labour Exchange and a District Office. The registrars of such Exchanges — often retired police detective-inspectors 'used to handling men and forming a quick and accurate judgment of them'[3] — maintained a Live Register of workmen who had signed the Free Labour pledge. This pledge was simply an agreement to work in harmony with union and non-union labour alike. In the context of the objectives of the N.F.L.A. what this pledge in fact amounted to was a willingness to act as a blackleg.

As part of its general hostility to trade unionism and in the name of the 'free' working men whom it claimed to represent, the N.F.L.A. kept up a steady criticism and comment on all aspect of trade-union affairs. Its declared object was to discredit unionism in general and to keep before public opinion in particular the ways in which the industrial organisations of the working people might be weakened. Thus at its second annual conference in November 1894 it was reported that the Association had received a number of replies from prominent politicians to whom a statement on picketing had been

---

[1] I am indebted to Mr. Chimen Abramsky for this suggestion. See, for example, the sympathetic account of Eleanor Marx in Collison's book, pp. 81-5 ; sentiments which Maltman Barry undoubtedly shared.

[2] The most useful sources in addition to those already noted are : J. M. Ludlow, 'The National Free Labour Association', *Economic Review*, January 1895, pp. 110-18 ; P. Mantoux et M. Alfassa, *La Crise du Trade-Unionisme* (Paris, 1903), pp. 194-216, 309-20, 323-7.

[3] Collison, *op. cit.* p. 101.

addressed. Among those who replied was Lord Salisbury, who wrote through his secretary that he was not willing to commit himself definitely :

> But he concurs with you in thinking that picketing, as at present practised, appears to be open to considerable objection in many ways where it appears to involve molestation and intimidation. This interpretation of the law is certainly not in accordance with the views of those by whom the Bill was framed.[1]

A few months after the first decision in the picketing case of *Lyons* v. *Wilkins*, the N.F.L.A. organised a National Conference on Picketing in the same Memorial Hall where the Labour Representation Committee was to hold its inaugural conference three years later. At all points the N.F.L.A. opposed the claims of the trade unionists. When the Society of Compositors sent a deputation to the Treasury to ask for the inclusion of a union clause in government printing contracts, the N.F.L.A. organised a counter-deputation ;[2] it protested to the Works Department of the London County Council against the refusal of that department to employ non-union labour ;[3] it agitated consistently against the alleged trade-union bias of the Labour Department of the Board of Trade ;[4] it organised a campaign against the Employers' Liability Bill of 1894 (on behalf of the interests of the Railway Companies).[5] When Ben Tillett sued the *Morning* newspaper for libel, Collison supplied the defending counsel, Edward

---

[1] *Free Labour Gazette*, 7 November 1894. Collison, *op. cit.* p. 202, quotes the letter in full, but incorrectly states that it was written in 1897.
[2] Report by Collison to Second Annual Congress of the National Free Labour Association, *Free Labour Gazette*, 7 November 1894.
[3] *Ibid.* [4] Collison, *op. cit.* p. 159 ff.
[5] Second Annual Congress Report, *Free Labour Gazette*, 7 November 1894. William Ellis, an employee of the London and North Western Railway Insurance Society, was a delegate to this Congress from London. For a later controversy concerning Ellis, the London and North Western Railway and the N.F.L.A., see *Parl. Deb.*, 4th Series, clxxi (19 March 1907), 756 ff. ; clxxiii, 352 ff. ; clxxiv, 644 ff. The point at issue was a denial by Colonel Lockwood that the London and North Western Railway, of which he was a director, had ever subsidised the N.F.L.A., or that Ellis had ever attended a Free Labour Conference. From the record of the *Free Labour Gazette* there was no doubt about Ellis's attendance, and according to the same journal of July 1895, a W. Ellis had been appointed District Secretary of the North of England F.L.A.

Unions and Free Labour: Background to Taff Vale Decision

Carson, with many of the facts which Carson used with such devastating effect.[1] Collison gave evidence against the unions in the 1903 *Royal Commission on Trade Unions*, and earlier had furnished much of the material which Pratt used in his famous 'Ca-Canny' articles in *The Times*.[2]

The importance of the National Free Labour Association must not be exaggerated. At its worst, it was no more than a marginal influence within the general trend of increasing hostility to the trade-union movement from the time of the great Dock Strike. Although the N.F.L.A. shed some of its criminal fringe — including most of the Kelly-Peters gang — early in its career,[3] it inevitably relied upon the *lumpen* elements for much of its labour force, as the engineering employers apparently discovered in the great lock-out of 1897.[4] In the nineties the N.F.L.A. was the creature of the Shipping Federation; in the early years of the new century the role of puppet-master was taken over by the Railway Companies. Where unskilled labour only was required, the N.F.L.A. could be of material assistance in strike-breaking; but over the range of skilled trades its usefulness to the employers was minimal, if not negative. What is of note, however, is that the N.F.L.A. could openly exist and could just as openly, and with only the thinnest of disguises, be publicly supported by influential sections among the property owners. By itself, the National Free Labour Association was only of limited importance; it is the political context within which it operated that underlines its significance.

---

[1] Collison, *op. cit.* p. 258 ff.; Ben Tillett, *Memories and Reflections* (1931), p. 183 ff.

[2] Mantoux et Alfassa, *op. cit.* p. 326.

[3] Report of Second Annual Congress, *Free Labour Gazette*, 7 November 1894. Collison, *op. cit.* p. 96, makes only a passing reference to what was a major upheaval in the internal affairs of the N.F.L.A. during the first year of its life, although in his report, quoted above, he refers to the Kelly-Peters gang as 'a body of brandy shifters and moochers'. The N.F.L.A. was not the only Free Labour organisation in the 1890s; but there are only incidental references to these other bodies.

[4] *Free Labour Frauds*, p. 4. The engineering employers took the initiative in forming a Free Labour Protection Association. See the important letter announcing this in *The Times*, 6 September 1897; and for an account of the new organisation by J. M. Ludlow, see his note, 'The Labour Protection Association', *Economic Review*, April 1899.

III

The industrial offensive in the early years of the 1890s was most successful against the dockers, the seamen, and in the casual trades where especially female labour was largely employed;[1] but all the New Unions lost heavily in membership by the middle of the nineties.[2] An important contributory factor to their decline was the worsening economic situation, and the growth of unemployment, after 1890. The gasworkers, partly because many among them were semi-skilled, partly because their union quickly spread its organisation over many other trades,[3] suffered less than most; and there were other organisations, like the National Amalgamated Union of Labour, as well as some pockets of semi-skilled labour in different parts of the country[4] which managed to hold themselves together more effectively than the Dockers' Union which Ben Tillett led. But there was, of course, no other employer's organisation quite as aggressive and as unscrupulous as the Shipping Federation. The continuing series of industrial conflicts which shook Britain in the years immediately following the Dock Strike, exercised a profound influence upon ruling-class opinion. *The Times*, as already noted, was in the van of all those who attacked New Unionism, the leaders of which were described by another Conservative journal as 'our national Mafia'.[5] The *Economist*, a soberly edited periodical, was convinced that the mass of the new unionists were bemused and beguiled against their real interests by professional agitators.[6]

---

[1] See *R.C. on Labour, Fifth and Final Report*, Part II (C. 7421), 1894, App. 3.

[2] Crowley, *op. cit.* ch. xi; E. J. Hobsbawm, 'General Labour Unions in Britain, 1889–1914', *Econ. Hist. Review*, 2nd Ser. I, Nos. 2 and 3 (1949), pp. 123-42.

[3] Crowley, *op. cit.* ch. xi. [4] Hobsbawm, *op. cit.* p. 128.

[5] *Quarterly Review* (April 1891), p. 507. The other side of the medal was the widespread discussion, in the liberal and conservative press, of ways and means by which the conflict between capital and labour could be diminished. Hence the emphasis upon conciliation boards, profit sharing, and the like. For a very interesting discussion of the whole question, Sydney Olivier, 'The Miner's Battle — and After', *Contemporary Review* (November 1893), pp. 749-64.

[6] For typical examples of the *Economist*'s attitude, 22 March 1890 ('Strikes and Poor Relief'); 12 July 1890 ('The Cause of the Epidemic of Strikes'); 31 January 1891 ('The Scotch Railway Strike').

Unions and Free Labour: Background to Taff Vale Decision

There arose a veritable crescendo of demands that the freedom of the non-unionist must be protected by the state against the 'tyranny' of the New Unions. This is the background to the widespread use of large police and military forces from the early nineties on by both Liberal and Conservative administrations.[1] When, as from the middle years of the decade, the decisions of the Courts began to echo the hostility of the employers and the prejudice of the politicians towards trade unionism, the working men found themselves in a world in which their accepted position was being rapidly undermined. Their last refuge was the law as enacted by Parliament; and this, by judge-made decisions, was now being turned against them.

The legal status of trade unions in the last quarter of the nineteenth century had been defined by the Trade Union Act of 1871 and the Conspiracy and Protection of Property Act of 1875.[2] Down to the early 1890s there were no major legal decisions affecting trade unions, and until this time the assumptions which had promoted the legislation of the seventies remained acceptable to those whose province it was to interpret the law. When Sir Frederick Pollock wrote his *Memorandum on the Law of Trade Combinations* as an Appendix to the Final Report of the *R.C. on Labour*,[3] the law as he understood it made no essential difference of principle between combinations of employers and combinations of workmen. Whatever could be said of an employer's freedom to choose his workmen could also be said of a workman's freedom to choose his employers, and industrial combinations of workmen were now broadly equal before the law with those of the employers. Trade combinations were expressly not a criminal conspiracy, strikes were legal, peaceful picketing was specifically provided for in s. 7 of the 1875 Act, and since trade unions were not legally constituted corporations, they could not be sued for damages in

---

[1] Cf. the comment on the 1893 mining lock-out, R. P. Arnott, *The Miners* (1949), p. 237.

[2] The Act of 1876 — Trade Union Act Amendment Act (39 & 40 Vict. c. 22), made only slight amendments to the law.

[3] *R.C. on Labour, Fifth and Final Report*, Pt. I, 1894 (C. 7421), pp. 157-62.

their corporate existence.[1] Their members, of course, could be individually proceeded against. On the crucial question of 'intimidation' (which was to result in increasingly hostile judgments against the unions in the decade before Taff Vale) Mr. Justice Cave in 1880 had ruled that intimidation within the meaning of s. 7 of the 1875 Act must involve threatened or actual violence; and in 1891, the Queen's Bench Division, in the cases of *Gibson* v. *Lawson* and *Curran* v. *Treleaven*,[2] pronounced in the same way.[3] Already, however, in the case of *Curran* v. *Treleaven* a lower court had awarded the decision against the unionists on grounds that were to become common in the middle years of the nineties. Certain unions in Plymouth had threatened to strike if an employer, Treleaven, did not dismiss non-union labour. The Recorder of Plymouth, Mr. Bompas, Q.C., held that this was intimidation within the meaning of the 1875 Act, in that such a strike, or threat of a strike, was not to benefit the workman, but to injure the employer. Commenting on the decision, *The Times* wrote:

> It decides in effect that every strike organised for the purpose of crushing free labour — that is to say, the majority of the strikes undertaken by the New Unionism — is illegal, and can be made the subject of criminal proceedings.[4]

The Times had to wait a few more years before the Courts were prepared to accept their point of view, for on this occasion the decision was reversed by the Court of Appeal, which held to previous judgments whereby 'intimidation' must involve violence to the person or damage done to property.[5]

A decision that was widely held to be applicable to trade unions, and one that clearly influenced the attitude of the Court of Appeal in the two cases just quoted was that of *Mogul Steamship Company* v. *McGregor, Gow & Company*.[6] The defendants were a group of shipowners who, in order to drive

---

[1] There is a useful summary of nineteenth-century legislation in H. Vester and A. H. Gardner, *Trade Union Law and Practice* (1958), chapter i.
[2] [1891] 2 Q.B. 545.
[3] See the comment on these two cases in *Law Quarterly Review*, January 1892, p. 7; *Memorandum*, by Sir Frederick Pollock, *op. cit.* p. 161.
[4] *The Times*, 12 January 1891.
[5] [1891] 2 Q.B. 545. And see Lord Coleridge, L.J., at p. 562.
[6] [1892] A.C. 25 affirming (1889) 23 Q.B.D. 598.

certain competitors out of the tea-carrying trade from Chinese ports, slashed freight charges and threatened a boycott of shipping agents who refused to deal exclusively with their group. It was held that these acts were the 'lawful pursuit to the bitter end of a war of competition urged by the defendants in the interest of their own trade '; and since it was granted that unfettered competition was good for the community, the consequences of competitive action, which might involve the ruin of some sections of commerce or industry, have to be accepted. It was recognised that to ruin a man's trade because of a personal animus against him was unlawful, but to ruin him in the furtherance of one's own economic interests was a legitimate and natural instinct.[1]

The Mogul case was to be much quoted in succeeding years. Applied to the activities of trade unions, it suggested that if the officials of a trade union threatened an employer with a strike for employing non-union labour (provided violence was not threatened or used or a breach of contract not involved) the employer would have no right of action against the members of the union, even though economic injury resulted. If coercion by a combination of businessmen was legitimate, it was just as legitimate in the relations of workmen towards their employers.

This was certainly the accepted interpretation of the law when Sir Frederick Pollock wrote his Memorandum for the *Royal Commission on Labour* in January 1892. A year later came the first of the many hostile decisions against the unions. This was *Temperton* v. *Russell*,[2] which concerned three trade unions in Hull that sought to compel a firm of builders to comply with certain building regulations. The plaintiff supplied building materials to the firm in question and the unions threatened to withdraw their members unless he desisted. The Court of Appeal held that an action was maintainable by the plaintiff against the unions both 'in respect of the interference with existing contracts and in respect of the prevention

[1] Summary of the case from Hon. Alfred Lyttelton, 'The Law of Trade Combinations' in *A Policy of Free Exchange* (ed. T. Mackay, 1894), pp. 287-9.
[2] [1893] 1 Q.B. 715.

of contracts being entered into in the future'.[1] The judgment relating to the breaking of contracts already entered into was in line with established decisions, but that regarding contracts in the future was without precedent. In effect, the power of a trade union to refuse the services of their members except upon stated terms was now being denied by the Courts.[2]

The effect of the decision in *Temperton* v. *Russell* (although the matter was not pronounced upon by the House of Lords) was to suggest that for workmen's combinations there were now different assumptions from those which applied to the employers. Sir Frederick Pollock attached a short supplementary note to his 1892 Memorandum on Trade Union Law,[3] in which he briefly set out the decision in *Temperton* v. *Russell*, and added his own opinion that 'with great submission, the reasons given in the judgment do not convince me that the decision is right on this point' (viz. 'that a combination to persuade workmen not to renew their engagements with a particular employer (this being within the workmen's rights, and coercion or intimidation of the workmen not being alleged) may be an actionable wrong, if "malicious")'. Other lawyers were similarly sceptical; and this decision in *Temperton* v. *Russell* is not only the starting-point in the series of hostile judgments that culminated in the Taff Vale case and *Quinn* v. *Leathem*, but it also marks the beginning of the growing confusion concerning the legal status of trade unions. In 1902 Asquith was able to declare in the Commons that the law relating to trade unions was 'in an unsatisfactory, confused, and I think I might almost say, chaotic state'.[4]

The reversal, by judge-made law, of the principles and assumptions which underlay the trade-union legislation of the 1870s, is an interesting commentary upon the political power of the Judiciary, and the much-discussed question of its independence. In the decade after 1889, the Courts followed, at only a short distance of time, the changes in public opinion towards the trade unions; and it is instructive to match,

[1] Lord Esher, at p. 730. [2] Lyttelton, *op. cit.* pp. 289-90.
[3] *Op. cit.* p. 163.
[4] *Parl. Debates* 4th Series, cviii (14 May 1902), 328.

Unions and Free Labour: Background to Taff Vale Decision

argument for argument, the attacks upon trade unions in the press and in Parliament, and the *obiter dicta* of the judges in decisions the result of which was the steady whittling away of the legal rights of the unions.

From the middle of the nineties, there was increasing comment in the press on the growing number of cases involving industrial questions.[1] It was a relatively new phenomenon, just as was the growing practice of using troops in trade disputes. The injunction was being increasingly accepted by the Courts to prohibit picketing in cases of strike action,[2] and in other ways to restrict the spread of unionism.[3] In *Trollope and Sons* v. *London Building Trades Federation*, it was held actionable for the officers of a trade union to publish a 'black list', the object of which was to prevent members of the building unions from working with or for any of the persons or firms named on the list. In the lower court the firm was granted an injunction to prevent publication of the list, the Court of Appeal upheld the decision, and in the action arising out of the case, damages of £500 were awarded 'to remind the defendants' said the foreman of the jury 'that they had made a mistake'.[4] The whole trade-union world had now become aware of the trend of legal decisions against the unions. Up to this time the skilled unions had been fairly passive spectators at the political and industrial attacks upon the New Unions; but now it was becoming clear even to the most conservative among the unionists that the whole movement was becoming

[1] Cf. the leading article in *The Times*, 29 July 1895: 'Questions as to labour have of late for some reason been more heard of in our Courts than used to be the case . . . both here and in America, and in the latter much more than with us, the recent actions of trade unions has brought them into collision with the Courts'.
[2] See *The Times*' report (28 to 30 July 1896) of *Wernam* v. *Stone*, and especially the remarks on picketing in the summing-up of Mr. Justice Grantham (30 July 1896).
[3] See *The Times*' report (27 July 1895) of *Wright and Company* v. *Hennessey* and the leading article of 29 July 1895. Hennessey was organising secretary of the National Association of Operative Plasterers. The union had withdrawn labour from an employer, Peck, to whom another master plasterer, Wright, had then lent men. Wright was blacklisted and union pressure was exercised against other firms with whom he was doing business. The jury awarded damages of £500 for libel and another £300 for causing breaches of contract from which Wright suffered.
[4] See *The Times*, 28 April, 1, 2, and 5 May 1896; 12 L.T. 373.

involved, and that the general position of all their organisations was being threatened. Few of the older unionists would have agreed with the remarks that Ben Tillett made to the Dockers' Union in 1896 — that the Courts were 'creatures of corruption' and the judges 'class creatures and instruments for the maladministration of the law'; but uneasiness was growing. The Parliamentary Committee of the T.U.C. issued a circular in April 1896 drawing the attention of its constituent members to some recent legal decisions and asking whether the whole movement should support appeals to the Supreme Court or should press for new legislation to remedy their now ambiguous position.[1]

The movement, however, while stirring, took yet a few more years to become fully aware of the dangers that threatened; and in the meantime both legal judgments and industrial defeats continued to make clear the dangerous situation in which the unions were now living. This year, 1896, saw the first stage in the most celebrated of all picketing cases, *Lyons* v. *Wilkins*.[2] J. Lyons and Sons, the plaintiffs, were leather goods manufacturers and the defendant, Wilkins, was the secretary of the Amalgamated Trades Society of Fancy Leather Workers. The society ordered a strike against Lyons and also against one of their sub-contractors. Both firms were picketed by order of the executive committee of the union. Lyons first applied for an injunction to restrain the unionists from picketing. On 13 February 1896 Mr. Justice North granted an order 'restraining the defendants from maliciously inducing, or conspiring to induce persons not to enter the employment of plaintiffs'. It was agreed that there had been no violence, or threat of violence, by the pickets. The union appealed, and it was heard on 18 and 19 March 1896, before three judges of the Court of Appeal. The restraining order, with only slight amendments to its wording, was upheld. Certain of the *dicta*

---

[1] *The Times*, 18 April 1896. For a statement of the law in 1896, see the Webbs's essay, 'The Legal Position of Collective Bargaining' in *Industrial Democracy* (1911 ed.), App. 1. While the Webbs recognised fully the meaning of the adverse decisions that had recently been made against the unions, they found it difficult to believe that they were not more than temporary aberrations. Cf. p. 858, note 1: 'So strong is *still* the legal feeling against Trade Unionism . . .' (my italics—J. S.).

[2] [1896] 1 Ch. 811.

of these appeal judges illustrate the way in which the political arguments for free labour were now finding legal justification. Lindley, L. J. (Sir Nathaniel Lindley, soon to become Master of the Rolls), said in the course of his judgment:

> Some strikes are perfectly effective by virtue of the mere strike and other strikes are not effective unless the next step can be taken, and unless other people can be prevented from taking the place of the strikers. This is the pinch of the case in trade disputes; and until Parliament confers on trade unions the power of saying to other people, 'You shall not work for those who are desirous of employing you upon such terms as you and they may mutually agree upon', trade unions exceed their power when they try to compel people not to work except on the terms fixed by the unions.[1]

Kay, L. J., was even more blunt:

> I hold distinctly that it is illegal to picket the work or place of business of a man by persons who are distributed and placed there for the purpose of trying by persuasion to induce the workmen of that man not to work for him any longer, or to induce people who want to work for him to abstain from entering into an agreement with him to do so. That seems to me illegal . . . (and picketing a sub-contractor) still more clearly is it illegal.[2]

This case of *Lyons* v. *Wilkins* was a long-drawn-out affair. So far all that had been decided was the legality of the order restraining picketing. The case itself was not heard until November 1897, and the judge, Mr. Justice Byrne, further postponed his decision until the House of Lords had pronounced judgment in an appeal that was currently before them. This was *Allen* v. *Flood* ([1898] A.C.1). On 3 February 1898 Byrne, J., finally gave judgment in *Lyons* v. *Wilkins* which, with only minor legal differences, underwrote the 1896 *dicta* as to the illegality of the union's picketing activities. The main point of the decision was that the type of picketing practised in this instance constituted 'watching and besetting' as distinguished from 'attending in order merely to obtain or communicate information' which was permitted under s. 7 of the 1875 Act. The union's appeal came before Sir Nathaniel Lindley, now Master of the Rolls, and two other appeal judges who affirmed the decision and dismissed the appeal.[3] The

[1] *Ibid.* pp. 822-3. [2] *Ibid.* p. 830. [3] [1899] 1 Ch. 256.

defending counsel, in a very able speech, argued that the intention of the 1875 Parliament had been to allow peaceful persuasion — an argument that the Master of the Rolls dismissed as irrelevant — and in this, and other matters, the defence was supported by many distinguished lawyers, including Sir Frederick Pollock who, in the *Law Quarterly Review*, both in 1896 and 1899, criticised the judgments in the Appeal Courts and argued, as a matter of urgency, that the House of Lords should pronounce.[1]

For a variety of reasons, however, *Lyons* v. *Wilkins* was never taken to the House of Lords.[2] The majority decision in *Allen* v. *Flood* [3] further muddled the whole question in that it was regarded as a victory for the unions. By the end of the old century the state of trade-union law was in considerable confusion, although the balance of decisions was markedly tipped against the unions. Picketing was being seriously questioned, heavy damages had been awarded against union officials and members arising out of strikes or the threat of strikes, and already there had been raised the question of the unions being sued in their corporate capacity. Then, close together, came the Taff Vale case and the decision in *Quinn* v. *Leathem*.

The Taff Vale case has been described in great detail.[4] In July 1901 the House of Lords unanimously reinstated the

---

[1] *Law Quarterly Review*, xlvii (July 1896), p. 201 ; lix (July 1899), p. 221.

[2] H. Pelling, *The Origins of the Labour Party, 1880-1900* (1954), p. 212, quoting *G.F.T.U. Conference Report, 1899*, p. 17 ; and *T.U.C. Reports*, 1899, p. 17, and 1900, p. 33 ff. ; and B. C. Roberts, *The Trade Union Congress, 1868-1921* (1958), p. 165. Both note that the failure to appeal to the House of Lords was due to a combination of factors, among them a technical error on the part of the solicitor handling the case, and the length of time it took the T.U.C. Parliamentary Committee to raise the necessary money. But in a debate on the state of trade-union law, after the decision on the Taff Vale case (*Parl. Deb.* 4th Ser., cviii, 299, 14 May 1902), Sir Charles Dilke intervened to say that the case was dropped on legal advice. In the same debate the Attorney-General taunted the opposition with the withdrawal of *Lyons* v. *Wilkins* from appeal to the Lords, the inference being that the T.U.C. Parliamentary Committee was, in fact, reluctant to have the matter definitively pronounced upon (*ibid.* 318-19).

[3] [1898] A.C.1. See the summary in E. Halévy, *A History of the English People, Epilogue*, i (1895-1905), p. 267 ff. Halévy, Pt. II, chapter 2, is still the best general introduction to these years.

[4] F. Bealey and H. Pelling, *Labour and Politics, 1900-1906* (1958), chapters 3 and 4.

decision of Mr. Justice Farwell, delivered ten months earlier, the main point of which was that a trade union could be sued in its corporate capacity for tortious acts committed on its behalf. This had been a recommendation of the *Royal Commission on Labour* in 1894,[1] opposed vigorously by the minority of trade unionists.[2] Henceforth, after the Taff Vale decision, trade unions would be liable for heavy damages for any actions arising out of their activities which could lie against them. In the particular event, the Amalgamated Society of Railway Servants paid the Taff Vale Railway Company £23,000 in settlement of damages and costs.[3]

A fortnight after the decision in the Taff Vale case, the House of Lords gave judgment in *Quinn* v. *Leathem*.[4] Quinn was the treasurer of the Belfast Journeymen Butchers' Association. The union tried to persuade Leathem, an employer, to dismiss his non-union assistants. Leathem refused but offered to pay any fee whereby his assistants might become union members. This offer the union refused, and threatened Munroe, who bought meat from Leathem, with a strike unless he ceased buying from Leathem. Munroe submitted to the threat, whereupon Leathem brought an action against Quinn and other officials on the grounds that they had conspired together to injure him and from which he had suffered damage.[5] A Belfast court awarded damages against Quinn and the decision was upheld by the House of Lords. Lord Macnaghten argued that *Quinn* v. *Leathem* was identical with the facts of *Temperton* v. *Russell* and all the law lords agreed that *Allen* v. *Flood* was not relevant, *dicta* that materially restricted the significance of this decision.[6] The effect of the judgment in *Quinn* v. *Leathem* was that a strike or boycott, or threat of strike or boycott, would be held in certain circumstances as a conspiracy to injure for which the union funds, as the result of the Taff Vale case, were now available for damages.

[1] 'Observations appended to the Report . . .', *Fifth and Final Report, R.C. on Labour*, Pt. I, paras. 1-11.
[2] Report by Mr. William Abraham . . . *ibid*. p. 146.
[3] Bealey and Pelling, *op. cit.* p. 71.
[4] [1901] A.C. 495.
[5] Summary from Vester and Gardner, *op. cit.* p. 9.
[6] [1901] A.C. 495 at pp. 508-9.

The unions were now in an extremely dangerous position. Not only did these legal decisions open the way to an increasing use of the 'free labour' weapon, but now the skilled unionists were as vulnerable to actions by the employers in the Courts as were their unskilled brethren. The industrial defeats of the last decade, and especially the failure of the engineers in 1897, underlined the difficulties of the general situation. Inevitably the leadership of the trade-union movement, however slowly their rank and file appreciated the position,[1] were pushed into political action to remedy the situation by legislation. The strengthening of the Labour Representation Committee, the greatly increased independent labour representation at the General Election of 1906 and the Trades Disputes Act of 1906, were the short-term results.[2]

[1] Bealey and Pelling, *op. cit.* chapter 4.
[2] I am indebted to my colleague Mr. H. K. Bevan for his comments on the latter part of this essay; but he must not be held responsible for any errors that I may have made.

INDEX

Titles of trade unions have been inverted where necessary to make them follow the general entry for the relevant occupation. References to trade unions mentioned only incidentally in the text are included in the general entry for the appropriate occupation. References to associations organised by place rather than occupation that are not indexed individually will be found in the general entry for the place.

ABERDEEN : branch of First International, 271 ; dock strike, 327
Adams, H., 219
Adderley, Sir C., 73 n. 3
Adullamites, 223
Agricultural workers, 132, 203
Allen, W., 177, 202, 216, 231
Allen v. *Flood*, 347, 348, 349
Alliance of Socialist Democracy, 244
Alsace, 117
America, *see* United States
American Civil War, 198-201, 218-220
American Society of Mechanical Engineers, 134
Anarchists, *see under* First International
Anti-Corn Law League, 53, 59, 61, 69 ; *see also* Corn Law Repeal
Anti-semitism, 260-1
Anti-war movements, 135
Applegarth, R., 198, 202, 203, 210, 214, 215, 216, 235, 247, 263-4
Arbeiterbildungsverein, 267, 269 n. 2
Arbitration, *see under* Labour management
Argenson, R. L. Voyer, Marquis d', 148-9
Armagh Co-operative Society, 84
Armit, R. H., 336
Armstrong-Whitworth, 135-6
Arnold, M., 69, 72
Asquith, H. H., 344
Assington, Owenite community, 78
Association of All Classes of All Nations, 90
Attwood, T., 51
Australia, labour legislation in, 321
Austria-Hungary, 136, 157, 165

Aveling, E., 278, 289
Avignon, section of Polish Democratic Society, 153-4

BABBAGE, C., 128
Babeuf, F. É., 145, 166, 172, 173
Bagehot, W., 71 n. 1
Baillie-Cochrane, A., 254
Bakunin, M., 172 ; *see also under* First International
Barcelona, support for Bakunin in, 244
Barker, H. A., 295
Barnsley, Owenite Labour Exchange, 87 ; co-operative movement, 92
Barry, Maltman, 249-52, 263, 264, 265, 274, 337
Bartley, J., 302, 306, 307
Basle Congress of the International, *see under* First International
Batley, and U.S. tariffs, 283 ; Fabian Society, 302 n. 1
Bax, E. Belfort, 269 n. 1, 275
Beaconsfield, Earl of, *see* Disraeli, B.
Beales, E., 189, 192 n. 3
Bee-Hive (afterwards *Industrial Review*) : origins, 174, 175-6, 180-1, 188-193 ; abolition of newspaper taxes a mixed blessing for, 182-3 ; and the London Trades Council, 174, 188-9, 190 ; financing, 183, 196-7, 198, 200-1, 202 ; constitution of Trades Newspaper Co., 183-6, 187-8 ; met need for trade-union newspaper, 181-2 ; aims, 184 ; choice of title, 180-1, 188 ; editorial staff, 186-7, 195, 201 ; popular appeal, 194-5 ; organ of different organisations, 174, 194, 202, 253 ; directors, 192-3, 195-6, 200-1 ; quarrel

between Potter and Dell, 188-9; successful start, 193-4, 197; and the American Civil War, 198-201, 218-20; and E. S. Beesly, 185, 213, 215-16, 230, 233, 234; and the Liberals, 230; quarrel between Potter and the directors, 200-1; conflict between Potter and the 'Junta', 183, 188; circulation, 174-5, 183, 194, 197-8, 201; price, 183

Beesly, Edward Spencer: early life, 205; at University College, London, 206, 212, 227-8; and Positivism, 206-7, 208-10, 217, 233; and the Christian Socialists, 212-13; and the *Bee-Hive*, 185, 213, 215-16, 230, 233, 234; and Potter, 215-16, 230, 231; and the American Civil War, 198, 218-20; and the education of public opinion, 209; and Marx, 211, 220, 228, 231, 232, 233, 241; and the trade-union movement, 213-214, 217-18, 220, 225-31, 234-8; and the nine-hours movement, 212; and the new model unions, 215-16, 240; on arbitration, 216-217; and the First International, 217-18, 220, 256 n. 4, 271 n. 1; and the Reform movement, 219-224; and Governor Eyre, 223, 226-7; and physical force, 224; and the Fenians, 225; Exeter Hall speech, 226-8; 'Programme for Trade Unions', 228; and the Irish question, 229, 238; marries, 231-2; and the Paris Commune, 232-4; politically inhibited by his Positivism, 238-9; general influence, 239-41. See also Positivism

Beever, J. H., 287 n. 1, 310

Behrens, Sir Jacob, originates Bradford committee on working-class conditions, 282

Belgium, industrial productivity, 117, 122, 125-6, 128, 138; influence of French Utopians, 140; Polish émigré socialists, 141; radicals from, and *La Tribune des Peuples*, 166; representatives at the 1871 London Conference of the First International, 245; support for Bakunin, 264

Berlin, 135, 273

Berne Anarchist Congress, 274
Besant, Annie, 293
Bethnal Green, branch of First International, 249, 252, 259, 274
Bevan, T., 192, 195
Bingley, co-operative movement, 92
Birkenhead, branch of First International, 259, 266; three-shift system in gasworks, 129 n. 1
Birmingham, co-operative movement, 84, 87, 88, 96; trade unionism, 215, 250 n. 4
Birmingham Political Union, 51
Birstall, co-operative movement, 92
Blackburn, disorders at, 231
Blackstone Edge, demonstration at, 298
Blanc, L., 168, 172
Bland, P., 289, 293
Blanquists, *see under* First International
Blatchford, R. ('Nunquam'), 278, 290, 308, 309, 312-13
Board of Trade Labour Department, 338
Boilermakers, 121, 136, 318
Bolte, F., 257
Bolton, 136, 278
Bookbinders, 177, 182, 185, 193, 214, 249 n. 2; London Consolidated Society of, 177, 185
Boon, M. J., 247, 257, 260
Boot and Shoe Operatives, 135, 136-137, 249 n. 2, 295 n. 2
Bradford, 228, 230, 289, 290-1, 293, 295; I.L.P. founded at, 302; I.L.P. in, 277, 278-9, 286, 288 n. 4, 311-12, 313; Manningham Mills strike, 278-9, 284 n. 4, 286, 303, 306-8; branch of Socialist League, 280, 293, 294, 301, 305; T.U.C. meeting, 281, 294, 305; social conditions, 282-3; and U.S. tariffs, 283; textile workers, 289; Labour Church, 291; Fabian Society, 301-2; Labour Union, 302, 307-8, 312-13; relations between I.L.P. and Trades Council, 303, 305, 310
Bradford Trades Council, 280, 281, 303, 305, 308, 310
Bradlaugh, C., 234, 250, 252, 271-2, 274, 333 n. 6, 334 n. 4
Bramwell, Baron, 225-6
Branicki, K., Count, 166
Brassey, T., 128, 270 n. 1

352

Index

Bratkowski, S., 172 n. 1
Bray, J. F., 92
Bremen, 244
Brentano, L., 128
Bricklayers, 175, 178, 179, 180, 182, 185, 189-90, 191, 198 n. 3, 200, 214, 247, 259, 283, 295
Bricklayers, Hull Operative, 185
Bricklayers' Society, Operative (*formerly* London Order of Bricklayers), 175, 178, 179, 182, 189-90, 191, 200, 247
Bridges, J. H., 205, 206-7, 230
Briggs co-partnership scheme, 101
Brighouse Trades Council, 309
Bright, J., 199, 218-19, 220, 221, 222-3, 224, 225, 228, 229, 288
Brighton, 81, 82-3
'Brighton system', *see under* Co-operative movement
Bristol, three-shift system in gasworks, 129 n. 1; 'team system' in boot-and-shoe industry, 135
Bristol Trades Council, 331
British Association for Promoting Co-operative Knowledge, 85
British Association for the Advancement of Science, 206
British Labour Exchange, 329
British Miner, The, 214
British Seamen's Protection Society, 332
Broadhead, W., 225, 226, 227, 237
Broadhurst, H., 238
Brotherhood (*Zbratnienie*), 161, 162
Brougham, H., 55
Brussels Anarchist Congress, 274
Bryan, W., 81, 82
Buchez, P. J. B., 146, 170, 172
Budapest, anti-war movement, 135
Builders, 86, 88, 122, 130, 131, 175-6, 177, 178, 179 n. 2, 181, 182, 184, 185, 186, 191, 206, 211, 295; *see also* Bricklayers, Carpenters, Painters, Plasterers, Plumbers
Building Trades Conference, 176, 177, 178
Buonarroti, M., 145, 146
Burgess, F. J., 192
Burgess, J., 278, 306, 309
Burke, E., 51
Burnley, 129 n. 1
Burns, J., 210
Bury, co-operative movement, 92
Butler, J., 195
Butler, R. D., 256

CABET, E., 146, 157, 159, 160-1, 172
Cabinet-makers, 236, 249 n. 2
Campbell, A., 84-5
Carbonari, 145
Cardiff, dock strike, 327
Carlyle, T., 47
Carpenter, E., 289, 291, 292, 298, 304, 305 n. 1
Carpenters, 87, 116, 175, 177, 178-9, 180, 185, 190, 192, 193, 195-6, 197, 198, 214, 215, 247, 254, 281 n. 1
Carpenters and Joiners, Amalgamated Society of, 175, 196, 197, 198, 214, 215
Carpenters and Joiners, Progressive Society of, 177, 178-9, 190
Carson, Sir E., 338-9
Chamberlain, J., 237
Champion, H. H., 277, 278, 304-5
Charter, The, 187
Chartism, 61-2, 68-9, 71, 90, 92, 104, 106, 181, 288
Cheap labour economy, *see under* Wages
Chernishevsky, N. G., 172
Chevalier, M., 131
Chipping Norton, 236
Christian Socialists, 90, 93-4, 102 n. 1, 106-7, 180, 181, 212-13
Cigar-makers, 249 n. 2
Class, as term describing social categories, 43, 47, 48-9, 50-1, 59 n. 4, 66-7, 69, 72 n. 2, 73; 'orders', 'ranks', and 'degrees', 43 n. 3, 44 n. 4, 48-9, 50, 59, 63 n. 3, 72 n. 2, 73 n. 3; class antagonisms, 45, 46-7, 48, 49, 60, 63, 64, 66-8, 69, 143, 148, 152, 173, 220, 221, 223, 226, 229, 303; class distinctions, 44-5, 48, 53, 57-8, 66-7, 69-73, 116-17, 142-3, 285, 295-6; concept of a 'working class', 46-7, 48, 60, 61, 62, 68-9, 73; 'productive' and 'non-productive' classes, 49-51, 88, 106; use of terms 'upper class' and 'middle class', 51-60; growing middle-class consciousness, 52-60, 72; middle classes and public opinion, 54-7
Clayton, Murgatroyd & Co., 310, 311
Clayworkers, 306
Coachmakers, 116, 254, 281 n. 1
Coal-tippers, 327
Cobbett, W., 45-6, 47, 65, 260
Cobden, R., 59, 60, 72, 288
Collett, J., 181-2, 192 n. 1

Collison, W., 334 n. 4, 336-9
Colne Valley, I.L.P. in, 277 n. 3, 280, 311; Labour Union, 308
Colquhoun, P., 49-50, 51 n. 1
Combe, A., 79, 80
Commonweal, The, 294
Commonwealth, The (formerly *Workman's Advocate*), 202, 204, 253
Communist League, 257
Compositors, 117, 187, 338; *see also* Printers
Comte, A., as social thinker, 206-7, 210-11; 'Religion of Humanity', 207, 208, 213; law of the three stages, 207-8. *See also* Positivism
Conference of Amalgamated Trades, 211, 230, 235
Congreve, R., 205, 206, 207, 222, 227, 228, 238
Conspiracy and Protection of Property Act (1875), 341, 342
Conspiracy Laws, 236, 341, 342
Cooper, W., 93, 98
Co-operative Magazine, 80, 81, 82, 103, 111
Co-operative movement, influenced by Robert Owen, 74-90, 94-5, 98-99, 100, 102, 111; as an organisation of communities, 76-80, 94-5, 96, 104-5, 114; working-class support for Owenite schemes, 79-80, 88-90, 104-5; financial problems, 78-80, 80-1, 82-6, 94-5, 96, 102; rapid growth in 1830s, 86; and Labour Exchanges, 86-7, 109; failure of Owenite phase, 86-90; Queenwood settlement, 74, 88; and capitalism, 86, 94, 99, 100, 102, 106, 107, 110; and the trade unions, 86-8, 109-10; and the I.L.P., 280, 287; transitional period of development around 1850, 90-8, 107; and the Redemption societies, 90-3, 96; and the Christian Socialists, 90, 93-4, 100, 102 n. 2; Rochdale Pioneers' Society, 74, 90-1, 92, 94-9, 107; as simply shopkeeping, 95-102, 107; Co-operative Congresses, 67 n. 3, 68, 77, 84, 86, 96, 100, 110; manufacturing societies, 97, 99, 110; wholesale societies, 74, 98; aims of co-operators, 88-90, 100, 111, 112; as self-help, 111, 112; a democratic movement, 110, 112. *See also* Owen, R.

Co-operator, The, 83, 85, 99, 107-8
Copley, Fabian society, 302 n. 1
Cordwainers, 250 n. 4
Cork, Owenite community, 78; branch of First International, 254
Corn Law Repeal, 56, 58-9, 90; *see also* Anti-Corn Law League
Cotton workers, 122, 136, 137, 138, 318
Coulson, E., 200, 202, 214
Coventry, 136
Craig, E. T., 99, 110
Crefeld, 306
Cremer, W. R., 230, 263
Criminal Law Amendment Act (1871), 234, 235-6
Critchett, T., 195
Crofters, 278
Crompton, H., 231, 235
Cunninghame Graham, R. B., 298
Curran v. *Treleaven*, 342
Curriers, 250 n. 4
Cutler, W., 236
Czartoryski, Prince A., 141, 164
Czynski, J., 156, 160, 163

Daily Telegraph, The, 176
Daly, J., 94
Danielson, N. F., 258
Defoe, D., 43 n. 3, 44, 45, 57 n. 2
Delegate Meeting of Trades, 332
Dell, W., 183-4, 185, 188-9, 192-3, 197, 198, 200
Dembowski, E., 157
Democratic Federation, the, 278, 293
De Morgan, J., 254, 272
Deptford Eye-Ball Buster Gang, 335
Derby Conference on the Nine-Hours Movement, 179
Dewsbury, 309-10; I.L.P. in, 277 n. 3; Ernest Jones invited to stand for, 287
Dewsbury Trades Council, 281
Dicey, A. V., 72
Dilke, Sir C., 348 n. 2
Disraeli, B., 47-8, 260
Dock Porters and Sugar Warehousemen, 332
Dockers, 319, 322, 324, 325-30, 340; London Dock Strike, 1889, 295, 317, 321, 322-3, 324, 325, 326-7; Hull strike, 328-30, 331 n. 1; Plymouth strike, 325, 326; Southampton strike, 325-6; other provincial strikes in 1891, 327-8

Index

Dockers' Union, 308, 324 n. 4, 325-6, 340, 346
Docks and Riverside Labourers' Council, 332
Doherty, J., 66
Donald, A. K., 298 n. 4
Dorchester Labourers' Committee, 187
Drew, W. H., 289, 291, 302, 305, 306, 307, 310
Drury, J., 109
Dublin, Owenite community, 78
Dundee, 129 n. 1; branch of First International, 259
Dunning, T., 177, 193, 195
Dupont, E., 252-3, 255, 262, 263, 264, 267
Durham, J. G. Lambton, 1st Earl, 56

EAST END FAIR TRADE LEAGUE, 332
Eccarius, J. G., 247, 249, 250 n. 4, 257, 258, 264, 269-70, 274
Economist, The, 319, 320, 340
Economist, The (Mudie), 79
Edinburgh, 186
Edwards, C., 324-5, 326 n. 5, 328 332
Égalité, 246
Eight Hour Day, demand for the, 286, 293, 297, 298, 299-301, 311, 320
Elcho, Lord, 236
Elliott, E., 61
Ellis, W., 338 n. 5
Employers' Liability Bill (1894), 338
Enclosures, 46
Engels, F., 48, 55, 63 n. 1, 233, 243, 248, 252-3, 255, 262, 263, 264, 266, 267, 268, 269, 278, 288, 289, 300
Engineers, 69-70, 107, 109, 110, 116, 118, 131, 134, 135-6, 137, 177, 196-7, 247, 281 n. 1, 294, 339, 340
Engineers, Amalgamated Society of, 69-70, 107, 109, 110, 135, 179, 196-7, 247, 280 n. 4, 294, 295, 301 n. 2, 305, 308
Européen, L', 146
Exeter, Owenite community, 78, 80
Extraordinary Black Book, 50-1
Eyre, E. J., 223, 224

FABIANS, 134, 211, 241, 301-2, 310
Factory Acts, 283, 286-7, 291
Factory system, 45, 47

Fair Trade movement, 331, 332, 334
Farn, J. C., 108
Federation of Trade and Labour Unions, 324
Fenians, 225, 250 n. 4, 252, 254
Firemen's Union, 323 n. 1
Firth, J. B., 333 n. 2
Ford, Isabella, 289, 292, 296-7, 307
Fourier, C., 146, 156, 160, 163, 172
France, mining productivity, 119, 121; trades-unionism, 130, 135; anti-war movement, 135; and the Polish émigré socialists, 141, 160, 165, 166, 168, 169; Beesly and, 232-4; and the First International, 245, 246, 264
Free labour, *see* Trade Unions
French Utopians, 140, 142, 144, 145, 164, 168, 172; *see also under names of individual writers*

GARNLWYD, Leeds Redemptionist community, 92
Garside, G., 280
Gaskell, P., 63
Gast, J., 187-8, 192
Gasworkers, 128-9, 236, 289, 296, 297, 298 n. 4, 299-301, 306, 309-310, 319, 323, 340
Gasworkers and General Labourers Union, 296, 297, 298 n. 4, 305
Gee, A., 289, 306
General Chamber of Manufacturers, 52-3, 60
Geneva, anarchist movement, 244, 246, 274
Germany, labour productivity, 117, 119-20, 121-2, 126, 130-1, 132, 136; influence of French Utopians, 140; Prussian rule in Poland, 141, 156, 157; radicals and *La Tribune des Peuples*, 166; support for Marx, 244, 252
Gibson v. *Lawson*, 342
Gide, C., 98
Gisborne, T., 52
Glasgow, Owenite Labour Exchange, 87; branch of First International, 259; dock strike, 328
Glass workers, 138, 182, 185
Glazier, W., 191
Glyde, C., 292
Gordon, G. W., 224
Gorgon, The, 64-5
Graham, Sir J., 56-7
Graham, R. B. Cunninghame, 298

355

Grand National Consolidated Trades Union, 86, 88
Grand National Moral Union of the Useful and Productive Classes, 88
Gray, J., 49-50, 76, 80, 103
Grayson, V., 292
Greening, E. O., 101, 287, 288
Greenock, branch of the First International, 274
Grey, Charles, 2nd Earl, 56
Grudziaz, 146
Guile, D., 202
Guizot, F., 206

HACKNEY, branch of the First International, 274
Hague, The, Fifth Congress of the International; *see under* First International
Hague and Another v. *Cutler*, 236 n. 6
Hales, J., 248-9, 250, 251-2, 257, 258, 260, 261-3, 266, 267-9, 271, 272, 274, 275
Halifax, 281-2, 287, 306; I.L.P., 277, 310, 311, 312; Fabian Society, 302 n. 1, 310; relations between I.L.P. and Trades Council, 303, 309; Labour Union, 310
Halifax Trades Council, 280, 303, 309, 310
Hall, C., 48
Halle, productivity in copper mines, 119
Hamburg, 244
Hamlyn, W., 195
Hardie, K., 278, 291, 294, 310, 312
Harnott, R., 193
Harris, G., 257
Harrison, F., 185, 205, 206-7, 210, 212, 213, 228, 232, 235, 237, 238
Hartlepool, dock strike, 328
Hartwell, R., 186, 187, 193, 195, 198, 199, 201-2
Hebden Bridge Co-operative Society, 280 n. 3
Heltman, W., 154-5
Herzen, A. I., 144, 149 n. 2, 172, 173
Hill, J., 272
Hinckley, branch of the First International, 259
Hodgskin, T., 65 n. 2
Hole, J., 93
Holyoake, G. J., 101, 104-5, 106, 110, 112

Hornby v. *Close*, 225
Howell, G., 182, 191, 198, 199, 200, 214, 230, 235-6, 237, 263, 320, 334
Hoxton Labour League, 278
Huddersfield, 280, 285, 289, 305, 309 n. 1; I.L.P. in, 277 n. 2, n. 3; Fabian Society, 302 n. 1
Huddersfield Trades Council, 280, 309
Hughes, T., 93, 101, 213
Hughes, T. W., 195, 196
Hull, 343; co-operative movement, 92; three-shift system in gasworks, 129 n. 1; branch of First International, 270; Operative Bricklayers and the *Bee-Hive*, 185; dock strike, 328-30, 331 n. 1
Hume, D., 208
Hungary, *see* Austria-Hungary
Hunt, H., 66
Huxley, T. H., 206, 207, 208
Hyndman, H. M., 211, 269 n. 1, 278, 290

ICARIANS, *see* Cabet, E.
Illingworth, A., 289, 290-1
Independent Labour Party: precursors of, 278; origins, 277-9, 279-292, 301, 302; branches, 277 n. 2, n. 3; and the co-operative movement, 280; and the Trades Council movement, 280, 303, 305, 309-11; as a reaction against established Liberalism, 286, 287-9, 311; and Radical Nonconformity, 289-92; a party of youth, 294, 299, 312; an authentic socialist party, 311-13, 316. *See also* Maguire, T.
Industrial and Provident Societies Act (1852), 93
Industrial Review, see *Bee-Hive*
Industry, modern sense of, 43 n. 1
International, First: Polish members, 172; *Bee-Hive* the organ of, 174, 202, 253; and the *International Herald*, 253; officers, 183, 248-9, 252; and Positivists, 217-18; Conservative view of, 242; English section, 242-3, 244, 246-7, 248-9, 250, 251, 252, 264-5; and the Paris Commune, 243, 245, 248, 249, 250, 252, 254, 265, 266; and the Bakuninists, 243-6, 256, 263, 264, 274; symbol of labour's aspirations, 243-4; absence of doc-

Index

trinal uniformity, 243; Basle Congress, 243, 247, 256; and the Blanquists, 245, 264; and Alliance of Socialist Democracy, 244; English support for Marx, 245, 263-4; headquarters in London, 245-8; 5th (Hague) Congress, 246, 253 n. 1, 263-5, 267-8, 269, 270; relations with London Trades Council and the unions, 247-8, 250 n. 4, 256 n. 4, 257, 263, 274; London Conference, 248, 249, 253; John Hales, 248-9, 250, 251-2, 257, 258, 260, 261-3, 266, 267-9, 271, 272, 274, 275; English branches, 249, 252-3, 255-6, 259-60, 265-7, 270-4; Maltman Barry, 249-52, 263, 264, 265, 274; accused of being a secret society, 250; and the Jurassian Anarchist Federation, 253, 268, 272, 274; failure of Irish branches, 254; Parliamentary attempt to suppress, 254-5; Universal Federalist Council, 256, 258; anarchist Section 12 of New York, 257, 261; transferred from London to New York, 257, 264-5; split in English Federal Council, 258-63, 266-74; later influence in England, 273 n. 2, 275. *See also* Marx, K.

International Herald, 253, 266, 268-9, 273; and anti-semitism, 260-1

Ireland, 78, 84, 254, 321

Ironworkers, 118, 125, 136, 197, 202, 247

Italy, anti-war movements, 135; influence of French Utopians, 140; Mickiewicz's Polish Legion, 165, 166; support for anarchists, 253, 264

JARVIS, H., 195
Jersey, Polish socialists in, 145, 146
Johnson, J. H., 333 n. 2, n. 3, n. 5
Joiners, *see* Carpenters
Jones, Edward, 262, 273
Jones, Ernest, 223, 224, 230, 258, 287, 288
Jones, Lloyd, 89, 93, 101, 108, 110
Jones, Thomas, 195, 196, 200
Jowett, F. W., 282, 289, 291, 299, 302, 312
Judge, J., 304
Jung, H., 264, 269, 275

'Junta', the, 183, 188, 202-4, 216, 231
Jurassian Anarchist Federation, *see under* International, First

KEEN, C., 252
Keighley Trades Council, 309
Kelly, T., 331, 332-5, 339
King, W., 82-3, 85, 111
Kingsley, C., 213
Kitson, Sir James, 311
Konarski, S., 156
Krepowiecki, T., 146, 155-6
Królikowski, L.: originally Saint-Simonian, 160; disciple of Cabet, 160-1; breaks with Cabet, 161; interprets Gospels in communistic sense, 161-3

LABOUR CHURCH MOVEMENT, 211, 291, 312
Labour Elector, The, 277
Labour Exchanges (Owenite), 86-7
Labour management, role of custom, 114; incentives, 114, 122, 124, 125, 126, 130-33, 134, 135-6, 137, 138-9; cheap labour economy, 124, 126-7, 128, 129; and coercion, 119, 120, 123-4, 125-6, 130, 134, 136-7; inefficient industrial organisation and, 127-9, 131; subcontracting, 125, 130, 131; scientific development of, 132-9; intensive utilisation of labour, 114, 124, 129, 130, 131, 135, 136, 138-139; 'continental system', 136-7; high wage economy, 132; payment by the hour, 179-80, 211-12; payment by results, 125, 126, 131-138; and mechanisation, 134-5; development of costing systems, 134; hours of work, 128-9, 131, 134; labour contracts, 124, 130; labour relations, 130, 137; arbitration, 216-17; shift system, 139. *See also* Wages
Labour productivity, 113, 114, 118-119, 120, 121-2, 124, 125-9, 130-1, 132-9; *see also* Wages
Labour Representation Committee, 243, 263, 338, 350
Labour Representation League, 174, 288 n. 4
Labour Unions, 278 n. 1, 298, 302, 303, 304, 307-9
Lamennais, F. R. de, 142, 146, 168 n. 2, 172

357

Essays in Labour History

Lancashire, 285 n. 3; demand for whole produce of labour, 66; builders' dispute, 88; wages, 118; productivity, 122, 137; and American Civil War, 218; I.L.P. in, 273 n. 3
Land and Labour League, 247
Lansbury, G., 275
Lassalle, F., 172
Law, H., 252
Laws, G., 327
Ledru-Rollin, A. A., 168, 171
Leeds, 283, 285, 288 n. 4, 295; I.L.P. in, 277 n. 2, n. 3, 302-5, 311; centre for new socialist ideas, 280; Socialist League branch, 280, 294, 295, 297, 298, 299, 301, 305; Labour Church, 291; open-air speaking, 295; organisation of unskilled labour, 295-6, 297, 305; tailoring trades, 296-7; 1890 May Day celebrations, 297; 1890 Gas Strike, 299-301, 303, 311; Labour Union, 303
Leeds Redemption Society, 91, 92, 93, 103, 107
Leeds Trades Council, 280, 281 n. 1, 295, 297-8, 301 n. 2, 303, 304
Leicester, branch of the First International, 272, 274
Leith, dock strike, 328
Lelewel, J., theory of communes, 142-4; association with Marx, 142; influence on the Polish left, 142-4; and Mickiewicz, 164
Le Locle, support for Bakunin in, 244
Lessner, F., 267
Libelt, K., 143-4 n. 1
Liège, productivity in mines, 125-6, 128
Limehouse, branch of the First International, 274
Lind, W. P., 331-2, 334-5
Lindley, Lord, 347, 348
Lister, J., 287-8, 289, 310-11, 312
Lister, S. C., 306, 311
Liverpool, co-operative movement, 87; three-shift system in gasworks, 129 n. 1; branch of First International, 252, 259, 266, 267, 270, 272, 274; dock strike, 328
Livesey, G., 323, 330, 331 n. 1
Lloyd, J., 332
Lloyd's Weekly, 181, 183
Lock-outs, *see* Strikes and Lock-outs

London, 185, 187, 188, 196, 197, 199, 219, 226, 236, 254, 285, 298; co-operative movement, 79, 80, 92; productivity in building trades, 122; Polish Democratic Society, 152, 169; nine-hours movement, 175-82, 211-12; branches of First International, 249, 252, 259-60, 267, 274; I.L.P., 277 n. 3; dock strikes, 295, 317, 321, 322-3, 324, 325, 326-7; United Labour Council, 324; South Metropolitan Gasworks strike, 323, 330, 331 n. 1; Wade's Arms Manifesto, 326; 3rd Co-operative Congress, 77-8, 84, 96; City Corporation, 333; University College, 206, 212, 227-8; Conference of the First International, *see under* International, First
London Co-operative Society, 79-80
London County Council, 332-4, 338
London Revolutionary Commune of the Polish People, *see under* Polish *émigré* socialism
London Rotunda, 66, 67 n. 5
London Trades Council, 174, 175, 178, 188, 189, 190-1, 193, 194, 196, 206, 213, 216, 219 n. 3, 238, 247, 256 n. 4, 275, 331
London United Riggers' Association, 335
London Working Men's Association, 62, 67 n. 3, 174, 187, 230
London Working Men's College, 93
Longuet, C., 250
Lorraine, productivity in ironworks, 136
Loughborough, branch of First International, 252, 259, 272
Lovett, W., 62, 187
Lucraft, B., 247, 250, 263
Lud Polski, *see under* Polish *émigré* socialism
Luddites, 290 n. 1
Ludlow, J. M., 93, 101, 108, 213
Lyons v. *Wilkins*, 338, 346-8

McCarthy, T., 326
McCulloch, J. R., 131
Macdonald, Alexander, 174, 214, 235, 236
MacDonald, James, 275
McDonnell, J. P., 252, 254
Mackinnon, W. A., 57-8

Index

McMillan, M., 292
Maddox, H. G., 273
Maguire, Tom: early life, 292-3; an atheist, 289, 293, 313, 314; character, 295, 298, 299, 303-5, 312, 313-14; verse of, 291, 293, 294, 297, 315-16; on land nationalisation, 288; friendship with Mahon, 293, 294, 295, 298, 303-5; and trade unions, 293, 295-6, 306, 308 n. 6, 309-10; and the Leeds tailors, 296-7; and the Socialist League, 293-4, 297, 301; and Leeds gas strike, 299-301; early death, 314. *See also* Independent Labour Party
Mahon, J. L., 278, 293, 294, 295, 298, 303-5, 308, 313
Malthus, T. R., 45, 50 n. 2, 77, 131
Manchester, 185, 221, 270, 271, 287; Engels' description, 48; and anti-corn law movement, 60; and the demand for the full produce of labour, 66; 1st Co-operative Congress, 84; establishment of *Weekly Wages*, 182; branch of First International, 252-3, 255, 259, 260, 262, 265, 267, 268, 272-273
Manchester School, the, 72, 199, 218
Manfred Weiss works, 135
Mann, T., 122, 292, 303, 308, 311, 312, 329
Manningham Mills strike, 278-9, 284 n. 4, 286, 303, 306-8
Marshall, A., 138
Marx, K.: on payment by results, 131; and Polish socialism, 142, 172; on Potter, 202; and Beesly, 211, 220, 228, 231, 232, 233, 241; on Bright, 223; on anarchists, 243; influence of Engels on, 269. *See also* International, First
Master and Servant Acts, 124, 130, 236
Mattison, A., 289, 291, 296, 298, 304, 305 n. 1, 306
Mayhew, H., 73
Mazzini, G., 243
Metaphysical Society, 206
Metropolitan Trades Committee, 187-8
Mickiewicz, A.: contradictory views of, 164, 165, 167-8; friendship with Czartoryski, 164; and revolution, 164, 167-8; forms Polish Legion, 165, 166; agrarian programme, 165-6; edits *La Tribune des Peuples*, 166, 167, 168
Middlesbrough, branch of the First International, 249, 252, 259, 267; dock strike, 328
Milan, anti-war movement, 135
Mill, James, 54-5, 64
Mill, John Stuart, 43-4, 206, 207, 208, 229
Millthorpe, 298
Milner, G., 254, 260, 267
Miner, The, 294
Miners, 119, 121-2, 124, 125-6, 128, 132, 174, 214, 216, 278, 293, 311, 318
Mineworkers, National Association of, 174, 214
Modrzewski, F., 146
Mogul Steamship Co. v. *McGregor, Gow & Co.*, 342-3
Moraczewski, J., 143-4 n. 1
More, H., 52
Morley, John, 60, 206, 231, 238
Morley, Samuel, 230, 232, 272
Morning Advertiser, The, 176, 181
Morris, W., 290, 291, 293, 294, 298, 299, 312
Morrison, J., 68
Motor industry, 137
Mottershead, T., 264, 266, 272
Mudie, G., 79
Mundella, A., 236, 287 n. 1
Murray, C., 259, 260, 267
Mutual Land Emigration and Colonization Company, 260

NAPLES, support for Bakunin in, 244
Napoleon III, 168
National Amalgamated Union of Labour, 340
National Associations of United Trades for the Protection, and for the Employment, of Labour, 109
National Free Labour Association, 337-9
National Political Union, 51 n. 3
National Reform League, 259, 260, 263, 267
National Republican Brotherhood, 271-2
National Union of the Working Classes, 66-7, 187
Neale, E. V., 93, 101

New Harmony, Owenite settlement, 78
New Lanark, Owenite settlement, 75, 78, 128
Newcastle, dock strike, 328
Nightingale, W., 192, 195
Nine-hours movement, 175-6, 179, 200, 211, 259, 271
Normanby, branch of the First International, 267
North, The (Pótnoc), 156
North British Daily Mail, The, 186
North Cave, co-operative movement, 92
Norwich, co-operative movement, 92
Nottingham: branch of the First International, 252, 255-6, 259, 262, 265-6, 267, 270, 271-2; Congress, British Federal Council, 261, 263
'Nunquam', *see* Blatchford, R.

OASTLER, R., 286
O'Brien, B., 68-9, 247, 257, 259, 260, 263, 266, 267, 274, 288
O'Connor, T. P., 324 n. 5
Odger, G., 189, 192, 194, 195, 196, 198, 199-200, 202, 210, 214, 215, 234, 247, 250, 263, 265
Oldham, labour productivity, 136
Operative Bricklayers, *see* Bricklayers
Operative Stonemasons, *see* Stonemasons
Orbiston, Owenite settlement, 78
Ossett, 292
Owen, R.: origins of social theory, 75; working-class support, 79-80, 88-90, 104-5; suspicious of radical reformers, 67, 68; Owenite communities, 76-86, 88-90, 94; New Lanark, 75, 78, 128; Queenwood, 74, 88, 94; and co-operative movement, 74-90, 85-6, 94-5, 98-9, 100, 102, 111; influence on Polish groups, 146, 172; and 'Labour Exchanges', 86-7; and the Redemption societies, 90-3; and the trade unions, 86-8; introduces the term 'working classes', 52 n. 3; and capitalism, 102, 104, 105-6, 108; on machinery, 76, 103-4, 105; on 'productive' and 'non-productive' classes, 49-50, 67, 88, 106. *See also* Co-operative movement

PAEPE, C. DE, 245, 246
Painters, 185, 192, 194, 195, 250 n. 4
Pall Mall Gazette, The, 234
Palmerston, H. J. Temple, 3rd Viscount, 71
Pare, W., 96, 99, 100, 110
Paris, bronzeworkers' strike, 247
Paris Commune, 172, 232-4, 242, 244, 245, 248, 249, 252, 254, 256, 265, 266, 293 n. 6
Parker, S. L., 271, 272
Paylor, T., 289, 294-5, 296, 298, 300, 306, 310
Peace, P., 73 n. 3
Peel, Sir R., 69
Peters, S., 331, 332-5, 339
Petherbridge, W., 193, 194
Petrograd, anti-war movement, 135
Pickles, F., 291, 293, 295
Pioneer, The, 68
Pitt, W., 52, 53
Place, F., 44
Plasterers, 195
Plumbers, 195, 281 n. 1
Plymouth, dock strike, 325, 326
Podolecki, J. K., 169, 170
Poland for Christ (Polska Chrystusowa), 161, 162 n. 1, 163
Polhill, J., 331 n. 1
Polish Democratic Society, *see under* Polish *émigré* socialism
Polish *émigré* socialism: origins, 140-2; Polish Democratic Society, 141, 144-5, 147, 151-6, 169-171, 172; The Polish People (Lud Polski), 145-51, 153 n. 3, 154, 155-6, 157, 158, 159, 160, 165, 170, 171; the Great Manifesto, 155; support by Polish gentry, 151, 155, 156-7; political divisions in France, 160; anti-semitism in, 150; London Revolutionary Commune of the Polish People, 171, 172; and the class-struggle, 148, 152, 173; and collective ownership, 141-2, 143-4, 145, 147, 149-51, 152-3, 154-5, 159, 169-70; communes, 142-4, 146, 149, 163, 165, 170, 171, 173; and industry, 149-50, 153, 154, 171-3; and education, 150, 158-9, 162; eclectic nature of, 172; influence of Lelewel, 142-4; influence of French Utopians, 142, 144, 145, 146, 150-1, 158, 160,

Index

161, 172 ; interpretation of Christianity, 148, 150-1, 153, 157-60, 169 ; and nationalism, 164, 173 ; originality of, 173 ; and peasant emancipation, 141, 143, 147, 152, 153-5 ; decline of, 168-72
Polish People, The, *see under* Polish *émigré* socialism
Pollock, Sir F., 341, 343, 344, 348
Polska Chrystusowa, *see* Poland for Christ
Ponson, A. T., 125-6, 128
Poor Law, English, 124, 130
Poor Man's Guardian, The, 66, 67 n. 3
Populaire, Le, 160
Portsmouth, The Polish People established at, 145-6
Positivism : three types, 206-7 ; and Comte's 'Religion of Humanity', 207, 208 ; and the trade unions, 180, 209, 210, 213-14, 217-18, 237, 239 ; and the working classes, 209, 210, 211 ; and capitalism, 209-10 ; and the Reform movement, 221
Pótnoc (The North), 156
Potter, G. : founds and promotes *Bee-Hive*, 174, 180-1, 182-6, 197, 201-2, 203-4 ; and nine-hours movement, 175-6, 179-80, 200 ; and power of the press, 176-7, 180 ; becomes a national figure, 177-8 ; and the 'Junta', 183, 188, 202-3 ; Troup on, 186-7 ; quarrels with Dell, 188-9 ; critics of, 188-93, 197, 198, 199-200, 202, 203-4 ; accepts Troup's views on American Civil War, 199-200 ; quarrel with *Bee-Hive*'s directors, 200-1 ; and Marx, 202 ; on new model unions, 215-16 ; and Beesly, 215-16, 230, 231 ; and the Liberals, 230 ; general influence, 203-4. *See also under Bee-Hive*
Pratt, D., 203 n. 1
Pratt, E. A., 339
Priestley, B., 291
Printers, 281 n. 1, *see also* Compositors
Proudhon, P. J., 146, 149, 150 n. 4, 154, 172, 243-4
Proudhonists, 243, 245, 256
Prussia, *see* Germany
Pudsey, co-operative movement, 92

Punch, 227
Putilov works, 135

Quarterly Review, The, 49
Queenwood, Owenite settlement, 74, 88, 94
Quelch, H., 290
Quinn v. Leathem, 317, 344, 348, 349

RAILWAY COMPANIES, 338, 339
Railway Servants, Amalgamated Society of, 349
Railwaymen, 121, 136, 349
Ralahine, Owenite settlement, 78
Redemption societies, 90-3, 96, 103, 106-7
Reform Club, 227
Reform League, 180, 220, 222, 223, 247, 287
Reform Union, 223
Reims, branch of Polish Democratic Society, 152-3
Reynolds, G. W. M., 181, 183
Reynolds, William, 192, 195
Reynolds's Newspaper, 176, 180, 181, 183, 190, 200
Ribbon workers, 136
Ricardo, D., 50 n. 2, 65 n. 2
Right to the Whole Produce of Labour, 64, 65, 66, 77, 91, 92, 97
Riley, W. H., 253, 266-7, 268, 275
Riverside Workmen's Council, 334 n. 4
Robb, T., 326 n. 5
Robinson, C. L., 288 n. 5
Rochdale Pioneers' Society, *see under* Co-operative movement
Roman Catholicism, 148 n. 2, 167, 254
Ropemakers, 190
Rotunda, *see* London Rotunda
Ruhr, productivity in mines, 119, 126
Rushton, B., 287, 290 n. 1
Russell, Lord Arthur, 234
Russell, Lord John, 55 n. 4
Russia : influence of Russian thinkers on Polish socialists, 172 ; the Polish commune and the Russian *mir*, 142, 143 n. 1, 144, 149
Rzewuski, L., 157

ST. LUKE'S (London), branch of First International, 251, 252, 259
Saint-Simon, C. H. de R., Comte de, 49, 150

Saint-Simonians, 142, 144, 146, 150-151, 155, 158, 160, 161, 172
Salisbury, 3rd Marquess of, 334 n. 4, 338
Sawgrinders, 225
Say, J. B., 131
Ściegienny, P., 157
Scotland, I.L.P. in, 277 n. 3
Scotland depot ship, 326
Seamen, 323 n. 1, 324, 327, 331, 335, 340
Seamen's and Firemen's Union, Amalgamated, 323 n. 1, 327
Seamen's Protection Society, Amalgamated British, 335
Shaftoe, S., 281 n. 1, 305, 308, 310
Shave, J., 195
Shaw, A., 301 n. 2
Shaw, G. B., 291, 308
Sheffield, 225; Owenite Labour Exchange, 87
Shipley, 302, 307, 311
Shipping Federation, 324, 326, 327-328, 330-1, 334, 335-9, 340
Shoemakers, 87, 116, 195, 259
Sibly, W., 192
Siemens-Schuckert (Vienna), 136
Siemens works (Charlton), 273
Silk workers, 265, 272
Sismondi, L., 131
Smith, Adam, 43 n. 1, n. 3, 45, 50 n. 2, 53, 58, 62, 64, 119, 124, 131, 320
Smith, Hawkes, 111-12
Smith, Thomas, 256, 262, 265-6, 267, 270, 272
Snowden, John, 287
Snowden, Philip, 292, 313
Social mobility, 45, 70, 71-3
Socialist League, 293, 294, 295, 297, 298, 301, 302
Society for the Diffusion of Useful Knowledge, 64
Sorge, F. A., 257, 261, 264, 266, 273
South Metropolitan Gasworks strike, 323, 330, 331 n. 1
South Wales, 132
Southampton, dock strike, 325-6
Sothey, R., 45, 46
Sowerby Bridge, Fabian society in, 302 n. 1
Spain, influence of French Utopians, 140; support for Bakunin, 264
Spectator, The, 227
Speedwell depot ship, 327
Spen Valley, I.L.P. in, 277 n. 3
Spen Valley Trades Council, 309

Spencer, H., 70, 206, 207, 320, 321
Sprow, W., 325-6
Standard, The, 250, 251
Stansfeld, J., 287
Steam power, 46, 63
Stefanski, W., 157
Stephen, W., 271
Stockport, co-operative movement, 92
Stonemasons, 116, 178, 180, 193, 194, 197, 198, 281 n. 1
Stonemasons' Society, Operative, 178, 193, 197
Stratford, branch of First International, 274
Strikes and Lock-outs, 87-8, 124, 130, 135, 176, 216; *see also under* Trade Unions *and under the names of individual firms, trades and towns*
Sub-contracting, *see under* Labour management
Sunderland, relations between Chartists and Anti-Corn Law Leaguers, 61; branch of First International, 259
Swansea, dock strike, 328
Świętosławski, Z.: and the Polish People (Lud Polski), 146, 156, 158; the Universal Church, 157-60, 162-3; forms London Revolutionary Commune of the Polish People, 171, 172
Switzerland, anarchist movement in, 243, 264; Eccarius on, 269-70

Tablet, The, 242
Taff Vale decision, 317, 348-9
Tailors, 87, 116, 117, 226, 247, 249 n. 2, 280, 281 n. 1, 286, 296-7
Tait's Edinburgh Magazine, 186, 187, 193, 199
Tapper, J., 192
Taylor, F. W., 133, 134-5, 139
Temperton v. *Russell*, 343-4, 349
Textile workers, 283-6, 289, 306-8
Thames Watermen and Lightermen, 332
Thompson, T. Perronet, 58-9
Thompson, William, 65 n. 2, 80, 94
Thorne, W., 296, 298, 300, 323 n. 2
Thring, E., 71-2
Tilers, 116
Tillett, B., 289, 290, 291, 303, 307, 308, 310, 312, 313, 324 n. 4, 325, 329, 338-9, 340, 341

Index

Times, The, 250, 254-5, 320, 322-3, 328, 330, 339, 340, 342
Tin-plate workers, 195, 196
Townsend, J., 123
Trades Disputes Act (1906), 350
Trade Union Act (1871), 234, 341
Trade Unions, 47, 62, 101, 104; and the co-operative movement, 86-8, 109-10; legal status, 109, 124, 130, 225-7, 228-9, 230-1, 234, 235-237, 240, 317-18, 341-50; fines for bad work, 121; and Positivism, 209, 210; New Unionism, 215-16, 240, 295-7, 299, 303, 309, 310, 317, 318, 320, 321-4, 328, 340-1, 345; and political action, 217-18, 220, 226-7, 229-31, 235-8, 240; and the Paris Commune, 234, 248, 250; and the Liberal Party, 234-8, 240; Beesly and the T.U.C. Parliamentary Committee, 235-8; and the First International, 243, 247-8, 257, 263, 274; decline of Yorkshire trade councils by early 1880s, 280-1, 285-6; and the unskilled worker, 295-6; public hostility towards, 317-18, 320, 321-2, 328, 337, 339, 340-1, 345-50; and strike-breakers, 318-19, 322-3, 326-8, 329-30, 336-9; and free labour, 319-20, 323, 326, 324-8, 329-30, 331, 336-339, 350; picketing, 236, 318-19, 322-3, 328, 337-8, 345, 346-8; and the *laissez-faire* dogmas, 320-321; National Free Labour Association, 337-9; and the closed shop, 342, 343
Trades Council movement, 309-11, 312; *see also under individual towns*
Trades' Newspaper, The, 187-8, 192
Trades Union Congress, 174, 203, 206, 235, 236, 237, 281, 294, 305, 346
Trafalgar Hotel group, 332-5, 339
Travis, H., 99
Tribune des Peuples, La, 166, 167, 168
Trollope and Sons v. London Building Trades Federation, 345
Troup, G., 186-7, 193, 195, 197, 198-9, 200-1, 202
Tuckerman, J., 48
Tufnell, H., 63

Turner, B., 280, 281, 289, 296, 299, 305, 306, 307, 309 n. 3, 310, 312
Tyndall, J., 206

UNION OF PLEBEIANS, 157
United Nations, Commission on Latin American Textile Industries, 127-8, 139
United States, 137, 270; effect of tariffs on Yorkshire textile industries, 283
University College, London, *see* London, University College
Urbanization, 47-8

VAUX, Clotilde de, 208, 213
Vickery, A., 192
Vienna, labour productivity in, 136
Vize, T., 195

WADE, J., 46-7
Wages: classical theory, 113; role of custom, 117; non-economic factors, 113-4, 118-19; unskilled labourers, 115; pre-industrial skilled workers, 115-16; historical continuity, 117, 120; differentials, 116-17; 'fair day's work for fair day's pay', 118-19, 121; incentives, 114, 122, 124, 125, 126, 131, 134, 135-6, 137, 138-9, 179-180; skilled workers, 117-18; cheap labour economy, 124, 126-127, 128, 129; and 'the rules of the game', 120-4, 133, 137; piece rates, 125, 126, 131, 136, 137, 138; high wage economy, 132; payment by the hour, 179-80, 211-212; payment by results, 125, 126, 131-8; trade unions and, 121; *see also* Labour management; Labour productivity
Wakefield, A. B., 288 n. 4
Weavers, 120 n. 3, 305
Webber, G., 282, 288
Weekly Mail, The, 181
Weekly Wages, 182
Weiler, A., 267, 275
Wernam v. Stone, 345 n. 2
Weston, J., 247, 269
Whitman, W., 291
Wilson, B., 288
Wilson, C., 328-9
Wilson, J. H., 324, 329 n. 1
Women's Provident League, 296 n. 5
Wood, W., 289, 300

Woolwich, branch of First International, 259, 273
Worcell, S., 146, 150, 155-6, 169, 170, 171, 172
Workingman, The (formerly *The Workman*), 181-2, 191-2, 193, 195 n. 1
Workingmen's Association for the Abolition of Foreign Sugar Bounties, 332
Workman's Advocate, The (later *The Commonwealth*), 202, 204, 253

Wright, T., 73 n. 1
Wright and Co. v. Hennessey, 345 n. 3

Yorkshire Factory Times, The, 279, 282, 295, 305-6, 307, 313
Yorkshire Federation of Trades Councils, 309, 312 n. 3
Yorkshire Labour Council, 297, 303
Yorkshire Socialist Federation, 298

Zbratnienie (*Brotherhood*), 161, 162 n. 1, n. 2

THE END